Contemporary Critical Theorists

Contemporary Critical Theorists

From Lacan to Said

Edited by Jon Simons

Edinburgh University Press

© The contributors, 2004, 2006

Edinburgh University Press Ltd
22 George Square, Edinburgh

Typeset in New Baskerville
by Norman Tilley Graphics

Transferred to digital print 2007

A CIP record for this book is
available from the British Library

ISBN 978 0 7486 1719 7 (hardback)
ISBN 978 0 7486 1720 3 (paperback)

The right of the contributors
to be identified as authors of this work
has been asserted in accordance with
the Copyright, Designs and Patents Act 1988.

Contents

Acknowledgements	vii
Notes on Contributors	viii
1 Introduction *Jon Simons*	1
2 Jacques Lacan (1901–81) *Yannis Stavrakakis*	18
3 Emmanuel Levinas (1906–95) *Arjuna Weerasooriya*	34
4 Louis Althusser (1918–90) *Steve Smith*	51
5 Roland Barthes (1915–80) *Andy Stafford and Susan McManus*	68
6 Jacques Derrida (1930–) *Adam Sharman*	85
7 Luce Irigaray (1932–) *Mary Eden*	102
8 Hélène Cixous (1937–) *Julia Dobson*	118
9 Julia Kristeva (1941–) *Moya Lloyd*	135

Contents

10 Jean-François Lyotard (1924–98) — 152
    Simon Tormey

11 Gilles Deleuze (1925–95) and Felix Guattari (1930–92) — 168
    Philip Goodchild

12 Michel Foucault (1926–84) — 185
    Jon Simons

13 Jean Baudrillard (1929–) — 201
    Paul Hegarty

14 Pierre Bourdieu (1930–2002) — 218
    Cheleen Mahar and Christopher Wilkes

15 Jürgen Habermas (1929–) — 234
    Martin Morris

16 Fredric Jameson (1934–) — 252
    Nick Heffernan

17 Edward Said (1935–2003) — 269
    Patrick Williams

Names Index — 286
Subject Index — 288

Acknowledgements

I would like first to thank the other contributors to this volume for the effort and care that they put into preparing their chapters. While each is an expert on the thinker or thinkers they have written about, it is always a challenge to translate expert knowledge into an accessible form, especially within the space of one chapter. I would also like to thank the University of Nottingham for a semester of study leave in 2002–3 during which I was able to do most of the editorial work for this volume. I am grateful to Peter Andrews for preparing a thorough index for this volume, as well as for its precursor which I also edited, *From Kant to Lévi-Strauss: The Background to Contemporary Critical Theory* (Edinburgh University Press, 2002). My main debt is to the pioneers of critical theory at the University of Nottingham whose dedication to and enthusiasm for their intellectual interests and teaching explain the success of the critical theory programme there. Their continuing willingness to give of their time and energy have attracted hundreds of students to the programme since 1983 (several of whom have contributed to this volume), encouraged new colleagues in the University of Nottingham to do likewise and provided me with employment. I dedicate this volume to them.

Jon Simons

Notes on Contributors

Mary Eden teaches cultural studies at Nottingham Trent University and Derby University. She has carried out postgraduate research on Irigaray's position on feminine subjectivity in a post-structuralist context. Her current research is about Irigaray and exchange, focusing on her neglected work on linguistics. She has published a critical review of Irigaray's *I Love to You*, for *The Journal of Contemporary French Thought*.

Dr Philip Goodchild is Lecturer in Religious Studies, University of Nottingham. He is the author of *Gilles Deleuze and the Question of Philosophy* (Fairleigh Dickinson University Press, 1996), *Deleuze and Guattari: An Introduction to the Politics of Desire* (Sage, 1996), and *Capitalism and Religion: The Price of Piety* (Routledge, 2002). He is also the editor of *Rethinking Philosophy of Religion* (Fordham University Press, 2002) and *Difference in Philosophy of Religion* (Ashgate Publications, 2002).

Dr Nick Heffernan teaches American Studies at University College, Northampton. His first book, *Capital, Class and Technology in Contemporary American Culture*, was published by Pluto in 2000.

Dr Paul Hegarty is a lecturer in the French department of University College, Cork, where he teaches philosophy and visual culture. He has published articles and a book on Georges Bataille, and articles on contemporary French theory, architecture, and most recently, on Japanese noise music. He is also involved in art/music/multimedia performance.

Notes on Contributors

Dr Moya Lloyd is a research fellow in the Centre for the Advancement of Women in Politics at Queen's University, Belfast. She is author of the forthcoming *Beyond Identity Politics?* (Sage); co-author of *Contemporary Social and Political Theory: An Introduction* (Open University Press, 1999) and *Political Ideologies* (Palgrave Macmillan, 2003); and co-editor (with Andrew Thacker) of *The Impact of Michel Foucault on the Social Sciences and Humanities* (Macmillan, 1997). She has written extensively on Michel Foucault and feminism, Judith Butler, feminist political theory and the body. She is currently completing a book, *Judith Butler: A Critical Introduction*, for publication in Polity Press's Key Contemporary Thinkers series.

Dr Susan McManus is currently a lecturer in Political Theory at Queens' University, Belfast. She completed her PhD at the University of Nottingham, where she also held an ESRC Postdoctoral Fellowship. Her first book, *Fictive Theories: Towards a Deconstructive and Utopian Political Imagination*, is forthcoming from Palgrave, New York.

Dr Cheleen Mahar is a professor of Anthropology at Pacific University. She has co-edited the book *An Introduction to the Work of Pierre Bourdieu: The Practice of Theory* and has recently completed a long-term ethnographic study of an urban poor population in Oaxaca, Mexico, titled *Constructing Habitus in a Disenchanted World: From Rural Migrant to Urban Citizen*. She has authored other journal essays on Mexico and New Zealand.

Dr Martin Morris teaches political science and communications at the University of Windsor. He is author of *Rethinking the Communicative Turn: Habermas, Adorno and the Problem of Communicative Freedom* (State University of New York Press, 2001), and guest editor of 'German Dis/Continuities', a special issue of the *South Atlantic Quarterly*, 96, 4, Fall 1997. He has published journal articles on political theory, critical theory and communications research on Canadian politics. His current research concerns the political dimensions of visual and linguistically mediated communication in the public sphere, which is supported by a major grant from the Social Sciences and Humanities Research Council of Canada.

Dr Adam Sharman is Lecturer in Hispanic and Latin American Studies, University of Nottingham. He works on the interface between critical theory and Spanish American literary culture. He has published essays on Foucault, postmodernism and diverse aspects of Spanish American literature, as well as editing a book on *The Poetry and Poetics of César Vallejo: The Fourth Angle of the Circle* (Edwin Mellen, 1997). He is currently working on a book entitled *Tradition and Modernity in Spanish American Literature.*

Dr Jon Simons is a senior lecturer in Critical Theory, University of Nottingham. He is the author of *Foucault and the Political* (Routledge, 1995), as well as other journal essays on Foucault, political theory, cultural theory and feminist theory. He has edited and contributed chapters to *From Kant to Althusser: The Background to Contemporary Critical Theory* (Edinburgh University Press, 2001) and is currently working on a book project, *Politics and Aesthetics: Style, Emotion and Mediation*, to be published by Edinburgh University Press and New York University Press.

Dr Steve Smith is a Lecturer in French at the University of Nottingham. He has published essays on critical theory, French literature, film and detective fiction.

Dr Andy Stafford is a senior lecturer in French Studies at Leeds University. He has published *Roland Barthes, Phenomenon and Myth: An Intellectual Biography* (Edinburgh University Press, 1998) and is currently writing a critical study of Barthes's *S/Z*, as well as a study of the relationship between writing and photography. He also works on Francophone Literature and is a member of the editorial board of the Association for the Study of Caribbean and African Literature in French.

Dr Yannis Stavrakakis studied political science in Athens and received his MA and PhD degrees from the Ideology and Discourse Analysis (IDA) programme at the Department of Government at the University of Essex. After lecturing for two years at Essex (where he directed the MA programme in IDA) he was awarded a three-year research fellowship at the School of Politics at the University of Nottingham. He has published extensively on psychoanalysis and politics, the analysis of Green ideological discourse and the politics of nature. He is the author of *Lacan and the Political* (Routledge, 1999) and co-editor of *Discourse Theory and Political Analysis* (Manchester University Press, 2000) and *Lacan and Science* (Karnac, forthcoming).

Notes on Contributors

Dr Simon Tormey is Senior Lecturer in Political Thought at the University of Nottingham. He is the author of *Making Sense of Tyranny: Interpretations of Totalitarianism* (Manchester University Press, 1995), *Politics at the Edge* (co-edited with C. Pierson – Macmillan, 1999) and *Autonomy, Contingency and the Postmodern: The Political Thought of Agnes Heller* (Manchester University Press, 2000).

Arjuna Weerasooriya is currently engaged in doctoral research on the themes of subjectivity and freedom, having already completed a postgraduate dissertation on ethics and politics in Derrida and Levinas. He teaches critical theory and modern thought at both postgraduate and undergraduate level at the University of Nottingham.

Christopher Wilkes is a professor of Sociology at Pacific University. He has written *In the Public Interest* (with Ian Shirley) and *The Tragedy of the Market* (with Mike O'Brien), and co-edited *An Introduction to the Work of Pierre Bourdieu: The Practice of Theory*. He is writing *Reinventing Culture* with Maria Alaniz, a semiotic study of advertising among Latinos in the Bay Area; *Philosophy and Sociology*, a historical critique of sociological epistemology; and an article on Jameson's epistemology.

Patrick Williams is Professor of Literary and Cultural Studies at Nottingham Trent University. He teaches in the areas of post-colonial studies, race, national identity and contemporary cultural production. His publications include *Post-Colonial African Cinema* (forthcoming), *Edward Said* (2001), *Ngugi wa Thiong'o* (1999), *Introduction to Post-Colonial Theory* (1997) and *Colonial Discourse and Post-Colonial Theory* (1993), as well as numerous articles and book chapters. His work has been translated into Korean and Turkish. He has also worked at the Open University, the University of Marrakech and the University of Strathclyde.

1

Introduction

Jon Simons

This volume offers sixteen introductory essays on key contemporary critical theorists. Critical theory in the broad sense used here includes the trends of Marxism and post-Marxism, semiotics and discourse analysis, structuralism and post-structuralism, ideology critique of all varieties, deconstruction, feminism, queer theory, psychoanalysis, postcolonialism, postmodernism, as well as the descendants of Frankfurt School Critical Theory. Those critical tendencies can be found across all the disciplines and interdisciplinary areas of the humanities, from architecture to theology, from American Studies to visual culture. This book is intended to be a good enough introduction to the thought of the critical theorists selected for the volume for readers to have an understanding of their main ideas, the most significant ways in which their ideas can be put to work in the humanities and some of the key problems identified in their work by critics. If this book succeeds in its aims, it will have whetted its readers' appetites to learn more about the critical theories it introduces. The following sections of the introduction explain what is meant by 'critical theory' and the scope of the book and suggests how best to use this book.

What is Critical Theory?

To provide a meaningful answer to the question 'what is critical theory?' I follow Wittgenstein in understanding that the meaning of a term involves invoking the practices and customs of a 'form of life'. The term 'critical theory' does not mean what it does because of some essential 'criticality' that is common to all modes of critical theory, but because of the ways in which the term is used in a particular 'form of life'. The 'form of life' in question is Anglophone academia since the late 1970s or so, when a range of theoretical approaches to different branches of the humanities began to be adopted on the margins of established disciplinary methodologies.

Within the social sciences there was already something known as Critical Theory which referred to the collective work of members of the Institute for Social Research first founded in 1923, also known now as the Frankfurt School, whose leading members were Max Horkheimer and Theodor Adorno. Critical Theory in this sense distinguishes itself from all forms of 'traditional' theory. It is a critical theory of Marxism developed in contrast to the crude materialist, determinist and allegedly scientific Marxism that had become orthodox in the Soviet Union. At the same time, Critical Theory denied the value-free character of positivist social science that was developing in the West. The neo-Marxism of the Frankfurt School regarded such unreflexive social science as one of the many ideologies that masked oppressive power relations. Critical Theory thus claimed to evaluate as well as explain and describe social reality. Practitioners were indebted to a philosophical and intellectual tradition that includes Kant, Hegel, Marx, Nietzsche, Freud and Weber, on the basis of which they widened Marxism from a focus on political and economic matters to include psychological and cultural matters.

Frankfurt School Critical Theory evolved first in the threatening context of 1930s Germany, against the background of the rise of fascism and Nazism. Forced into exile, mostly in the United States, because of their Jewish background and their left-wing politics, the main insights of the school were soon applied as vigorously to the capitalist consumer mass culture of post-Second World War North America and Western Europe as they had been to fascist society. Technological, instrumental rationalism, a tyranny of administration and the ideological distraction of mass culture precluded the emancipatory potential of Enlightenment from being realised in the democracies of the United States and West Germany as well as in fascist regimes. These ideas were well received by the radicals of the New Left social protest movements, including the student revolts, that emerged out of widespread dissatisfaction with the post-war West in the 1960s. West German economic success and conservatism troubled a younger generation that had questions about their parents' past. Cold War America also enjoyed suburban prosperity, but embroilment in the Vietnam War (1964–73) affected the younger generation particularly. Critical Theory was thus clearly connected with political events.

Frankfurt School Critical Theory already displayed some of the features that would characterise the heterogeneous set of theories that would become known as critical theory in the more general sense. First, it was an interdisciplinary project, both in that members addressed a range of social issues, including politics, jurisprudence, culture and psychology, and also in that it applied the theoretical insights that had developed in some disciplines to others. Second, it regarded itself as critical not only, or perhaps not primarily, in relation to its object of inquiry but also in relation to traditional or conventional approaches and methodologies with which it contrasted itself. Critical theory requires an allegedly uncritical Other in order to identify itself. Third, Critical Theory was nurtured by the rich ground of an intellectual tradition with which it engaged deeply and productively by both criticising it and by drawing on its best ideas. Fourth, both the ground from which it grew and Critical Theory itself is predominantly continental European, subsequently exiled and exported to the Anglophone world.

New Left radicalism had affinities not only with Frankfurt School Critical Theory but to a varied range of theories emerging in France. Even before 1968 the French intellectual scene had already nurtured its own version of unorthodox, Western Marxism, in the work of Louis Althusser. The most famous of post-war French philosophers, the existentialist Jean-Paul Sartre was, like the Frankfurt Critical Theorists and the post-Stalin French Communist Party, interested in a humanist Marxism. Althusser, however, drew on the structuralism of both the psychoanalyst Jacques Lacan and the anthropologist Claude Lévi-Strauss to displace man as the centre and driving force of history. The Situationists, a group of radical cultural practitioners active from 1958, rejected conventional Marxism as anachronistic, proposing instead a 'revolution of everyday life' in personal relationships and cultural perspectives. Guy Debord, an editor of the group's journal, published in 1967 his *Society of the Spectacle*, which was an ideology critique of commodified, mediated culture.[1] Along different lines, in the 1950s Roland Barthes was deploying structuralist analysis of signs, or semiotics, to demystify everyday bourgeois consumer culture, as did Jean

Baudrillard in his earliest work. Although Michel Foucault later denied that he had ever been a structuralist, his 'archaeological' studies of madness, medicine and the human sciences shared with structuralism an emphasis on the analysis of language and cultural practices, in the form of systems of discourse. His *The Order of Things*, published in 1966, predicted the erasure of the figure of man as the foundation of knowledge. By 1967 Jacques Derrida was already deconstructing structuralism in addition to the more dominant philosophical trend of phenomenology, while also decentring the human subject as author by examining the gap between authorial intention and textual meaning. In the background to all this intellectual ferment had been not only youth lived out under the shadow of Nazi occupation, collaboration, resistance and the promise of liberation, but also Algeria's anti-colonial struggle for independence from France, from 1954 to 1962. Another alternative left-wing group which was very much concerned with the Algerian situation as well as workers' struggles and daily resistance was Socialism and Barbarism, of which Jean-François Lyotard was a prominent member.

The explosion of French thought after 1968 led to Frankfurt School Critical Theory losing its monopoly on the title of critical theory in a more general sense. The most dramatic manifestation of the student movement in France had brought the republic to crisis in May 1968, during which Situationist graffiti appeared as slogans on the walls and Socialism and Barbarism came into prominence. But revolution was averted and order was restored. Radicals already dissatisfied with the official Marxism of the French Communist Party felt their misgivings had been confirmed by the latter's reluctance to participate in the momentum of May 1968. Post-1968 France became host to a dazzling eruption of theoretical innovation which might not unreasonably be interpreted in part as an intellectual sublimation of disappointed political radicalism. In addition to the figures mentioned above, Gilles Deleuze and Felix Guattari, who wrote a 'philosophy of desire' that spoke to the ferment of 1968 and its suppression by the establishment, were part of a vibrant intellectual scene.

Critical theory in the broader sense, though, is not a French term or invention, but an effect of the appropriation and integration of both Frankfurt School Critical Theory and the various streams of French and other thought into Anglophone academies. American universities in particular had been radicalised by a combination of the civil rights movement, experimental youth cultures (most notably the hippies), expansion of higher education that gave access to a broader sector of the population, anti-Vietnam War protests and student revolts. Intellectual culture felt the pressure to change just as established hierarchies and cultural values were being challenged across the Western world. The 1960s, in all their manifestations, were the background in which what became known as critical theory took root. The feminist movement was a major element in the new social movements that then emerged. Feminism's 'second wave' from 1968 onwards was motivated partly by a critique of sexism evident to women activists in student and anti-war protests. The dominant theoretical paradigm for the radicalism of the 1960s was Marxism, generally in its non-orthodox Western and neo-Marxist forms. Yet, even those forms seemed ill-equipped to explain and critique forms of oppression that are not only economic, namely, sexism, racism, militarism and the domination of nature.

The Anglophone world certainly produced its own intellectual figures for the movements that criticised and resisted these oppressions, but the influence of the explosion of French thought that had distanced itself from Marxism was evident here too. Juliet Mitchell, for example, who initially tried to fashion a socialist feminism that would win the respect and attention of her male colleagues in Britain's New Left, drew substantially on Althusser and Lacan, as well as Marx, Freud and Lévi-Strauss.[2] She sparked an interest in French psychoanalytic, structuralist and post-structuralist theory in Anglophone academia that opened the way for the influence of what became known as 'French feminism', despite the differences between the work of Luce Irigaray, Julia Kristeva and Hélène Cixous, as well as the work of other French feminists. Feminist, anti-racist and ecological or green thought are all critical theories in that they criticise the methodologies, analyses and conclusions of conventional or traditional approaches to their subject matter, yet what has come to be regarded as critical theory 'proper' often seems to need the additional cachet of originating from Continental Europe, as in the case of French feminism.

In the social sciences, approaches and methodologies that modelled themselves on the natural sciences, often referred to as behaviourism, were the convention or tradition against which critical theory was pitched. In spite of its claims to scientific value neutrality, behaviourism became regarded as a form of covert ideological justification for the status quo, which obscured objections to a repressive social order by studying people externally as objects rather than subjects, ignoring the subjective meaning inherent in social action. Given the similarity of this sort of criticism to the objections of the Frankfurt theorists to positivist social science, it is not surprising that a leading light in a revised form or second generation of critical social theory was Jürgen Habermas, who had been Adorno's assistant after the Second World War. Habermas associated critical theory with a human interest in emancipation, in identifying ideological distortions and revealing coercive power relations in the operations of the administrative state and capitalist economy. He distinguished critical theory from both positivist social science and hermeneutic approaches which emphasise the meaning that people attribute to social action, meanings which constitute the presuppositions of any social inquiry. In a more general sense, however, critical social theory refers to qualitative theories which both adopt hermeneutic strategies in seeking to interpret and understand social action in contrast to quantitative approaches and at the same time evaluate as well as describe and explain social action. Significantly, this interpretative turn in social science drew on a wide range of literary and cultural theories by means of which society can be 'read', just as a literary text is read.

The literary connection is significant as critical theory in the broader sense took root in Anglophone academia primarily in the field of literary studies. In this domain, critical theory denotes a broad range of approaches to literary interpretation that stand in contrast or opposed to the 'traditional' methodologies that are concerned with the aesthetic qualities of 'great' literature that constitutes the cultural canon. Literary criticism had become professionalised in twentieth-century universities, which is probably reflected by the development of New Criticism, an effort to make criticism rigorous and methodical rather than an expression of subjective judgement. New Criticism (a term first used in 1910) was itself an eclectic collection of methods, but most of them shared a concern for close textual analysis while many were prepared to use extra-literary tools, such as contextualisation, for literary analysis. To some extent, then, there was an internal dynamic in the discipline of literary criticism that made room for further methodological innovation and imports. Just as in visual art the avant-garde modernism of the early twentieth century had by the 1960s become the established art of the museums favoured by professional critics, so had New Criticism become 'traditional' theory in relation to

Introduction

Russian formalism, reader-response theory and Marxism, followed by psychoanalysis, feminism, semiotics, structuralism, post-structuralism, deconstruction, postmodernism, postcolonialism and queer theory. Some of these terms and ideas were imports from the European continent, while some of them were home grown. Even the latter, though, showed an affinity to what is known in the Anglophone world as 'Continental philosophy'. Indeed, the philosophies of Heidegger, Gadamer, Levinas, Derrida and others were and are much more commonly welcomed and studied in literature than in Anglophone philosophy departments.

However, the impetus behind the movement whereby critical theory became almost synonymous with all theory in literary studies was not merely to multiply the possible interpretations of literary texts and stock the supermarket of new ideas. There was something, maybe a great deal, of the radicalism of the 1960s and the New Left in critical literary theory. Critical theory is always in some way, even if obscure and indirect ways, politically engaged. While this point may be more obvious for critical social theory, critical literary theory has its political edge too. For one thing, just as Frankfurt School theory challenged the value-neutrality of positivist social science, critical literary theory targets the assumption of 'tradition' literary interpretation to be apolitical, as a scholarly or aesthetic exercise. Critical theory exposes the bourgeois, capitalist, racist, (neo)-colonialist, (hetero)sexist bias at work in literature and criticism. It also reads into literary texts the ways in which those forms of social and political oppression constitute the contexts for aesthetic, cultural and literary texts. Through such readings, critical literary theories indicate, even if obliquely or implicitly, a world without such oppression.

A good deal of the political impetus of all forms of critical theory was absorbed by 'campus wars', the struggle to introduce critical theory into the curriculum, to disseminate it through publications and conferences, to appoint critical theorists to academic positions and to establish new, often interdisciplinary programmes as institutional bases for further development. In the 1970s and 1980s critical theory was defined to a considerable extent by its embattled position within academic institutions, forming common ground in opposition to mainstream conventional and traditional approaches across the humanities. Retrospectively, the critical theorists seem to have done quite well out of those struggles in many disciplines, though with varying degrees of success. Anglophone philosophy departments are still dominated by analytical philosophy, but a few have built up a reputation for Continental philosophy while others accept it as part of the curriculum. In the United States in particular, comparative literature departments often became safe havens for theorists, especially of French structuralism, post-structuralism, deconstruction, Lacanian psychoanalysis and later postcolonialism. English literature departments also often developed theoretically oriented curricula and were also often the breeding grounds for new interdisciplinary programmes or even new disciplines, notably cultural studies, media studies and film studies, all of which rely on critical theories as their main methodological approaches. Sociology and social studies departments served as bases for interdisciplinary programmes in women's studies (also based in psychology departments), race and ethnicity or, in the United States, African-American and other ethnic-group studies. Critical theory is generally welcome, if not an expectation, in these programmes.

The bigger story is that critical theory made inroads into almost all of the arts and social sciences departments during the 1980s and 1990s from accountancy to art history, from management to media studies, from religious studies to rhetoric. Often labelled rather broadly and inaccurately as post-structuralist or postmodernist theories, critical theory found itself ensconced as branches within even quite conventional and scientifically oriented disciplines, such as critical legal studies and human geography. In the new disciplines and interdisciplinary programmes, critical theories would often predominate, whereas in more traditional disciplines such as political theory, anthropology or sociology critical theories tended to become accepted as part of the intellectual terrain, sometimes in a genuine atmosphere of pluralism, sometimes under a truce called after acrimonious arguments in departmental seminars and conference panels.

The experience of the Critical Theory group at the University of Nottingham is a good, if not typical, example of how critical theory came to be what it is understood to be in Anglophone academia. It is not typical in that it is quite rare to find programmes dedicated to critical theory per se in its broad, trans-disciplinary form, but it does illustrate what that form is and how it relates to interdisciplinary as well as narrower disciplinary settings. Faculty members based mostly in language departments and American Studies in Nottingham formed a reading group to satisfy their common interests as there was not sufficient enthusiasm, if not suspicion and hostility, in their home departments to delve into critical theory in research seminars. After a few years, there was enough interest in critical theory per se for the group to set up a masters course in critical theory that started in 1983 along with a PhD programme, and for the group to be recognised by the university as the Postgraduate School of Critical Theory, under the umbrella of the Arts Faculty. Several years later, after the group had invested a great deal of effort and enthusiasm into teaching and supervision, the university agreed to fund a full-time position in critical theory, with the possibility of further expansion which came several years later, reaching three full-time members of staff in 2003. By this time, 'critical theory' had been re-branded as 'critical theory and cultural studies', the single masters course had proliferated to include joint courses of critical theory with architecture, politics, cultural studies and modern languages, while the number of undergraduate classes offered had increased dramatically.

The experience at Nottingham illustrates some relevant themes for the development and fate of Critical Theory in Anglophone academia in general. First, the critical theory group covered diverse intellectual interests and proclivities, which did not always coexist easily. There are tensions in critical theory between an emphasis on social and political theory, on theories that directly analyse and critique social and political power relations, and theories which are mostly concerned with the human subject, self or psyche, often analysed through cultural texts. There are similar tensions between materialist (mostly Marxist) theories that focus on what they take to be the real structures of human practice and action and theories that focus on language and signification, on the relations between signs and symbols, as the most pertinent aspect of social interaction. There are tensions between critical theories, such as Habermas's, that are modernist in that they adhere to the promise and values of the Enlightenment for emancipation, universal truth and ethics, and those who are postmodernist in that they have no faith in that grand narrative of emancipation, such as Lyotard's. The most interesting critical theories typically transgress such boundaries, attempting to overcome or subsume the tensions, as did Frankfurt School Critical Theory with its blend of Freud and Marx, of psychology and social theory. Barthes, for example, put the semiotic analysis of signs to work in an ideological critique of consumer society, while Althusser deployed Lacan's psychoanalytic theory of the subject to refigure ideology not as a set of false beliefs about social relations but as the imaginary relation of individuals to their real conditions of social existence. However, the tensions between the disparate approaches and even incommensurable paradigms that are considered to be 'critical theory' suggest that it coheres as a definable field of scholarship most obviously in opposition to traditional theory, when it is embattled.

The experience at Nottingham also reflects the way in which critical theory's sense of marginalisation has declined as victory or truces in the campus wars have taken place. The original members of the Critical Theory group who once felt like an underground are now mostly professors, some of whom have taken on senior managerial roles in their departments and the university. Their successful careers reflect the extent to which critical theory has become accepted across the humanities, albeit unevenly. In some sense, critical theory has become part of the academic establishment, which makes claims for political radicalism and engagement seem less credible. It has often been noted how markets have a knack of appropriating cultural radicalism, so it is not surprising to find that critical theory is another intellectual commodity sold to a student market by higher education institutions driven by neo-liberal management principles.

The questioning of critical theory's continuing radicalism is also internal to the field itself. For some practitioners of critical theory, too many of their colleagues by the 1990s were wrapped up in 'identity politics', championing the differences of sexual, cultural and postcolonial identities and hybridities and the resistances of popular appropriations of hegemonic cultural practices, instead of challenging material inequalities and structural power imbalances. 'Postmodernism' was blamed by other branches of critical theory for debilitating scepticism about truth, morality and aesthetic value that precludes political and cultural commitment. At the same time, traditionalists in the humanities were hitting back in a fairly widespread backlash against critical theory, which was regarded as a part of the broader campus war, especially in the United States, about political correctness, multiculturalism, the literary canon and curriculum content. Academically, the backlash proclaims the traditional value of mainstream literary and cultural canons, dismissing 'theory' as mere obfuscation or misplaced politicisation. The backlash, though, is at least as political as critical theory, bearing resemblance to the neo-conservative agenda. Certainly, if critical theory is to retain its radical, engaged reputation into the twenty-first century it will have to rely less on embattlement within the academy alone and more on its connection to the radical opposition to Anglophone political and economic hegemony, the anti-capitalist and anti-globalisation movements which are today's version of the New Left. The success of Michael Hardt's and Tony Negri's *Empire*, which is a critique of the current political order of globalisation, gives every indication that critical theory is indeed moving along this path.[3]

Another inevitable consequence of the successful dissemination of ideas is that theories which were novel and groundbreaking in 1980 have become familiar twenty years later. There is no doubt that the emergence of critical theory in Anglophone academia was the consequence of a remarkable burst of intellectual creativity, particularly in France. The first generation of academics to disseminate, adapt and appropriate the mostly imported ideas of critical theory in effect created their own 'critical canon', a body of scholarship and knowledge that could be passed on to eager students looking for new, sharper tools to understand and challenge their social and cultural worlds. As I will explain below, this volume covers this 'critical canon', the 'classical' critical theorists who have been familiar, increasingly so, since the late 1970s or 1980s. But not only did key figures in this critical canon continue to produce new work since then, either until their deaths or until today, but they have been supplemented by new figures active in the academies of both Continental Europe and the Anglophone world, including figures originating from outside the First World. So, while the 'classical critical theory' is taught to undergraduates, critical theory replenishes itself constantly to keep a sense of 'cutting-edge' scholarship. Moreover, the new theorists build on the work of their predecessors, such that an understanding of the theoretical canon (and probably its precursors too) is necessary when dealing with the most contemporary theory. A good example here would be the extensive use of Lacanian theory by Slavoj Žižek.

One of the primary areas in which critical theory has become part of the staple intellectual diet of undergraduates is cultural studies. To a large extent, cultural theory has become a synonym for critical theory, just as literary theory, and to a lesser extent, social theory and radical political theory have. Cultural studies, especially in its British, Birmingham School form, has always had a similar commitment to political engagement as critical theory. It also has a very broad brief, especially if not limited to popular culture, covering a significant swathe of the range of topics to which critical theories are most often applied. It is thus not surprising that within two years of opening a masters course in critical theory with cultural studies at the University of Nottingham, the new joint course was attracting more students than the well-established and reputed course in critical theory alone. There are some places in which the distinction between critical theory and cultural studies is maintained, such as the University of California, Davis, which has separate programmes for each, but there critical theory retains a close association with the Frankfurt School. But critical theories have become entrenched in so many disciplines that cultural studies can by no means claim a monopoly over them, especially when they are labelled social theory or literary theory. It is harder now to identify critical theory in contrast to other theories because its success means it is found throughout the humanities.

The Scope of this Book

The type and range of critical theory covered in this volume refers to the broad sense of the term described above, as it is used in Anglophone academia as a catch-all phrase for a divergent set of theories that distinguish themselves from conventional or traditional theories. Critical theory designates a range of 'isms' including Marxism and post-Marxism, semiotics and discourse analysis, structuralism and post-structuralism, ideology critique of all varieties, deconstruction, feminism, queer theory, psychoanalysis, postcolonialism, postmodernism, as well as the successors to Frankfurt School Critical Theory. The range of critical theorists covered by the book provides an overview of the general field without privileging one particular area of critical theory. The thinkers covered in sixteen essays are those who had established significant transdisciplinary reputations in the Anglophone world by 1990, who will thus also be referred to as literary, cultural and social theorists. These are theorists who travel across disciplinary boundaries, whose work has been found useful and insightful within a wide variety of disciples as well as in the interdisciplinary work of, say, African-American Studies and visual culture studies.

The selected thinkers belong to what I have described above as the 'canon' of 'classic' twentieth-century critical theory, who are the theorists most often referred to by more recent thinkers. The

Introduction

selected theorists were all born within forty years of each other, between 1901 (Lacan) and 1941 (Kristeva). World War One was thus a significant experience in the youth of only Lacan and Levinas, whereas World War Two overshadowed the early lives of all the other thinkers except perhaps for Kristeva who was still an infant. The majority of the theorists come from Continental Europe, especially France, for reasons which I have also explained above. Not all of them were born in France: Levinas was born in Lithuania; Althusser, Cixous and Derrida in the French colony of Algeria (which was under Nazi-allied Vichy rule during the war); Irigaray in Belgium; and Kristeva in Bulgaria. Lyotard and Bourdieu spent part of their early careers in Algeria and Foucault did in Tunisia. The Eurocentric bias of the canon of critical theory selected here is somewhat softened by Said's birth in Palestine, from which he became exiled when Israel was established in 1948. Jameson is the only native of the Anglophone world in which critical theory has the meaning it does, though Said settled in the United States and many others have been or are still welcome visitors to American campuses. The gender bias in the selection shows that it is still difficult for women to rise to academic fame, especially without doing so on the feminist ticket. Derrida, Irigaray, Cixous, Kristeva, Baudrillard, Habermas and Jameson are still living and active, but the ideas of the others who have died are still very much alive too, so the 'critical canon' is by no means dead.

There are inevitably some omissions from a volume this size. In part these are compensated for by the publication of an earlier volume that covers the precursors to the canon of contemporary critical theorists selected for this volume. That volume deals with the intellectual 'tradition of critique', meaning the range of Continental philosophy and theory which has had a significant impact on the contemporary figures discussed here. There are individual chapters on Kant, Hegel, Marx, Nietzsche, Weber, Freud, Lukács, Adorno and Horkheimer, Husserl, Heidegger, Gadamer, Wittgenstein, Arendt and Lévi-Strauss.[4] In the opposite direction, a planned second volume is intended to include more contemporary critical theorists than those here, though in some cases it is difficult to determine precisely which have become influential in Anglophone academia only since the 1990s. The planned volume will cover Ernesto Laclau and Chantal Mouffe, Slavoj Žižek, Gayatri Spivak, Giorgio Agamben, Judith Butler, Alain Badiou, Donna Haraway, Homi Bhabha, Jacques Rancière, Bruno Latour, Antonio

Table 1.1 Chapters recommended for reading before or along with other chapters

When you read …	It is recommended that you also read …
Levinas	Derrida
Althusser	Lacan
Derrida	Levinas, Cixous
Irigaray	Lacan, Levinas
Cixous	Lacan, Derrida
Kristeva	Lacan
Jameson	Lacan, Althusser, Derrida, Baudrillard
Said	Foucault

Negri, Cornelius Castoriadis, Zygmunt Bauman, Paul Virilio, and a chapter on Green critical theorists.

Taking that into account, though, this volume could have gone further to represent home-grown Anglophone critical theorists, such as Richard Rorty for the American pragmatist tendency, which bears some strong affinities to European Continental philosophy. Charles Taylor would characterise the continuity of the hermeneutic tradition for contemporary notions of selfhood and identity. There would also be a good case for including a chapter on Stuart Hall as the main figure in the influential Birmingham School of Cultural Studies. The range of feminist theory could also be widened by including Anglophone theorists such as Juliet Mitchell, Catherine MacKinnon and Nancy Chodorow, as well as more French feminists such as Monique Wittig.

How to use this Book

Most readers will probably pick up this book to read individual chapters as required, to obtain a basic, general grasp of each thinker either before delving deeper or after being stymied in an attempt to read a primary text or a commentary designed for a more knowledgeable reader. Each chapter opens with a biographical and intellectual contextualisation of the theorists, presents and explains their key concepts, indicates how their work is applied across the humanities and presents some of the main criticisms of their work. There are also suggestions for further reading at the end of each chapter. While each chapter is designed to be free standing, there

Introduction

Table 1.2 Contemporary critical theorists and the main influences on them from the critical tradition

Contemporary theorist	Significant precursors
Lacan	Hegel, Freud, Lévi-Strauss
Levinas	Kant, Hegel, Heidegger
Althusser	Hegel, Marx, Freud, Lévi-Strauss
Barthes	Marx, Lévi-Strauss
Derrida	Hegel, Nietzsche, Husserl, Heidegger, Gadamer, Arendt, Lévi-Strauss
Irigaray	Hegel, Marx, Nietzsche, Freud, Heidegger, Lévi-Strauss
Cixous	Freud, Heidegger
Kristeva	Hegel, Marx, Freud, Lévi-Strauss
Lyotard	Kant, Hegel, Marx, Nietzsche, Freud, Wittgenstein
Deleuze and Guattari	Kant, Marx, Nietzsche, Freud, Lévi-Strauss
Foucault	Kant, Nietzsche, Marx, Weber, Freud, Heidegger, Lévi-Strauss
Baudrillard	Marx, Nietzsche, Lévi-Strauss
Bourdieu	Kant, Marx, Husserl, Weber, Heidegger, Lévi-Strauss
Habermas	Kant, Hegel, Nietzsche, Weber, Freud, Adorno and Horkheimer, Husserl, Heidegger, Gadamer, Wittgenstein, Arendt
Jameson	Marx, Hegel, Lukács, Adorno
Said	Marx, Lukács, Adorno

are some chapters from which greater benefit will be gained if they are read after or along with some other chapters. These cases are listed in Table 1.1.

In addition to reading about the immediate influences on the theorists included in this volume, readers may also find it helpful at some stage to learn more about some of the intellectual precursors to this 'canon' of critical theory. Readers will find accessible introductory essays on many figures in this 'tradition of critique' in the volume referred to above, *From Kant to Lévi-Straus*. Table 1.2 indicates which essays in that preceding volume would be most

Table 1.3 Thematic clusters

Theme	Relevant theorists
Psychoanalysis	Lacan, Irigaray, Cixous, Kristeva, Lyotard, Deleuze and Guattari
Structuralism and post-structuralism	Lacan, Althusser, Barthes, Derrida, Irigaray, Cixous, Kristeva, Foucault, Bourdieu, Jameson
Semiotics	Barthes, Kristeva, Bourdieu
Marxism, neo-Marxism, post-Marxism	Althusser, Barthes, Baudrillard, Bourdieu, Habermas, Jameson
Self and Other	Lacan, Levinas, Derrida, Irigaray, Cixous, Kristeva, Deleuze and Guattari, Bourdieu, Habermas, Said
Postmodernism	Lyotard, Baudrillard, Habermas, Jameson
Feminism	Irigaray, Cixous, Kristeva
Postcolonialism	Said
Socio-political power relations	Althusser, Kristeva, Deleuze and Guattari, Foucault, Baudrillard, Bourdieu, Habermas, Jameson, Said
Literary criticism and writing	Lacan, Althusser, Barthes, Derrida, Cixous, Kristeva, Jameson, Said
Phenomonology	Levinas, Derrida

relevant to understand the main intellectual influences on the theorists in this volume.

The book is not arranged in any definitive chronological order, such as by the date of birth of the thinkers, so there is little to be gained by working through the book from start to finish. Nor is it possible to divide the theorists into neatly separated tendencies, such as 'structuralists' and 'postmodernists' without enforcing the categories violently. However, various overlapping clusters of theorists do suggest themselves for reading along thematic lines, which are listed in Table 1.3. The real benefit of collecting these chapters on key contemporary critical theorists in one volume is to enable readers to draw their own connections, discern the multiple lines of influence and antagonism, to attempt their own combinations and syntheses and, by doing so, to carry on the tradition of critique themselves.

Notes

1. Guy Debord, *Society of the Spectacle*, rev. trans. (Detroit: Black and Red, 1977).
2. Juliet Mitchell, *Women's Estate* (London: Penguin, 1972); and *Psychoanalysis and Feminism* (London: Allen Lane, 1974).
3. Michael Hardt and Antonio Negri, *Empire* (Cambridge, MA: Harvard University Press, 2000).
4. Jon Simons (ed.), *From Kant to Lévi-Strauss: The Background to Contemporary Critical Theory* (Edinburgh: Edinburgh University Press, 2002).

2

Jacques Lacan (1901–81)

Yannis Stavrakakis

Lacan: A Life in Context

Lacan is arguably the most influential psychoanalyst after Freud. Adored by his followers and loathed by his opponents, he left a deep mark in the history of psychoanalysis in the twentieth century and contributed enormously to broadening the appeal of psychoanalytic ideas. Apart from claiming the loyalty of almost half of the psychoanalysts practising worldwide today – located mainly in France, Spain and Latin America – Lacan's work has also been extremely influential in Anglophone post-conventional philosophy, cultural criticism and political theory.

Lacan was born in 1901 in Paris. In 1919, he started his medical training leading to a specialisation in psychiatry (1926). His doctoral thesis, entitled *On Paranoid Psychosis in Its Relation to the Personality*, was a detailed study of his psychotic patient Aimée. He soon started his training analysis and, in 1934, became a candidate member of the Paris Psychoanalytic Society, being recognised as a full member four years later. Already in 1936, in his famous paper on the 'mirror stage', he articulates his first important contribution to psychoanalytic theory by pointing to what he calls the imaginary, and ultimately alienating, character of ego formation. The 'imaginary' is the first term in Lacan's conceptual triad of 'imaginary, symbolic, and real', which will be discussed in detail below.

During the 1930s Lacan became closely involved with the Surrealist movement, developing friendships with Breton, Picasso and Dali and publishing a series of articles in the acclaimed

Jacques Lacan (1901–81)

surrealist journal *Minotaure*. At the same time he followed closely the literary and philosophical developments of the period. He attended Joyce's first public reading of *Ulysses* and studied the work of Heidegger and Jaspers. He was also one of the regular attendants of Alexandre Kojève's legendary seminar on Hegel, also attended by Queneau, Merleau-Ponty, Aron, Klossowski and Bataille. Indeed his life was marked by his friendship with figures such as Claude Lévi-Strauss and Roman Jakobson while many more were invited to his seminar or his country house (among them Heidegger and Foucault). In that sense, Lacan had taken very seriously Freud's idea that the study of language and society, literature and art, is a necessary prerequisite for the understanding of clinical experience and the broadening of psychoanalytic theory.

After the Second World War Lacan was recognised as one of the major theorists of the Paris Psychoanalytic Society. Soon he became President of the Society but aspects of his analytic technique (especially his introduction of analytic sessions of variable duration) sparked a controversy that eventually led to his resignation from the society and to the formation of a new psychoanalytic group, the Société française de psychanalyse (SFP). In 1953 Lacan started his public seminar at the Saint-Anne hospital. Although focusing on analytic theory and technique the themes discussed in the seminar also encompassed philosophy (from Plato and Aristotle to Descartes, Kant and Hegel), linguistics (from Saussure to Peirce and beyond), and anthropology, as well as literary and artistic creation (from *Antigone* and *Hamlet* to Holbein's *Ambassadors* and Velasquez's *Las Meninas*). This is the period in which he initiates his 'return to Freud' which involves a rereading of the Freudian corpus with the aid of an appropriation of elements from structuralist linguistics. Lacan's focus now turns from the imaginary to the symbolic dimension of human experience: to the role language and signification play in the constitution of the desiring subject.

When the new psychoanalytic society asked for recognition from the International Psychoanalytic Association the IPA demanded the termination of Lacan's training programme, thereby forcing him to resign and suspend his seminar. This 'excommunication' triggered his lifelong struggle with the international psychoanalytic establishment and with American Ego-Psychology in particular. With the help of Fernand Braudel and Louis Althusser, Lacan soon resumed his seminar, by then a major cultural and theoretical event, at the Ecole normale. Indeed the 1960s marked Lacan's canonisation as an autonomous force in the psychoanalytic/cultural landscape. He founded his own psychoanalytic society, the École freudienne de Paris (EFP); his reputation was boosted by the publication of a 900-page collection of his essays, the *Écrits*; while in 1969 a Lacanian department of psychoanalysis was founded at the new Université de Paris VIII at Vincennes.

In 1973 the first edited transcript of his seminar appeared, *The Four Fundamental Concepts of Psychoanalysis*. During the late 1960s and throughout the 1970s Lacan continued his seminar, focusing on the concept of the real, the third term in his conceptual triad. The real accounts for what cannot be represented by the image and the signifier but keeps distorting and dislocating our imaginary and symbolic representations and identifications. In order to approach this unrepresentable real in a non-reductionist way, Lacan's focus now shifts from linguistics to areas of mathematical formalisation such as topology. His fame and intellectual reputation is firmly consolidated. French television broadcasts a two-part interview with Lacan, who is invited to lecture in a variety of American Universities (Yale, Columbia, MIT). He dies in 1981 after a controversy caused by the participation of his son-in-law and editor of his seminars, Jacques-Alain Miller, in the board of directors of the EFP forces him to dissolve the society and found the École de la cause freudienne.

Accessing Lacan: From Psychoanalysis to Critical Social Theory

Notwithstanding his continuous engagement with philosophy, social and cultural theory, Lacan was neither a philosopher nor a social scientist. He was first of all a clinician and psychoanalytic theorist, indeed a theorist who has often been accused of obscurantism. Thus, any reference to his work within the fields of the social sciences and critical theory is bound to create scepticism and accusations of reductionism and inaccessibility. I will deal with these obstacles to the reception of Lacan before moving to a presentation of some key Lacanian concepts and discussing their relevance for critical theory.

The very application of psychoanalysis to the socio-political domain might itself seem inappropriate. Clearly, psychological reductionism, that is to say, the understanding of socio-political phenomena by reference to some sort of psychological substratum, an essence of the psyche, is something that should clearly be avoided. Psychoanalysis, however, cannot be reduced to the essentialist psychology of an isolated individual. Quite the contrary. Psychoanalytic theory is based on the experience of a social relation: that between an analyst and an analysand. The analytic relationship provides a thorough insight into the nucleus of the social bond, leading to a knowledge which is thoroughly social and has important socio-political implications. In this vein, Lacan deconstructs the essentialist opposition between the individual and the collective by registering the socio-symbolic dependence of subjectivity and by addressing in a non-reductionist way the incomplete (lacking) constitution of both the subject and the Other – a Lacanian term partly denoting the socio-symbolic order, about which more will be said below.

But even if Lacan's discourse avoids psychological reductionism, this does not make it any more accessible or less difficult. Much of the inaccessibility of his work can be ascribed to the preferred form of Lacan's teaching: a series of oral seminars (twenty-six in total) which are not yet published in their entirety owing to a long process of editing. This has led to a variety of misreadings and misunderstandings; for example, depending on the particular phase of his teaching with which they are most familiar, different commentators have categorised Lacan as a structuralist or a post-structuralist. Although bearing a multitude of family resemblances with these and other trends, his theoretical trajectory defies all these categorisations; something which becomes clear when one gets a more 'global' picture of his work – especially the last phase of it. In any case, most of his seminars are gradually becoming available, as are Lacan's written texts, in French and in translation. There is also a proliferation of secondary works further illuminating and developing Lacanian theory and making it more accessible to the international psychoanalytic community and the wider public.

Another significant problem has to do with the difficulty of Lacan's prose, with his baroque style. Lacan is not an easy read. It is even more frustrating for many readers that this is a conscious strategy on his part. One may ask for example: 'If what he says is so insightful, why is it written in such an obscure language? Why is everything stated in such an allusive, ambiguous manner?' His teaching aims to have certain effects on the reader other than the usual academic meaning effects: he seeks to evoke, to provoke, to unsettle us, to jolt us out of our conceptual complacency. Related to this is his aim to put us to work, to remind us that in fact we do not understand what we think we understand and that we may have to make numerous attempts to express or conceptualise something, without ever achieving a perfect understanding.[1] The ambiguity of Lacan's discourse is a challenge for every reader, a difficulty that has to be assumed; only by acknowledging the irreducible ambiguity and indeterminacy of his discourse can one develop a desire to work with it. Furthermore, one should not overlook the fact that behind Lacan's often labyrinthine discourse, it is possible to discern a certain theoretical systematicity, albeit one premised on a 'negative' ontology. In the militant deconstructionist climate of the 1970s this has even become one of the main points of criticism in Lacoue-Labarthe and Nancy's reading of Lacan.[2] In any case, there is clearly more to Lacan's teaching than French intellectual snobbery. In fact, as Derrida has recently pointed out in a text partly withdrawing his earlier criticisms of Lacan,[3] the alterity of his language can also be seen as an act of resistance against intellectual neo-conformism, as a call for theoretical innovation and originality.

Mapping Human Experience: Imaginary, Symbolic and Real

One way through which Lacanian theory expands the horizons of cultural, social and political theory and critique is by introducing a new conception of subjectivity, the subject as lack, the lacking subject. The roots of this conception of subjectivity can be traced back to the Freudian idea of *Spaltung* (splitting). Lacan, for his part, sees this split as something constitutive of subjectivity in general. Ignoring its implications would amount to a betrayal of psychoanalysis:

> But if we ignore the self's radical ex-centricity to itself with which man is confronted, in other words, the truth discovered by Freud, we shall falsify both the order and methods of psychoanalytic mediation; we shall make of it nothing more than the compromise operation that it has, in effect, become, namely, just what the letter as well as the spirit of Freud's work most repudiates.[4]

According to Lacan the subject of psychoanalysis is not the self-sufficient, 'autonomous' subject of knowledge as it is constructed in the tradition of philosophy, that is to say, as corresponding to consciousness, to the conscious *cogito*, but the ex-centric subject, one structured around a radical split, a radical lack.

From a philosophically aware socio-political point of view, the benefits of such a conceptualisation are obvious. First, it avoids

Jacques Lacan (1901–81)

positing a positively defined essence of subjectivity and thus moves beyond psychological reductionism. Second, it permits a thorough grasping of the socio-symbolic dependence of subjectivity: if lack is clearly central in the Lacanian conception of the subject it is because subjectivity constitutes the space where a whole 'politics' of identification takes place. The idea of the subject as lack cannot be separated from the recognition of the fact that the subject is always attempting to cover over this constitutive lack at the level of representation, through continuous identification acts. This lack necessitates the constitution of every identity through processes of identification with socially available objects of identification such as political ideologies, patterns of consumption and social roles. And vice versa: the inability of all identification acts to produce a full identity – subsuming subjective division – (re)produces the radical ex-centricity of the subject. In that sense the notion of the subject in Lacan does not only invoke lack but also all our attempts to eliminate this lack which, however, does not stop re-emerging.

Two points are extremely important here. First, the resources available to the lacking subject in order to attempt a (re)constitution of her identity are, broadly speaking, of two distinct types: imaginary and, primarily, symbolic. This emphasis on the symbolic has sometimes been misinterpreted as a sign of adherence to a rather simplistic version of structuralism. In Castoriadis's words, 'linguistic structuralism, an illegitimate extrapolation of *some* aspects of the organisation of language as a *code*, was pressed by Lévi-Straus into the service of ethnology, and by Lacan into the service of psychoanalysis'.[5] Lacan's structure, however, is never presented as a closed circuit – as in classical structuralism – but always as a lacking and incomplete order. In this point Lacan seems to be much closer to a post-structuralist radicalisation of structuralism. Second, as we shall see, Lacan points to the ultimate inability of both these planes to provide anything resembling a full identity, because of their inability to master an always escaping real (which in Lacanian terms is always distinguished from reality). This stress on the (extra-discursive) real has caused unease in many post-structuralists, who have warned against any tabooing or ahistorical essentialisation of such a category.[6] This criticism, however, fails to engage with Lacan's primary objective, which is to explore the interaction of these three registers – imaginary, symbolic and real – in structuring human experience, personal and collective history. This exploration also marks a gradual passage from Lacan's theory of the 'subjective' to his understanding of the 'objective', of (imaginary and symbolic) reality and the real.

The imaginary register is first approached by Lacan in his work on the 'mirror stage'. This stage refers to a particular period in the infant's psychic development – roughly located between the sixth and the eighteenth month of her life – in which the fragmentation experienced by the infant is, for the first time, transformed into an affirmation of her bodily unity (through the assumption of her image in the mirror or through similar experiences). In that sense the mirror stage has to be understood as an identification: 'We have only to understand the mirror stage as an identification, in the full sense that analysis gives to the term: namely the transformation that takes place in the subject when he assumes an image'.[7] This assumption of a spatial imaginary identity is, however, indicative of the ambivalence involved in ego formation. As Lacan observes, acquiring a first sense of identity is a cause not only of jubilation but also of alienation. At first the infant appears jubilant because of her success in integrating her fragmentation into an imaginary totality and unity. Later on, however, jubilation is followed by alienation:

> The fact is that the total form of the body by which the subject anticipates in a mirage the maturation of his powers is given to him only as ... an exteriority in which this form is certainly more constituent than constituted, but in which it appears to him above all in a contrasting size (*un relief de stature*) that fixes it and in a symmetry that inverts it, in contrast with the turbulent movements that the subject feels are animating him.[8]

By virtue of its inability to represent the turbulent real of the infant's body and of its exteriority, imaginary identification 'prefigures its alienating dimension'.[9] Thus, what was supposed to be the basis of a stable ego-identity is revealed as a mark of radical ex-centricity: 'the human being has a special relation with his own image – a relation of gap, of alienating tension'.[10]

If the imaginary representation of ourselves, the mirror image, is ultimately incapable of providing us with a stable identity, the only option left for acquiring one seems to be the field of linguistic representation, the symbolic register. After all, the symbolic is already presupposed in the functioning of the mirror stage since the infant, even before her birth, is inserted into a symbolic network constructed by her parents and family (her name is often discussed and decided in advance, inserting her into a pre-existing family mythology). In Lacan's work it is clear that the symbolic has a far more important structuring role than the imaginary: 'While the image equally plays a capital role in our domain, this role is completely taken up and caught up within, remoulded and reanimated by, the symbolic order'.[11] By submitting to the laws of language the child becomes a subject in language, it inhabits and is inhabited by language, and hopes to gain an adequate representation through the world of words: 'the symbolic provides a form into which the subject is inserted at the level of its being. It's on this basis that the subject recognises himself as being this or that'.[12] The subject truly comes to being as long as 'it agrees' to be represented by the signifier: 'the subject is the subject of the signifier – determined by it'.[13]

This, however, should not lead to the conclusion that entering the symbolic overcomes alienation by acquiring a solid identity. On the contrary, the subject constituted on the acceptance of the laws of language, of symbolic Law – a function embodied, within the Oedipal setting, by what Lacan calls 'the Name of the Father' – is the subject of lack par excellence. Alienation is not resolved but displaced into another (symbolic) level, to the register of the signifier, to what Lacan calls the Other. Owing to the 'universality' of language, to the linguistic constitution of human reality, the signifier offers to the subject an almost 'immortal', 'neutral' representation; only this representation is incapable of capturing and communicating the real 'singularity' of the subject. In that sense, it is clear that something is always missing from the symbolic, the Other is a lacking Other. The emergence of the subject in the socio-symbolic terrain presupposes a division between reality and the real, language and *jouissance* (a pre-symbolic, real enjoyment), a division that consolidates the alienation of the subject in the signifier and reveals the lack in the Other.

If the subjective is no longer 'subjective', in the sense of a self-sufficient, autonomous consciousness, the objective is also no longer 'objective' in the sense of a closed structure, of an entity capable, under certain circumstances, of filling the lack in the subject. This is the 'big secret of psychoanalysis', as Lacan calls it already from his 1958–9 seminar, a secret that is not limited to the subject but touches on the incomplete constitution of social reality itself. Something is missing in the Other; there is no Other of the Other.[14] The field of representation is itself revealed as lacking because it attempts the impossible, that is to say, the representation of something ultimately unrepresentable. Both at the subjective and at the objective level there is always a real which escapes our attempts to master it, to represent it, to symbolise it. It is this impossibility of mastering the real which splits subjective and objective reality.

Lacanian theory accounts for this lack in the Other, the lack that splits subjective and objective reality, as a lack of *jouissance*. This lack is always posited as something lost, as a lost fullness, the part of ourselves that is sacrificed – castrated – when we enter the symbolic system of language and social relations. This lack of *jouissance* should not be viewed, however, as a nihilistic conclusion. It is, rather, what constitutes and sustains human desire: the prohibition of *jouissance* – the nodal point of the Oedipal drama – is exactly what permits the emergence of desire, a desire structured around the unending quest for the lost, impossible *jouissance*. As a result the dimension of fantasy acquires a central role in personal as well as in social and political life: fantasy denotes all the imaginary scenaria, all the discursive constructions, in which we are promised an encounter with our lost *jouissance* – consider, for example, political or consumerist utopias – or, most crucially, in which the lack of *jouissance* is explained as the result of someone else's action – and not as an integral part of the constitution of social reality.

Lacanian Social and Political Criticism: Advertising, Racism and Nationalism

Undoubtedly, critical theory can draw numerous implications from Lacan's teaching. Various components of the Lacanian conceptual and theoretical universe have been reappropriated by film studies, feminism, philosophy, literary theory and political analysis. His work on the imaginary and the gaze has been taken up by film theorists, while feminists have long been debating the proper interpretation of his work on sexual difference, the role of the phallus and his distinction between phallic and feminine *jouissance*. Philosophers have also used Lacan's work in exploring issues in ethics, while literary theorists have focused on his reading of important literary works. In the context of this chapter we will limit ourselves to a brief discussion of Lacan's relevance for socio-political analysis and cultural critique.

Lacan's conceptualisation of the symbolic, especially the importance he assigns to the role particular signifiers play in structuring whole fields of signification, has influenced enormously the study of political discourse and ideology. Lacan's understanding of signification stresses the importance of the laws of metaphor and metonymy, but that does not mean that he subscribes to the postmodern idea of an unending fluidity of meaning. Certainly, each signification refers to another one and so on, and both metaphoric substitution and metonymic combination can, in principle, be described as infinite. Yet, for Lacan, this endless movement of signification is partially halted by the prominent role attributed (retroactively) to certain signifiers. These signifiers he calls *points de capiton* ('quilting points' or 'nodal points' in Laclau and Mouffe's rendering). The *point de capiton* is the signifier which 'stops the otherwise endless movement (*glissement*) of the signification'.[15] These signifiers fix the meaning of whole chains of signifiers:

> Everything radiates out from and is organized around this signifier, similar to these little lines of force that an upholstery button forms on the surface of material. It is the point of convergence that enables everything that happens in this discourse to be situated retroactively and retrospectively.[16]

Thus, meaning is produced in the relations between signifiers through the (contingent) establishment of certain *points de capiton*. Without the reference to this structural position all meaning would be impossible and discourse would disintegrate into chaotic rumbling.

Given the importance of the *point de capiton* in creating a sense of unity, it is no surprise that the logic of *capitonage* has been central for the development of a Lacanian analysis of ideology. Let me illustrate this logic of discursive articulation with an example often used by Slavoj Žižek. In the ideological discourse of communism a series of floating signifiers or proto-ideological elements (previously articulated in other ideological discourses) such as democracy, state and freedom acquire a certain meaning through their quilting by the signifier 'Communism'. Thus, they are transformed to internal moments of the communist ideological discourse. Democracy is conceived as real democracy opposing bourgeois democracy, freedom acquires an economic connotation, and so on. In other words, the terms acquire the meaning imposed by the *point de capiton* 'Communism'; this is how communism can hegemonise a set of available signifiers. The same, of course, applies to all signifiers that acquire a central political role and aspire to hegemonise a given politico-discursive field. It is in this sense that 'the Lacanian concept of the *point de capiton*, the nodal point that fixes meaning, is profoundly relevant for a theory of hegemony'.[17]

Beyond all the semiotic conditions we have highlighted up to now, the construction of social reality, the illusion of the world as a stable and well-structured whole, would not be possible without the intervention of the element of fantasy. Although discursive coherence is important, the lack in the Other forces ideological discourse to position itself vis-à-vis the lack of *jouissance* marking human life. No discourse can offer itself as a desirable object of identification without dealing with this important issue. In Lacan's view, 'everything we are allowed to approach by way of reality remains rooted in fantasy'.[18] If social and political reality is a symbolic construction produced through metaphoric and metonymic processes and articulated around *points de capiton*, it nevertheless depends on fantasy in order to constitute itself.

Broadly speaking, there are two ways in which social discourse and political ideology deal with the lack of *jouissance*. They can either promise an encounter with the lacking *jouissance* in the future and/or blame someone else for this lack, thus reassuring us that its filling remains possible. The discussion that follows about, first, advertising and, then, racism and nationalism will reveal how *jouissance* can serve as an important explanatory ingredient for various socio-political phenomena and will clarify these two operations at stake.

If advertising attempts to stimulate, to cause, our desire, this can only mean that the whole mythological construction it articulates around the product which is advertised is structured as a fantasy and, furthermore, that this product is offered to us as an object that can satisfy our desire. In Lacanian terms, the condition of possibility for this complex play is, of course, the loss, the prohibition, of a 'mythical' pre-symbolic enjoyment (*jouissance*) which stands at the Oedipal roots of (social) subjectivity. It is a piece of this enjoyment that is promised in slogans like 'Enjoy Coca-Cola' – a slogan that Lacan himself has associated with what he called *le sujet de la jouissance*. In other words, within the advertising universe, every experience of social lack (from sexual frustration to social and political alienation) is projected to the lack of the product that is being advertised, that is to say, to a lack that one simple move promises to eliminate: the purchase of the product. Advertising fantasies reduce the constitutive lack in the subject to the lack of the product that they simultaneously offer as a solution, as a promise for the final elimination of this lack. Thus, advertising fantasy attempts to exorcise the malaise of everyday life by reproducing the system within which this malaise is constitutive.

The harmony, however, promised by fantasy cannot be realised; the advertised object can function as the object-cause of desire only insofar as it is lacking. As soon as we buy the product we find out that the enjoyment we get is partial, that it has nothing to do with what we have been promised: '"That's not it!" is the very cry by which the *jouissance* obtained is distinguished from the *jouissance* expected'.[19] And with every such experience a lack is re-inscribed in the subject. But this resurfacing of the inability of fantasy to lead us to a full satisfaction of our desire does not put in danger the cultural hegemony of advertising in late capitalist societies. The aim of fantasy is not to satisfy our desire, something that is ultimately impossible. It is enough to construct it and support it as such: through fantasy we 'learn' how to desire. As far as the final satisfaction of our desire is concerned this is postponed from discourse to discourse, from fantasy to fantasy, from product to product. It is this continuous displacement that constitutes the essence of consumer culture. The important 'by-product' of this process is, however, a specific structuration of our desire. It is this particular economy of desire, articulated around the advertised product that guarantees, through its cumulative metonymic effect, the reproduction of late capitalism within a distinct 'promotional culture'. In other words, the hegemony of the market depends, to a large extent, on the hegemony of this particular economy of desire, on the hegemony of this particular administration of enjoyment.

Another crucial example of the relevance of *jouissance* to critical theory is the phenomenon of racism. In *Television* Lacan replies to the following question posed by Jacques-Alain Miller:

– [W]hat gives you the confidence to prophesy the rise of racism? And why the devil do you have to speak of it?
– Because it doesn't strike me as funny and yet, it's true. With our *jouissance* going off track, only the Other is able to mark its position, but only insofar as we are separated from this Other. Whence certain fantasies – unheard of before the melting pot.

Leaving this Other to his own mode of *jouissance*, that would only be possible by not imposing our own on him, by not thinking of him as underdeveloped.[20]

Miller takes up these comments in his seminar *Extimité* which leads him to argue that racism, as a hatred of difference, is founded on 'the fact that the Other takes his *jouissance* in a way different from ours' – something clearly reflected in racist discourse.

> All the arguments employed by racists to justify their hatred ultimately focus on the way in which the Other obtains some *plus-de-jouir* [surplus enjoyment] that he does not deserve; either he does not work, or he works too hard, or he eats smelly food or he has too much sex, etc.[21]

It follows from this line of argumentation that intolerance and racism are directly associated with the intolerance towards the (supposed) *jouissance* of the Other.[22]

Clearly all these insights are crucial not only for the analysis of racism but also for the analyses of all sorts of discourses of hatred. In *Tarrying with the Negative*, Žižek conducts an insightful analysis of nationalism around this same Lacanian insight, building on Miller's idea of 'the theft of enjoyment': 'The question of tolerance or intolerance … is located on the level of tolerance or intolerance toward the enjoyment of the Other, the Other as he who essentially *steals* my own enjoyment'.[23] Nationalist hatred is explained then as a way societies or social groups attempt to deal with their lack of enjoyment, attributing this lack, this structural impossibility, to the action of an external force, the national enemy or the general Other who is fantasised as enjoying more (having already stolen what is thought of as 'essentially ours').

Given this background, it should come as no surprise to find *jouissance* acquiring special importance for those contemplating seriously theories of ideology and, especially, critiques of ideological discourse. For in this view, 'the element which holds together a given community cannot be reduced to the point of symbolic identification: the bond linking together its members always implies a shared relationship toward a Thing, toward Enjoyment incarnated', an enjoyment structured in fantasies and directly linked to the hatred of Others.[24]

In that sense, the importance psychoanalysis attaches to the notion of the real *qua* fantasmatically-structured *jouissance* suggests that symptomal analyses of the discursive, deconstructive or interpretative kind, though perhaps a necessary prerequisite, are often not sufficient to effect a displacement in the social subject's psychic economy. We often encounter cases in which subjects fully acknowledge the contingency of their situation, subjects who accept how things could be otherwise and how an even minor change (in behaviour or attitude) would lead to a different life visited less by suffering. Yet the subjects cannot help themselves; they cannot stop repeating. Why? Lacan's answer is, as should be clear by now, *jouissance*, the same *jouissance* that animates the consumerist desire that sustains late capitalism, the same *jouissance* that supports racist and nationalist discourses – in fact, discursive structures in general.

The structure of fantasy defines a mode of *jouissance* that often resists all interpretive and deconstructive strategies. Thus, if psychoanalytic intervention (and, by extension, political intervention and critical theory) is to have any effect in these cases, it must aim between the lines, so to speak, at the whole field of *jouissance*, at the way it constitutes our desires and sustains the economic, cultural and political parameters of our societies. This will be the first step in opting for an alternative administration of enjoyment, an administration that will aim at the 'crossing of the fantasy', one of Lacan's definitions for the end of analysis. In socio-political terms this crossing implies a particular ethics of relating to the lack in the Other, a new positioning of our social and political arrangements beyond the illusions of consumerist, racist and nationalist utopias.

Notes

1. Bruce Fink, *A Clinical Introduction to Lacanian Psychoanalysis: Theory and Technique* (Cambridge, MA: Harvard University Press, 1997), p. 220.
2. See Phillippe Lacoue-Labarthe and Jean-Luc Nancy, *The Title of the Letter* (Albany: SUNY Press, 1992).
3. See Jacques Derrida, 'For the Love of Lacan', *Cardozo Law Review*, 16, 3–4, 1995, pp. 699–728.
4. Lacan, 'The Agency of the Letter in the Unconscious or Reason since Freud', *Écrits*, p. 171.
5. Cornelius Castoriadis, 'Psychoanalysis: Project and Elucidation', *Crossroads of the Labyrinth* (London: Harvester Press, 1984), p. 100.
6. See, for example, Judith Butler, *Bodies That Matter* (New York: Routledge, 1993).
7. Lacan, 'The Mirror Stage as Formative of the Function of the I', *Écrits*, p. 4.
8. Ibid., p. 2.
9. Ibid., p. 2.
10. Lacan, *The Seminar. Book II*, p. 323
11. Lacan, *The Seminar. Book III*, p. 9.
12. Ibid., p. 179.
13. Lacan, *The Seminar. Book XI*, p. 67.
14. Lacan, Seminar of 8 April 1959.

15. Lacan, 'The Subversion of the Subject and the Dialectic of Desire in the Freudian Unconscious', *Écrits*, p. 303.
16. Lacan, *The Seminar. Book III*, p. 268.
17. Ernesto Laclau, 'Metaphor and Social Antagonisms', in G. Nelson and L. Grossberg (eds), *Marxism and the Interpretation of Culture* (London: Macmillan, 1988), pp. 249–57 (255).
18. Lacan, *The Seminar. Book XX*, p. 95.
19. Ibid., p. 111.
20. Lacan, *Television*, pp. 32–3.
21. Dylan Evans, 'From Kantian Ethics to Mystical Experience: An Exploration of Jouissance', in Dany Nobus (ed.), *Key Concepts of Lacanian Psychoanalysis* (London: Rebus Press, 1998), pp. 21–8.
22. Ibid.
23. Miller cited in Slavoj Žižek, *Tarrying with the Negative* (Durham: Duke University Press, 1993), p. 203, emphasis added.
24. Ibid., p. 201.

Major Works by Lacan

Écrits, A Selection, trans. Alan Sheridan, ed. Jacques-Alain Miller (London: Tavistok/Routledge, 1977 [1966]). A much anticipated new translation of the *Écrits* by Bruce Fink appeared in 2002 (New York: Norton).

The Seminar. Book I. Freud's Papers on Technique, 1953–4, trans. with notes John Forrester, ed. Jacques-Alain Miller (London: Cambridge University Press, 1987).

The Seminar. Book II. The Ego in Freud's Theory and in the Technique of Psychoanalysis, 1954-5, trans. Sylvana Tomaselli, with notes John Forrester, ed. Jacques-Alain Miller (London: Cambridge University Press, 1988).

The Seminar. Book III. The Psychoses, 1955–6, trans. with notes Russell Grigg, ed. Jacques-Alain Miller (London: Routledge, 1993).

The Seminar. Book VII. The Ethics of Psychoanalysis, 1959–60, trans. with notes Denis Porter, ed. Jacques-Alain Miller (London: Routledge, 1992).

The Seminar. Book XI. The Four Fundamental Concepts of Psycho-analysis, trans. Alan Sheridan, ed. Jacques-Alain Miller (London: Penguin, 1977).

The Seminar. Book XX. Encore, On Feminine Sexuality, The Limits of Love and Knowledge, 1972–3, trans. with notes Bruce Fink, ed. Jacques-Alain Miller (New York: Norton, 1998).

Television, a Challenge to the Psychoanalytic Establishment, trans. Dennis Hollier, Rosalind Krauss and Anne Michelson, ed. Joan Copjec (New York: Norton, 1990).

Lacan, Jacques, and the École Freudienne, *Feminine Sexuality*, ed. Juliet Mitchell and Jacqueline Rose (New York: Norton, 1985).

Jacques Lacan (1901–81)

Suggestions for Further Reading

Bracher, Mark, Marshall Alcorn, Ronald Corthell and Françoise Massardier-Kenney (eds), *Lacanian Theory of Discourse* (New York: New York University Press, 1997). A wide-ranging collection demonstrating the importance of Lacanian theory – and Lacan's theory of the four discourses in particular – in approaching a variety of discursive formations.

Dean, Tim, *Beyond Sexuality* (Chicago: University of Chicago Press, 2000). An innovative argument demonstrating the possible uses of the Lacanian conception of desire in queer theory.

Fink, Bruce, *The Lacanian Subject: Between Language and Jouissance* (Princeton: Princeton University Press, 1995). One of the most sophisticated but, at the same time, extremely readable introductions to Lacanian theory.

Glynos, Jason and Yannis Stavrakakis (eds), *Lacan & Science* (London: Karnac Books, 2002). A collection of articles focusing on the relation between Lacanian psychoanalysis and science and including, among others, discussions of causality, truth and knowledge, sexual difference, clinical diagnosis and addiction.

Grosz, Elisabeth, *Jacques Lacan: A Feminist Introduction* (London: Routledge, 1990). The standard feminist introduction to Lacan's work.

Nobus, Dany (ed.), *Key Concepts of Lacanian Psychoanalysis* (London: Rebus Press, 1998). An accessible but not simplistic introduction to a variety of Lacanian categories such as *jouissance*, the mirror stage, fantasy, desire and the subject.

Roudinesco, Elisabeth, *Jacques Lacan*, trans. B. Bray (Cambridge: Polity, 1997). One of the few biographies of Lacan, this is an extensive, well-documented, but somewhat controversial work.

Stavrakakis, Yannis, *Lacan and the Political* (London: Routledge, 1999). A systematic exposition of some basic aspects of Lacanian theory and their relevance for social and political analysis. Particular attention is also paid to Lacan's importance in radicalising modern democracy.

Žižek, Slavoj, *The Sublime Object of Ideology* (London: Verso, 1989). The first book by Žižek in English and arguably one of his best so far. It opened the road for the emergence of a whole tradition of Lacanian political theory.

Žižek, Slavoj, *Looking Awry: An Introduction to Jacques Lacan through Popular Culture* (Cambridge, MA: The MIT Press, 1991). Here Žižek introduces some central Lacanian themes through his unique take on popular culture.

Žižek, Slavoj (ed.) *Everything You Always Wanted to Know about Lacan (But Were Too Afraid to Ask Hitchcock)* (London: Verso, 1992). Stimulating essays that explain the relevance of Lacan for the analysis of film – and the relevance of Hitchcock for explaining Lacanian theory.

3

Emmanuel Levinas (1906–95)

Arjuna Weerasooriya

Introduction

Emmanuel Levinas is a key figure in twentieth-century Continental philosophy, whose highly original description of ethics is frequently utilised in other disciplines. He takes ethics to be an asymmetrical relation with an opaque other that decentres the ego-subject. This relation is concretely produced as 'my infinite responsibility to the other person'. Enlightenment ethics was founded upon the notion of an autonomous moral agent, but was significantly undermined by the Nietzsche-inspired critique of such metaphysical assumptions. Hence, the recent revival of the term, contentiously called 'the ethical turn', has found in Levinas an invaluable basis for thinking about ethics without a return to foundationalism and the sovereign subject.

Levinas was born into the important Jewish community in Kaunas, Lithuania, in 1906. The complex trajectory of his life intersects most of the major political fault-lines of the twentieth century, starting with the flight from German-occupied Lithuania during the First World War. He witnessed the Russian Revolution and the Civil War as an eleven-year-old refugee in the Ukrainian city of Kharkov. Then, in 1923, as a student of the University of Strasbourg, Levinas experienced the post-war upsurge of Republicanism in France that set the tone of his critical engagement with liberal politics and values. At Strasbourg he was introduced to Henri Bergson's revolutionary thinking of time as 'creative duration', and Emile Durkheim's concept of 'organic solidarity'. These ideas would resonate in his own deeply original thoughts on time and community. But the main stimulus for his rethinking of fraternity on the basis of alterity was the abiding interest shown by his teachers toward reassessing the universality of the trinitarian legacy of 1789, in the light of the widespread anti-Semitism revealed by the Dreyfus Affair. It was also at Strasbourg that Levinas began a rigorous study of Husserl's phenomenology.

In 1928, having moved on to the University of Freiburg, he first encountered Martin Heidegger's critique of Husserl's thesis of intentionality. Heidegger's analysis of the human being who is inextricably implicated in the world through a priori structures, such as understanding, moods and discourse, had a profound formative influence upon Levinas. But Heidegger's capitulation to Nazism in the 1930s, especially his subsequent refusal to provide either explanation or apology for his terrible act, deeply injured Levinas. Consequently, Levinas repudiated Heidegger's later philosophy, remaining thoughtfully critical of his early work. He claimed that the values central to National Socialism were prefigured throughout Heidegger's thought. Throughout his life Levinas remained faithful to phenomenology's essential practice of describing reality in terms of reconstructing the tacit horizons that constitute the appearance of an object to consciousness. He practised phenomenology on its own thesis of intentionality by interrogating the notion of 'horizon' itself, thereby revealing how phenomenology originates in a suspension of the failure of its own intention to describe consciousness as a return to self. This heteronomy of consciousness, according to Levinas, is ethics, or the transcendence of intentionality.

Levinas obtained French citizenship in 1930. Captured while serving in the army in 1940, he remained incarcerated until the end of the war, narrowly escaping the death camps only because of the prisoner of war status conferred by his French uniform. The Nazis murdered his family in Lithuania. If not for Maurice Blanchot, his friend from the Strasbourg days, Levinas's wife and daughter would have met the same fate. The *Shoah* haunted Levinas all his life, as the political horror that is the ubiquitous horizon of his work. After the war, as director of an organisation training teachers for schools in the Mediterranean basin, Levinas keenly felt the repercussions of the violent inception of the State of Israel, and the reverberations of decolonisation struggles in the region. Between 1947 and 1949 he learned Talmudic exegesis from an itinerant scholar named Monsieur Chouchani, which combined with his training in phenomenology to produce a unique approach. Beginning in 1964, Levinas taught philosophy at the universities of Poitiers, Nanterre and the Sorbonne, retiring in 1976, but continuing to conduct his seminars until 1980, fifteen years before his death.

Levinas's discourse is a sustained encounter between the Western philosophical tradition and Talmudic Judaism, resulting in a radical account of human subjectivity and a notion of community that challenges the fundamental assumptions of traditional political theory. This ethical subjectivity, receiving its unity from alterity instead of identity, is foremost a corporeal being, not a rational or abstract ego of any kind. Levinas asserts that ethics is not a rational category, such as the Kantian 'categorical imperative' nor an affectivity such as Scheler's notion of sympathy. It is 'pre-originary': prior to distinctions between subject and object, reason and emotion, matter and idea, and philosophy and religion. Nor is ethics an experience, not even of the highest kind, but a radical exposure to the other that underpins all experience. Consequently, Levinas defines ethical subjectivity as a radical passivity, whose freedom occurs in the form of an 'election' to unlimited responsibility for the other person. In his first major work, *Totality and Infinity*, Levinas presents ethics as a complete separation between the ego and the other, which is also a relation between the two. A profound critique of ontology, especially of Heidegger's philosophy, which allegedly privileges impersonal being over each being, pervades the book. Through intricate and nuanced phenomenological analyses of everyday phenomena, Levinas explores the multiple ramifications of the ethical relation. The culmination of his endeavours is the ethical figure of the 'face'. This profound conjuncture of phenomenon and expression is even more importantly the moral injunction against killing.

Levinas's second magnum opus, *Otherwise than Being or Beyond Essence*, further intensifies the ethical tropes, consciously resorting to performative language in order to counter the previous work's adoption of ontological terminology in the very critique of ontology. The later book describes an intensified ethics, now presented as a subjectivity become hostage to the other. Levinas explores the movement from the interpersonal level to that of wider society on the basis of justice. This way of apprehending subjectivity enables Levinas to formulate a notion of human community that is united by neither primordial individual freedom, nor by universalism, but by the interminable quest for social justice. Thereby Levinas establishes a radically critical relationship with the entire Enlightenment tradition, from Descartes to Hegel, for whom justice is a function of freedom. However, he differs also from the political philosophers, such as Rawls, who consider justice as the first value of society. Levinas would say that justice, better still, the 'work of justice', cannot be valorised because it is what calls for values. There are two aspects to the account of justice in Levinas's discourse. The first describes the origin of institutions in terms of a universalisation of ethics necessitated by the primordial presence of the 'third party' who without delay complicates the ethical immediacy. The second is far more profound, because, here, justice distresses ethics. Justice is the problem of the political, because of the mutual corruption, in this case of ethics and justice, intrinsic to supplementarity. Levinas's work demonstrates that not only justice, but also ethics, is political. Hence the return to a politics, informed by 'prophetic witnessing', capable of carrying out the work of justice.

'Prophetic politics' is the encounter between ontological and epistemological philosophy, on the one hand, and religion, in the specific Levinasian sense of the term, on the other. Operationally, it takes the form of a biblical supplement to the Greek philosophical heritage. Basically, Levinas inscribes the ethical message of the Bible within the very origin of philosophy. His groundbreaking notion of the 'trace' or the 'pre-original' describes our everyday tripartite sense of temporality in deformalised or ethical terms. The pre-original is also what passes for a method in Levinas's work, by operating performatively in his text. Moreover, unlike the entire post-Nietzschean tradition, especially post-structuralism, dismantling the history of philosophy is not Levinas's technique. Instead, he emphasises instances showing a propensity toward transcendence, in a tradition where otherwise the immanence of being and presence reigns supreme. Plato's 'Good beyond being', Descartes's 'idea of infinity', Rosenzweig's critique of Hegelian totality, Bergson's *'elan vital'*, Buber's 'I–thou' relation are some such moments. Strictly speaking, Levinas does not formulate concepts. Nor does he engage in systemic articulations. Instead he prefers the *mise en scène*, the dramatic staging, a third way between concept and inchoate ethical protest, leading to many quasi-transcendental tropes.

This chapter presents Levinas through three levels pivotal to his thought: ethics, justice and prophetic politics. Levinas locates justice, community and peace in language and discourse, contrary to traditional political theory that attributes them to the universal state. Levinas's thought, taken as a mutually transforming confluence of philosophy and religion, offers us a novel description of the human being that shows the way to a better polity. Prophetic politics claims to transcend, for example, Kantian cosmopolitics, Hegelian historicism, Marxist realism, Sartrean existentialist humanism and the cultural relativism of current anti-humanism. It appeals to a discourse of rights (the other person's), rather than subscribing to the doctrine of civic identity based upon the universality of the state. But in exposing politics to prophetic correction, Levinas also runs the risk of triggering a fundamentalist invasion of prophecy, in which the forgetting of self could have lethal consequences, or the state might forcibly universalise that which is merely particular.

Ethics

A comprehensive critique of ontology underpins Levinas's discourse. Ontology posits the philosophical sovereignty of being and the priority of presence over past and future. Being and presence are manifest in the concrete as 'economies of the same', that is to say, the magnification and perpetuation of self-identity by the reductive absorption of alterity. However, amidst this violent natural perseverance of being, Levinas also observes the incidence of morality, that is, conscience, or a being's deference to another. His well-worn phrase 'ethics is first philosophy' is primarily a reference to this reflexivity of being that provides the pre-original impulse for philosophy, redescribed in turn as 'the work of justice'. Ethics, variously defined as 'Desire', 'metaphysics', 'infinity', that is, an asymmetrical and non-reciprocal relation between the other and me, is in the concrete, a superlative affectivity, or 'sensibility'. This passivity, or 'infinite responsibility', extends right up to the level of my 'substitution' for the other person. In substitution I am 'elected', prior to the advent of a will that is capable of choice, as irreplaceable in responsibility for the other person.

The concrete problem of war and peace is the background for this profound meditation upon subjectivity. In liberal political theory war and peace are regarded as constituting a fundamental opposition in which peace is instituted as politics, as an overcoming of human beings' primitive propensity toward war. Levinas shatters this conventional contrast. Modern society, he argues, is in a permanent state of war, and politics is 'the art of foreseeing war and winning it by every means'.[1] Where society is conceived as merely a debate in the management of self-interest, politics cannot be other than the institutionalisation of war. 'The struggle of each against all becomes exchange and commerce.'[2] However, the frequent breakdown of commerce into war betrays the permanent latency of war within exchange. Hence the dialectic of war and peace is really the distinction between two modalities of self-interest. Aware of this 'interpenetration of opposites', Hegelian speculative dialectic envisions a society where war would become absent by virtue of the incremental coincidence of self-interest and the common good, in the historical actualisation of reason. Reduced to civic identities, their subjective freedom realised in the objectivity of the political state, beings would no longer go to war. However, the rational totality has not proved to be the promised expulsion of war. Instead, what becomes clear to Levinas is that 'the visage of being that shows itself in war is fixed in the concept of totality, which dominates Western philosophy'.[3]

The notion of totality was raised to the level of a concept mainly during the flowering of German idealism, reaching its apotheosis in Hegel's notion of the 'absolute'. It is constituted as a permanent state of unrest by two conflicting movements. Whilst the natural thrust of totality comprises a drive toward self-identity, it is also continuously undermined by the exterior it strives to internalise in the process. In the concrete, totality at any given moment shows the ascendancy, in sum, of either totalisation or pluralisation. Strictly speaking, in Levinas's discourse the term 'totality' refers to the dominant orientation toward totalisation that encompasses both commerce and war. Going in the opposite direction one finds the differentiating affects of exteriority, that manifests its recalcitrance to totalisation as the subversion of totality. It is the latter movement that Levinas calls ethics.

Totality labours endlessly at multiple levels to absorb the external, that is, to apprehend and reduce the foreign to an internal difference reproducible by an algorithm. In theory this reduction is accomplished as 'comprehension', for which 'the general title ontology is appropriate'.[4] Furthermore, 'Western philosophy has most often been an ontology: a reduction of the other to the same by interposition of a middle and neutral term that ensures the comprehension of being'.[5] The function of the neutral third term is mediation between thought and being. Plato's 'Forms', Descartes's 'cogito', the Kantian 'I think' of transcendental constitution, Hegel's concept of history, Husserl's 'intentionality', and Heidegger's notion of 'Being' are examples of mediation in the philosophical tradition. What all these different terms have in common is the constant of 'freedom', that is, the supposedly inalienable capacity of a being to grasp and absorb anything that it encounters. The two modalities of being that characterise totality are violent identification by war, on the one hand, and the calculus of rational peace, that is, politics, law and commerce, on the other.

Levinas's critique of totality is aimed at the fatal primacy granted freedom, especially in Hegel's system where it becomes a constitutive ideality: the potentiality of subjective freedom is insignificant until actualised in the objective freedom of the state and civil society. In other words, politics and commerce, by giving it rational expression fulfil primitive spontaneity. But Levinas discovers that the potential for war that attends subjective freedom is inevitably carried over into the universal categories, making them highly unstable. Levinas's analysis of totality assumes several related forms in his various writings. Beginning with the fundamental dependence of Western political thought upon the philosophical category of freedom, he extends his critique to objectification, for example, in institutions and labour, where freedom and creativity are transformed into law and objects, respectively. Capitalism's closed system of possession and exchange, too, comes under fire. But the undimmed horror of totality is truly captured only in the historical instances of National Socialism and the Cold War, in which universality and force were combined, demonstrating the devastation wrought by totalisation. Levinas makes it very clear that totality cannot generate peace, for it cannot abide plurality, which, he argues, is the sole possible basis of peace. Totality must be ruptured at the risk of war because 'only beings capable of war can rise to peace. War like peace presupposes beings structured otherwise than as parts of a totality'.[6] But war is itself derived and secondary. For 'war presupposes the transcendence of the antagonist; ... it aims at a presence that comes always from elsewhere, a being that appears in a face'.[7] A being that appears in a face is the other.

'The way in which the other presents himself, exceeding *the idea of the other in me*, we here name face.'[8] Levinas is well aware that an everyday term such as 'face' brings to mind the physical visage. He does not deny this phenomenality of the face but describes the manner in which its plastic physicality is relentlessly rearranged by expression. In fact, when Levinas uses the term he is not considering the visual aspect at all, but language in the form of address. Thus he is able to say, 'this infinity, stronger than murder, already resists us in his face, is his face, is the primordial *expression*, is the first word: "you shall not commit murder"'.[9] The absolute nudity and defencelessness of the face reveals a troubling ambiguity. On the one hand the lack of resistance in terms of force is an exposure to violence; on the other it is absolute moral resistance that forbids violence.

War is just one of the possibilities open to beings who are related to one another without the totalising mediation of a third term. Figures such as 'Desire', 'infinity', 'sensibility', 'proximity' and 'substitution', that Levinas utilises in order to describe the asymmetrical ethical relation, are all a 'calling into question of my spontaneity by the presence of the Other'.[10] This term operates at two related levels, a reference to 'otherness', that is to say, the irrecuperable residue of totality, and also to the human other. The other is the one who orders me to responsibility, but is also the most impoverished in terms of power. The other is a figure of superlative height; he/she also is indigence personified. Because of the mutual corruption of levels, the 'quality' that concretely describes the other is ambiguity, through which the other enjoins me to ethics. It is not that I do not know enough about the other, but that the other is not given to cognition. In a passage that epitomises the ambiguity of the other, Levinas states,

> the alterity of the other does not result from its identity, but constitutes it: the other is the Other. The Other qua Other is situated in a dimension of height and of abasement – glorious abasement; he has the face of the poor, the stranger, the widow, and the orphan, and at the same time of the master called to invest and justify my freedom.[11]

If totality is the violation of the independence of the other person, infinity sketches the form of a relation in which the I remains I and the other is other. Levinas borrows the notion of infinity from Descartes's Third Meditation, where the idea of infinity appears in the finite cogito as a form that could not encompass its content, thereby resulting in the undoing of the cogito's unity. What is pivotal here is that the idea of infinity is not thought but undergone. Put another way, the idea of infinity ruptures the way in which consciousness grasps its object in comprehension. Instead, 'at stake is a passivity that one could not assimilate to receptivity'.[12] Infinity in thought assumes the irreducible figure of the negation of the finite. The subject's inability to comprehend infinity is a positive relation, demonstrating what Levinas calls infinity's 'non-indifference' toward the subject. The passivity of subjectivity in relation to infinity is called 'sensibility'.

The passivity of the ethical relation, crucially, occurs as 'sensibility', at the level of corporeal existence. In this sense, it is opposed to the rationalist theories of ethics maintained against sentiment. The I of passivity is formed, as 'interiority', separated from totality. 'Interiority' is an incessant process of identification. This labour of identification is what Levinas calls 'the same'. It occurs as a concrete relationship between an I and a world that is other. The process is not tautological, such as the formalistic 'I am I', but involves its apophantic version, that is, incessant recovery. The I maintains itself and is at home (*chez soi*), by perpetually divesting its world of alterity.

> The 'moments' of this identification – the body, the home, labour, possession, economy – are not to figure as empirical and contingent data, laid over the formal skeleton of the same; they are the articulations of this structure. The identification of the same is not the void of a tautology nor a dialectical opposition to the other, but the concreteness of egoism.[13]

The essential teaching here is that the entire ethical venture depends on a being that eats and sleeps, a being who lives its life rather than one who is concerned for its existence. To have needs and to require their satisfaction is not grafted onto a more primordial existence as its conditions. They are the very articulations of that life. Moreover,

> life is a body, not only lived body [*corps propre*], where its self-sufficiency emerges, but a cross-roads of physical forces, body-effect. In its deep-seated fear life attests this ever possible inversion of the body-master into body-slave, of health into sickness. *To be a body* is on the one hand *to stand* [*se tenir*], to be master of oneself, and, on the other hand, to stand on the earth, to be in the *other*, and thus to be encumbered ...[14]

While maintenance, or being a body, is enabling, it also generates fatigue. The I is burdened by its own existing, seeking distractions. But even Levinas's deepening of the subject's involvement in the world as 'enjoyment', that is to say, being nourished by the world before acting in it, does not succeed in discovering a genuine break in the immanence of subjectivity. An absolute departure from self would only come in the subject's relationship with death. The world and light open up only relative horizons of temporality, but death is an absolute because it refuses to be a horizon. To a being death is an absolute event, a mystery that cannot be grasped and thus mastered. The subject and death do not share a common border. It is as if death were patient, in affecting the subject as the event always about to happen. Not available to consciousness as an object, death is undergone rather than assumed. The subject is rendered absolutely passive by death's affectivity. Furthermore, the modality of a subject's relationship with the other, according to Levinas, resembles this trauma. The uniqueness of this form lies in the de-phasing or unsettling of the subject by its encounter with a mystery or enigma. It is this 'quality' that the other shares with death. This encounter, which took the form of a 'relation' in *Totality and Infinity*, is described as 'proximity' in *Otherwise than Being*.

Levinas calls the deposed subject 'subjectivity'. However, he goes a step further than typical post-structuralism, in arguing for a unity of the subject decentred by the loss of sovereignty. The subject, impossible as a freedom for itself, is reformed by responsibility for another. The meaning, according to Levinas, of the first person singular is responsibility. 'The word *I* means *here I am*, answering for everything and everyone.'[15] In this manner, subjectivity is a 'hostage' of the other.

> It is, however, not an alienation, because the other in the same is my substitution for the other through responsibility, for which, I am summoned as someone irreplaceable. I exist through the other and for the other, but without this being an alienation: I am inspired. This inspiration is the psyche. The psyche can signify this alterity in the same without alienation in the form of incarnation, as being in one's skin, having-the-other-in-one's-skin.[16]

Now Levinas is in a position to revive reason and truth too. The other, essential to subjectivity as the heterogeneity that defines the latter, is both the locus and the focus of reason and truth. Reason, instead of being a reified freedom, is, according to Levinas, always the plural form of reasons offered to the other person in justification of one's being. Truth, the primordial site of intelligibility in the philosophical tradition, where thought and reality purportedly coincide, is subjected to justice. Thereby, knowledge, science and technology are subordinated to humanity. These elements of epistemology are shown not to possess an objective value in themselves that set them above the ephemeral human being. The genuine 'essence' of truth lies in its being sought to facilitate the work of justice. But before exploring what Levinas means by the work of justice it is necessary to state how he extrapolates the interpersonal relation to wider society briefly, for this move will have a profound bearing on his notion of justice.

Levinas's concept of community is far removed from the Hegelian rational universality, arrived at by the actualisation of primordial subjective freedom. 'Fraternity' is a constellation of terms, which could probably be called the most profoundly religious moment in Levinas's discourse. 'Election' through responsibility, in which the I is chosen; 'paternity' and 'filiality', both references to the non-causal, creator–creature relationship between the human being and the divine father of monotheism; and 'fecundity'; give rise to a plural community of singularities. Yet, as it is with most of Levinas's figures, fraternity too is an orientation rather than a state. In defining fraternity as a unity of singularities, 'whose logical status is not reducible to the status of ultimate differences in a genus'; also involving 'the commonness of a father, as though the commonness of a race would not bring together enough',[17] Levinas not only challenges the pillars of political theory but also redefines religion, especially what is meant by monotheism. Through the notion of fecundity, Levinas argues for a community, whose subject is the flesh-and-blood human being of sensibility, not the ageless 'absolute' where history is but an eternal present.

Justice

In *Totality and Infinity*, justice appears synonymous with ethics. Although frequent statements such as 'we call justice this face to face approach, in conversation',[18] seem to reinforce this impression, there is a crucial displacement between ethics and justice. Ethics, or the interpersonal relationship of proximity, is transformed into justice by the 'third party'. The 'third', synthesis in Hegel, here refers to an increase in the level of plurality, that is to say, the third party is not anthropological, but the other's other who is another to me. The advent of the third complicates Levinas's ethical discourse because the fact that the other also has an other introduces a contradiction into ethics. Ethics demands that we

> sternly reduce each one's uniqueness to his individuality in the unity of the genre, and let universality rule. Thus we need laws ... institutions and the state, to render justice. And thus no doubt an entire political determinism becomes inevitable.[19]

Moreover, Levinas derives philosophy itself from the moment

of justice. The questioning form, 'what is?', originates in the need for distributive justice. But, unfortunately, this return to the order of calculation reduces philosophy, as ethics, to a form of critique, and politics to administration. Justice itself seems to be reduced to the law, albeit subjected to infinite corrections. Nowhere is this form of 'tinkering' better epitomised than in the hackneyed subject of language and its relation to justice. Throughout his discourse Levinas asserts that language is justice, and that it demonstrates an intrinsic form that resembles the movement of justice.

Levinas begins by stating that the word is always a metaphor asserting the ideality of the same across the diverse. A word supplies the background presupposed by every relation between the individual and the universal. But language is also a performative speech act, or 'saying', in addition to the constative statements, or 'said' that constitute its propositions. The saying is analogous to ethics, while the said is ontological. Saying is the 'essence' of signification but is betrayed by the said during statement. The relationship between the two is captured well, as the need to reduce the said, in an un-saying, in order to 'liberate' the saying: 'The *otherwise than being* is stated in a saying that must also be unsaid in order to thus extract the *otherwise than being* from the said in which it already comes to signify but a *being otherwise*'.[20] The reduction to ethical saying has a precedent, according to Levinas, in the relationship between philosophy and scepticism. Even as scepticism, refuted time and time again, returns to haunt philosophy as its original repression, so is the said unravelled by the antecedent saying.

Prophetic Politics

A closer look at the 'structure' of the translation of ethics to justice, however, reveals a troubling complication. The third party is not added onto a preceding relationship of proximity but makes its demand upon the ethical immediately. Hence, contrary to the assumption of many, who purport to take away a pure ethical formula from Levinas's discourse, ethics never finds itself uncomplicated by the question of the third. It is already corrupted by institutions. Although this can lead to treating ethics as a form of custom, Levinas returns to the political, which he had denounced as 'war by other means'. In *Otherwise than Being*, under the section called 'witness and prophecy', Levinas intensifies the encounter between philosophy, religion and politics. Here prophecy, defined as a bearing witness to infinity, is constituted by two related moments. They are monotheism, or the separation from universal history, and the battle against idolatry. For Levinas, the modern idols are not statues of pagan gods but ideology, Hegelian historicism and its idea of progress, and foremost, the political state. In the face of these idols, prophecy is the designation of the meaning of justice without awaiting the end of universal history. It is the troubling of philosophy by religion, which is not the supplanting of the former by the latter, but the generation of a 'messianic eschatology' of peace. Levinas presents this as a precarious balancing act between war and peace.

However, the ethical troubling of politics does not authorise ethics to govern institutions. Instead ethics itself becomes politicised. Thus, we return to the starting point of a general economy, where the work of justice is seen inextricably bound to political orientation. This is the other face of the third, pointed toward pluralisation without guarantee of which political form would gain ascendancy. Consequently, the ethical disturbance of ontology can lead to different political manifestations. Totalitarianism is as equally possible as an egalitarian and pluralistic polity. Here, we are presented with a much more realistic account of politics. It is this danger that prompts Levinas to, as it were, anchor ethics in the universality of the Judaic tradition; in the justice of its Torah. But as the case of Israel shows, this can also lead to an attempt to concretise the messianic, thus leading to cataclysmic violence in the name of justice. Perhaps a better approach is found in Levinas's examination of the 'Rights of Man' as the workings of prophetic politics.

As a development of 'prophetic politics', during the 1980s Levinas begins to reflect upon the topic of human rights. Levinas argues that human rights have an a priori normative character if they are derived from alterity. Although Levinas rejects individualism as a basis for rights, he is not a communitarian either. Arguing the universal importance of 'prophetic politics', he presents human rights based upon alterity as a corrective to political institutions. Furthermore, the sociality of ethics, arising from responsibility for the other, is antecedent to that of humanism and is therefore capable of revealing the internal contradictions inherent to ontologically oriented rights. Such possession-based and entitlement-based rights can easily be used against themselves. Right opposes right resulting in war.

Emmanuel Levinas (1906–95)

The other important aspect of Levinas's rights discourse is its separation from 'natural right'. Human rights based upon the humanism of the other man, that is, in terms of 'substitution' and 'proximity', transcend the fatalism of society and the inhuman quality of nature. From the 'thou shall not kill' of responsibility to the other person, Levinas derives the 'right to life'. But Levinas is not satisfied with simply formulating rights. He seeks to discover and endorse the political conditions for realising them. By showing how starvation and hunger are incompatible with the 'right to life', Levinas attacks economic inequality. It is toward the alleviation of scarcity and need that he supports the growth of science and technology. If they are to be realised, rights must be institutionalised. However, this makes them vulnerable to abuse and perversion. In addition, the development of technology can lead to the terrifying proliferation of the means of destruction. Therefore, 'prophetic politics' and its vigilance are necessary to defend the rights of man. To summarise, 'prophetic politics' reinvents the triple republican legacy as follows: a peaceful fraternity answering for the rights of the other, from which are derived freedom invested in responsibility for the other and equality resulting from singularity, produced in substitution for the other.

Levinas in Contemporary Theory

Since the 1980s the thought of Emmanuel Levinas has continued to have a significant impact in disciplines as diverse as philosophy, theology, Jewish studies, feminism, social and political theory, literature, pedagogy and psychotherapy. The thesis of the essential opacity of the other, revealing an irreducible non-thematisability in every theme has led to a renewed wave of self-reflexivity in theory. However, attempts to privilege the secular or the religious in Levinas's thought have produced some poor interpretations. Antipolitical and sentimental readings have abducted Levinas from the political sphere, asphyxiating his thought by removing its vital political atmosphere. Political readings, with some notable exceptions, have tended toward formalism. The singular aim, in both camps, has been the isolation of a pure formula of ethical alterity. The result has been a fetishism of 'the other', whether it appears in the form of a nauseatingly naive 'love for the other', war with a bad conscience, or, even worse, the advocacy of 'humanitarian intervention' in order to save the other, usually from herself. Both

Slavoj Žižek and Alain Badiou are utterly sceptical about any discourse based upon the 'other'. For Badiou, Levinasian ethics is 'decomposed religion' which reduces philosophy to non-philosophy.

However, Derrida's careful reading of Levinas evokes the political stakes of ethics as first philosophy. Derrida's brilliant essay 'Violence and Metaphysics' poses the options open to a discourse that claims to transcend ontology: either admit its complicity with ontological language or relinquish philosophy for empiricism. Derrida's 'ethical turn', having as its axis scepticism about the ethical import of deconstruction, is inspired by Levinas's unique notion of ethics. Not only has Derrida concentrated on constructively problematising Levinas's 'concepts' (for example, the 'concept' of infinite responsibility in *The Gift of Death* and the translation of ethics to politics in *Adieu to Emmanuel Levinas*), but used them in his own discourse: for instance the quasi-transcendental concept of 'hauntology' in *Specters of Marx*, and the long meditation upon 'fraternity' and 'friendship' in the *Politics of Friendship*. Coinciding with a religious turn in continental thought, Levinas's contention that ethics is neither teleology nor foundation but a 'messianic eschatology' has been directly responsible for important work in political philosophy. Its influence is key in the critique of 'immanentism' and in articulations of democracy considered as an irrecuperable future affecting the present as an urgent demand for justice.

Notes

1. Levinas, *Totality and Infinity*, p. 21.
2. Levinas, *Otherwise than Being*, p. 4.
3. Levinas, *Totality and Infinity*, p. 21.
4. Ibid., p. 42.
5. Ibid., p. 43.
6. Ibid., p. 222.
7. Ibid.
8. Ibid., p. 50 (emphasis in the original).
9. Ibid., p. 199 (emphasis in the original).
10. Ibid., p. 43.
11. Ibid., p. 251.
12. Levinas, *Of God Who Comes to Mind*, p. 64.
13. Levinas, *Totality and Infinity*, p. 38.
14. Ibid., p. 164 (all emphases and parentheses in the original).
15. Levinas, *Otherwise than Being*, p. 114 (emphasis in the original).

16. Ibid.
17. Levinas, *Totality and Infinity*, p. 214.
18. Ibid., p. 71.
19. Ibid., p. 174.
20. Levinas, *Otherwise than Being*, p. 7.

Major Works by Levinas

Collected Philosophical Papers, trans. Alphonso Lingis (The Hague: Martinus Nijhoff, 1987).
Existence and Existents, trans. Alphonso Lingis (The Hague: Martinus Nijhoff, 1978 [1947]).
Nine Talmudic Readings, trans. Annette Aronowicz (Bloomington: Indiana University Press, 1990 [1968]).
Of God Who Comes to Mind, trans. Bettina Bergo (Stanford: Stanford University Press, 1998 [1986]).
Otherwise than Being or Beyond Essence, trans. Alphonso Lingis (Pittsburgh: Duquesne University Press, 1998 [1981, 1974]).
Time and the Other, trans. Richard A. Cohen (Pittsburgh: Duquesne University Press, 1985 [1947]).
Totality and Infinity: an Essay on Exteriority, trans. Alphonso Lingis (Pittsburgh: Duquesne University Press, 1969 [1961]).

Suggestions for Further Reading

Bernasconi, Robert, and Simon Critchley (eds), *Re-Reading Levinas* (Bloomington: Indiana University Press, 1991). Important collection of essays examining Levinas's impact on reading, and the consequences of Levinas's figure of the feminine for feminism.
Caygill, Howard, *Levinas and the Political* (London: Routledge, 2002). A brilliant political reading of Levinas's ethics in the light of his own concrete political writings.
Critchley, Simon, and Robert Bernasconi (eds), *The Cambridge Companion to Levinas* (Cambridge: Cambridge University Press, 2002). Pre-eminent scholars of Levinas exploring his key concepts and discussing the significance of his relationship to Judaism, aesthetics, feminism, philosophy of religion and philosophy of language.
Critchley, Simon, *Ethics-Politics-Subjectivity: Essays on Derrida, Levinas and Contemporary French Thought* (London: Verso, 1999). Contains important essays on Levinas's relationship to psychoanalysis and Critchley's original work on developing an ethics of finitude through the comic rather than tragic.
Derrida, Jacques, 'Violence and Metaphysics: An Essay on the Thought of Emmanuel Levinas', in Jacques Derrida, *Writing and Difference*, trans.

Alan Bass (London: Routledge and Kegan Paul, 1978), pp. 79–153. This is the first essay that rigorously and sympathetically explored Levinas's work, setting the tone for subsequent Levinas criticism.

Derrida, Jacques, *Adieu to Emmanuel Levinas*, trans. P.-A. Brault and M. Naas (Stanford: Stanford University Press, 1999). Reading the passage between ethics and politics as an aporia, Derrida explores the resulting implications for both.

Peperzak, Adriaan (ed.), *Ethics as First Philosophy: The Significance of Emmanuel Levinas for Philosophy, Literature and Religion* (New York: Routledge, 1995). A compilation of important thematic and comparative essays by an international group of Levinas scholars discussing the impact of his thought.

4

Louis Althusser (1918–90)

Steve Smith

Introduction

Along with Gramsci and Lukács, Althusser is among the most important Marxist theorists of the twentieth century. Althusser described himself first and foremost as a reader of Marx, his apparently modest aim being to investigate 'the specific nature of the principles of the science and philosophy founded by Marx'.[1] Althusser's work is a radical attempt to reinvigorate Marxist philosophy in the wake of what he saw as the theoretical void left by Western Communism's belated acknowledgement of the theoretical and political errors of Stalinism in the late 1950s. Such an undertaking was given its immediate intellectual impetus by the theoretical ferment of 1960s Paris, with the then pre-eminent discourses of psychoanalysis, structuralism and a nascent post-structuralism providing an important influence on his thinking. Althusser's commitment to the political cause of communism never wavered, but the Marxism that emerged from his writings was unapologetically unorthodox. For some, Althusser's entire project was as foolhardy as it was ambitious, precipitating the very decline which he sought to arrest – not least because of the acuity of his diagnosis of Marxism's theoretical shortcomings. Such a judgement may be somewhat harsh, but it is undeniable that Althusser is the last Marxist philosopher to attempt to reform Marxist philosophy at a time when the broader political stakes of such an undertaking were even thinkable at all.

Louis Althusser was born in Algeria in 1918. A gifted student in philosophy, he secured a teaching post at the elite École nationale supérieure in Paris in 1948, where he supervised students (including Foucault and Derrida) preparing for the prestigious agrégation examination. His early career gave little indication of his future pre-eminence, nor even of his Marxist leanings; a notably reverential doctoral thesis on Hegel was followed by translations of Feuerbach and a slim volume on Montesquieu. Althusser's engagement with Marx began only later in the early 1960s with a series of seminars, essays and collaborations that led to the publication of two key texts, *For Marx* and *Reading 'Capital'*. His work, however, was constantly interrupted by treatment for a longstanding manic-depressive illness. His public career ended in 1980 following his murder of his wife, Hélène, an act for which he was pronounced unfit to plead. He continued to write though legally unable to publish in his own name in France, completing an autobiography and other theoretical writings which were eventually published after his death in 1990.

Marxism and Philosophy

Althusser was exercised throughout his published work by the peculiarity of the articulation of Marxism with philosophy which is neatly summed up in the title of his 1975 retrospective essay: 'Is It Simple to Be a Marxist in Philosophy?'.[2] Althusser's obvious reference-point for such a question was his contemporary, Jean-Paul Sartre, whose stance as a non-card carrying Marxist 'fellow-traveller' preoccupied him. The issue is raised in the preface of *For Marx*, where he refers to the 'imaginary Debt' contracted by Marxists of petty-bourgeois origin (like himself and Sartre) as a result of their 'not being proletarians', a debt that was typically discharged 'in pure activity, if not in political activism'.[3] In *Reading 'Capital'*, he describes as Sartre's 'profoundest problem' a reticence in the face of the theoretical complexity proper to Marxism as a philosophical enterprise. This he attributes to the sheer weight exerted on Sartre's theoretical project by the prospect of 'the suffering of a poor wretch reduced by imperialist exploitation to hunger and agony' in whose name Marxist intellectuals feel obliged to speak.[4] Althusser's stance was the precise opposite of Sartre's; his writings are oriented solely by the requirement of conceptual rigour, while he sought to secure his narrowly political credentials (thereby countering accusations of excessive theoretical abstraction) through a stubborn allegiance to the French Communist Party (PCF) during a period when leftist intellectuals were abandoning it in droves. Central to his whole project was a Leninist commitment to the primacy of the party at a time when the PCF was the dominant party of the left in France. Althusser was not afraid to attack the party's lack of 'theoretical culture',[5] but it never ceased to represent for him the only conceivable prospect of political change. Without it, theory was inevitably condemned to abstraction.

In broader theoretical terms, Althusser's project brings to mind (and was arguably modelled upon) Lacan's contemporary 'return to Freud', which was a thoroughgoing rereading of Freud that sought to take on what Lacan felt to be the misreading of Freud's work implied in mainstream psychoanalysis, notably ego psychology. Althusser's work suggests implicitly a comparable 'return to Marx', an attempt to renew Marxism by means of a critical engagement with an embedded tradition of misreadings. Althusser's reading of Marx is a notably eclectic one, read through perspectives provided by a range of non-Marxist sources – Spinoza, Machiavelli, Freud, Bachelard, Lacan and Lévi-Strauss, among others. Furthermore, like Lacan, while he is aware that the moment of theory entails an institutionally situated practical field of application (therapeutic for Lacan, political for Althusser), the relation is left indirect enough to secure a space for the theory to develop on its own terms, leaving the question of its practical implementation a matter for others, for a different kind of discourse and practice. In this regard, Althusser was unapologetic about his requirement for theoretical rigour, for patient, detailed conceptual elaboration, despite its seeming indifference to the plight of the 'poor wretch'.

Theoretical Antihumanism

Althusser's conception of his work as, at once, 'a political intervention in existing Marxist philosophy ... and a philosophical intervention in politics'[6] is apparent in his engagement with what he termed 'theoretical antihumanism'. While antihumanist approaches to the human sciences were certainly in the air at the time he was writing (through recent translations of Heidegger and the work of Lacan, Lévi-Strauss and Foucault) official Marxism, anxious to de-Stalinise, was proclaiming a full-blooded return to the values of humanism, taking its cue from recently uncovered early texts by Marx such as the *Economic and Philosophical Manuscripts*. For Althusser, this was a paradigm instance of an instrumental, at best pragmatic, invocation of theory to deal with the political problem of the Stalinist legacy. Now that the first stage of the passage to communism in the USSR was complete, 'socialist humanism' was heralded as the 'liberalisation' of the Soviet system, a radical loosening up of the (historically necessary) rigours of State Socialism, allowing for individual rights, human dignity, citizenship and so on. Judging by the wry, disingenuous tone of the opening section of his 1965 essay 'Marxism and Humanism',[7] Althusser was more than a little sceptical about this historical narrative. Worse, the new line was also being taken on board by the Western communist parties. Its adoption seemed to authorise the PCF's accommodation to a reformist agenda of social-democratic values and the forging of strategic alliances with the non-Marxist left.

In Althusser's view this renewed emphasis on humanism constituted a serious theoretical regression. For him, Marx's fundamental discovery points toward the displacement of 'Man' as the driving force of historical development and a radically historical conception of humankind as such. While Marx was profoundly influenced by a post-Enlightenment philosophical tradition marked by humanism, his achievement was having thought beyond his inherited 'problematic'. Althusser discerns two discrete, though related, 'stages' in Marx's early humanist thinking. In the first, Marx maintains an Enlightenment belief in the potential for the post-feudal state to embody reason and freedom. Marx's politico-philosophical intervention at this stage took the form of an injunction that the state should realise this potential. In the second stage, however, Marx, disillusioned by the descent of the contemporary Prussian state into despotism, found in Feuerbach's humanism a means of understanding the persistence of unreason in terms of alienation, the paradigm example being wage-labour. Alienation, which for Marx can only be overcome in the political realm by communism, is also conceptualised negatively in terms of loss. The final goal of communist politics becomes the redemption of this loss through the recovery of man's 'own essence alienated in property, religion and the State' through their overthrow. As Althusser puts it, emphasising the Hegelian roots of this conception: 'Then the proletariat will negate its own negation and take possession of itself in communism.' Revolution is the very practice of the logic immanent in alienation: 'it is the moment in which criticism, hitherto unarmed, recognises its arms in the proletariat'.[8] Thus the proletariat, rather than the recognition by the state of its own unreason, becomes the vehicle by which the essence of humankind will be realised.

Marx broke with theoretical humanism first and foremost, according to Althusser, through a protracted and rigorous theoretical labour as a result of which Marx discovered that an unchanging or evolving human essence was not a pre-social empirical or ideal given that happens to find itself opposed to 'real history', but is a concept appropriated by and operative wholly within that history. In other words, humanism mystifies to the extent that it regards 'real history' as ultimately no more than a contingent impediment to human self-realisation. In a well-known quotation from one of his middle-period texts, Marx writes: 'Men make their own history, but they do not make it just as they please; they make it under circumstances directly encountered, given and transmitted from the past.'[9] This formulation remains indebted to the humanist problematic in that it leaves open the prospect of 'men' taking control of their 'historical circumstances'. By the time Marx wrote *Capital*, Althusser argues that Marx had dropped alienation as an operative concept, passing instead to the terminology of 'mode', 'forces' and 'relations' of economic production. Moreover, the social relations of production (which humanism views as alienated human relations) become indivisible from the specific material conditions in which they function. Unlike Marx's early writings, *Capital* does not derive from an 'ethical inspiration',[10] but is a rigorous conceptually based analysis of the anonymous mechanics of capitalist production. Within this new perspective, for example, the motif of the worker's alienation through commodity production disappears, replaced by the pivotal concept of surplus value whose extraction or appropriation is enabled by the inequalities of ownership. Similarly, Marx no longer uses the language of 'needs' (which can only make sense if needs are viewed as some essential quality of the human as such), but of the economic and social conditions for the reproduction of labour-power (which are subject to enormous historical and cultural variability). In short, because 'Man' can no longer be abstracted from the economic circumstances in which his so-called 'sensuous practical activity' takes place, humanism is theoretically incoherent. As theory and politics are never very far apart, Althusser further contends that a politics grounded in humanist premises (whether it be conservative, social democratic or even communist) is equally incoherent, based on a false promise of plenitude, satisfaction or self-realisation, upon which it cannot hope to deliver.

Historical Causality

Althusserian antihumanism is not necessarily incompatible with a conception of dialectical materialism of the kind that had dominated orthodox Marxism before its humanist turn in the late 1950s. In its hardline version, known as economism, Marxism was a deterministic theory in which the central determining element and the driving-force of historical development is the state of the economic contradiction at any given moment. Two consequences followed: first, the non-economic elements of a given society (the legal, political, and cultural 'superstructure') merely reflect the economic base that wholly determines them; second, the (historically inevitable) exacerbation of the economic contradiction will lead to a point of crisis that can only be resolved by the revolutionary passage to communism.

Althusser certainly holds that structures not 'men' make history, but he is suspicious of the reduction of such structures to the realm of the economic. In 'Contradiction and Overdetermination'[11] he traces the theoretical underpinnings of economism to a Hegelian misreading of Marx. For Hegel, contradiction is fundamentally 'simple' in that the totality of relations within which the conflict of opposites is played out constitutes an 'expressive totality'. Hegel's *Philosophy of History* is premised on the assumption that the realm of empirical factuality is, in principle, nothing but the concrete manifestation of 'a unique internal principle',[12] and that analysis seeks a level of abstraction at which this principle may be adequately identified and articulated. Althusser readily concedes Hegel's influence on Marx as 'the first consciously to expose [the] general movement [of history] in depth', but his argument is that, in attempting to think a new kind of object (the mode of production) within the framework of dialectics, Marx was obliged to go beyond Hegel, rethinking the 'characteristic determinations and structures' of the dialectic, thereby preparing the ground for a quite distinctive conception of contradiction.[13]

For Althusser such a conception is realised in the theoretical lessons of Lenin's revolutionary strategy in the period preceding the October Revolution. A revolutionary movement succeeded in industrially backward Russia rather than in one of the advanced Western capitalist societies where the purely economic contradiction was rather more developed and acute because the economic dialectic was not in itself enough to ensure the success of the Bolsheviks.

Numerous 'exceptional' factors intervened that are not directly attributable to the historic development of capitalism: the survival of pre-capitalist social structures in Tsarist Russia; the relative underdevelopment of the state machine; the advanced state of the revolutionary movement, nourished by the lessons of its failure in 1905; Russia's difficulties in the 'imperialist' World War One, among many others. What was decisive was not the 'sole, unique power of the general "contradiction"', but a 'ruptural unity' constituted by a 'vast accumulation' of heterogeneous contradictions, none of which was enough in itself to bring about revolution, but which achieved that outcome only as a function of their particular coincidence at a given historical moment.[14]

In order to develop the theoretical lesson of this analysis Althusser draws on the Freudian concept of 'overdetermination'. He argues that Marxism must begin to think of historical development not, as per the Hegelian model, as the expression or evolution of its 'inner logic' but as the effect of the overdetemined relations holding within a complex totality. In the Freudian sense, overdetermination describes the processes of condensation and displacement at work in the constitution of dreams, viewing them as complex structures whose elements cohere within a network of cause and effect in which no single causal element may be specified which is not itself already the effect of some other element. The dream thus constitutes a totality insofar as each of its elements is related to all the others, but it is a totality that can only be grasped in the very disposition of those elements. It is not an arbitrary construct, but neither can its necessity be attributed to any external factor in relation to which the dream might be viewed as a translation or expression. The unity of the dream is purely conjunctural, so dream-analysis is immanent in approach, its object given only in the often surprisingly diverse relations holding within it. In the context of Althusser's critique of economism, the Freudian analogy suggests a model of causality that is more appropriately characterised as one of relationality (which is not unrelated to the structuralist notion of the primacy of synchronous relations). Once the Marxian contradiction is understood as overdetermined 'in its principle' it can no longer function as a grounding causal instance, logically prior to the social totality within which its 'effects' are felt. In other words, the superstructures cannot be conceived as the concrete expression of the economic contradiction; the whole base/superstructure model, in effect, must be rejected.

Such are the theoretical stakes in what Althusser terms 'structural causality', though his conception hardly entails causality at all. The paradox of structural causality lies in its insistence on the coextensive space of causes and effects, such that it is impossible to separate them out at all. What analysis confronts, then, are 'effects' made possible by a structure of relations at a given synchronic moment of the structure's broad diachronic development. Therefore, the effective horizon of Marxist inquiry is constituted by what he terms the 'conditions of existence' that produce and sustain any particular superstructural phenomenon. Such an orientation, owing to the effects of overdetermination, always points in the direction of 'complexity'. It is not a question of analysing discrete objects or effects in their own right, but rather of viewing their identity as a structural effect that is governed by the relations of autonomy and dependence that sustain it.
    Such a conception implies that all relations are equally determinant, at least in principle. As a Marxist, however, Althusser is constrained to acknowledge the dominant role of the structure of economic relations within the 'conditions of existence' of the elements of the superstructure. He therefore further qualifies the Marxist concept of totality as a 'structure in dominance', meaning that superstructural elements may be adequately understood only in relation to the economic. The role played by the economic is given only in concrete analyses, remaining theoretically an open question. If all social phenomena are to be analysed through a relation to the social organisation of economic production, they are nevertheless not explained with reference to it alone. The key to such irreducibility lies in their inscription within the totality of concrete social practices; they have their own realm of effectivity, their own histories and structure. But their autonomy remains 'relative', subject to a certain determination from without, the 'external' determination which is dominant within capitalism being economic. Every institutional social practice carries the mark of exploitative social relations at some point or other, although the question of precisely where this point is located for any given practice cannot be specified in terms of an abstract causal model. The economic thus does not constitute the essence of those practices: it is not its hidden cause, but it does constitute an inescapable element of the conjunctural relations that constitute it. Analysis is thus inadequate without such a reference, yet reductive by reference only to it.
    Althusser's argument may be a timely rejoinder to a humanist

account of the political, legal, cultural or ethical superstructure that would acknowledge only a purely contingent relation to the economic, but it hardly represents a call to revolution in the manner of the *Communist Manifesto*. It is a sobering message as to the non-inevitability of revolution and the constitutive inability of communist political practice to occupy the driving-seat of historical development. Its positive value is a theoretical one: in the light of Althusser's recognition that 'the theory of the specific effectivity of the superstructure and other "circumstances" remains to be elaborated',[15] at stake is the more modest imperative of the kind of patient, rigorous theoretical labour that orthodox Marxism had long felt to be simply superfluous to the more pressing business of class struggle.

Ideology

Althusser's rethinking of the concept of ideology is arguably his most unorthodox and innovative contribution to Marxist theory. Ideology, however, was never the central focus of his theoretical project, discussion of ideology per se being restricted to a section toward the close of 'Marxism and Humanism' and the 1969 essay, 'Ideology and Ideological State Apparatuses (Notes towards an Investigation)' (ISAs), which is his most anthologised single work.[16] It is no coincidence that Althusser should first broach the thorny issue of ideology in the context of antihumanism given that the then prevailing conception of ideology (particularly within the PCF) drew on the same Hegelian sources that were being invoked to underpin Marxist humanism. For the broad Hegelian-Marxist tradition, ideology is theorised as a superstructural element through which the economic base is represented by and in consciousness, but in a distorted form. In *The German Ideology* Marx and Engels argue for the causal priority of (social) being over consciousness, 'ideology' being precisely the mechanism through which the opposite relation had been assumed by Marx's radical contemporaries. Ideology effects an inversion whereby the realm of ideas is abstracted from its properly material origin; ideas and other phantoms of the human brain, which are sublimates of material life-processes, present themselves spontaneously as free-floating tools of understanding. Ideology is thus held to explain how individuals, when constituted collectively as a social class by their role within economic production, effectively acquiesce to exploitative social relations. Concepts such as freedom or equality are 'ideological' in that they are held to have been already realised or to be potentially realisable under capitalist relations of production. Such was Engels's thesis of ideology as productive of 'false consciousness' which in its most hardline version unites humanist and economic determinist perspectives. Ideology is viewed as a necessary impediment to the self-understanding of the proletariat, a negative, 'alienated' stage of its development to be overcome through its eventual and 'inevitable' assumption of its historically appointed role as the agent of human emancipation.

Althusser's opening move in his reworking of ideology in 'Marxism and Humanism' draws on the thesis of the relative autonomy of the practices. He argues boldly that ideology is a specific kind of production whose operative procedures constitute an object of study in their own right. The first consequence of such a position, rhetorical as much as it is theoretical, is that ideology can no longer be considered as peculiar to the capitalist mode of production. Actually existing ideological formations should be considered as instances of an invariant, transhistorical structure ('ideology in general'). Implicitly targeting the Hegelian-Marxist thesis that ideology will perish along with capitalist relations of production, he writes: 'historical materialism cannot conceive that even a communist society could ever do without ideology'. Ideology is an 'organic' element of society, the essential function of which is to 'form' and 'equip' individuals 'to respond to their conditions of existence'.[17]

Perhaps the key moment of Althusser's thinking comes in his outright rejection of any reduction of ideology to the realm of knowledge. Ideology is not fundamentally concerned, as it is according to the false consciousness thesis, with truth and falsity. Ideology is, strictly speaking, unfalsifiable. In ideology what matters is 'the practico-social function' rather than the 'knowledge function'. Despite this stipulation, ideology comprises a 'system of representations' that remains beyond the quasi-epistemological scrutiny and judgement of Marxist science because 'in ideology men do indeed express, not the relation between them and their real conditions of existence, but *the way* they live the relation between them and their conditions of existence'. Ideology involves an irreducibly subjective dimension, its basic function being to engage and validate that dimension. While it may function as the frame within which individuals are able to make truth-claims or express beliefs about their world, the purpose of such utterances lies less in what is enunciated than in their enunciation .

The human subject itself is represented in and by ideology, through which the autonomous, 'productive' role of consciousness is 'lived' and constantly reaffirmed. The relation it underwrites between individuals and 'their real conditions of existence' is 'invested' in their 'imaginary relation'. Ideology does not represent the world to the individual, but represents the individual in their world: hence, 'men "live" their "consciousness" ... as their world itself'. The imaginary relation is saturated with non-cognitive elements: 'in ideology, the real relation is inevitably invested in the imaginary relation, a relation that expresses a will (conservative, conformist, reformist, or revolutionary), a hope or a nostalgia rather than describing a reality'.[18]

In conceptualising ideology in a sense that is coextensive with the ostensibly broader domain of consciousness and the 'lived', Althusser has moved a considerable distance in the direction of ideology as a neutral, descriptive notion. In more directly political terms, if ideology is able to authorise subject-positions at both ends of the conservative-revolutionary spectrum, ideology would not be a problem as such for Marxism. It would be a locus of political struggle in which people become conscious of their place and fight it out. Althusser's position at the time of 'Marxism and Humanism' is certainly very close to this position and its corollary that Marxist intervention at the wider political level is fundamentally oriented by the need to 'alter the "lived" relation between [men] and the world'.[19] Althusser nevertheless seeks to reconcile his position with an account of the human subject consistent with the thesis of theoretical antihumanism. While the feeling individuals have that their actions derive from and reinforce their subjectively experienced individual identity has concrete effects, he nevertheless maintains that the effective sense of autonomous agency implied in the 'imaginary relation' (as it is for Lacan from whom the term is borrowed) is illusory.

In this sense the notion of the subject is profoundly contradictory for Althusser. He argues that there can be no resolution of this contradiction in a theoretical sense, but only by intervening in the material conditions in which it occurs. Marxist analysis remains purely descriptive unless it is conceived as a practice in existing ideological relations. With this in mind he states categorically that Marx 'never fell into the idealist illusion of believing that the knowledge of an object might ultimately replace the object or dissipate its existence', nor, in consequence, can one necessarily expect that 'an ideology might be dissipated by a knowledge of it'.[20] Marxist science, moreover, cannot seek to dispel the ideological relation, only to modify it. Marxist science is opposed to ideology, not as truth to falsity, but as two kinds of practice whose field is concrete social formations. Marxist theory can understand the 'conditional necessity' of the concrete forms taken by the ideological relation and seek to engage the imaginary of the exploited (that is, to enable them to subjectivise their exploitation in a different modality, to imagine notions of freedom and equality as something other than some unrealisable ideal and to adjust their actions accordingly). Science has no efficacy of its own, as there is no scientific subject-position; theoretical antihumanism cannot be 'lived'. But it is only through science that the specular mirror-relation that characterises the ideological relation can be challenged. Science is thus a necessary condition for Marxist politics.

Lacking in such a conception of politics is any account of the class dimension of ideology. Althusser's approach does not necessarily rule it out, but the emphasis on the structure of ideology in general and its transhistorical function (meaning that ideology is not necessarily related to a class subject as it will persist in a classless society) lent weight to the accusation that Althusser's Marxism was a rather abstract, academic affair, unconcerned with politically engaged analysis of a given socio-historical conjuncture. The ISAs essay was clearly envisaged by Althusser as a response to such criticisms, made more pertinent by the events of May 1968 which had reinstated class antagonism and revolution on the radical agenda. Its publication also coincided with Althusser's broader attempt to stress the political import of his own work by explicitly repudiating 'theoreticism' and reconceptualising Marxist philosophy, the ongoing critique of philosophical idealism, as 'class struggle' in the field of theory.

The ISAs essay addresses an important lacuna in 'Marxism and Humanism': the functioning of ideology within 'mature' capitalism. Althusser opens with a standard Leninist account of the state playing a central role in securing the economic, social and political conditions necessary for the functioning and continual reproduction of capitalism, such that the capitalist mode of production acquires a viable measure of historical stability. At its disposal the state has two distinct but related kinds of coercive instrument to secure this: the repressive state apparatuses (RSAs) and the ISAs. The former comprise the public face of state power (law courts, police, army, state functionaries) and are grounded in a more or less explicit code of constraints and obligations. They rely on violence in that failure to comply usually elicits some form of statutory state sanction (fines, incarceration and so on). The ISAs, in contrast, function not by force but by ideology. They constitute those sites within which subjects acquire and exercise their individual rights and 'freedom'. Among the ISAs Althusser includes such institutions as the family, trades unions, the media, the church and 'cultural ventures', but it is the education system that, in the modern era, assumes the role of the dominant ISA. In a notably polemical passage, the educational ISA is characterised as little more than a ruthless machine churning out workers with the appropriate skills, attitudes and values to take up their appointed place within economic production.

Passages like this give the first half of the essay a markedly 'sociological' air of describing socialisation or conditioning. In the second half, however, Althusser returns to the ground staked out in 'Marxism and Humanism', but with two important advances. First, he proposes that the effectiveness of ideology does not derive from the extent to which individuals internalise beliefs or values. Ideology is not about beliefs at all, except insofar as they rationalise social actions or practices which individuals habitually and unquestioningly 'perform'. Second, while the earlier essay focused on the process of subject-constitution through the implicit references to Freud's theory of narcissism and Lacan's mirror stage, a new element is introduced in the form of Lacan's notion of the symbolic. Althusser interprets Lacan's notion rather narrowly as something like a voice of culture and authority with which subjects must come to terms in order to constitute themselves as normal, socially functional individuals, in the process of 'interpellation'. Interpellation, as well as ideology's imbrication in everyday social practices, is well illustrated in the following scenario:

> There are individuals walking along. Somewhere (usually behind them) the hail rings out: 'Hey, you'. One individual (nine times out of ten it is the right one) turns around, believing/suspecting/knowing that it is for him, i.e. recognising that 'it really is he' who is meant by the hailing.[21]

In turning around to acknowledge the address of his interlocutor, the individual in the street 'becomes a subject'. The agency through which this is effected is always external and prior; it is only through the act of acknowledging its authority or right to hail that the individual is constituted as an 'autonomous' subject. Before this moment the subject has no social existence at all. Such a moment, though, is strictly unthinkable: we are always already subjects. Moreover, the moment of recognition in the above scenario is not conceivable as the effect of anything like a conscious choice; it can only be retrospectively considered as such.

Althusser notes that even before birth the conditions of interpellation are secured by a whole series of actions on the part of parents and family, crucial among which is the practice of naming. Individuals may spontaneously regard their name as innately 'theirs', but a name is also a social fact, conferred from without upon individuals, which, from the moment it is officially 'registered', constitutes an essential formal condition for their existence as social actors. Only later does it pass over to the realm of (ideological) obviousness, allowing them to respond to the hailing of others: 'Yes, that's me'. The name we receive at birth bears the mark of paternity, in that the vast majority of people (at least in Anglo-French cultures) bear the name of their father (or their mother's father); the psychoanalytic resonances of the point are unmistakable. In his earlier essay, 'Freud and Lacan', Althusser is already considering the metaphorical extension of the Oedipus complex beyond what he calls its role within 'familial ideology'. As he puts it, 'the Oedipus complex is ... imposed by the Law of Culture on every involuntary and constrained candidate to humanity'.[22]

By the time of the ISAs essay, when Althusser was considering a more 'top-down', causal account of ideology than that outlined in 'Marxism and Humanism', the 'Law of Culture' provides a suitably deterministic framework in which to explain the subjugation of the 'involuntary' worker to the all-embracing requirements of capital through the combined resources of ISAs and RSAs. That the process should be so fully realised recalls the very Hegelian problematic he had earlier been at pains to reject. It also fails to account theoretically for the few examples of resistance even he evokes in the ISAs essay (such as those 'heroic' teachers who try to work against the grain). He gives little sense of the process of subjectivisation (becoming a subject) being partial, contradictory or precarious. Furthermore, the playing down of 'theoreticism' also means that the opposition of ideology to science is notably absent. What emerges, despite a postscript that suggests vaguely that resistance to ideology is possible only through 'class struggle', is a political (though decidedly not a theoretical) pessimism that would be increasingly to the fore in Althusser's later writings.

Althusser's Influence

Despite their often austere tone, Althusser was always insistent that his theoretical texts should be regarded as part of an ongoing project, subject to revision and extension by others working the broad field of Marxist theory. In France his initiatives were carried forward in various disciplines by a group of like-minded collaborators such as Pierre Macherey (literary theory), Michel Pêcheux (linguistics) and Nicos Poulantzas (political theory). But Althusserianism was too closely aligned with the PCF to survive the latter's decline amid a general fragmentation of the political left following the events of May 1968. Althusser's work and that of his collaborators has had its main impact in the Anglo-American world. In the field of political and social theory, Althusser was a key point of reference in the project of the long-standing journal *Economy and Society*, and, to a lesser extent, in the cultural theory of Stuart Hall. Latterly, the largely USA-based movement of post-Marxism has sought in Althusser a key reference in its synthesis of Marxism with a broad swathe of post-structuralist, anti-essentialist thinking in politics, sociology and economics.

Althusserianism has had its most long-lasting influence in literary and cultural studies. Taking their cue from Macherey's *A Theory of Literary Production*[23] as well as from Althusser's occasional interventions in the field, critics such as Terry Eagleton and Fredric Jameson have theorised relative autonomy in the literary and cultural domain. What emerges is a model of analysis that both acknowledges textual specificity and rejects traditional appeals to aesthetic unity and autonomy by means of careful attention to the ways in which the sheer ideological weight of its source materials prevent the text from saying quite what it explicitly wants to say. Textual production is thus conceived as a productive tension between the ideological and purely formal dimensions of its 'conditions of possibility'. In a similar vein, Althusser's co-option of psychoanalytic concepts in his theory of ideology has given rise to a mode of analysis, notably in the area of film studies, that focuses on the ways in which subjectivity is construed as an effect of the practice of spectatorship. Althusserian criticism examines film and other texts from the perspective of the subject-positions which they encode and make available, theorising such possibilities in terms of their broader socio-political determinants. Such approaches tend not to operate on Althusser's preferred ground of social class, but it is a fitting testament to the flexibility and open-ended character of his thinking about ideology that it has proven to be adaptable to the contemporary agenda of a politics of gendered, racial and sexual identity.

Notes

1. Althusser, *For Marx*, p. 9.
2. In Louis Althusser, *Essays in Self-Criticism*, trans. Grahame Lock (London: NLB, 1976).
3. *For Marx*, p. 27.
4. Althusser and Balibar, *Reading 'Capital'*, p. 142.
5. *For Marx*, p. 23.
6. Louis Althusser, *Positions (1964–1975)* (Paris: Éditions Sociales, 1976), p. 144 (my translation).
7. In *For Marx*.
8. *For Marx*, p. 221.
9. Karl Marx, *The Eighteenth Brumaire of Louis Bonaparte*, trans. E. and C. Paul (London: Allen and Unwin, 1926), p. 96.
10. *Reading 'Capital'*, p. 139.
11. In *For Marx*.
12. Ibid., p. 102.
13. Ibid., p. 91.
14. Ibid., p. 100.
15. Ibid., p. 114.
16. In Althusser, *Lenin and Philosophy and Other Essays*.
17. *For Marx*, p. 235.
18. Ibid., pp. 231, 233, 234.
19. Ibid., p. 235.
20. Ibid., p. 230.
21. *Lenin and Philosophy*, pp. 174–5.
22. Althusser, 'Freud and Lacan', p. 29.
23. Pierre Macherey, *A Theory of Literary Production* (London: RKP, 1978).

Major Works by Althusser

For Marx, trans. Ben Brewster (London: Verso, 1990 [1965]).
'Freud and Lacan', in *Writings on Psychoanalysis*, ed. Olivier Corpet and François Matheron, trans. Jeffrey Mehlman (New York: Columbia University Press, 1996), pp. 7–32.

Lenin and Philosophy and Other Essays, trans. Ben Brewster (London: NLB, 1971 [1969]).

(with Etienne Balibar) *Reading 'Capital'*, trans. Ben Brewster (London: Verso, 1979 [1968]).

Suggestions for Further Reading

Gregory Elliot, *Althusser: The Detour of Theory* (London: Verso, 1987). A general survey. Particularly good on the philosophical, historical and political contexts of Althusser's work. Contains a comprehensive bibliography.

Alex Callinicos, *Althusser's Marxism* (London: Pluto, 1976). Acute, though generally sympathetic, philosophically orientated exposition of Althusser's work.

E. Ann Kaplan and Michael Sprinkler, *The Althusserian Legacy* (London and New York: Verso, 1993). Consistently interesting essays on Althusser's influence on a wide range of disciplines. Includes an interview with Jacques Derrida.

Warren Montag, *Louis Althusser* (New York: Macmillan, 2003). Interesting perspectives on Althusserianism as a model of (mainly literary) textual analysis.

5

Roland Barthes (1915–80)

Andy Stafford and Susan McManus

Barthes: Between Theory and Writing

There are singular difficulties in the task of exposition of the work of Roland Barthes. How to find the meaning of the theorist who taught us to unpack the conditions in which meanings become possible? How to express the significance of the critic who sought to 'unexpress the expressible'?[1] How to narrate the intellectual life of a thinker and writer of fragments, of the dispersal of meanings? How to pin down the legacy of the theorist, critic and writer who proposed analytical codes and categories only to exceed them, and to leave them in his wake as an obstacle to writing when they had once been a provocation to write? This chapter traces the interplay of theorist and writer in the work of Barthes, giving a sense of the movement and the activity of thought that Barthes both performs and bequeaths us, as he multiplies the sites of critique, theory and writing. For while Barthes is known primarily as a critical and literary theorist, his theorising was mobile, never ossifying into stricture or systematising dogma.

Barthes was born in Cherbourg, France, in 1915. His youth was marked by illness, tuberculosis, and he spent 1934 and between 1941 and 1946 in sanatoria in the Alps. He worked as a journalist and a teacher, gaining his first academic post in 1960. During the *événements* in France of May 1968, Barthes was associated with the left-wing, theoretically and aesthetically avant-garde journal *Tel Quel*. When he died in 1980, he held the distinguished position of Professor at the Collège de France. To narrate briefly: his intellectual journey saw him move by means of engagements with Jean-Paul

Sartre and Bertolt Brecht; with Ferdinand de Saussure, semiology and structuralism; and in the 1960s, with Claude Lévi-Strauss, Michel Foucault and Jacques Lacan. Finally, he gained notoriety as post-structuralist and theorist of *écriture* (writing). Yet the range of his interventions and the idiosyncratic qualities of his writing practice precluded the development of a 'Barthes School' of thought: his work cannot be 'captured', contained, or understood via the impulse to codify as 'Barthes-ian/ism'.

From this sketch, we can begin by pointing to two guiding concerns: one, via his encounters with Sartre and Brecht, is the possibility of critique, and of the political responsibility of the intellectual. The second, stemming from his semiological interests, is the possibility of a metalanguage. Barthes's vital contribution to critical and literary theory has to do with the ways he wrote between the poles of theorist/writer, holding these roles in productive tension and play. The task of theory, it may be claimed, is to seek an epistemologically privileged, authoritative way of writing (so authoritative that it is no longer simply language but truth). Theory, then, is distinct from its object (literature, culture, society, politics and so on), analysing from a position of detachment. In the case of a critical theory, the task is one of exposure of the pretensions to innocence and neutrality in literature, culture and politics, and critique of the concomitant status quo of ostensibly universal liberal, humanist values. The writer, in contrast, accomplishes the neutralisation of the opposition between theory and its object, denying theory both its autonomy and its status. The paradox of Barthes, then, is the co-existence of the writer with the theorist, the essayist with the structural analyst, and emotive sensibility with critical acuity. The force of his work is to deny the opposition between theory and its object, and yet still to theorise, still to write, and indeed implicitly to redefine the task of theory itself (as writing). It is common to note a distinction between an 'early' Barthes (the critical work from around 1950–60) and a 'late' Barthes (1970–80, emphasising the writing body and its pleasures). This maps onto the shift from theorist to writer, or from structuralist to post-structuralist, with a pivotal turning point identifiable in the early 1960s. This chapter follows that chronological framework, but should not be read as a teleological exposition (where the meaning of a process or a life is contained in an authoritative end point).

The Politics of Form

In his Inaugural Lecture at the Collège de France, Barthes stated, 'it seemed to me that a science of signs [semiology] could stimulate social criticism, and that Sartre, Brecht and Saussure could join forces in this project'.[2]

> There isn't a day [he writes in 1965] when reading a newspaper, watching a TV programme, listening to a taxi driver, I don't want to transform what I read or hear into what I call mythological material, that is precisely into a discourse which is between criticism and the novel.[3]

In 1962, he wrote, 'what has interested me passionately all my life is the way men [*sic*] make their world intelligible to themselves. It is, if you like, the adventure of the intelligible, the problem of meaning'.[4] This 'adventure of intelligibility', however, does not simply involve making meanings: the task of the critic as Barthes sees it in 1964 is to 'unexpress the expressible'.[5]

Barthes's first work, *Writing Degree Zero*, critically engages with Sartre's views on political responsibility and engagement, of being 'in situation'. On the one hand, Sartre's *What Is Literature?*, written in 1947, had a restricted, content-based perspective on the political aspects of literature. Language, for Sartre, should be used as a tool, meaning should be clear, revealing the world as it is as a means towards political commitment. For Barthes, on the other hand, the very form of writing held within it historicity as well as political implications. Barthes saw the 1848 revolutions as the harbinger of modernity; and also as the moment when the interested and partial, rather than universal, character of bourgeois writing became evident and marked. Writers, then, had to reflect on writing practices self-consciously: language either continued to perpetuate bourgeois orderings of the world of meaning, or could become a self-conscious engagement with that world, and thus a questioning, reordering and weakening of bourgeois ideological hegemony. This identification of two ways of writing is itself a persistent concern for Barthes, particularly in *S/Z* and *The Pleasure of the Text*. *Writing Degree Zero* is a complex interrogation of literary form itself, and the significance of experiment at the level of form. 'Zero degree writing', as exemplified by Albert Camus, or in the *nouveau roman* of the 1950s (Alain Robbe-Grillet, Nathalie Sarraute and Jean Cayrol) 'struggles against literature and its presumptions of meaning and order'.[6] Unexpressing the expressible, then, is, as Culler notes, 'to problematise the meanings our cultural codes otherwise confer, and thus to unwrite the world as it is written by prior discursive practices'.[7]

Avant-garde writing exposed the processes of construction of intelligibility, showing discursive codes to be by no means natural. This concern with meaning and connotation, and the possibility of political critique inherent in the form in literary history, is also evident in Barthes's exploration of accounts of contemporary culture. Throughout the early 1950s, Barthes was a keen advocate and supporter of the French popular theatre movement, especially the Marxist theatre of Brecht. Brechtian theatre worked by means of estrangement, which encouraged and provoked a critical distance (rather than emotive identification) in its audience. It was a politically critical move that encouraged the audience to recognise human agency at work in both the theatre and in history. Barthes explains, referring to Brecht's *Mother Courage*:

> [T]he point is to show those who believe in the fatality of war, like Mother Courage, that war is precisely a human phenomenon, not a fatality ... because we *see* Mother Courage blind, we *see* what she does not see ... We understand, in the grip of dramatic obviousness which is the most immediate kind of persuasion, that Mother Courage is the victim of what she does not see, which is a remediable evil.[8]

This demystifying ethos, a combination of critique and intellectual responsibility, inspired *Mythologies*, which collects a series of monthly feature articles Barthes wrote between 1954 and 1956 for *Les Lettres nouvelles*. Barthes uncovers and decodes another level of signification. As he puts it, 'in short, in the account given of our contemporary circumstances, I resented seeing Nature and History confused at every turn, in the decorative display of *what-goes-without-saying*, the ideological abuse which, in my view, is hidden there'.[9] Reading cultural artefacts as diverse as wrestling, wine, striptease, film and advertising, Barthes exposed the ways in which the mass ideology effaced historical explanation, unquestioningly accepted the world as it was, and so worked to maintain order. This is the function of 'myth' in contemporary society:

> Myth does not deny things, on the contrary, its function is to talk about them; simply, it purifies them, it makes them innocent, it gives them a natural and eternal justification, it gives them a clarity which is not that of an explanation but that of a statement of fact ... In passing from history to Nature, myth acts economically: it abolishes the complexity of human acts, it gives them a simplicity of essences, it does away with all dialectics, with any going beyond what is immediately visible, it organises

a world which is without contradictions because it is without depth, a world wide open and wallowing in the evident, it establishes a blissful clarity; things appear to mean something by themselves.[10]

Barthes's acts of demystification are semiological: 'semiology has taught us that myth has the task of giving an historical intention a natural justification, and making contingency appear eternal'.[11] For example: 'I am at the barber's, and a copy of *Paris-Match* is offered to me. On the cover, a young Negro in a French uniform is saluting, with eyes uplifted, probably fixed on a fold of the tricolour.'[12] In the midst of France's deep colonial crisis, Barthes invokes Saussure's distinction between signifier and signified to uncover what is at stake. The image reinforces colonial ideology by implying, though not showing, the soldier saluting the French flag. The myth of French imperialism is thus latent: the signifier (the salute) denotes this. Its connotation, however, the signified, is that French imperialism is a great civilising force appreciated by Africans. The photograph, asserts Barthes, is a myth: 'the Negro suddenly hails me in the name of French imperiality; but at the same moment the Negro's salute thickens, becomes vitrified, freezes into an eternal reference meant to *establish* French imperiality'.[13] The myth then, does not efface French imperialism; on the contrary, what is effaced is 'the contingent, historical, in one word: *fabricated* quality of colonialism'.[14] As myth naturalises, reifying meanings so as to imply the world could not be otherwise, the mythologist unveils:

> The unveiling which it carries out is therefore a political act: founded on a responsible idea of language, mythology thereby postulates the freedom of the latter. It is certain that in this sense mythology *harmonises* with the world, not as it is, but as it wants to create itself.[15]

Mythologies returned the responsibility for the construction and dissemination of meanings to the producers themselves (humanity), effectively opening critical spaces in everyday life. And yet, the totalising methodology Barthes suggests in 'Myth Today', the extended essay which concluded the collected articles, seems to efface the very contingency and timeliness of the essays themselves. This tension illustrates a central problem within the structuralist method that Barthes was at this time working with: what is the relationship between effective political critique and metalanguage? The essay returns to this question under the heading of a 'parametric' form of criticism.

Barthes's early work took shape and force under the dual

problematic of critique and of metalanguage. Barthes's structuralist 'phase' is where these concerns, along with the conflict between theorist/writer, become most evident. In *Critical Essays*, Barthes attests, 'the goal of all structuralist activity ... is to "reconstitute" an object so as to make manifest the rules of its functioning'; and further, 'what is new is a mode of thought (or a "poetics") which seeks less to assign completed meanings to the objects it discovers than to know how meaning is possible, at what cost and by what means'.[16] Semiology showed that meaning in language depended upon a synchronic (rather than diachronic) positioning within a system: words mean not because they have a history, but because they differentiate themselves from other words. Barthes and others applied this differential philosophy of meaning – in which system replaces etymology as the basis of communication – to the social sciences in general, in what is now known as structuralism. The classic example illustrating structuralist thought is the Argonauts' ship, which, though every single plank, nut and bolt on it had been replaced at some stage, was still entitled to be called the 'Argo', because its captain, crew, ethos, mission and so on, remained unchanged: '*Argo* is an object with no other cause than its name, no other identity than its form.'[17] In other words, the material that determines the mechanical functioning of the ship was irrelevant in maintaining its identity: its identity was maintained by its 'structural' (or 'systemic') difference in relation to all other ships on the sea. Structural analyses, by virtue of this 'differential' approach to social phenomena, show that meaning is not determined by material reality, but by positions in systems of discourse.

Barthes's *Elements of Semiology* and *The Fashion System* are attempts to show the workings of the science of signs. Structuralism and semiology were, however, accused of being anti-historical. Since semiology treated not just language but all phenomena as part of a system (or synchronically), it was not difficult to see how this tended to ignore or down-play the diachronic, historical background or origins. Barthes's work is implicated in this 'error'. His earliest work on fashion involved an investigation into how historians have analysed the forms that clothes have taken. Barthes's conclusion in 1957 (ten years before publishing his study of fashion) was that a purely historical approach failed to account for the changes that have taken place. A Roman soldier might have thrown a piece of cloth around him to keep warm (historical explanation), but why did this become a red tunic, of a certain length and with a brooch worn on the breast? For Barthes, a structural and semiological reading of clothing forms had to take into account the relationship each form had in relation to the contemporary society around the wearer. So tunics were a sign of military and centurion status for a Roman soldier, which, though arbitrary in that the status could have been signified in many other ways, was integral to the clothing system operating at that time. It is clear from this example that it is hard to square the synchronic/systemic with the diachronic/historical.

Barthes's suppleness of thought enabled him, just as he was publishing *Elements of Semiology* and completing *The Fashion System*, to suggest already that semiology was a flawed system unless it recognised its own status as language. In the second half of the 1960s Barthes would carry out this search for an appropriate self-reflexive semiology by establishing what J. G. Merquior has called the 'literarisation of thought',[18] a Nietzschean avant-garde recognition that 'we are scientific out of a lack of subtlety'.[19] As semiology and structuralism became orthodoxy, Barthes tired of the scientific claims. Structuralist analyses were merely revealing the paucity of forms in human social and cultural phenomena. Thus, a crucial component of post-structuralism was the move 'From Science to Literature' (as Barthes's 1967 essay was aptly titled), or from theory to writing, a move which problematised both metalanguage and critique.

Polemics and Parametrics

In an interview in 1963 Barthes talks of how he has 'often dreamed of a "parametric" form of criticism which would modify its language according to the work offered to it'.[20] The work of the late 1960s and early 1970s can usefully be viewed under the aegis of self-reflexive methodological experimentation, with a concomitant commitment to empowering the reader in a participatory reading-as-rewriting critical praxis. Barthes is best known for 'The Death of the Author' thesis. Ironically, this article was due to appear in May 1968, and was a crucial part of Barthes's politicisation during the *événements* in France at that time, when students led prolonged demonstrations and ten million workers came out on strike. Publication of the article was delayed until November of that year. *S/Z*, perhaps Barthes's most militant text, was also written in the heat of May 1968. Originally worked through as a series of post-graduate seminars in

Paris, Barthes's reading, which was interrupted by the student and worker uprising, was inflected by the events. Whereas the pre-May 1968 notes for his seminar show a concern with 'structural analysis', the notes written for the seminars when colleges and universities reopened in the Autumn of 1968 show a marked shift in Barthes's perspective. The post-May 1968 Barthes now believed that to use a purely structuralist methodology gave credence to the very scientific arrogance that the students had been questioning. In post-May 1968 France, structuralism and a non-self-reflexive semiology were perceived as technocratic modes of theorising. His work of this period is caught in the nexus of several core problems: metalanguage and critique, as well as the politics, possibilities and, indeed, convergence of structuralist and post-structuralist modes of theorising.

'The Death of the Author' sought to release the hold of the authorial voice as the guarantor of the meaning of a text. As with structuralist analysis, the text should be approached, not in order to explain its meaning (in the singular), but in order to explore the possibilities of meaning (in the plural). The 'distancing' or removal of the author effects a change in the nature of texts:

> [W]e know now that a text consists not of a line of words releasing a single 'theological' meaning (the 'message' of the Author-God), but of a multi-dimensional space in which are married and contested several writings, none of which is original.[21]

This is, then, an explicitly anti-authoritarian manoeuvre: 'an activity which we may call countertheological, properly revolutionary, for to refuse to halt meaning is finally to refuse God and his hypostases, reason, science, the law'.[22] Finally, Barthes asserts, 'the birth of the reader must be requited by the death of the author'.[23] With the death of the author comes the refusal to privilege the role of the critic; but the newly empowered reader can no longer be a passive consumer of texts, but must, instead, be actively involved in generating new meanings by rewriting the text. Barthes's exemplary reading of Balzac's short story in S/Z demonstrates this.

Performative and singular, S/Z has been seen, as Jonathan Culler points out, as a 'meeting ground for projects often held to be contradictory. On the one hand, it displays a powerful scientific and metalinguistic drive, breaking the work into its constituents, naming and classifying'; on the other hand, Barthes suggests that Balzac's story can be read/rewritten as it 'outplays the codes on which it seems to be based'.[24] Just as methodologically innovative is Barthes's introduction which thematises this congruence and shift between structuralist and post-structuralist. Barthes here distinguishes between two 'types' of text: the *scriptible* (or readerly) and *lisible* (or writerly). The writerly is privileged, 'because the goal of literary work ... is to make the reader no longer a consumer but a producer of the text'.[25] However, the 'writerly' text has a tenuous existence: 'Where can we find them? Certainly not in reading (or at least very rarely: by accident, fleetingly, obliquely, in certain limit-works): the writerly text is not a thing, we would have a hard time finding it in a bookstore'.[26] The qualities which would enable the reader to distinguish between the readerly and the writerly do not inhere within texts themselves – they are not 'given' qualities. The distinction between writerly/readerly can be seen as an active differential: a difference that is activated in the very process of reading as rewriting. This is clear from Barthes's own choice of text to read/rewrite: Balzac's *Sarrasine*, pre-Barthes's reading, was a classic 'readerly' text. This choice illustrates some of what is at stake in Barthes's argument, in literary, critical and political terms. By rereading a classic, 'readerly' text, Barthes disrupts the establishment of literary values and literary history itself, preventing the recuperation of the classic as such by showing the ways in which Balzac's text also 'struggles against literature and its presumptions of meaning and order'.[27] Textuality or *écriture* also disrupts the status of criticism and the role of the critic, as the opposition between critical writing and creative writing is undone:

> its model being a productive (and no longer representative) one, it demolishes any criticism which, once produced, would mix with it: to rewrite the writerly text would consist only in disseminating it, in dispersing it within the field of infinite difference. The writerly text is a perpetual present, upon which no *consequent* language (which would inevitably make it past) can be superimposed; the writerly text is *ourselves writing*, before the infinite play of the world ... is traversed, intersected, stopped, plasticised by some singular system (Ideology, Genus, Criticism) which reduces the plurality of entrances, the opening of networks, the infinity of languages.[28]

There can no longer be the authoritative critical moment of closing the text. The writerly text is constructed via an active process of reading which cannot and should not be stabilised: 'The writerly is ... production without product, structuration without structure. But the readerly texts? They are products.'[29] Reading a text by rewriting it, then, becomes a political interpretative activity which saves texts from mere endless reproduction and repetition. A parametric form renounces metalanguage to save critique as ongoing process.

Barthes is deeply involved with the radical Leninist (then Maoist) literary journal *Tel Quel* from 1968 to 1970. Alongside its main theorists, Phillipe Sollers and Julia Kristeva, Barthes applies his rewriting strategies to some heretical and complex writers. The distinction between writerly/readerly can be seen as an active differential: a difference that is activated in the very process of reading as rewriting. Barthes illustrates his approach by writing on the Marquis de Sade (a pornographer), the Utopian thinker Charles Fourier (a socialist) and the Jesuit spiritualist Ignace de Loyola (a mystic) in *Sade, Fourier, Loyola*. Barthes argued that they were all 'logothets', designing new ways of using language. The following suggestion on reading Sade exemplifies his approach:

> The Sadian combination ... can appear monotonous to us only if we send our reading off in an arbitrary fashion, away from Sade's discourse and towards the 'reality' which it is supposed to be representing: Sade is boring only if we become fixated by the crimes reported, instead of the performances of the discourse.[30]

The emphasis is clearly on 'discourse', how language 'functions', on us in the here and now, and in comparison to its history of reception, dissemination and reuse. The 'scandal' of the eighteenth-century Sade's writing for 1970s France is no longer its pornographic and debased content, but its capacity to theatricalise language.

The Pleasure of the Text explores the newly thematised pleasures of the reader by transforming the writerly/readerly distinction into a further active differential of pleasure: *plaisir* (pleasure) and *jouissance* (bliss). *Plaisir*/pleasure concerns the kind of reactive joy of the readerly, a confirmation of 'what goes without saying'; *jouissance* denotes the bliss/ecstasy of the writerly, as affectively experienced by the subject as reader-rewriter who also experiences the concomitant dispersal of coding. Concern with the reader as rewriter does not, for Barthes, mean a revalorisation of individuality or subjectivity. Just as the text is composed of a multiplicity of codes, so too is the subject:

> Then perhaps the subject returns, not as an illusion, but as *fiction*. A certain pleasure is derived from a way of imagining oneself as *individual*, of inventing a final, rarest fiction: the fictive identity. This fiction is no longer the illusion of a unity; on the contrary, it is the theater of society

in which we stage our plural: our pleasure is *individual* – but not personal.[31]

Subjectivity is itself a 'text' for Barthes. To summarise the concerns of this crucial period between structuralist and post-structuralist: finding a 'parametrical' form of criticism meant self-reflexive methodological experimentation. With the death of the author the reader is newly empowered; but the role of the reader, the active reader, is not to reconfirm existing codes and discourse, but to enact an avant-garde dispersal of such codes. The reader as rewriter of the text is not the origin of meaning, but merely a privileged site where meanings interweave. Textuality leads, then, to the deconstruction of subjectivity. The institutions of literature – the author as creative origin, narrative as referential representation, the critic as the privileged preserver of a history of literary genius – are thoroughly questioned. Where does that leave the text?

> What relation can there be between the pleasure of the text and the institutions of the text? Very slight. The theory of the text postulates bliss, but has little institutional future: what it establishes, its precise accomplishment, its assumption, is a practice (that of the writer) not a science, a method, a research, a pedagogy; on these principles, this theory can produce only theoreticians or practitioners, not specialists.[32]

What, indeed, is the institutional future of Barthes's work?

Barthes Today

Barthes's final works can be read as only one answer to the question he posed, a singular writing practice rather than the inevitable, teleological outcome of his theoretical development. The final works are distinctive, singular, evocative, sometimes melancholy. Barthes's last writings, involving the textualising of love (*A Lover's Discourse: Fragments*), of writing the self (*Roland Barthes by Roland Barthes*), of photography (*Camera Lucida*) and cruising (*Incidents*). This work ranges from the delicate, parodic, astute, deeply sad, humorous, lonely and, in places, forthrightly scatological. At stake is the possibility of meaning and that which is not given to significance. For, as we have seen, textuality is not an alternative to the bodily or material.

The relation of meaning and significance is prefigured in *Empire of Signs*. If logothets and empowered readers were one way of defying the recuperative power of the established order of values, another way is to free processes of signification from meaning. The place where Barthes found this emptying of meaning was in the Orient, specifically Japan. Two visits there in 1966 and 1968 led to his seminal, if deliberately fantastical, ethnography of the country which symbolised the 'Other' of the West. Bankrupt for its facile insistence on plenitude, completion and monotheism, and characterised by its serial consumption and acquisitive mentality, the West was contrasted directly by Barthes to Japan, and in particular to Buddhist philosophy. *The Empire of Signs* was Barthes's fictional (literally, for Barthes denied all scientific or sociological pretensions) account of a decentred world. Presents with nothing inside, cities with no centre, meals without a main course, and short poems, *haïku*, without definite meaning, Japanese culture was presented as the polar opposite of its advanced European counterpart. Even its puppet theatre, *bunraku*, displayed all the traits that Barthes had found inspiring in Brecht's radical popular theatre. He even contrasts the Japanese student demonstration, *Zengakuren*, highly organised, to the 'spontaneity' so cherished in the European student movement. But, above all, it was the concentration on writing, the material act of tracing the hand across paper, which fascinated Barthes, already celebrating the practice of *écriture*. It is not surprising that, after his visits to Japan, he became an amateur calligrapher, using the gestural forms typical of this ancient art in his own creative drawings.

Barthes found in Japan a celebration of artifice and form that did not naturalise those fictions. In short, he found a different answer to the question of what 'science' is appropriate to humanity, and to forms of experience suffered or enjoyed. His final book *Camera Lucida*, subtitled *Reflections on Photography*, surprised most critics and friends by indeed avoiding a stark and searching semiological account of the photographic medium, preferring instead a romantic search for his recently deceased mother through photographs which touched him personally, written in an almost confessional tone:

> I have always wanted to *argue* my feelings; not to justify them, even less to fill the textual stage with my individuality; but on the contrary to offer, to tender this individuality to a science of the subject; the name of this science does not matter, as long as it reaches (which hasn't happened yet) a generality which does not reduce nor squash me.[33]

As well as a meditation on the possibilities of refinding someone in photography (both materially and physically, as well as emotionally), this shows the deeply personal journey that Barthes was undertaking in his last year of life. It is nevertheless, at the same time, a deeply theoretical one, trying to account for and record an existence without locking this individuality into a box (or a 'science').

Rather than become a novelist – something Barthes always hesitated in doing – he would take the Nietzschean option and become 'literary'. However, despite his fascination with Proust, this would not focus on the grand stuff of literary imagination, but rather on the day-to-day act of living (including the writing act itself). As he stated in *A Lover's Discourse*, in relation to Proust's search for lost time in the classic novel *À la recherche du temps perdu*, amorous interaction in today's modern world has none of the grandeur of the Novel:

> This theatre of time is the very opposite of the search for lost time; because I remember pathetically, on the spot, and not philosophically, discursively: I remember to be happy/unhappy – not in order to understand. I don't write, I don't lock myself away to write the great novel of recaptured time.[34]

Roland Barthes by Roland Barthes, his collection of fragments that constitutes the 'image-repertoire' of his self, is prefaced by 'it must all be considered as if spoken by a character in a novel'; or, better, given the necessary plurality of the subject, 'by several characters'.[35] *A Lover's Discourse: Fragments* continues this practice by textualising the body of the lover, reading, through the unfashionable sentimental language of love, the excess of signs to which the heightened sensitivity of the lover is prone.

All of which leads to difficulties in addressing Barthes's own question: what, indeed, is the relation between pleasure of the text and the institution of the text? Barthes provides one possible answer in thematising his intellectual journey in terms of 'doxa/paradoxa' (orthodoxy and its other):

> At the work's source, the opacity of social relations, a false Nature; the first impulse, the first shock, then, is to demystify (*Mythologies*); then when the demystification is immobilised in repetition, it must be displaced: semiological *science* (then postulated) tries to stir, to vivify, to arm the mythological gesture, the pose, by endowing it with a method; ... the goal of a semiological science is replaced by the (often very grim) science of the semiologists; hence one must sever oneself from that, must introduce into this rational image-repertoire the texture of desire, the claims of the body: this, then, is Text, the theory of the Text. But again the Text risks paralysis ... Where to go next?[36]

And again:

> Such oppositions are artefacts: one borrows from science certain conceptual features, an energy of classification ... the opposition is *struck* (like a coinage), but one does not seek to *honor* it. Then what good is it? Quite simply, it serves *to say something*: it is necessary to posit a paradigm in order to produce a meaning and then be able to divert it, to alter it.[37]

It is important to recall that for Barthes, 'artefact' is by no means a pejorative term. However, for a literary theorist such as Jonathan Culler, Barthes should not be read through this kind of assessment. For Culler, what remains of importance is semiology, the science of signs. That commitment, Culler argues, enables Barthes, and us, to identify the processes by which meaning happens, rather than simply assuming meaning. In terms of application and relevance now, then, Culler would privilege semiological approaches: cultural studies and media studies have benefited enormously, reading and demystifying the products of everyday life as 'texts' which produce the effect of 'reality'.

Diana Knight, however, takes a more holistic approach. She identifies a utopian impulse at work throughout Barthes's career: 'the mark of the utopia, as the "political form of fantasy" is therefore, the everyday – it is less a matter of theoretical proclamations than of a minutely detailed conjuring up of the organisation and quality of everyday life'.[38] The 'everyday', in this reading, is amenable to demystification – but also to pleasure, as one does not necessarily exclude the other. As we have argued, a parametric form of criticism lies at the heart of a radical theoretical and practical guide to judgement that in no way excludes pleasure; but neither does it exist as a once-and-for-all formula. For Barthes, the interplay of theorising and writing means renouncing the drive to an authoritative and all-encompassing metalanguage and, in turn, this leaves us with the multiplication of spaces of theorising and writing.

Notes

1. Barthes, *Critical Essays*, p. 15.
2. Barthes, 'Inaugural Lecture', *A Roland Barthes Reader*, p. 471.
3. 'Les artistes devant la politique', *Arts*, 10 (1965), p. 10.
4. Barthes, *The Grain of the Voice*, p. 8.
5. Barthes, *Critical Essays*, p. 15.
6. Jonathan Culler, *Barthes: A Very Short Introduction* (Oxford: Oxford University Press), p. 19.

7. Ibid., p. 129.
8. Barthes, *Critical Essays*, pp. 33–4.
9. Barthes, *Mythologies*, p. 11.
10. Ibid., p. 143.
11. Ibid., p. 142.
12. Ibid., p. 116.
13. Ibid., p. 125.
14. Ibid., p. 143
15. Ibid., p. 156.
16. Barthes, *Critical Essays*, p. 218.
17. Barthes, *Roland Barthes by Roland Barthes*, p. 46.
18. J. G. Merquior, *From Prague to Paris: A Critique of Structuralist and Post-Structuralist Thought* (London: Verso, 1986), p. 247.
19. Barthes, *Roland Barthes by Roland Barthes*, p. 161.
20. Barthes, *Critical Essays*, p. 275.
21. Barthes, *The Rustle of Language*, pp. 52–3.
22. Ibid., p. 54.
23. Ibid., p. 55.
24. Culler, *Barthes*, p. 74.
25. Barthes, *S/Z*, p. 4.
26. Ibid., pp. 4–5.
27. Culler, *Barthes*, p. 19.
28. Barthes, *S/Z*, p. 5.
29. Ibid.
30. Barthes, *Sade, Fourier, Loyola*, p. 36 [translation modified].
31. Barthes, *The Pleasure of the Text*, p. 62.
32. Ibid., p. 60.
33. Barthes, *Camera Lucida*, p. 18 [translation modified].
34. Ibid., p. 217.
35. Barthes, *Roland Barthes by Roland Barthes*, p. 119.
36. Ibid., p. 91.
37. Ibid., p. 92.
38. Diana Knight, *Barthes and Utopia*, p. 87.

Major Works by Barthes

Camera Lucida: Reflections on Photography, trans. Richard Howard (London: Fontana, 1984 [1980]).

Critical Essays, trans. Richard Howard (Evanston: Northwestern University Press, 1972 [1964]).

Criticism and Truth, trans. Katrine Pilcher Keuneman (London: Athlone 1987 [1966]).

The Eiffel Tower and Other Mythologies, trans. Richard Howard (New York: Hill and Wang, 1979 [1964]).

Elements of Semiology, trans. Annette Lavers and Colin Smith (London: Jonathan Cape, 1967 [1964]).
Empire of Signs, trans. Richard Howard (London: Jonathan Cape, 1983 [1970]).
The Fashion System, trans. Matthew Ward and Richard Howard (London: Jonathan Cape, 1985 [1967]).
The Grain of the Voice, trans. Linda Coverdale (New York: Hill and Wang, 1985 [1981]).
Image, Music, Text, trans. Stephen Heath (Glasgow: Fontana, 1977).
Incidents, trans. Richard Howard (Berkeley: University of California Press, 1992 [1980]).
A Lover's Discourse: Fragments, trans. Richard Howard (London: Jonathan Cape, 1979 [1977]).
Mythologies, trans. Annette Lavers (London: Jonathan Cape, 1972 [1957]).
New Critical Essays, trans. Richard Howard (Berkeley: University of California Press, 1990).
The Pleasure of the Text, trans. Richard Miller (London: Jonathan Cape, 1976 [1973]).
The Responsibility of Forms: Critical Essays on Music, Art and Representation, trans. Richard Howard (Oxford: Blackwell, 1985 [1982]).
Roland Barthes by Roland Barthes, trans. Richard Howard (London: Macmillan, 1977 [1975]).
The Rustle of Language, trans. Richard Howard (Oxford: Blackwell, 1986 [1984]).
Sade, Fourier, Loyola, trans. Richard Miller (Berkeley: University of California Press, 1976 [1971]).
The Semiotic Challenge, trans. Richard Howard (Oxford: Blackwell, 1987 [1985]).
S/Z, trans. Richard Miller (London: Jonathan Cape, 1975 [1970]).
Writing Degree Zero, trans. Annette Lavers and Colin Smith (London: Jonathan Cape, 1967 [1953]).

Suggestions for Further Reading

A Barthes Reader, edited by Susan Sontag (New York: Hill and Wang, 1982). Important collection of essays by Barthes, introduced by the American writer.

Calvet, Jean-Louis, *Roland Barthes: A Biography*, trans. Sarah Wykes (Oxford: Polity, 1994). Standard account of Barthes's life.

Knight, Diana, *Barthes and Utopia: Space, Travel, Writing* (Oxford: Oxford University Press, 1997). Wide-ranging analysis, original and thought provoking.

Knight, Diana (ed.), *Critical Essays on Roland Barthes* (New York:

G. K. Hall, 2000). Barthes's reception in France and English-speaking world.

Lavers, Annette, *Roland Barthes: Structuralism and After* (London: Methuen, 1982). Sophisticated, early overview of Barthes's career.

Moriarty, Michael, *Roland Barthes* (Oxford: Polity, 1991). Excellent introduction to the main aspects of Barthes's work.

Stafford, Andy, *Roland Barthes, Phenomenon and Myth: An Intellectual Biography* (Edinburgh: Edinburgh University Press, 1998). Sees Barthes's life as comprised of three spheres – journalist, academic, essayist – and contextualises the resultant theories.

6

Jacques Derrida (1930–)

Adam Sharman

Introduction

Jacques Derrida is most commonly associated with the textual practice of deconstruction, though Derrida himself has expressed reservations concerning the fortunes of that name. Derrida's work consists of a series of frequently dazzling readings of texts drawn largely from the Western philosophical tradition (though by no means from the canonical fragments of that tradition), but from many other places besides. Derrida begins with texts since there is no concept that is not bound to a specific text or textual tradition. The readings he produces typically alight on a dominant concept which seeks to preserve its position of mastery by erecting borders between itself and those subordinate elements which might contaminate and hence undermine it. Often accused of being disrespectful towards the texts of the philosophical tradition, in fact Derrida shows these texts utmost respect by refusing to tear the concepts they treat out of their textual locus. Indeed, from one perspective, Derrida's approach is highly traditional. He constantly upholds the need to understand the internal logic of a textual system by dint of close reading, respect for a text's detail (including its margins) and much patience. In truth, however, in their content and form Derrida's texts are at once respectful and heretical. And while he has always stressed the political force of intellectual work, he has been no less insistent on the intellectual rigour which must accompany a philosopher's 'ethico-existential pathos'.[1] Such rigour is one reason why one should not expect instant access to Derrida's writing. Access to a common idiom and a common opinion, hence to a common knowledge, does not necessarily make the best servant of democracy.

Contexts

Derrida was born in El-Biar, near Algiers, in 1930. At the time, Algeria was a French colony, and Derrida, born into a Jewish family, a figure on the periphery of one of the margins of French culture. Expelled from secondary school in Algiers in 1942 by an official anti-semitism implemented more keenly in the colony than in German-occupied France, Derrida describes the child he was at the time of the expulsion as a 'little black and very Arab Jew'.[2] Derrida resumed his education first in a Jewish school, and subsequently at a series of *lycées* which eventually led him to France's prestigious École normale supérieure in Paris. Both the path to the École normale supérieure and his career at that institution – traditionally entrusted with producing the country's philosophical elite – were marked by set-backs and ill health. Derrida finally qualified in 1956 and then, at the height of the Algerian war, did French military service between 1957 and 1959 as a teacher near Algiers, before returning to French academic life. He is a founder-member of GREPH (the International Group for Research into the Teaching of Philosophy) and currently holds the position of Director of Studies at the École des hautes études en sciences sociales in Paris. Derrida has enjoyed notable international success and not a little notoriety. But despite this success, or perhaps because of it, this no longer so black, and, as he puts it, now excessively acculturated, Arab Jew has consistently met with institutional opposition in France. Derrida describes himself as 'a sort of *marrane* of French Catholic culture',[3] the name *marrane* indicating a troublesome rather than homely relationship to the question of belonging.

The political context of Derrida's formative years in Algeria and France was marked by the Algerian war, the return to power of de Gaulle, the *événements* of May 1968, and the totalitarian regimes of Stalin and the eastern European states. Derrida kept a sceptical distance from the extreme Marxist and Maoist militancy prominent among French intellectuals of the time, but maintains that, despite palpable divergences from it, Marxism constitutes an indispensable part of the element in which deconstruction developed. Three other intellectual forces of the time also left their imprint on Derrida's work: first, the phenomenological tradition which runs (with detours) from Edmund Husserl to Martin Heidegger and

Jacques Derrida (1930–)

Maurice Merleau-Ponty, the first two thinkers being of particular importance to Derrida; second, the practice of a critical-artistic avant-garde (formed by the likes of Georges Bataille, Maurice Blanchot, the Tel Quel group including Philippe Sollers) which worked at the interface between literature and philosophy; finally, structuralism, the systematic character of which is much tempered in Derrida's work by his cultivation of a heretical, transgressive writing practice, closer to the spirit of the aforementioned avant-garde. Derrida's context is constituted by texts drawn from the entire history of philosophy and thought. We might cite those of Plato, Aristotle, Kant and Rousseau, but perhaps, above all, those of Kierkegaard, Nietzsche and Freud. Derrida will insist repeatedly that a context, and indeed a critical theorist, is never simply contemporary.

Some Concepts and Methods

Deconstruction and différance

Although profoundly alien to one of the spirits of deconstruction, it is possible to identify something like a deconstructive system. One of the recurring themes of this system is Derrida's deconstruction of the metaphysics of presence. Derrida maintains that the idea of presence provides the support for a series of founding concepts or centres which have variously aspired to govern the Western philosophical tradition:

> Successively, and in a regulated fashion, the center receives different forms or names. The history of metaphysics, like the history of the West, is the history of these metaphors and metonymies. Its matrix ... is the determination of Being as *presence* in all senses of this word. It could be shown that all the names related to fundamentals, to principles, or to the center have always designated an invariable presence – *eidos, archē, telos, energeia, ousia* (essence, existence, substance, subject), *alētheia*, transcendentality, consciousness, God, man, and so forth.[4]

Each of these centres hopes to rule over the system of thought by remaining unsullied and unimpeachable, by belonging to itself, in such a way that it remains spatially and temporally self-present and self-identical.

Deconstruction begins by identifying the centre of a system, or the privileged term in a violent conceptual hierarchy, and represents an intervention to make that system or hierarchy tremble. Derrida is faithful in this respect to a tradition of thought which includes Heidegger's insight concerning our being-in-the-world, together with Nietzsche's lesson on the interestedness of any and all knowledge. There is no neutral, no detached or absolute vantage point of knowledge; rather, our language and conceptuality are already bound up with the object of thought. Thus, for Derrida, the starting point for deconstruction can never be justified absolutely. For the same reason, the intervention which inaugurates a deconstruction does not mean that a pure ethics provides the foundation of deconstruction. On the contrary, *différance* stands at the origin of all ethics as of all would-be centres. *Différance* is the spatialisation and temporalisation which precede all centres, all concepts and all of reality, making these things possible. The neologism *différance* itself exemplifies the complexity of this simple idea. The neologism taps into the resources of the French word *différer*, which means both to differ and to defer. The difference between *différence* (the usual word) and *différance* (the neologism) lies neither in the 'a' nor in the 'e'; it is actively produced in the constant shuttling process – over time and across space – between the two words. As such, *différance* is not a matter of space and time, so much as spacing-timing.

On the basis of this spacing-timing which underpins all concepts and all reality, Derrida departs from the traditional philosophical, and everyday, view of language and reason as essentially unified and unifying forces. In his view, language and rationality operate on the basis of discontinuity. If there were no gap, no physical break on the page, between the letters T-h-i-s, there would be no language and no communication. It is rather like the idea of a family feud which produces what is commonly called a 'broken relationship'. For Derrida, every relationship, no matter how loving, is broken. If the child were not separated from the mother at birth, there would be no identifiable child to speak of and no possibility of a relationship to it. This is why Derrida can say that language does not belong to the father, as psychoanalysis maintains, since language and meaning necessarily become disseminated (the father-author sows his seed and it duly scatters) in order to be what they are. It is true, of course, that not everything is discontinuity, rupture and dissemination. There is something in a specific word which marks it out from other words. One way to understand Derrida's view of meaning is to see it as a modification of Ferdinand de Saussure's theory of linguistic meaning. For Saussure, to be schematic in the extreme, linguistic meaning is produced by difference, by the interaction of opposites

Jacques Derrida (1930–)

– the meaning of 'night' only having value in relation to 'day'. Derrida pushes at the logic of Saussure's basic insight. For Derrida, meaning is indeed differential, but is produced by the interaction of a potentially limitless number of terms, not just by the difference between two. Meaning is the product of a play of differences plural, never presenting itself in one place or at one time.

Différance takes time and needs a bit of space to work. Derrida's point is that differences between words are not to be found in any one place, but are, rather, both scattered across the network of language and bound up with the unique instance of articulation. (Hence Derrida's concern with the question of translation: if words are not simple concepts floating freely in a universal ether which assures stable semantic relations, there can be no simple passage of meaning from one language to another; concepts take on singular resonances depending on the language in which they are articulated.) In order to arrive at a provisional understanding of a word, we rifle through our private mental, and shared cultural, archive of words, checking sounds and concepts against each other. Because we carry out this process so rapidly and so automatically, we forget that this play between the same and the different underlies all meaning. But meaning is not simply given in advance in the system of language; meaning is actively produced in the linguistic utterance which must draw on the system (the structure) but which will always produce singularities (the event).

Derrida's understanding of meaning sets him on a collision course with the concept of the sign, whose revived fortunes lay at the heart of French structuralism and semiotics of the late 1950s and early 1960s. Both in the classical understanding of the sign, in which the sign is deemed to point beyond itself arrow-like to the referent or thing, and in the Saussurean model, according to which the signifier is indivisibly wedded to the signified like the two sides of a piece of paper, the sign always functions on the basis of meaning's self-presence. Derrida's notion of trace, in contrast, approximates the idea that meaning is never simply located in a self-identical element:

> The play of differences supposes, in effect, syntheses and referrals which forbid at any moment, or in any sense, that a simple element be *present* in and of itself, referring only to itself. Whether in the order of spoken or written discourse, no element can function as a sign without referring to another element which itself is not simply present. This interweaving results in each 'element' – phoneme or grapheme – being constituted

on the basis of the trace within it of the other elements of the chain or system. This interweaving, this textile, is the *text* produced only in the transformation of another text. Nothing, neither among the elements nor within the system, is anywhere ever simply present or absent. There are only, everywhere, differences and traces of traces.[5]

In short, there is neither transcendental signifier nor transcendental signified to stabilise the system of meaning. What happens when I look in the dictionary in the hope of finally grasping the meaning of the word 'trace'? Among a number of definitions, the first I encounter is this: '*n*. Track left by person or animal walking or running or by moving pen or instrument etc.' I then check 'track': '*n*. Mark or series of marks left by person, animal, or thing, in passing along.' I then go to 'mark', and so on. In effect, each concept or signified (trace, track, mark) is inseparably a signifier which relays me elsewhere.

The hasty conclusion reached by critics of Derrida is that this understanding of meaning is anarchistic. Derrida's conclusion, in contrast, is: (1) that if language did not operate thus there would be no meaning in the first place; (2) that, yes, we must attempt to arrive at provisional meanings in order to achieve a minimal intelligibility; (3) that the problem occurs when these provisional meanings are taken for definitive ones. The same misguided accusation of anarchism is often levelled at deconstruction itself, which has passed into common usage as a synonym for a purely destructive practice. But it would be fairer to say that deconstruction submits the key concepts of the tradition to scrutiny and displacement, without thinking to annihilate them. One could not begin to speak about the sign, for instance, without engaging with the word 'sign' and with all the related words and concepts which provide the very medium in which thought on such matters has taken place. Any attempt to dispense with them altogether would constitute an impossibly violent razing of language and thought. This appreciation of the impossibility of destroying, or 'abandoning', metaphysical concepts such as truth is what most distinguishes Derrida's work from that of other French thinkers of the time with whom he has too hastily been grouped as 'post-structuralists' or even 'postmodernists'.[6]

Writing, speech and logocentrism

One understands from Derrida's deconstruction of the metaphysics of presence that a critique of the vulgar concept of time that has been with us in the West since Aristotle lies at the heart of Derrida's philosophy, which here draws on the work of Heidegger and Husserl. To think of time as made up of a succession of clean and proper presents, each identical to itself and necessarily distinct from the preceding and following instants, affords us a series of snapshots but no film of the movement or passing of time itself. In short, for Derrida the vulgar conception of successive time cannot think succession; it freezes out time from the thinking of time. Derrida is particularly close here to Husserl's work on internal time-consciousness – specifically, the idea that the present moment must retain something (a trace) from the preceding instant and likewise already be inscribed by the future one. Thus time as such does not exist, if by time we understand in traditional manner that which exists in a permanent now. Rather, time must be thought of on the basis of the trace. This idea underpins Derrida's oft-quoted but much misunderstood phrase 'il n'y a pas de hors-texte' (there is nothing outside the text, there is no outside-text).[7] It is the moment when Derrida brings together and radicalises the insights of phenomenology and structuralism. The phrase has been taken as proof that Derrida holds a linguistic, idealist view of the world: we have no access to past or even present reality, we are stuck in language, we have only signs which relay us to other signs, and so on ad infinitum.[8] In fact, Derrida is not to be read as a social constructionist, much less a postmodern relativist. What he means by the phrase is that the reality of the external world, which is a very real, very material thing, does not give itself in an instant or in an unmediated way. As Derrida says in the great essay 'Violence and Metaphysics: An Essay on the Thought of Emmanuel Levinas', for ethical reasons one must take seriously the reality of the external world or the egoity of another person, but this does not mean that access to that reality or that other is immediate. When Derrida speaks of textuality, then, it is to emphasise the fact that reality, including the brute facticity of the other, is a weave of spacing-timing, not a frozen simultaneity accessible in the instantaneity of God's vision.

On the basis of his suspicion of the metaphysics of presence, Derrida takes issue with many of the traditional key concepts – the right and proper currency – of philosophical debate. We can see this in his well-known deconstruction of the concepts of speech and writing. In *Of Grammatology* Derrida maintains that if the Western philosophical tradition has been 'logocentric', that is, premised on a series of centres which would found the system of thought while somehow remaining uncontaminated by the system's other elements, it has been no less 'phonocentric', that is, based on the primacy of the living voice (*phonē* is Greek for 'voice'). The living voice is that which stands in the relation of greatest, because most intimate, proximity to the self. My voice comes from deep within me; it is the exteriorisation of my most personal, unique interior, my spirit or soul. From Plato through to Jean-Jacques Rousseau and Saussure, speech in the Western tradition is assigned the values of spontaneity, immediacy, authenticity, originality, self-presence. Writing, in contrast, is considered secondary, derivative, impersonal, the product of technique, contrivance and machination. Speech is nature, writing artifice. Writing is that dangerous supplement that always threatens to carry my meaning off to a place where I will not be able to exercise control over it.

Derrida latches onto Rousseau's use of the word *supplément* in relation to the latter's discussion of the dichotomy between nature and culture. The word *supplément* in French pulls in conflicting directions. It means 'that which is added', but also 'that which makes up for a lack'. If culture is a supplement to nature, or if writing is a supplement to speech, this is because nature and speech exhibit an originary lack. If nature is so wholesome and complete, why does Rousseau argue that man's best natural instincts can only be drawn out by education (that is, by culture)? If speech is so full, why do we need writing? Derrida insinuates into his discussion of the supposed opposition speech/writing the bothersome concept of archi-writing or what he calls writing in general, which is designed to shake that opposition. Writing in general does not come after speech but precedes it. Before speech there must already be a system of differences which makes speech possible, which makes it possible for me to say 'I am an original and no one speaks like me'. This archi-writing does not determine what the subject says (it does not compel me to say 'I am an original ...'), but it does make the subject possible (if there were no archi-writing, no spacing-timing, there would be nothing and certainly nothing to say).

The implications of this expanded concept of writing, and of Derrida's deconstruction of certain discourses on the origins of language, go beyond linguistics. Derrida's exposition of the violent hierarchy speech/writing works through an analysis of an ethnographic 'writing lesson' made by the anthropologist Lévi-Strauss. Lévi-Strauss recounts how he introduced the practice of writing to

Jacques Derrida (1930–)

the Nambikwara of the Mato Grosso region of Brazil, showing this advanced Western technique to the chief of the tribe. According to the anthropologist, the chief proceeded to produce his own squiggly lines in order to convince his people that he had mastered the new technique. Lévi-Strauss frames the scene as a classic instance of Western ethnocentric invasiveness: impersonal Western technique and traditional instrument of domination corrupts primitive, non-violent, authentic other who knows only speech. But, as Derrida points out, the Nambikwara already have social hierarchies and divisions of their own, and already have a system of names which presupposes differentiation or writing in general. In sum, Lévi-Strauss's analysis betrays a linguistico-philosophical prejudice intimately bound to an anthropological one – an antiethnocentric nostalgia for the primitive. Here antiethnocentrism is a form of ethnocentrism ('they' know neither writing nor violence) which effectively misconstrues its object. The philosophical prejudice programmes the supposedly most empirical, most immediate contact between anthropologist and object of knowledge.

Ethics

Derrida is also, then, a philosopher of ethics, illustrated here by his later work on the concept of responsibility, which is tied to the idea of the aporia. The relationship between the two will take us close to the paradoxes which Derrida sees inscribed in any thinking of ethics. Aporia (from the Greek) designates a difficult, impracticable, or indeed impossible, passage, the experience of a non-passage. Derrida uses the word aporia to name the point in argumentation where one appears to arrive at a place of contradiction or paradox from which no simple exit is possible. In *The Gift of Death* he attempts to disturb the Kantian foundation of ethics at the heart of which lies the notion of the absolute duty or responsibility, formalised as universal law, which all citizens have to respect and to which they must respond. Apropos of the work of the Czech philosopher Jan Patočka, Derrida writes of the aporia of the concept of responsibility, which is explained thus: on the one hand, a responsible decision can only be taken in the light of knowledge (a decision made without one being minimally informed of the facts, without one knowing what one is doing, would be the height of irresponsibility); on the other hand, if decision-making amounts merely to following a body of knowledge given in advance, then it is irresponsible (since it becomes instead the mechanical application of a programme). In other words, responsibility demands that one be responsible (follow the guidance offered by knowledge) and irresponsible (not always follow that guidance) at the same time. In a sense, then, and simplifying greatly, the concept of responsibility is tied to the notion of heresy, that is to say, to a departure from the official, publicly stated doctrine. Moreover, insofar as this heresy maintains a certain distance with regard to what is publicly or officially declared, responsibility is not to be thought of as an absolutely public affair which must always take place in the full glare of publicity; rather, from this point of view, responsibility is bound to a type of secrecy. The fate of the concept of responsibility is thus once more linked to the (im)possibility of presence.

Derrida illustrates the paradox of responsibility by drawing on and developing Kierkegaard's discussion of the biblical story of Abraham's willingness to sacrifice his son Isaac. Without giving him any reason, God commands Abraham to sacrifice his only son on Mount Moriah, staying his hand only at the last minute. The story of Abraham and Isaac is the most extreme, most abominable instance of the obedience to absolute duty. And yet, Derrida says, it is also the most common and everyday experience of responsibility. In order for any human society to maintain itself along ethical lines, each individual must recognise and respect the alterity of another individual: I must be responsible in the face of the other as other and answer for what I do before him or her. That is my duty and obligation to the other. Such a duty might not prove difficult to fulfill if there were just one other. But there are an infinite number of others, to whom I am in principle bound by the same responsibility. Each time I fulfill my obligation to a specific other, I neglect the other others. I sacrifice them. At the precise moment that I dedicate all my care and compassion, all my physical and emotional energy to another, I betray all other others. This paradoxical condition does not just affect a situation in the real world, as it is called; it affects thinking itself:

> The concepts of responsibility, of decision, or of duty, are condemned a priori to paradox, scandal, and aporia. Paradox, scandal, and aporia are themselves nothing other than sacrifice, the revelation of conceptual thinking at its limit, at its death and finitude. As soon as I enter into a relation with the other ... I know that I can respond only by sacrificing ethics, that is, by sacrificing whatever obliges me to also respond, in the

same way, in the same instant, to all the others ... I don't need to raise my knife over my son on Mount Moriah for that. Day and night, at every instant, on all the Mount Moriahs of this world, I am doing that, raising my knife over what I love and must love, over those to whom I owe absolute fidelty, incommensurably.[9]

Borders

Because Derrida is interested in the ways in which impurity is denied and contamination suppressed, he pays constant attention to the places and figures (limits, frontiers, boundaries, demarcations; identities, essences, proper names) which attempt to separate out that which belongs from that which is alien, the proper from the improper, the official member of the group, nation or state from the outsider. All of Derrida's work takes place on and at the border. Be it the border that passes among things (territories, cultures or languages) or the border that passes between two apparently opposed concepts. Whence all those oppositions which seem to populate his writing (the singular and the general, the personal and the impersonal, the event and the system or structure, philosophy and everyday language, the literal and the figurative, nature and culture, the inside and the outside) and which might mislead the unwary reader into thinking that Derrida has a penchant for oppositions. Derrida's practice of reading tries, rather, to demonstrate that, in their etymological or philosophical origins, and in their historical development and contemporary resonances, words and concepts disturb oppositional reasoning, spilling over into each other to form a knotted fabric of associations.

Such a fabric can be seen in Derrida's analysis of metaphor in 'White Mythology: Metaphor in the Text of Philosophy' (in *Margins of Philosophy*). The question of metaphor, Derrida says, derives from a theory of value, according to which things are equated with each other on the basis of their resemblance or similarity. Because, in the Greek tradition, the sun is the source of light and life which produces the essence of what is, the sun is also what makes resemblances possible, it is the 'nonmetaphorical prime mover of metaphor', around which and towards which everything turns. Thus the 'flowers' of rhetoric (rhetoric is traditionally regarded as ornamentation) are turned towards the sun (as natural origin, source of truth and philosophical logic). But since we can never know what is proper to the sun, that is, since we can never see or touch the sun properly, so the sensory object par excellence, the sun, paradoxically becomes the paradigm both of the sensory (or literal truth of nature) and of metaphor (or tropes), since it turns (itself) (trope means to turn) and hides (itself). If metaphor is a heliotrope, then, it is so inasmuch as it designates both a movement towards the sun (as the source of truth) and the turning movement of the sun (which henceforth cannot act as the stable origin of the system). Western metaphysics attempts to reduce this play of metaphor by having metaphor, like the sun, return full circle to itself without loss of meaning. This specular circle is shared by the trajectory of the sun, by metaphysics and by the Western concept of Man. Thus, if the sun rises in the east, it reaches its completion in the west and in the eye of Western Man. In other words, for Derrida, metaphysics is an attempt to interiorise and master the metaphorical division between the origin and itself, the Oriental difference (this is why metaphysics is 'white mythology'). And yet, the heliotrope can always become a dried flower in a book, that is, a figure of excess that endlessly displaces the book's closure. Moreover, heliotrope, Derrida writes in the final sentence, is also the name of a precious stone – a kind of oriental jasper.

The oppositions which fill Derrida's pages, and whose usefulness to thought he does not deny, are identified as simplifications of this associative network, generally working to maintain the privilege of one of the terms. As soon as the clean and proper categories (of nature, of speech, of the inside, of logic, of the nation) are contaminated by that which was considered exterior to them but which was always already in their midst, they are 'no longer thoroughly what they are or what one thinks they are, that is, they are no longer identical to themselves, hence no longer simply identifiable and to that extent no longer determinable'.[10] Hence, finally, the reason for Derrida's list of quasi-concepts, or undecidables, which dislocate thought and force us to enter a conceptual passage from which there is no simple exit. We have already seen the supplement and the aporia. Then there is the double-bind, the pharmakon (poison and remedy), the *hôte* (host and guest), hymen (virginity and consummation). Such concepts are serious interventions made to expose the flaws in the logic of philosophy. But they also produce a certain pleasure. We can say of Derrida what he says of Hegel when he speaks of the German philosopher's 'delight' that a single word should express two opposed meanings.[11]

Jacques Derrida (1930–)

We will still, in truth, have understood little about Derrida and deconstruction if we remain at the level of this presentation of concepts and methods. It has always been said by Derrida's admirers that deconstruction is not a theory, but a practice. The claim should be understood strategically. Derrida willingly concedes that deconstruction is not alien to theory, system or method. On the whole, however, he is deeply mistrustful of systematic systems and methodical methods, of theories boiled down to theorems which can simply be applied to produce foreseeable results. This unease with systems doubtless cannot be divorced from a deterministic strain in the dominant Marxist and structuralist systems of thought in the 1950s' and 1960s' French academy.

Some Criticisms

Derrida has been largely ignored, rather than criticised, by the analytical philosophical tradition – partly because of the latter's general antagonism towards Continental Philosophy, and partly because of the idiosyncratic character of Derrida's writing. In a famous encounter over Derrida's critique of J. L. Austin's speech act theory, John R. Searle took Derrida to task for his lack of seriousness and unwillingness to respect the traditional and commonly accepted coinage of the debate on linguistic communication. Hans Georg Gadamer argues similarly that the success of philosophical dialogue depends on the willingness of interlocutors to allow a text to say what it means in a gesture of mutual understanding.

The criticism levelled at him by Jürgen Habermas of the Frankfurt School is that, despite his engagement with Enlightenment philosophy, Derrida follows Nietzsche's lead in seeking to overturn the age-old privilege accorded by philosophy to logic over rhetoric. By dissolving all of the foundationstones of intersubjective communicative rationality (that is, subjectivity and all the elements that comprise the communication model), Derrida's work finds its home firmly in the relativist tradition which extends directly, in Habermas's view, from Nietzsche to the French postmodernists. The criticism made of Derrida by other thinkers in the broadly Marxist tradition of critique is that Derrida is a textualist who pays insufficient attention to the conditions of production of knowledge and none at all to the question of class relations. The central issue here bears on the degree to which so-called external historical factors determine philosophy and social thought. Though no Marxist, this is also the gist of Michel Foucault's critique of Derrida (one is again reminded of the heterogeneity of the so-called French postmodernists). Foucault chides Derrida for failing to appreciate the ways in which Descartes's discursive exclusion of madness from his philosophical meditation is determined by the larger historical tableau of seventeenth-century France's generalised internment of the insane. Against Foucault and certain Marxist spirits (Derrida says that deconstruction remains faithful to one of the spirits of Marxism), Derrida maintains the need to respect the relative autonomy and ruptural force of the event of thought – without which there would be no philosophy.

There have been abundant criticisms of Derrida by traditional literary critics, but it is noticeable that the best of these have chosen either not to engage directly with the texts of Derrida or to engage and then disavow the contact absolutely. George Steiner, Frank Kermode, Gerald Prince and, among the disavowers, Harold Bloom, tilt at the shibboleths of a practice which, now fully institutionalised (above all in the US academy), has become an -ism (deconstruction*ism*). While being the one who perhaps least understands Derrida, it is Steiner who has best encapsulated the dangers of the 'Secondary City' – that place where students of literature read 'Theory' in ignorance of the literary texts and traditions to which said theory is then happily applied. Derrida himself has added his voice to this debate, warning of the capitalisation of deconstruction and consequent neutralisation of it as an effective political intervention.

Applications

Apart from the influence on contemporaries like Roland Barthes and on a younger generation of philosophers (most notably perhaps Jean-Luc Nancy), Derrida's influence in France has been limited. Elsewhere, Derrida's work has been hugely influential on contemporary critical theory. Often, it is true, applications of Derrida's ideas typically consist in little more than the peremptory identification of a binary opposition, followed by a simple inversion of terms. Derrida has always maintained that inversions which are not followed by a questioning of the underlying oppositional logic do little to shake the order of things.

Derrida's work on the 'white mythology' of Western metaphysics has been taken up by, and to a certain extent helped open up, the fields of postcolonial studies and race (or critical race) theory – notably in the work of Gayatri Chakravorty Spivak, Homi Bhabha and Henry Louis Gates. Derrida's work on the irreducibility of justice to the categories of law (an irreducibility which prevents justice from becoming a mere calculating machine) has proved important for developments in the field of legal theory. As has already been indicated, the import of Derrida's idea of textuality, together with his critique of the traditional model of communication and constant recourse to literature, has not been lost on literary studies. The most famous, if misleadingly named, group of literary critics to develop the insights of deconstruction for literature is the Yale School of critics, including Paul de Man, J. Hillis Miller, Geoffrey Hartman and, for a time, Harold Bloom. Of these, De Man's work on rhetoric and Bloom and Hartman's work on the Jewish traditions of Kabbalah and Midrash respectively are perhaps the most notable 'applications' of deconstruction.

Derrida's work has also been taken up in architectural theory; in feminist textual studies (most prominently in the work of French feminists Julia Kristeva, Luce Irigaray and Hélène Cixous); and, again to particular effect in the Anglo-Saxon academy, in work done under the aegis of cultural studies (Stuart Hall, for instance). Derrida himself has signalled a disquiet with that branch of cultural studies which would reject the study of 'high' cultural texts. But, as Derrida once said apropos of the nefarious appropriations of Nietzsche's doctrine of the cultural leader or *führer*, there is something in the text in question which allows for such 'applications'. Given the constant wearing away of the borders between opposing categories of culture which takes place in Derrida's texts, and in view of the primary place he gives to the political dimension of intellectual work, Derrida must accept his share of responsibility for the rejection of the high tradition. There is no secure guardrail that would prevent applications of deconstruction slipping into the more politically satisfying, but altogether less painstaking, form of a traditional destructive critique.

Notes

1. Jacques Derrida and Maurizio Ferraris, *A Taste for the Secret*, trans. Giacomo Donis (Cambridge: Polity Press, 2001), p. 40.
2. Geoffrey Bennington and Jacques Derrida, *Jacques Derrida*, p. 58.
3. Ibid., p. 170. The *marrane*, from the Spanish *marrano*, is the christian-

ised Jew or Moor in medieval Spain who professed conversion in order to avoid persecution.
4. Derrida, 'Structure, Sign, and Play in the Discourse of the Human Sciences', *Writing and Difference*, pp. 279–80.
5. Derrida, *Positions*, p. 26.
6. See for example Fredric Jameson, *Postmodernism, or, the Cultural Logic of Late Capitalism* (London and New York: Verso, 1996), p. 12.
7. Derrida, *Of Grammatology*, p. 158.
8. See, for example, Jameson, *Postmodernism*, p. 18.
9. Derrida, *The Gift of Death*, p. 68.
10. Derrida, *Aporias: Dying-Awaiting (One Another at) 'the Limits of Truth'*, trans. Thomas Dutoit (Stanford, CA: Stanford University Press, 1993 [1993]), p. 7.
11. Derrida, 'Violence and Metaphysics', *Writing and Difference*, p. 114.

Major Works by Derrida

Dissemination, trans. Barbara Johnson (Chicago: University of Chicago Press, 1981 [1972]).
Margins of Philosophy, trans. Alan Bass (Brighton: Harvester Press, 1982 [1972]).
Of Grammatology, trans. Gayatri Chakravorty Spivak (Baltimore and London: Johns Hopkins University Press, 1976 [1967]).
The Postcard: From Socrates to Freud and Beyond, trans. Alan Bass (Chicago and London: University of Chicago Press, 1987 [1980]).
Specters of Marx: The State of the Debt, the Work of Mourning, and the New International, trans. Peggy Kamuf (New York and London: Routledge, 1994 [1993]).
Speech and Phenomenon: Introduction to the Problem of Signs in Husserl's Phenomenology (Evanston: Northwestern University Press, 1973 [1967]).
Writing and Difference, trans. Alan Bass (London, Melbourne and Henley: Routledge and Kegan Paul, 1978 [1967]).

Suggestions for Further Reading

Bennington, Geoffrey, and Jacques Derrida, *Jacques Derrida*, trans. Geoffrey Bennington (Chicago: Chicago University Press, 1993). Two books in one: the first an unbeatably clear systematisation (a 'Derridabase') of Derrida's thought; the second an extended autobiographical piece by Derrida designed to jam the former.
Chakravorty Spivak, Gayatri, 'Translator's Preface', in Derrida, *Of Grammatology*. Excellent commentary on Derrida's work.
Derrida, Jacques, *A Derrida Reader: Between the Blinds*, ed. Peggy Kamuf (New

York: Harvester Wheatsheaf, 1991). Good compilation of key excerpts from Derrida's work.

Derrida, Jacques, *Positions*, trans. Alan Bass (London: The Athlone Press, 1981 [1972]). Three interviews with Derrida which provide an accessible commentary on many of his key concepts.

Gasché, Rodolphe, *The Tain of the Mirror: Derrida and the Philosophy of Reflection* (Cambridge, MA: Harvard University Press, 1986). High-level meditation on Derrida's philosophy.

7

Luce Irigaray (1932–)

Mary Eden

Biographical and Intellectual Contextualisation

Luce Irigaray is arguably one of the most significant thinkers writing in French since Simone de Beauvoir. She is most well known in Anglo-American contexts for her radical position on sexual difference via the feminist philosophy espoused in *Speculum of the Other Woman* and *This Sex Which Is Not One*. However, as more of her works are being translated critics are acknowledging the contributions which she has made to gender studies across a much wider variety of disciplines, including: linguistics, jurisprudence and ecology.

Irigaray was born in Belgium in 1932 and received an MA in Philosophy and Literature at the University of Louvain in 1955. Around 1960 she moved to France where she took further degrees in psychology and linguistics. From the early 1960s she was employed at CNRS (National Centre for Scientific Research) as a research assistant. At this time Irigaray became involved in a collaborative research programme with the departments of neurology and psychiatry at the Saint Anne hospital in Paris. As a psycholinguist working in the pathology of language she was part of a multi-disciplinary research team made up of psychiatrists, neuro-linguists and psychologists. This research group in neurolinguistics were attempting to carry out more systematic studies of aphasias by utilising advances made in both structural and Chomskyan linguistics as well as in the neurosciences.[1] Her first doctoral thesis published in 1973 as *Le Langage des déments* (The Language of the Demented) was a result of the work carried out in the neuro-linguistic tradition. She was first noted in the *Le Répertoire biblio-*

Luce Irigaray (1932–)

graphique de la philosophie (an extensive bibliography of publications in philosophy) for the essay 'Linguistic and Specular Communication', and other studies in linguistics.[2]

During the 1960s Irigaray also attended and participated in the seminars of Jacques Lacan. By the mid-sixties she was a member of the École freudienne and remained in private practice until 1990. In 1973 she was awarded a second doctoral thesis in philosophy (now published as *Speculum of the Other Woman*). Her first major work on sexual difference and sexuate subjectivity, *Speculum* contained explicit criticism of psychoanalytic theory. As a consequence, Irigaray was sacked from her teaching post and expelled from the École freudienne. At present Irigaray is Director of research in philosophy at CNRS. Her most recent research has been on the sexuation of discourse and sexuate communication. Whilst carrying out her studies in language pathology Irigaray inadvertently discovered differences in language use which corresponded to the sex of the subjects in question. This led her to study the spontaneous discourse of male obsessionals and female hysterics from within the psychoanalytic session. Subsequently, Irigaray was interested to find out if the stereotypical responses of the latter study would be refuted or supported by socio-linguistic studies carried out on 'normal' men and women. In her role as Director of research at CNRS and in collaboration with other feminist linguists and semioticians, Irigaray organised a series of conferences and seminars aimed at researching the sexuate characteristics of discourse across a variety of languages.[3] I shall be discussing the results of these studies in more detail below. Irigaray now divides her time between this work on the sexuate characteristics of discourse and organising lectures and conferences on the importance of sexual difference around the world.

With respect to the women's liberation movement, Irigaray does not adhere to any one group. The French movement is well known for its factions and she welcomes this diversity. However, as an advocate of difference she differentiates herself from orthodox feminisms which argue simply for equality. For Irigaray, equality signifies a suppression of female difference and an acceptance of masculine values. Nevertheless, she has always campaigned on individual issues such as legal abortion and the right to contraception and she worked to bring together a variety of disparate groups in Paris in October 1979 for a demonstration on women's right to choose abortion. For the last four years she has maintained connections with the PCI (Italian communist party) now the PDS

(Democratic socialist party). At the moment, in conjunction with Renzo Imbeni, a member of the European parliament and communist mayor of Bologna, she is constructing a code for citizenship (to be included in the Maastricht treaty) which takes cognisance of sexual difference in the form of a specific civil identity for women.

To a certain extent Irigaray's work can be contextualised with that of other French feminists such as Julia Kristeva and Hélène Cixous since they also utilise post-Lacanian psychoanalysis and focus on sexual difference. However, there are crucial differences between the theoretical positions taken up by these women. Kristeva argues that women's revolutionary potential lies in their marginality to the symbolic realm and the fact that woman can never be defined. In this sense, she is much more the dutiful daughter of Lacan than Irigaray. Cixous is associated with *écriture féminine*, privileging a radical form of bisexuality in her writing which does not fit well with Irigaray's stance. Irigaray argues against the Lacanian notion that woman can never exist or be defined and for the inscription of sexual difference at all levels of socio-symbolic exchange.

Key Concepts and Methods

The central issue at stake in Irigaray's work is of course sexual difference. In the essay of the same name she insists:

> Sexual difference is one of the major philosophical issues, if not the issue of our age. According to Heidegger, each age has only one issue to think through, and one only. Sexual difference is probably the issue in our time which could be our salvation on an intellectual level.[4]

Irigaray's search for an ethics of sexual difference is a threefold project. Initially, in the negative moment, she engages in a critique of the sexual indifference of the masculine economy. In the second stage, she attempts to symbolise other forms of socio-symbolic exchange or another libidinal economy which would allow for the construction of a feminine subjectivity. In the third phase of her work, she focuses on intersubjectivity. That is, she attempts to define a new model of possible relations between the sexes.

Irigaray's critique is clearly informed by her formation in linguistics, psychoanalysis and philosophy. In fact, she assigns primacy to philosophy as the principal discourse in the historical production of knowledge, meaning, subjectivity and power, stressing the fact that whilst patriarchal culture has always tolerated women's participation in literary projects it has always excluded them from doing philosophy. It is not therefore surprising that she tends to play down the importance of her writing project and her involvement with psychoanalysis preferring to emphasise her status as a philosopher. Irigaray regards herself as a philosopher who utililises both linguistics and psychoanalysis as tools in her critique of patriarchal culture.[5]

Irigaray takes issue with psychoanalysis from the viewpoint of sexual difference. That is, she sees it in both its Freudian and Lacanian formulations as phallocentric and phallomorphic. In other words, psychoanalysis is still trapped in the metaphysical tradition and as a therapeutic practice it serves only to normalise patriarchy. Nevertheless, despite the critical distance she maintains from psychoanalysis, her critique of patriarchy is deeply indebted to it. This is evidenced in the way she uses psychoanalysis against itself in her deconstruction of the major discourses of Western culture. Being a psychoanalyst means that for Irigaray all forms of exchange and economy are libidinised (marked by desire and unconscious effect). Thus, like other French feminist critiques, her work is informed by a merging of political and libidinal economy that is quite alien to the Anglo-American reader.

Irigaray engages with most of the prominent thinkers in the Western metaphysical tradition such as Aristotle, Plato, Descartes, Kant, Hegel, Marx, Heidegger and Nietzsche as well as more modern philosophers such as Levinas, Merleau-Ponty, Sartre and Derrida. As with the psychoanalysts, her relationship with all these thinkers is marked both by an indebtedness and critical distance. It is therefore difficult to speak of sources in Irigaray's work. One of the consequences of her mimetic intertextual and therefore always intersexual style is that every writer she engages with becomes a source. That is, she tends to appropriate the concepts of individual writers, reworking and redefining them from the viewpoint of sexual difference.

Irigaray is well aware that she cannot stand outside the phallogocentric system; she thus takes up the position of arch hysteric mimicking the masculine position and reworking language in order to create a new feminine position of enunciation or a feminine style. She comments as follows:

> to put it another way: the option left to me was to *have a fling with the philosophers*, which is easier said than done ... in the first phase, there is perhaps only one path, and in any case it is the one to which the female condition is assigned: that of mimicry.

And again: 'to play with mimesis is thus for woman, to try to recover the place of her exploitation by discourse, without allowing herself to be reduced to it'.[6] The recuperative aspect of the mimetic process is of course possible because there is always an excess on the feminine side.

Irigaray's intercourse with the metaphysical tradition is thus an attempt to retraverse the masculine imaginary and to locate the repressed and unacknowledged maternal/feminine which is its foundation. In her deconstructive reading of the philosophical canon, nature, the body and the material world in general (by way of a metaphorical process) have been coded maternal/feminine and systematically denigrated. The maternal/feminine can be seen to stand in opposition to what gives form, the founding principle of idealism, mind and reason, which Aristotle (for example) makes clear are attributes of masculine extraction.[7] Thus, she is attempting to undo the hierarchical way in which sexual difference has been articulated in philosophical discourse.

It is characteristic of her mimetic writing practice to quote substantial passages from the thinker in question, allowing the text to speak for itself whilst insinuating her own discourse (often in the form of questions) between the cited passages. Other linguistic formulae associated with the interlocutory process, as well as typological features such as ellipsis, characterise her textual practice, resulting in dialogic style which foregrounds the notion of an exchange or dialogue taking place. Irigaray also creates meaning by playing with the structure of the text. For example, *Speculum* begins with a symptomatic reading of Freud's essay on femininity and ends with a reading of Plato's myth of the cavern, inverting the natural order of the philosophical canon.

Irigaray's textuality is at its most compelling and persuasive when she engages in close readings of individual writers. See in particular, *Marine Lover of Freidrich Neitzsche, Elemental Passions* and *Forgetting of Air in Martin Heiddeger* and *To Be Two*. In so far as her philosophy utilises aspects of dialectical, phenomenological and deconstructive methods, she is perhaps most indebted to Hegel, Marx and Nietzsche as well as to thinkers in the phenomenological tradition such as Heidegger, Merleau-Ponty and Levinas. Irigaray's position with regard to Derrida is more complex. Whilst there is clearly a deconstructive aspect to her work, she is highly critical of male writers who can be seen to take part in what has been referred to as the feminisation of philosophy. That is, the critique of phallogocentrism which has as its corollary the trope of woman as undecidability or *différance*. Irigaray sees these writers as not making their own position of enunciation as male writers clear. She summarises: 'In other words the masculine is not prepared to share the initiative of discourse. It prefers to experiment with speaking writing enjoying "woman" rather than leaving to the other any right to intervene, to "act", in her own interest'.[8]

The Critique of patriarchy

Underpinning Irigaray's arguments about the sexual indifference (monosexuality) of Western society is the related claim that the latter has been founded on a cultural matricide: 'Culture has taught us to consume the body of the mother – natural and spiritual – without being indebted and as far as the world of men is concerned to label this appropriation in their name'.[9] Irigaray expands on this claim that Western culture has been built not on a patricide as Freud postulates in *Totem and Taboo* but on a matricide. In a reinterpretation of the Greek myth of Clytemnestra she puts forward an account of the installation of the patriarchal economy which is subtended by this matricide. Whereas Freud founds his account of culture on the primal horde, and his account of psychoanalysis on Oedipus, thus focusing on the sons who kill the father, Irigaray focuses on Clytemnestra, the mother killed by her son.[10] What interests Irigaray here is that the mythology underlying patriarchy has not changed. Irigaray indicts psychoanalysis further, arguing that the latter's stress on Oedipus, the incest taboo and on castration upholds the fact that the major taboo in the West is the relation to the maternal body.

Irigaray points out that whilst psychoanalysis has little to say about this bodily relation, 'which brought us whole into the world', it has much to say about the genital drive: 'Thanks to which the phallic penis takes back from the mother the power to give birth, to nourish to dwell and to centre. The Phallus erected where once there was an umbilical cord? It becomes the organiser of the world'.[11] For Irigaray then, the relation to the mother must be symbolised and understood in order to stop the perpetuation of negative fantasies associating the maternal/feminine with madness, castration and death. Irigaray argues that 'a double syntax' or another libidinal economy which embraced feminine difference might have been possible in our culture if the male subject 'was not wounded, threatened by castration, by anything he cannot see directly, anything he cannot perceive as like himself'.[12] Elsewhere in a similar context, she states that the threat of castration drives the masculine subject to 'the Empire of the same'.[13]

To gloss, in Irigaray's reading all forms of symbolic and sociosymbolic exchange in patriarchal capitalist society are predicated on the negation of material difference (a difference which Irigaray always takes to be of maternal/feminine extraction) and the substitution or putting in place of a system of values or standards (whether this be the phallus in the libidinal and discursive economies, money in the political economy or a transcendental god in the monotheistic religions) which is always of masculine extraction. She is thus positing a structural isomorphism between symbolic and socio-symbolic systems. This explains the way in which she moves so fluidly between the maternal/feminine as 'prime matter', the figure of woman and real women in society. That is, just as the maternal/feminine is seen to be the unacknowledged resource, the *sang rouge*, of discursive practices (and by extension of masculine subjectivity), so women as mothers are seen to be the infrastructure of the social world. Put another way, if exchange (as social relation) in the masculine economy requires a currency then woman as object of exchange is that currency.

The commodification of women is a recurrent theme for Irigaray. She reads this notion through a variety of disciplines and conceptual systems, often blurring the boundaries between them in order to highlight the fact that women are excluded from being subjects in the masculine economy. Drawing on the work of both Claude Lévi-Strauss and Marx she argues controversially that exchange in patriarchal culture is Hom(m)osexual. That is, in the *société l'entre homme* (the society between men) exchanges occur between men, whereas women are mere objects of exchange. Using Marx's critique of commodity fetishism against itself, she argues that women are *les marchandises* or fetishised commodities. Just as commodities are a product of labour power whose value is to be found in comparison to a general equivalent (gold or money), so women, in patriarchal society, are a product of man's labour. Furthermore, their exchange value is to be found in comparison to another standard or general equivalent, namely, the phallus, the supposedly universal signifier of desire and difference. For Irigaray, woman as virgin is pure exchange value (functioning as a sign in Lévi-Strauss's account). As a mother she has a use value whilst the prostitute has both a use value and an exchange value. All these roles are de-subjectivised roles in Irigaray's reading. Women therefore urgently need their own subjective identity distinct from the maternal role.

Irigaray wants to bring into being a sexuate culture which is not built on this hierarchical split between the material and the ideal, the sensible and the intelligible, male and female. In so far as she attempts to re-valorise the maternal/feminine (the material world) in all its dimensions her philosophy is fundamentally a materialist philosophy. However, it is a materialism which goes beyond orthodox Marxism. Irigaray is highly critical of capitalist modes of production and social relations. She goes as far as to posit complicity between the political economy of capitalism and the masculine libidinal economy. That is, just as the political economy of capitalism is based on the appropriation and accumulation of wealth, so the libidinal economy is quantitative and economic in the sense that it is based on the (re)production of the species. Although she acknowledges that Marx identified the latent slavery within the family, she suggests that orthodox materialist philosophies have been inadequate in addressing the problem of gender relations as well as environmental issues. With respect to ecological issues, in Irigaray's reading the earth re-valorised by Marx's rereading of the Hegelian dialectic is still an earth to be conquered and exploited. Significantly, Irigaray's radical or divine materialism involves a re-evaluation of our relation to 'mother-matter-nature' (the material world) in all its manifestations. Irigaray introduces the notion of a sensible transcendental to refer to a socio-symbolic system which is not built on the split between the sensible and the ideal.

In her most recent writings Irigaray has turned to Eastern philosophies and in particular to yoga and tantric Buddhism. She is attracted to a variety of factors here. Initially, she finds a different non-hierarchised articulation of the mind–body dualism in which matter and the body are not denigrated but made spiritual. For example, in the texts of Hinduism she locates representations of feminine deities or female ideals. In tantrism in particular, she finds another libidinal economy which does not correspond to Freud's economic model of the psyche which is based on the thermodynamic principles of tension–release and a return to homeostasis. Rather, tantrism proposes a carnal ethics in which sexuality is not solely based on reproduction but is an end in itself, a regenerative spiritual act.

From imaginary to symbolic configurations of the feminine

Irigaray goes as far as to say that the move into a patriarchal symbol (the condition for sanity in psychoanalytic accounts) is actually pathological for women, leaving them open to madness, to melancholia, hysteria and even to a latent psychosis. Subsequently, the issue of women's auto-eroticism and of women's subjectivity and identity becomes central to her account. In order to disturb the logic of phallocentric and phallomorphic systems of representation Irigaray attempts to put in place: 'A mode of specularisation that allows for the relation of woman to "herself" and to her like. Which presupposes a *curved* mirror'.[14] In the context of Irigaray's critique of psychoanalytic accounts of subjectivity and sexuality, the speculum, with its feminine connotations, can be read simultaneously, as a deconstruction and a reconstruction of the phallomorphic Lacanian mirror within which woman is represented as a lack or a hole. The mirror stage is the imaginary structure upon which the bodily ego is built. Significantly, it corresponds to the ego-ideal in Freud and refers not just to the mirror image or the mother but to all identificatory processes or relations with others. Imaginary identity may be based on misrecognition. However, since it is the only place from which we can know ourselves it becomes central to Irigaray's project with respect to feminine identity.

Irigaray uses a variety of tropes in an attempt to articulate a feminine libidinal economy. In *This Sex*, she states:

> woman 'touches herself' all the time, and moreover no-one can forbid her to do so, for her genitals are formed of two lips in continuous contact. Thus, within herself she is already two and not divisible into one(s), that caress each other.[15]

In place of one, visible, erect organ Irigaray presents a figure of at least two erogenous zones and more than one sexuality. It can therefore be read as an attempt to reconceptualise women's auto-, homo- and heterosexuality beyond the confines of the masculine conceptual system. Elsewhere, she presents the image of the two lips caressing and speaking. As Irigaray reiterates throughout her work women have more than one pair of lips. The image of the two lips therefore refers crucially to woman as a speaking being as well to a new libidinal and discursive economy. Beyond this, it can be seen as a figure which stands for new, more qualitative forms of exchange. That is, the figure of the half-open lips can be seen to disrupt the classic dichotomies which underpin the economy of meaning within masculine discourse.

For Irigaray, the lack of a possible feminine ideal, of mediation in general, is responsible for the lack of self-love in and between women. A feminine symbolic therefore also involves the symbolisation and rebuilding of the mother–daughter relationship, the construction of a female genealogy and a woman-to-woman sociality. Without a maternal genealogy the mother cannot transmit respected images of women whilst the daughter can only see her mother in one of two ways: (1) as an omnipotent phallic mother whom she must flee in order to retain some autonomy or; (2) as a castrated mother to whom she does not wish to turn, turning instead towards the father. The benefit of Irigaray's analysis here is that it shifts the blame from mothers themselves to an effect of the patriarchal symbolic. As Irigaray states: 'Woman needs to develop words, images and symbols to express her intersubjective relationship with her mother, and then with other women, if she is to enter into a non-destructive relation with men'.[16] Elsewhere, she comments that: 'Women need a religion, a language, and a currency of exchange, or else a non-market economy'.[17]

Most importantly, this desire for new forms of relationships and exchange between women and the requirement that their specificity be collectively and publicly recognised needs to be translated into public and social forms. Irigaray's feminine symbolic therefore also includes the issue of women's civil rights. In two essays she therefore puts forward the idea that each gender should have rights and responsibilities which correspond to their own specificity.[18] Irigaray's stress on feminine subjectivity and identity has been criticised as being essentialist. That is, she is accused of positing an essence of woman which is problematic from a variety of feminist perspectives. Early critiques, focusing mainly on the image of the two lips, regard her as biologically essentialist.[19] That is, they suggest that Irigaray is working with a model of the body unmediated by language. Other psychoanalytically inspired critiques suggest that she has not understood the importance of the symbolic in Lacan's theory of subjectivity and is trying to return women to some pre-symbolic imaginary space.[20]

However, given her theoretical base in linguistics and psychoanalysis, it is clear that, whilst she is critical of his position on sexual difference, Irigaray accepts Lacan's linguistic and structural reformulation of subjectivity as constituted in and through the three orders of the real (drives), imaginary (phantasy) and symbolic (language and culture). This view is supported by a series of more complex studies. These studies argue that dismissals of Irigaray's work as essentialist were premature and based on misreadings of Irigaray's theoretical base. They also suggest that in stating the problem of women's identity at all Irigaray is obliged to return to the language of essentialism. Irigaray's 'essentialism' if it is one is seen from their perspective as a discursive strategy. Irigaray's stress on sexual difference and feminine subjectivity has also been defended and taken up in particular by the Milan Bookstore collective and by other feminists such as Rosi Braidotti who advocate difference as a strategy within feminism. In particular, the idea of a feminine symbolic and a maternal genealogy has been adopted by the Italian Feminist Movement. In an attempt to create more positive relations between women, these notions have been translated into the idea of *affidamento* or entrustment which is enacted in the creation of symbolic mother/daughter relations.

The Double Dialectic

In *I Love to You* and *To Be Two* Irigaray addresses the issue of more qualitative relations between the sexes. For Irigaray, the establishment of a political ethics requires a dialectic appropriate for each of the sexes and one for their relationship in the community. She argues passionately that love between the sexes cannot find its *raison d'être* in property and reproduction. What she is seeking to articulate here is a relation between the sexes in which men and women avoid reducing each other to objects. Again, only the recognition of sexual difference can create the conditions necessary for this new ethical relation between the sexes. In a rereading of the Hegelian concepts Irigaray argues in particular for the bringing about of a double dialectic and two universals, which would allow a relation of reciprocity between the sexes, a carnal relation not solely based on the reproduction of the species. It could be argued here that Irigaray is attempting to return women to a compulsory heterosexuality. However, this would be to ignore both Irigaray's critique of the patriarchal bias in Freud's reading of female homosexuality as well as her attempts to reconceptualise homoeroticism in *This Sex*.

Luce Irigaray (1932–)

The Sexuation of Discourse

The lack of attention which has been paid to Irigaray's work in linguistics has led to a plethora of misunderstandings around her statements about language. One of the most obvious examples is that when Irigaray speaks of a women's language, she is usually referring to *langage* and not to *langue*.[21] She is therefore referring to language use or practice rather than a completely new language. Subsequently, Irigaray has been incorporated into current debates on *écriture féminine* and compared to both Kristeva and Cixous. Significantly, Irigaray rejects this association with *écriture féminine* arguing that as a labelling process it tends once again to marginalise women and objectify them. Irigaray is much more concerned about *parler-femme* (speaking as woman) and the sexuation of discourse, terms which refer to the enunciation and thus to the representation of subjectivity in and through language.

The enunciation refers in general terms to the speech act or to the activity of speaking. However, in linguistics it refers specifically to the linguistic formulae of the enunciation, that is, to eidetic markers, such as personal pronouns, demonstratives, the performative verbs, certain tenses and adverbs. Enunciation thus refers to the linguistic markers of subjectivity which indicate the intentions and agency of the subject. Since the process of the enunciation is always an instance of discourse the two terms (*parler-femme* and the sexuation of discourse) are clearly interrelated and need to be understood in the context of Irigaray's work in empirical linguistics and psychoanalysis. Whilst in *Speculum* and *This Sex* Irigaray focused on revealing and disrupting the masculine bias in philosophical and scientific discourse, in recent years she has returned to empirical studies. In fact, she returned to the initial language tests she first developed to examine pathological subjects in order to assess the representation of subjectivity and sexual difference in the everyday language use of non-pathological subjects.

In her earlier work on pathological subjects, Irigaray developed language tests specifically to examine the process of the enunciation and beyond that the dynamics of the communication between two interlocutors. These tests required very few changes to apply them to the question of sexuate subjectivity, the only modifications being the choice of words used to elicit a linguistic performance from the subject. So far, the results from these empirical studies seem to reveal that women and men occupy different subjective positions in their relationship to language, the object of discourse, the world, and the other. That is, their utterances differed in choice of subjects, interplay of pronouns, verbs, verb tenses and modes, types of predicate transformation, grammatical categories chosen and in their attitude towards the other interlocutor.

To summarise briefly, she found that:

1. Men are much more likely to use I and take up a subjective position. However, their discourse tends to be circular and does not encourage the other (woman) to participate.
2. Women are less likely to take up a subjective position by using the pronoun I. Even when they do use the first person, their discourse is constructed in such a way that responsibility for the utterance is left to the other interlocutor: the you.
3. Women's discourse is much more likely to encourage dialogue and privilege personal relations. Men's dialogue privileges their relation to themselves and their world – a world of objects.
4. Men play much more with language whilst women concentrate on the message or the communication.
5. Women tend to use concrete adjectives and adverbs, whereas men use more abstract language.

In order to examine the performance of a group the linguist requires both a model of language and a model of the subject. With respect to her model of language Irigaray takes a syncretic approach utilising aspects of generative and transformational grammars to construct the tests. She then undertakes a distributional analysis of the immediate constituents of the statements constructed and analyses the latter utilising theories of enunciation developed by Émile Benveniste and Roman Jakobson. The originality of Irigaray's method of analysis is that it focuses on the act of enunciation in order to specify the subject's way of structuring language. In addition, she is working with a complex model of the subject. A subject constructed in and through discourse as well as material practices. This is a sophisticated model of performance compared to Anglo-American feminist linguistics.

Most sociolinguistic studies utilise orthodox socio-psychological approaches which focus solely on the content of the utterance and do not work with any model of the subject. This empirical research is still in progress and not yet all in translation. It is therefore difficult to assess it comprehensively. However, it is clear that these studies have played an important role in the development of

Irigaray's theories of subjectivity and they promise to provide significant insights into our understanding of the linguistic representation of sexuate subjectivity and theories of the enunciation.

Notes

1. Neurolinguistics (a relatively new discipline in the 1960s) is the study of the correlations between anatomical/clinical typologies and linguistic typologies.
2. This essay and most of Irigaray's important language studies in the pathology of language are now translated in *To Speak Is Never Neutral*.
3. Irigaray's research into the sexuate characteristics of discourse culminated in the following publications: 'Le Sexe linguistique', *Langages*, 85, 1987, pp. 81–123; 'Genres culturels et intercultural', *Langages*, 3, 1993, pp. 12–23; and *Sexes et genres à travers les langues: éléments de communications sexuées* (Paris: Grasset, 1990). The last publication focuses on sex differences in communication or in discourse across a variety of languages including French, English and Italian. A translation is forthcoming from Routledge.
4. Irigaray, *Irigaray Reader*, p. 165.
5. Stephen Pluhacek and Heidi Bostic, 'Thinking Life as Relation: An Interview with Luce Irigaray', *Man and World*, 29, 1996, pp. 343–60.
6. Irigaray, *This Sex*, pp. 150–1.
7. Irigaray, *Speculum*, pp. 160–1.
8. Irigaray, *This Sex*, p. 157.
9. Irigaray, *Irigaray Reader*, p. 54.
10. Irigaray's reinterpretation of the story of Clytemnestra reads the myth as an account of the installation of patriarchy, built over the sacrifice of the mother and her daughters. One daughter, Iphigenia, is literally sacrificed by her husband Agamemnon, while the other, dutiful daughter Electra is abandoned to her madness.
11. Irigaray, *Irigaray Reader*, p. 38.
12. Irigaray, *Speculum*, p. 139.
13. Irigaray, *This Sex*, p. 141.
14. Ibid., p. 155.
15. Ibid., p. 24.
16. Irigaray, *Sexes and Genealogies*, p. 196.
17. Ibid., p. 79.
18. Irigaray, *Irigaray Reader*, pp. 199–212.
19. See Toril Moi, *Sexual Textual Politics: Feminist Literary Theory* (London: Methuen, 1985); and Plaza, 'Phallomorphic Power'.
20. Mitchell and Rose, *Feminine Sexuality*; and Kaja Silverman, *The Acoustic Mirror: The Female Voice in Psychoanalysis and Cinema* (Bloomington: University of Indiana Press, 1988).

21. *Langue* refers to the corpus of language (French or English) and in a structural sense to the rules of language. It is opposed to *parole*, which refers to the individual utterance. *Langage* in contrast refers to the individual use of language as it is used by speakers. It is thus possible to distinguish between uses of *langage* (idiolect or register). A problem arises because of the polysemy of the word language in English.

Major Works by Luce Irigaray

Democracy Begins between Two, trans. Kristeen Anderson (London: Athlone Press, 2000 [1994]).
Elemental Passions, trans. Joanne Collie and Judith Still (London: Athlone Press, 1992 [1982].
An Ethics of Sexual Difference, trans. Carolyn Burke and Gillian C. Gill (London: Athlone Press, 1993 [1984]).
The Forgetting of Air in Martin Heidegger, trans. Mary Beth Mader (London: Athlone Press, 1999 [1983]).
I Love to You: Sketch for a Possible Felicity in History, trans. Alison Martin (London: Routledge, 1996 [1992]).
The Irigaray Reader, ed. Margaret Whitford (Oxford: Basil Blackwell, 1991). This collection contains several lectures and essays by Irigaray which are not translated elsewhere. Each section has an informative introduction.
Je, tu, nous: Toward a Culture of Difference, trans. Alison Martin (London: Routledge, 1993 [1990]).
Le Langage des déments (The Hague: Mouton, 1973).
The Marine Lover of Friedrich Nietzsche, trans. Gillian C. Gill (New York: Columbia University Press, 1991 [1980]).
Sexes and Genealogies, trans. Gillian C. Gill (New York : Columbia University Press, 1993 [1987]).
Speculum of the Other Woman, trans. Gillian C. Gill (Ithaca: Cornell University Press, 1985 [1974]).
Thinking the Difference: For a Peaceful Revolution, trans. Karin Montin (London: Athlone Press, 1994 [1989]).
This Sex Which Is Not One, trans. Catherine Porter (Ithaca: Cornell University Press, 1985 [1977]).
To Be Two, trans. Mary Beth Mader (London: Athlone Press, 1999 [1997]).
To Speak is Never Neutral, trans. Gail Schwab (New York: Routledge, 2002 [1985]).

Suggestions for Further Reading

Benveniste, Émile, *Problems in General Linguistics*, trans. Mary Elizabeth Meek (Coral Gables, FL: University of Miami Press, 1971). The chapters on subjectivity in language are particularly helpful for understanding Irigaray's work on enunciation.

Brennan, Theresa (ed.), *Between Feminism and Psychoanalysis* (New York: Routledge, 1989). This collection contains a little-known essay by Irigaray, 'The Gesture in Psychoanalysis' and seminal essays by both Margaret Whitford and Rosi Braidotti on Irigaray.

Chanter, Tina (ed.), *Ethics of Eros: Irigaray's Rewriting of the Philosophers* (New York: Routledge, 1995). A readable exposition of Irigaray as a philosopher. This collection also contains a discussion of Irigaray's only essay on Derrida, 'The Rape of the Letter'.

Fuss, Diana, *Essentially Speaking* (New York: Routledge, 1990). An excellent discussion of the debates around essentialism with a chapter devoted to Irigaray.

Gallop, Jane, *Feminism and Psychoanalysis: The Daughter's Seduction* (London: Macmillan, 1982). Contains a sympathetic reading of Irigaray's relation to Lacan and her poetics of the body.

Grosz, Elizabeth, *Jacques Lacan: A Feminist Introduction* (London: Routledge, 1990). The standard feminist introduction to Lacan and essential reading for those interested in Irigaray's post-Lacanian position with respect to psychoanalysis.

de Lauretis, Theresa, 'The Essence of the Triangle or, Taking the Risk of Essentialism Seriously', *Differences*, 1 (2), 1989, pp. 3–37. Contains a succinct discussion of essentialism as a discursive and political strategy.

Lemaire, Anika, *Jacques Lacan*, trans. David Macey (London: Routledge, 1991). An excellent account of the role linguistics plays in Lacanian theories of subjectivity. Recommended for the reader interested in Irigaray's work on enunciation in both psychoanalysis and linguistics.

Milan Women's Bookstore Collective, *Sexual Difference: A Theory of Social–Symbolic Practice* (Bloomington: University of Indiana Press, 1990). A study of Irigaray's influence on the Italian women's movement.

Mitchell, Juliet, and Jaqueline Rose, *Feminine Sexuality: Jacques Lacan and the École freudienne* (London: Macmillan Press, 1982). Translations of Lacan's seminars where he makes his most controversial pronouncements about femininity. Essential reading for an understanding of Irigaray's critique of Lacan.

Plaza, Monique, '"Phallomorphic Power" and the Psychology of "Woman"', trans. Miriam David and Jill Hodges, *Ideology and Consciousness*, 4, Autumn, 1978, pp. 4–36. A materialist critique of Irigaray as essentialist.

Whitford, Margaret, *Philosophy in the Feminine* (London: Routledge, 1991). This comprehensive critique remains the best overall exposition of Irigaray's work.

8

Hélène Cixous (1937–)

Julia Dobson

Hélène Cixous's oeuvre is prolific, including a dazzling range of forms and issues. Approaches to her work tend to divide her output up in order to present several different authorial identities; Cixous the theorist, Cixous the writer of 'fictions', Cixous the 'French feminist', Cixous the playwright, Cixous the teacher and so on. Such an approach to her work runs the risk of concealing or potentially undermining the central cohesive principles and concerns which underpin all of these different activities and writings. The fundamental engagement at the core of Cixous's work remains that of the relationship between self and other, a dynamic which extends to personal, national and historical constructions of identity. In her quest to subvert dominant constructions of alterity and to build more positive representations of difference itself, Cixous has identified the site and process of writing as the most productive arena in which new intersubjective structures can be imagined and realised. Thus her writing transcends traditional definitions of theoretical discourse in its articulation of both the theory and practice of her thought. The concepts expressed in her writings should not be regarded in isolation from the innovations in form and genre displayed in her work from her early fiercely political and poetic essays to recent 'fictions' and plays.

Cixous occupies very different positions within French and Anglophone cultural landscapes. In France she is known mainly as a playwright, author of fiction and leading academic, whilst within Anglophone academic communities she is regarded almost exclusively as a theorist and her work continues, to a considerable degree, to be associated with definitions of 'French feminism', the concepts of *'écriture féminine'* and 'writing the body' in response to her seminal works of the mid-1970s. After a brief introduction, this chapter will provide an exploration of the concepts of *écriture féminine* whilst attempting to give a broader picture of Cixous's work and to situate it within wider discursive and theoretical contexts.

Biography

Since 1990 Cixous's texts have articulated a more explicit exploration of her own personal position on the margins as woman and as Jewish (more specifically combined in her term *juifemme*), revisiting events, people and places of her personal past. Hélène Cixous was born in Oran, Algeria, in 1937 into a familial and social situation inseparable from reductive discourses of exclusion and difference. Her mother from an Austro-Jewish family and her father of Jewish Spanish descent, Cixous was educated within the French system in Algeria whilst both French and German were spoken in the home. Cixous describes this plurilingual environment as the source of her fascination with the play of the signifier and the musicality of language.

The family experienced a series of exclusions; her mother had fled the Nazi regime, and her father was prevented from practising as a doctor in Algeria by the Vichy regime of occupied France. Cixous was profoundly marked by her father's death from tuberculosis when she was 11; and in 1955, during the Algerian war, the family left Algeria for France. This series of losses, that of her father and of Algeria, combine to form a powerful trope throughout her work, that of exile from paradise, a loss which she suggests can be inscribed and acknowledged through the act of writing itself.

Cixous studied English and published her doctoral thesis on James Joyce in 1968.[1] Following the dramatic events of May 1968 in France, Cixous was appointed as part of a team to found the groundbreaking University of Paris VIII, where she continues to work as Professor of English Literature and where she established the interdisciplinary Centre de recherches en Etudes féminines in 1974. It is, however, misleading to regard Cixous's status as unproblematic in relation to the French academic establishment; indeed the French government has attempted to prevent the Centre de recherches en Etudes féminines from awarding postgraduate qualifications, while threats of the withdrawal of basic funding continue. She has spoken out against the conservatism of the university establishment in France, remarking that 'the French have taken the Bastille but not the Sorbonne'.[2] Cixous's close involvement with the theatre began in 1976 and her work in this form has increased progressively since then. She is now one of the most successful contemporary playwrights in France and has forged a strong collaborative working relationship with Ariane Mnouchkine and the Théâtre du soleil.[3] She continues to teach and live in Paris, while her seminar programme, run as part of the postgraduate course in Etudes féminines, is open to all. The seminars engage in close readings of texts by a recurring group of authors who have come to form a Cixousian canon of writers inherently associated with her own constructions of poetic identity.

Intellectual Contextualisation

Cixous's oeuvre which extends over forty written 'fictions', articles and plays constitutes a consistent interrogation and subversion of dialectics and all constructions of difference which invoke hierarchical binaries. Her work began in a post-war France whose intellectual landscape was dominated by the discourses of existentialism and phenomenology, which posit different but persistent assertions of an oppositional division between the subject and object, the self and other. A key influence in this context is to be found in the work of Jacques Derrida, particularly in the theorisation of *différance* – a conceptualisation of difference that is not founded upon opposition, but explores the way in which meaning is always constructed in a space–time continuum, and so relies upon structures of deferral that can never be closed. Cixous's and Derrida's longstanding intertextual dialogue has led to a jointly authored text of meditation on the act of seeing and the assumptions of sight.[4]

In Cixous's published doctoral thesis on the novels of Joyce, the central belief in the potential links between writing and revolution, the assertion that change can be attained through revolutionary forms of writing, first emerges in her work. This marks the continuing coexistence in her writing of the search for new representations of subjectivity and innovations in language which speak for, to and of a newly constructed radical subject.

The point at which Cixous's voice emerged was one of vital importance to the feminist movement in France. Many feminist

Hélène Cixous (1937–)

groups had been involved in the call for social and political reform that informed the events of May 1968, but now found that the extent of women's exclusion from politics had not changed. Cixous aligned herself with a distinctive group called Psych et Po (Psychanalyse et politique) which was associated with Antoinette Fouque and the publishers 'des femmes'. As suggested by the organisation's title, the group's main interests lay in an engagement with psychoanalytic theory which, through writing and the dissemination of particular avant-garde modes of writing, would, they argued, lead to social change. Conflict between Psych et Po and other feminist groupings was intense, often personal, extended over a lengthy period and served, amongst other things, to overdetermine the critical and popular reception of many of Cixous's early fictions.[5] Cixous's writing has been identified as representative of 'French feminism' alongside the work of Luce Irigaray and Julia Kristeva. Whilst their work shares an interest in the linguistic and the psychoanalytical in their search for redefinitions of female subjectivity, such groupings are misleading, reductive and motivated more by the simplistic positing of an 'exotic' other to Anglo-American feminist discourses than by any national cultural specificity.

Writing the Body and *Écriture féminine*[6]

Cixous's essay 'The Laugh of the Medusa' and the expansion of its central arguments in her collaborative text with Catherine Clément, *The Newly Born Woman* (*La Jeune née*) are powerful and poetic texts which constitute an attack on dominant representations of woman in Western culture. Throughout Cixous's oeuvre, language is foregrounded as a political arena:

> [N]o political reflection can dispense with reflection on language, with work on language ... For as soon as we exist, we are born into language and language speaks (to) us, dictates its laws, a law of death; it lays down its familial model, lays down its conjugal model, and even at the moment of uttering a sentence, admitting a notion of 'being', an ontology, we are already seized by a certain kind of masculine desire that mobilises discourse.[7]

The closely argued denunciations are followed importantly by a rousing manifesto which calls upon women to reclaim a positive relationship with their selves and their bodies through the creative potential and visceral practice of writing. These pieces, which were first published in 1975, have, within an Anglo-American context, been predominantly presented as symptomatic of the cultural otherness of French feminism, a move which also served to construct a reductive response to the work of Cixous, Luce Irigaray and Julia Kristeva as a homogenous and often elitist discourse and which has glossed over the many important differences between their oeuvres.

The Newly Born Woman remains undoubtedly Cixous's most well-known work outside France and is a politically projective exercise – the rich wordplay of the title in French accommodates amongst other meanings the three main movements of the text. First, the laying bare of the exclusion of the female subject from dominant cultural discourse, and the resultant alienation felt by the female subject – *Là je n'est* – (There I is not/The female I is not) an assertion of exclusion and a radical rupture between subject and discourse. The central question is broached in the first pages of the text:

Where is she?
Activity / Passivity
Sun / Moon
Culture / Nature
Day / Night

Father / Mother
Head / Heart
Intelligible / Palpable
Logos / Pathos
Form, convex, step, advance, semen, progress.
Matter, concave, ground – where steps are taken, holding and dumping ground
Man
Woman[8]

This list of oppositions, whose hierarchical nature is revealed in the last line, introduces Cixous's insistence upon the importance of undoing models of difference (sexual, personal, historical) which rely upon the establishment of a rigid oppositional binary. The terms associated with the feminine in the list above are also those which are devalued, which provide the negative of the masculine 'norm'. The inherent presence of this hierarchical opposition between man and woman at the core of Western philosophy and ontology is thus seen to relegate the female subject to roles defined by passivity or invisibility.

Whilst recognising the cultural and historical value of Freud's work on the unconscious, Cixous's writing at this point contains a

Hélène Cixous (1937–)

detailed and passionate engagement with the definitions of female identity and sexual difference constructed through the narratives of both Freudian and Lacanian psychoanalytic theory. It is her concern with the role of writing in identity formation, and indeed transformation, that motivates her consistent critique of Lacanian models of gendered identity, models which themselves posit language acquisition as a central element. Lacan suggests that the child at first enjoys a 'symbiotic' relationship with the mother, and cannot conceive of itself as a separate being. A gradual separation then takes place as the child misrecognises itself as a whole and distinct identity, which is termed the 'mirror stage'. Language occupies a central role here as, Lacan argues, the child can distinguish objects as separate from itself through their absence – an absence which is acknowledged in the substitution of the signified by the signifier, the very structure of language which relies upon loss. The oedipal intervention of the father is thus allied in Lacanian theory with the acquisition of language as the necessary entrance into law and social order (the Lacanian 'symbolic') which is dominated by the phallus as signifier of the central lack which permits systems of language and exchange to function. In this model the subject's sense of self and language are underwritten by loss and the practice of language constitutes a ceaseless attempt to recover an illusory unity.

Cixous identifies the repression of the feminine and the invisibility of the mother as the founding principles of such constructions of identity. Dismissing Freudian and Lacanian constructions of sexual difference, she reveals that, as a consequence of their privileging of the phallus as transcendental signifier, Freudian and Lacanian discourse on the development of the subject insists upon the disadvantaged position of the female subject in relation to the symbolic and language which originates in a privileging of the male subject in an oppositional construction of sexual difference. Cixous states that dominant cultural representations of the female subject inscribe her body as lack and thus confine her to an essential state of alienation from her body, maternal genealogy and language:

> Because they want to make us believe that what interests us is the white continent with its monuments to Lack. And we believed. We have been frozen in our place between two terrifying myths: between the Medusa and the abyss ... For the phallo-logocentric *aufhebung* is there, and it is militant, the reproducer of old schemes, anchored in the dogma of castration. They haven't changed a thing: they have theorised their

desire as reality. Let them tremble, those priests; we are going to show them our sexts!'[9]

Cixous argues for a reinstatement of the role of the mother in relation to identity and language and a recognition of the unconscious as inherently feminine. This would ensure that a female self, which cannot identity with the phallus as transcendental signifier and therefore, under Freudian and Lacanian models, experiences a disadvantaged entry into language and the Law, is not solely identified by lack. The apparently problematic relationship between women and patriarchal Law is seen by Cixous as a positive element in that it enables women to occupy the powerfully disruptive position of the marginal.

Cixous proceeds from this rejection of models of sexual difference and gendered identity to suggest an escape from the binary that they establish through what she describes as a different libidinal economy. The analysis of psychoanalytic discourse is thus undertaken in tandem with an engagement with the economic and libidinal economies of capitalist patriarchy 'The empire of the selfsame (L'Empire du propre)',[10] in which, Cixous argues, the other is maintained in its alterity only for its repression to shore up the illusion of unified subjectivity and mastery of the self. Drawing on Marcel Mauss's analysis of gift economies, George Bataille's subsequent radical interventions in concepts of spending and excess and Derridean notions of *différance*, Cixous suggests a different mode of difference that could be celebrated rather than repressed.[11] This is configured as an apparently innate bisexuality open to the female subject and which, in contrast to a fantasy of unity which does nothing to disrupt dominant tropes of gender and exchange, creates an open and non-excluding celebration of multiple differences.[12] Cixous argues for a movement away from a discourse of sexual difference based on the anatomical and its consequent constructions of the female subject as lack, to a consideration of *jouissance*, a term which denotes sexual pleasure and which escapes both anatomical definition and 'the strange importance that is accorded to exteriority and that which is specular in sexuality's development'.[13]

Working within the different contexts of Greek mythology, the history of women's oppression and the values upheld within Freudian and Lacanian discourses, Cixous asserts the potentially liberating impact of an insistence upon the presence of the body which does not deny maternal genealogy. The text addresses central cultural narratives and analyses the representation and function of female figures such as Dido, Electra and Cleopatra. Cixous argues that these figures remain complex and, by way of their potentially powerful position on the margins of their respective narratives, accommodate some promise of escape from dominant representation. Cixous illustrates her argument with a dazzling range of examples from Western culture, which uphold her assertion that woman serves as the oppressed other of patriarchal culture. Such detailed engagement with cultural meta-narratives foregrounds the central role of cultural and literary narratives in construction of self (image). The assertion that philosophy and literature are founded on the consistent subordination of the feminine to the masculine leads Cixous to imagine the consequences of revealing and subverting the harmful relationship between logocentrism and phallocentrism in which the former acts as naturalising agent for the latter:

> So all the history, all the stories would be there to retell differently; the future would be incalculable; the historic forces would and will change hands and change body – another thought which is yet unthinkable – will transform the functioning of all society. We are living in an age where the conceptual foundation of an ancient culture is in the process of being undermined by millions of a species of mole (Topoi, ground mines) never known before.[14]

The site of writing

Following the denunciation of the restricted and marginalised position of the female subject, the second movement of the text is an affirmative insistence upon the potential to subvert this position and assert a positive identity: this is inscribed within the multi-layered meaning of the text's title '*Là je une nais* – There I (a Feminine Subject) Am Born'. Cixous argues that the site which is inherently suited to the embrace of the other and the articulation of a different libidinal economy is that of writing. It is through writing that different modes of personal, economic and social intersubjective relationships can be realised – modes that do not insist upon an oppositional structure which invokes hierarchy and domination, and ultimately denies difference – but one which is open and seeks to embrace rather than to appropriate the other:

> Everyone knows that a place exists which is not politically or economically indebted to all the vileness and compromise. That is not obliged to reproduce the system. That is writing. If there is an

somewhere else that can escape the infernal repetition, it lies in that direction, where it dreams, where it invents new worlds.[15]

Cixous maintains that it is this positive celebration of the potential of writing as a utopian site which will enable the reconnection, reconfiguration and retelling of female subjectivities:

> She must write herself because, when the time comes for her liberation, it is the invention of a new insurgent writing that will allow her to put the breaks and indispensable changes into effect in her history. At first, individually, on two inseparable levels: woman, writing herself, will go back to this body that has been worse than confiscated, a body replaced with a disturbing stranger, sick or dead, who so often is a bad influence, the cause and place of inhibitions. By censuring the body, breath and speech are censored at the same time.
>
> To write – the act that will 'realise' the un-censored relationship of woman to her sexuality, to her woman-being giving her back access to her own forces; that will return her goods, her pleasures, her organs ... that will tear out the superegoed, over Mosesed structure where the same position of guilt is always reserved for her (guilty of everything, every time: of having desires, of not having any; of being frigid, of being too 'hot'; of not being both at once; of being too much of a mother and not enough; of nurturing and of not nurturing ...). Write yourself: your body must make itself heard. Then the huge resources of the unconscious will burst out. Finally the inexhaustible feminine Imaginary is going to be deployed.[16]

An assertion of the presence of the female body will thus overcome censorship and writing will bring the female subject to a life and a language which are no longer dependent on patriarchal definitions of female subjectivity. Through a typically playful Cixousian use of language the two main movements of *écriture féminine* are described: 'flying/stealing is the gesture of woman, flying in language/stealing from language, making it fly'.[17] The combined sense of transcendence, exhilaration (flying) and subversion (theft) encapsulates the relationship between *écriture féminine* and the conventions of language.

Practising *écriture féminine*

Many immediate reactions to these essays articulated a desire to reveal different authors as champions of *écriture féminine*. However, the textual identification or application of such concepts is extremely difficult:

Hélène Cixous (1937–)

> At the present time, defining a feminine practice of writing is impossible with an impossibility that will continue; for this practice will never be able to be theorised, enclosed, coded, which does not mean it does not exist. But it will always exceed the discourse governing the phallocratic system; it takes place and will take place somewhere other than in the territories subordinated to philosophical–theoretical domination. It will not let itself think except through subjects that break automatic functions, border runners never subjugated by any authority.[18]

Cixous maintained that the status of *écriture féminine* is consciously non-prescriptive and in permanent flux, as Conley summarises: 'Always becoming, it never becomes the system to be applied'.[19] This liberating writing should rather be seen as a utopian process rather than model or analytical tool, a sense of what a feminine imaginary could be that remains a potent cultural and political image. At first reading the use of terms such as 'feminine' (or indeed masculine) to describe modes of writing might seem reductive, or at best naive. However, Cixous defended her use of the terms which she claims are employed to differentiate, to 'mark the distance',[20] in her search for a decipherable libidinal femininity characterised by openness, inclusion and the acceptance of difference. She does not posit any innate and consistent gendered differences between the writing of men and women.

Despite the difficulty in identifying *écriture féminine* in its finished form, Cixous does discuss writers whom she feels display great affinity with the main characteristics of this writing. It is perhaps surprising that the main examples cited by Cixous as existing exponents of this radical form are male canonical writers such as Shakespeare, Kleist and Genet, yet this last name is already contained in the wordplay and homonyms of the text's title as 'La Genet'.[21] *Écriture féminine* does not entail a reductive gender specificity but could be written by men or women who are capable of demonstrating an openness to the other in their writing.

Cixous's own fictions have been discussed as examples of *écriture féminine* as their linguistic innovation, transgressive forms and representations of permeable and changing subjectivities combine polemical and poetic discourses. The subversion of mythical narratives and figures creates empowering images of female creativity, whilst the texts articulate an awareness of the delicate balance to be struck between adopting such figures with subversive intent and risking recuperation by the dominant discourse. The Cixousian canon of writers, a group whose works feature repeatedly in her essays and seminar programme, are writers whose works, and indeed life stories, reflect the central tropes of poetic identity constructed in her work. Those tropes include multiple exiles (from an allegorical paradise lost, from the father, from language itself), a reinscription or subversion of myth and metanarratives, linguistic playfulness and subversion of literary forms.

Staging Writing

Since 1984, writing for the theatre has become an increasingly central part of Cixous's oeuvre. Her work with Ariane Mnouchkine and the Théâtre du soleil must be recognised as one of the richest and most important partnerships between a writer and company in contemporary Europe. Cixous's work expressed an early hostility towards the theatre as a site where archetypal modes of patriarchal oppression of the feminine were rehearsed and reinstated. Her article 'To Go to the Sea/Mother' criticised the formal structure of theatre for being inflexible, addressing the marginalised status and lack of agency of many female characters of classical theatre.[22] Two plays, which coincide with the publication of this article, engage with two metanarratives of Freudian psychoanalytical discourse, that of the oedipal narrative and the analysis of hysteria as a gendered disease.[23] Both plays' dramatisations of the repression of the female subject in language and society draw on the narrative tropes and figures discussed in *The Newly Born Woman* and contain radical formal innovations which subvert the classical structure of theatre to represent a subject-in-process through the reconfiguration of spatio-temporal relationships between spectator, character and stage.

In the early 1980s, the theatre becomes a metaphoric model for the staging of Cixous's continuing search for a site in which inter-subjective relationships can be restructured. This site is based on the perceived relationship between actor and character established in rehearsal, which is characterised by openness, fluidity and loss of self and is clearly linked to the libidinal economies of writing as described in *The Newly Born Woman*. 'The theatre is the palace of others. It lives off the desire of the other, of all others.'[24] Cixous's strategic use of theatre enables her to address a rethinking of structures of alterity which go beyond the personal to engage with questions of national and historical identity. Her plays represent the partition of India, the struggle for control of Cambodia, repression under Stalin and recent corruption in French political and medical establishments.²⁵ The consistent premise of these plays is the harmful nature of dialectic structures which insist upon the hierarchical opposition between self and other and lead to oppression, exploitation and paranoia. Moreover, Cixous maintains that theatre is the site in which both levels of *histoire* can be addressed – narrative and history. The figures within Cixous's theatre who speak out against reductive notions of difference (Gandhi, Aeschylus, Snorri Sturlusson, Anna Akhmatova) are clearly identifiable as constructions of poetic identity and continue the central importance to her oeuvre of asserting the ethical role of the writer. This Cixousian model is highly influenced by the Heideggerian notion of the poet as purveyor of truths and link between the individual and society.²⁶ Indeed, several of these plays end with the poet-figure addressing the audience directly.

As Cixous's 'fictions' often foreground the process of writing and reading and suggest a positive re-evaluation of constructions of identity based on models of creativity and textual reception, so her theatre explores the generic specificity of writing for the stage and, in particular, the different relationship to time experienced by both writer and spectator of theatre. The ability of theatre to be (in the) present reveals the influence of arguably more radical discourse on the revolutionary potential of catharsis, and identifies it as a form in which she can combine the two central motivations of her writing, namely, the inscription of memory, the bearing of witness and the insistence upon the fluidity of narrative and identity. Theatre is thus identified, through the temporal acrobatics of her plays, as a 'manifestation of memory in the present'²⁷ that can both inscribe forgotten or repressed stories and act as a site of change and transformation for writer and spectator.

Major Angles of Criticism

Cixous's work has at times been received with the same response afforded many French intellectuals who came to the fore following the events of May 1968, namely, with charges of elitism and utopianism. Many feminist theorists expressed deep concern about Cixous's use of bodily metaphors particular to the potential of the female body (those of giving birth, of producing milk) to describe writing as creative process and cultural activity, seeing in them a dangerous lack of distinction from patriarchal discourses of biological essentialism, which erase any consideration of women as social subjects and construct models of Woman as abstract other.[28] Cixous acknowledges the difficulty of working with terms which are already so heavily determined:

> It is impossible to predict what will become of sexual difference ... But we must make no mistake: men and women are caught up in a web of age-old cultural determinations that are almost unanalyzable in their complexity. One can no more speak of 'woman' than of 'man' without being trapped within an ideological theater where the proliferation of representations, images, reflections, myths, identifications, transform, deform constantly change everyone's Imaginary and invalidate in advance any conceptualization.[29]

Whilst several of the bodily metaphors of *écriture féminine* may indeed seem easily recuperable and open to caricature, this would underestimate the complexity of Cixous's project which endeavours to reclaim the body, but the body as text, a body whose cultural construction and mediation is inherently understood. For Cixous, this remains a positive choice and a rejection of any pernicious complicity in the positing of the female body as a site of shame, silence and alienation. Indeed, Cixous's assertion of a reformulated relationship between language and the body counters the discourse of such critiques which persist in a logocentric Cartesian discourse that posits the mind as the source of writing.

The employment in Cixous's theatre of the historical narratives of India, Cambodia and the Soviet Union as settings in which to undertake ambitious allegorical narratives of personal and national difference have drawn criticism that she unwittingly reinforces Romanticised and Orientalist discourse which posits the Western intellectual (and audience) as locked in self-reflexive crisis in opposition to an uncomplicated other identity. However, Cixous's position as outsider in relation to discourses of national, sexual and academic orthodoxy ensure that her engagement with such narratives is consistently aware of the dangers of fixing and reducing the other.

Conclusions

Cixous's writing has been highly influential in many fields. Her discussion of *écriture féminine* has changed the reception of the work of writers across many national literatures and periods, ranging from Kafka to Clarice Lispector. The radical rethinking of intersubjective relationships articulated in Cixous's work has had immeasurable influence within the broad field of cultural studies and across disciplines as diverse as translation studies and fine art (see, for example, the textual incorporation of her writing in the work of Maria Chevska).

Cixous's work articulates many concerns common to intellectuals of the Left in post-1968 France including the insistence upon a link between the personal and the political:

> [T]he political – it's banal, I'm ashamed of having to say it – does not arise simply from the political scene, political events reported by the media; it begins obviously with the subject's discourse of themselves. What I mean to say is that everything that makes up the political scene – there are the relations of power, oppression, the imposition of slavery, exploitation – all of this commences at home I would say first of all within the family and then inside myself, the tyrants, despots, dictators, capitalism, in short all that which represents for us the visible political arena is nothing but the theatricalised and visible photographable projection of my conflicts with the other. I cannot even imagine that one could think otherwise.[30]

Her work reveals the centrality of language to identity formation and the political and economic investments of a gendered view of language and culture which assigns the function of lack, negative or marginal to the female subject and representations of femininity.

Throughout her writing, from the polemical and poetical essays of the 1970s to her most recent theatre and fiction, we find a specific assertion of the role of the text as transformative site and experience for writer, reader and spectator. Cixous's consistent advocacy and practice of a form of writing which enables different modes of thinking and a rethinking of difference itself retains clear philosophical and political motivations. She rejects a classification of her work as philosophy:

> The difference with philosophical discourse is that I never dream of mastering or ordering or inventing concepts. Moreover I am incapable of this. I am overtaken. All I want is to illustrate, depict fragments, events of human life and death, each unique and yet at the same time exchangeable. Not the law, the exception ... I always work on the present passing ...[31]

Indeed she has suggested that the motivation behind her writing in all its forms is 'a question of writing today's pain and making it heard without betraying it',[32] a summary which expresses the unceasing work on alterity, voice and love which permeate her writing.

Notes

1. The thesis was published as *The Exile of James Joyce or the Art of Replacement*, trans. Sally Purcell (London: Calder, 1976; and New York: Riverrun, 1980).
2. Cixous in conversation: seminar given at Centre for Cultural Analysis, Theory and History, University of Leeds, November 2002.
3. Her recent play *Drums on the Dyke* (Tambours sur la digue) received overwhelming critical and audience acclaim. For further details of her writing for the theatre, see my *Hélène Cixous and the Theatre*.
4. Hélène Cixous and Jacques Derrida, *Voiles* (Paris: Galilée, 1998).
5. For a detailed discussion of these conflicts see Duchen, *Feminism in France*.
6. The translation of *féminin* is highly problematic and I will leave the term in the French throughout so as to sidestep both the different set of gender connotations which beset the English word 'feminine' and the potential erasure of notions of gender as construction which are implied by the use of 'female'.
7. Cixous, 'Castration or Decapitation', trans. Annette Kuhn, *Signs*, 7, 1981, pp. 41–5, p. 45.
8. *Newly Born Woman*, p. 63.
9. Ibid., pp. 68–9.
10. Ibid., p. 79.
11. Marcel Mauss, *The Gift*, trans. Ian Cunnison (New York: Norton, 1967); and Georges Bataille, *The Accursed Share: An Essay on General Economy*, trans. R. Hurley (New York: Zone Books, 1988).
12. *Newly Born Woman*, p. 84.
13. Ibid., p. 82.
14. Ibid., p. 65.
15. Ibid., p. 72.
16. Ibid., p. 97.
17. The French text reads: 'voler c'est le geste de la femme, voler dans la langue, la faire voler' (*La Jeune née* (Paris: Union Générale des Editions, 1975), p. 146).
18. *Newly Born Woman*, p. 92.
19. Conley, *Hélène Cixous*, p. 6.
20. Ibid., p. 129.
21. This is also a clear reference to Derrida's study of Genet which had recently been published as *Glas*, trans. J. P. Leavey and R. Rand (Lincoln: University of Nebraska Press, 1986).
22. Hélène Cixous, 'Aller à la mer', *Le Monde*, 28 April 1977, p. 19; 'Going to the Seashore', *Modern drama*, 27, 1984, pp. 546–8.
23. Hélène Cixous, *Le Nom d'Œdipe: Le chant du corps interdit*; and *Portrait de Dora* (Paris: des femmes, 1976).
24. Hélène Cixous, 'L'Incarnation', in Hélène Cixous, *L'Indiade ou l'Inde*

de leurs rêves (Paris: Théâtre du soleil, 1987), p. 260.
25. For detailed analysis of these plays see my *Hélène Cixous and the Theatre*.
26. See Martin Heidegger, 'What Are Poets for?', in Martin Heidegger, *Poetry, Language, Thought*, trans. Albert Hofstadter (New York: Harper and Row, 1975), pp. 91–142.
27. Hélène Cixous in discussion at Cerisy La Salle, July 1998.
28. For examples of this see: Alice Jardine, *Gynesis: Configurations of Woman and Modernity* (London: Cornell University Press, 1985); and Donna Stanton 'Difference on Trial: A Critique of the Maternal Metaphor in Cixous, Irigaray and Kristeva', in Nancy Miller (ed.), *The Poetics of Gender* (New York: Columbia University Press, 1986), pp. 157–82.
29. *Newly Born Woman*, p. 83.
30. Interview 'Guardian of Language', Kathleen O'Grady, *Women's Education*, 23, January 1996.
31. Hélène Cixous, 'Preface', in Susan Sellers (ed.), *The Hélène Cixous Reader* (London: Routledge, 1994), p. xxii.
32. Hélène Cixous interviewed in *Qui parle*, 43, 1989, p. 9.

Major Works by Cixous

With Catherine Clément, *The Newly Born Woman*, trans. Betsy Wing (Minnesota: University of Minnesota Press, 1986 [1975]).

The Book of Promethea, trans. Betsy Wing (Lincoln: University of Nebraska Press, 1991 [1983]).

'From the Scene of the Unconscious to the Scene of History', trans. Deborah Carpenter, in Ralph Cohen (ed.), *The Future of Literary History* (New York, Routledge, 1989 [1980]), pp. 126–33.

Coming to writing and Other Essays, trans. Deborah Jenson, Sarah Cornell, Ann Liddle and Susan Sellers (Cambridge, MA: Harvard University Press, 1991 [1977]).

Readings: The Poetics of Blanchot, Joyce, Kafka, Lispector, Tsvetaeva (Seminar 1982–1984), trans. Verena Conley (London: Harvester Wheatsheaf, 1992).

Stigmata. Escaping Texts, trans. Catherine A. MacGillivray, Keith Cohen and Eric Prenowitz (London: Routledge, 1998).

Suggestions for Further Reading

Conley, Verena Aldermatt, *Hélène Cixous: Writing the Feminine* (Lincoln: University of Nebraska Press, 1984). A good introduction to Cixous's early writings.

Dobson, Julia, *Hélène Cixous and the Theatre: The Scenes of Writing* (Oxford: Peter Lang, 2002). A detailed investigation of the place of Cixous's theatre within her oeuvre.

Duchen, Claire, *Feminism in France. From May '68 to Mitterrand* (London: Routledge and Kegan Paul, 1986). A well-contextualised introduction to the main issues and groupings.

Rye, Gill, *Reading for Change: Interactions between Text and Identity in Contemporary French Women's Writing* (Oxford: Peter Lang, 2002). A detailed discussion of the practices and tropes of reading and writing evoked in texts by a range of women authors.

Shiach, Morag, *Hélène Cixous: A Politics of Writing* (London: Routledge, 1991). An excellent study of the details and connections between elements of Cixous's work.

Sellers, Susan (ed.), *The Hélène Cixous Reader* (London: Routledge, 1994). Invaluable collection of translated pieces with clear introductions.

9

Julia Kristeva (1941–)

Moya Lloyd

Biography and Intellectual Context

Consistently positioned as one of the three leading French feminists alongside Hélène Cixous and Luce Irigaray, Julia Kristeva was born in Bulgaria in 1941. After studying for an undergraduate degree in linguistics at the University of Sophia, Kristeva emigrated to Paris in late 1965 to study for a doctorate. Almost immediately, Kristeva became steeped in the intellectual life of Paris. Assisted initially by fellow Bulgarian linguist Tzvétan Todorov, Kristeva met many of the leading intellectuals of the day, including structuralists Lucien Goldmann, Roland Barthes and Claude Lévi-Strauss. Through Barthes, Kristeva met theorist, novelist and left activist, Philippe Sollers, the co-founder of *Tel Quel* (an avant-garde journal, which disseminated structuralist and post-structuralist ideas in France). Kristeva and Sollers married in 1967; their only son David was born in 1976.

From the outset, Kristeva had a significant intellectual influence on those around her. Together with Todorov, Kristeva was responsible for bringing to the attention of French structuralist intellectuals (and indeed to Western intellectuals in general) the work of Russian literary scholar and philosopher of language, Mikhail Bakhtin. In contrast to the structuralist account of signification (derived from the work of Ferdinand de Saussure) that dominated in France at that time, where texts were treated as discrete units to be analysed in terms of general laws, and whose meaning was inherent within them, Bakhtin offered a dialogical approach. Here language is seen to be dynamic and meaning to be contextual, that is, to be dependent upon factors such as circumstance or the specific cultural and social context in which it operates. Kristeva's utilisation of the ideas of Bakhtin, combined with her training in Marxist theory, a critical approach to Hegelian dialectics and a burgeoning interest in Freudian psychoanalysis, helped to shape the original approach to linguistic theory that has characterised her work and that has made her such an influential philosopher. This work in linguistics led to the publication in 1969 of *Séméiotiké: Recherches pour une sémanalyse* and in 1970 *Le Texte du roman*. It culminated in 1974 in the publication in France of her hugely influential doctoral thesis *Revolution in Poetic Language*, a work that helped to inaugurate a specifically post-structuralist theory of language.

The same year that her doctorate was published, Kristeva was awarded a chair in linguistics at the University of Paris VII, a post she still holds. (She is also currently permanent visiting Professor at Columbia University, New York.) In 1979, after undergoing psychoanalysis herself during the 1970s, she became a practising psychoanalyst. The influence of this training is increasingly evident in the works she has published since then (see for instance *Powers of Horror, Tales of Love, Black Sun: Depression and Melancholia*). Here Kristeva brings psychoanalysis to bear on questions of, for instance, motherhood, femininity and love, as well as treating problems to do with analytic practice. As several commentators have observed, this shift appears to betoken a new phase in her work, a movement away from the semiotic and linguistic. Semiotician, literary critic, philosopher and psychoanalyst, in 1990 Kristeva became a published author with the first of her three novels to date: *The Samurais*. This was followed in 1991 by *The Old Man and the Wolves* and in 1996 by *Possession*. Such is her intellectual significance in her adopted country, that in 1997 she was awarded the esteemed *Légion d'honneur*.

It would, however, be a mistake to represent Kristeva as a scholar confined in the ivory tower of academe. Throughout her career, she has been intensely involved in political activism. She was, for example, a participant in the events of May 1968 (about which she talks in *Revolt, She Said*). In 1974, whilst still an adherent of Maoism, she travelled to China with the *Tel Quel* group, the journal she kept during the trip being published that year as *About Chinese Women*; and in 1989 she accompanied François Mitterand on a diplomatic trip to Bulgaria. In all this, however, Kristeva's relation to one particular political movement, feminism, has been a highly ambivalent

Julia Kristeva (1941–)

one. This is somewhat ironic given the extent to which feminists have repeatedly appropriated her ideas.

The Thought of Julia Kristeva

'Semanalysis': the role of the speaking subject in semiotics

The first appearance in English of Kristeva's semiotic work was not *Revolution in Poetic Language*, the heavily abridged translation of which came out only in 1984, but an essay entitled 'The System and the Speaking Subject' which appeared in the *Times Literary Supplement* in 1973.[1] This short theoretical piece outlines in succinct fashion the approach Kristeva developed in more depth in her later work. Of particular note in this essay is the distinction she draws between 'semiology' and what she coins 'semanalysis'. Structuralist semiology endeavours, according to Kristeva, to treat language scientifically and in doing so presents it as a static system, governed by rules, a social code. As such:

> what semiotics has discovered is the fact that there is a general social law, that this law is the symbolic dimension which is given in language and that every social practice [e.g. myth or kinship] offers a specific expression of that law.[2]

What this theory of language fails to grasp, however, is 'anything in language which belongs not with the social contract but with play, pleasure or desire'.[3] It is at this point that semiology reaches its limit as an explanation of language since it cannot understand the process of change.

In place, then, of this static conception focused on practice, Kristeva offers a more 'dynamic' account of language that takes as its starting point 'a theory of the speaking subject'. 'Semanalysis' combines semiology (the study of sign-systems) with psychoanalysis to produce a conception of language as '*a signifying process*'.[4] This fusion of semiotics and psychoanalysis allows Kristeva to develop a dual approach to signification: to 'bring the body, replete with drives' into semiotics and to 'reinscribe language within the body'.[5] It thus enables her to trace both the ways that the divided subject of psychoanalysis impacts upon signification and the production of meaning and the mechanisms whereby language operates as one of the necessary conditions of human existence. (See the next section for further explication.)

The integration of the work of the unconscious into semiotics, in particular, requires supplementing an understanding of language apprehended as social code with an exploration of elements extraneous to that system (such as the 'drives' as Sigmund Freud calls them). Semanalysis challenges, therefore, the notion of a science of language by introducing the idea that the system will be haphazardly disrupted by these extraneous elements. Semanalysis interweaves system with negativity, suggesting the potential for transgression of the system. The interplay between the two aspects functions not only to sustain the social code but also and crucially to renew it. This is why Kristeva sees signification as a dynamic process (as opposed to a static system). To understand the relation between system and negativity, it is necessary to consider in more detail Kristeva's analysis of the speaking subject.

The speaking subject: the symbolic and the semiotic

In place of the transcendental subject of semiology, Kristeva proposes a theory of the speaking subject as split between the conscious and unconscious. Kristeva describes this speaking subject as the 'subject of a heterogeneous process'.[6] Semanalysis must, therefore, explore the distinct kinds of operation that characterise the two sides of this split process. These she labels the semiotic and the symbolic.

The semiotic, for Kristeva, is a pre-linguistic or pre-symbolic space, the realm of the 'unspeakable' or the 'unnameable', or what Kristeva following Plato calls the 'chora'. It is the site of energies and bodily drives, and is thus associated with rhythms and forces, movements and gestures, intonations and melodies. It is related to what psychoanalysts call the pre-oedipal, that is, to a time before sexuality has been ordered, to a time when the infant child is in a symbiotic state with the mother in which it cannot distinguish between its own body and hers. It is for this reason that the semiotic is conceived as intrinsically associated with the maternal body, a body that provides the first source of rhythm, touch, sound and movement for all humans. By contrast, the symbolic is the realm of language understood as a rule-governed system, of grammar and syntax and what Kristeva refers to as 'propositions' and 'positions'. In a more general sense it is also the realm of social order and law. It is, in psychoanalytic terms, post-oedipal, that is, it relates to a time when the mother/baby dyad is separated and the child becomes conscious of

Julia Kristeva (1941–)

itself as an individuated, linguistic being. Broadly speaking, where the semiotic is dominated by the figure of the mother, then the symbolic is governed by the law of the father. Two questions immediately arise: what is the purpose of this distinction in relation to the subject; and, second, what is its relation to signification?

In order for the speaking being to come into existence, s/he must cross a particular threshold, what Kristeva calls the 'thetic'. This is a two-stage process. The first stage relates to what Jacques Lacan calls the 'mirror stage'. This is the stage at which the child is able to distinguish its own reflection in a mirror. It marks the phase, therefore, when the child is able to substitute an image or representation (its image in the mirror) for its immediate experience. In terms of language, the mirror stage initiates the differentiation, in a very simple way, of signifier from signified.[7] It sets up, that is, the separation of the image and the object. The second stage relates to the oedipal situation and to the threat, therefore, of castration.

According to Freud, all children believe that every human being has a penis. When they see a human – their mother – who lacks such an organ, children are said to assume that she has been castrated. A fear of his/her own castration then ensues. The boy fears castration as a form of paternal punishment for desiring his mother. Renouncing the mother and accepting the law of the father, that is, submitting himself to socio-cultural rules, becomes his path to 'normal' male subjectivity. The boy identifies with patriarchal authority. Symbolic castration is thus overcome. For the girl, the path is slightly more complicated. Like the boy, the girl also desires her mother. Believing, however, that the mother has robbed her of her penis, the girl feels her lack in a particular way. Since she can never have a penis of her own, accepting castration and thus paternal law means that the resolution of the oedipal complex for the girl requires her to direct her desire away from her mother and towards her father, desiring his penis and then, by implication, his (or a) child (a penis substitute). It should be noted here that where the term 'penis' connotes the biological organ, Kristeva following Lacan, talks rather of the 'phallus' – the signifier of the social power of the father. This is how the thetic works in relation to subjectivity, but what is its importance for language?

Where the mirror stage led to a rudimentary distinction between signifier and signified, the resolution of the Oedipus complex, generates signs, organises them according to the rules of grammar, syntax, introduces order and coherence and so on in order to make discourse possible. The thetic (combining the two stages discussed above) thus establishes a gap between reality and signification. For children of both sexes rejecting the mother and, for Kristeva, the maternal sphere of the semiotic is crucial in allowing the child to enter the symbolic sphere, the sphere of language and paternal authority. (Importantly, a subject who was to remain in this pre-linguistic state would remain outside language and society; s/he would be psychotic).

The child's entry into language marks the repression of the semiotic into the unconscious. However, for Kristeva that repression is never complete or absolute. Instead the relation between the semiotic and symbolic is a dialectical relation. This is significant in several ways. First, from time to time, the semiotic breaks through conscious representations, disrupting symbolisation with hetero-geneous unconscious contents. This can be adduced in poetry, for instance. (Note that Kristeva focuses in many of her own works upon literary texts.) According to Kristeva, poetic language through its greater attention to rhythm and sound exposes the subject's link with the pre-linguistic realm or semiotic chora; it is, in effect, a memory trace of a time when the relation of mother to child was undifferentiated and bodily. It is an instance of what Freud referred to as 'the return of the repressed'. Significantly for Kristeva, the kinds of crises of representation betokened in avant-garde litera-ture, for instance (which challenges, amongst other things, textual coherence), are just as important as, say, economic upheaval. For, crises of representation indicate moments of crisis in the symbolic itself, moments that might be amenable to political intervention, to revolution.

Second, since the relation between the semiotic and symbolic is a dialectical relation, this has profound implications for subjectivity. Here Kristeva introduces the idea of the subject-in-process/on trial. The oscillations between semiotic and symbolic mean that the speaking subject is not stable and his/her identity is not secure. S/he is always in the process of desiring identification with figures of authority (aspiring to a stable identity) at the same time as s/he is drawn back to the archaic maternal space of the semiotic. In essence, for Kristeva, this means that the subject is always in the process of renewing her/his identity, a process with the creative potential to allow both the subject and meaning to change. In both cases, the importance of moments of transgression and negativity cannot be underestimated.

Julia Kristeva (1941–)

The first phase of Kristeva's work is marked, thus, by an interest in the relation between semiotic and symbolic both in terms of moments of disruption of the symbolic by the semiotic and of how the semiotic becomes accessible to symbolic codification. As her work progresses, however, this interest is displaced somewhat in favour of a more psychoanalytic approach. Continuing to explore the relation between the mother/child dyad of the semiotic and the maternal function, Kristeva also examines two issues of interest to us: abjection and ethics.

Abjection

In *Powers of Horror*, a text that draws on the work of anthropologist Mary Douglas, Kristeva sets out her discussion of abjection. As Megan Becker-Leckrone notes, 'In this work Kristeva elaborates ideas that were incipient in much of her earlier work, such as the role of otherness in the production of meaning, and the foreignness that besets the speaking subject'.[8] The abject, like the semiotic, is both a precondition of and an element that disrupts subjectivity and the symbolic. Reiterating the idea that the subject is always split, Kristeva notes that the separation that is necessary for the subject to construct an identity is present from its birth when it is expelled from the mother's body. This is where abjection becomes important. For Kristeva, the abject 'is not an ob-ject facing me, which I name or imagine' and it is not a subject; it is, rather, what makes the identity of both impossible. The abject is 'the jettisoned object', that which is 'radically excluded',[9] in order for the subject to exist but which remains nevertheless part of its body. Its tears, saliva, faeces, urine, mucus and vomit, though expelled, are never entirely separate or distinct from it. Neither are those objects that are ingested: mother's milk, for instance. However repugnant these expelled and ingested objects may be, they are absolutely necessary to bodily existence, and thus are inescapable. Abjection is also thus itself an inescapable process.

Recalling the earlier discussion of the Oedipus complex, abjection also relates to the messy process of separation or differentiation that marks the shift from the semiotic to the symbolic; it signifies that which needs to be expelled in order that a 'clean and proper body' can be established. This relates not only to the individual (who must learn to control their bodily functions) but also to the collective body. Here forms of cultural taboo such as the incest taboo and defilement rites that structure and organise social life are particularly pertinent but so are moments of immorality and horror. Crime, but especially premeditated crime, is abject 'because it draws attention to the fragility of the law', it exposes the 'sinister, scheming, and shady' and it threatens identity, order, system and certainty. As Kristeva notes of one of recent history's most vile affairs: 'The abjection of Nazi crime reaches its apex when death, which, in any case, kills me, interferes with what, in my living universe, is supposed to save me from death: childhood, science, among other things'.[10] Such episodes of profound abjection reveal the death within life, and demonstrate the precariousness of human existence.

Abjection in all its guises – both individual and social – relates to what Kristeva calls 'violent, dark revolts of being'.[11] The abject is that which consciously we recoil from, which horrifies us, but which is nevertheless part of our subjectivity and part of our culture; it is that which paradoxically repels as it fascinates. As with the semiotic, the abject/abjection is that which must be repressed in order for symbolic and cultural order to be established, but which is ever present, looming and haunting the security and stability of that order, threatening its dissolution. This repression may well be productive: much of the book is devoted to an exploration precisely of literature as a mechanism whereby unconscious forces (abjection) can be channelled into more acceptable forms of expression, but it can never finally be overcome. Culture and symbolic order are achieved at a cost: the repression of the disorderly, the unconscious and the unassimilable.

Maternal function

It should be apparent by now that a consistent feature of Kristeva's work is her engagement with that which is repressed or contained in order for culture, language and subjectivity to function. One way of looking at this interest is to see it as a concern with liminal or borderline states. Here pregnancy becomes important to Kristeva's later work, as she interrogates the maternal body and thus opens the way to a new discourse of maternity.

Unlike Freud and Lacan who give priority to the paternal function and specifically to the paternal threat of castration, Kristeva, drawing on the work of psychoanalyst Melanie Klein, focuses on the maternal function. She contends that the maternal body plays a crucial role in the formation of subjectivity and in access to the symbolic. Giving birth is for Kristeva the first form of separation experienced by the subject: their expulsion from the safety of the maternal body into the world. In addition, during the period leading up to the mirror phase, it is the maternal body that imposes some form of regulation or 'law' on the operation of the infant/mother dyad – through the denial or granting of access to the breast. Moreover, and this will be returned to in the discussion of ethics below, the maternal body is the exemplification of divided subjectivity, since the pregnant body contains alterity within it. Finally, as that which must be symbolically murdered in order that the child may enter language, the maternal body (mother) is located at the cusp of the nature/culture, semiotic/symbolic divide. Maternity, through the pre-linguistic symbiosis of mother and child, has to be denied or rendered unspeakable in order for signification to occur. There is, however, no easy alignment here between women and the semiotic; for although pregnancy is a bodily process, over which women have no control, and thus mothers are not subjects of their pregnancy, the mother is, nonetheless, a speaking subject who has attained language.

As part of her quest to contemplate the maternal function, Kristeva observes that the discourses of maternity that currently exist fail to acknowledge the role of the maternal function in the accession to language and culture. In the essay 'Stabat Mater', the title of which derives from the Latin hymn on the agony of the Virgin Mary at the crucifixion of Christ, Kristeva explores representation of the Virgin Mary within Catholicism. The decline of religion in general and of the cult of the Virgin in particular, has rendered this Christian discourse redundant or, at least, ineffectual in understanding women's continued desire to have children (particularly in the face of feminist castigation of motherhood as a form of patriarchal oppression). What is needed, is thus a new discourse. A discourse, that is, which can combine an understanding of the maternal body with the 'corporeal and psychological suffering of childbirth'. Moreover, one that appreciates the 'self-sacrifice' mothers face in passing on 'the social norm' (the law of the father) even when they might be keen to repudiate it, and which apprehends the 'war between mother and daughter'. Finally, it must be capable of acknowledging female desire for power.[12] This new discourse Kristeva calls 'herethics', an ethics of love.

Ethics

Accounts of ethics and morality are frequently based upon the idea of the autonomous agent who has certain obligations or duties towards others. The other, in this context, is viewed as the same as the agent (entitled to the same rights, with the same capacities and so on). As we have seen, however, the account of subjectivity that Kristeva deploys has a more complex understanding of the relation between self and other. Conceptions of the autonomous subject tend to treat it as having a stable identity. This can be compared with the subject-in-process/on trial, pulled between the paternal realm of the symbolic and the maternal semiotic. There is, for Kristeva, therefore, an otherness (or alterity) at the very heart of the subject. Take the case of the maternal body. According to Kristeva, pregnancy involves the 'splitting of the subject: redoubling up of the body, separation and co-existence of the self and an other, of nature and consciousness, of physiology and speech'. Pregnancy or maternity, as a model for ethics, reveals that alterity or otherness is contained within the subject. It offers a fundamental challenge, therefore, to the assumption of identity associated with the autonomous subject and to any conception of ethics based on that identity. Instead, Kristevan ethics – herethics – reconceives fundamentally the relation to the other by revealing the other within.

Maternity is important in another way: the birth of the child 'leads the mother', she contends, 'into the labyrinths of an experience that, without the child, she would rarely encounter: love for an other'.[13] This is not love for a being that is the same as the self, but for difference, including the difference within the self. What is crucial about the maternal function, in contrast to the paternal function, is precisely, therefore, that it is one of love and not fear. (Recall that paternal authority is based on fear, the child's fear of castration). Moreover, this love of the mother is not only love of her child but also of her self and her own mother. As a model of ethical love, therefore, it is always already collective. It is important to point out that maternity is not the only model of ethics as Kristeva conceives it (psychoanalysis is also seen as an ethical relation of love). What maternity reveals most starkly, however, is the concept of otherness as intrinsic to subjectivity (since we are all, to borrow the title of another of Kristeva's books, *Strangers to Ourselves*), and thence to ethics.

Julia Kristeva (1941–)

It should be apparent by now that Kristeva does not present herethics as a form of morality, as a system of obligations and duties or moral laws. Rather, it is tied in with negativity and transgression, with that which is repressed in order for the social to function but which returns from time to time to disrupt the Law. Ethics, for Kristeva, is about accepting or recognising transgression so that it can be articulated and understood in the social-symbolic realm. It is about acknowledging the unconscious and the semiotic and about allowing love to speak.

Critical Responses

Unsurprisingly, given the breadth and range of Kristeva's work, her ideas have been the subject of intense debate. Aside from the frequent contention that her work is opaque and difficult to read, substantive criticisms tend to centre on a number of themes: that her work is essentialist and that it is politically conservative, lacking a collective politics, and thus is of no use to feminism.

Essentialism

The charge of essentialism has been commonly used within contemporary political thought, including feminism, to contest the viability of many different kinds of ideas and theories. Indeed, such is its use – or overuse – that it has become a pejorative term, a way of dismissing ideas out of hand, though philosophically it is simply a description or form of categorisation. The term relates to the belief in a true essence, something that is unchanging and irreducible about a thing or a person. It is, thus, an ontological claim. In the context of Kristeva, she is regularly perceived as operating with either an essentialist conception of maternity, woman and/or the feminine. Implied here is that Kristeva pays insufficient attention to history and its effects on maternity and femininity, and that her theory is universalist (applying in all times and all places). She is seen to reduce women to their biological functions. Thus, Nancy Fraser argues that for Kristeva the only way that women can access the semiotic is through pregnancy and childbirth, through their biology that is, whereas men 'do it by writing avant-garde poetry'.[14] Femininity thus comes to be linked, in an essentialist fashion, with maternity. Conception, pregnancy, childbirth and child rearing are then treated apart from the socio-political context in which they actually operate, a context that colours their operation in different ways at different times. (Think here, for instance, of the advent of reproductive technologies, from the contraceptive pill to *in vitro* fertilisation, and their effects on conception or of the impact of nurseries on child rearing). In a parallel fashion, Elizabeth Grosz, whilst acknowledging that Kristeva does not essentialise women (that is, she does not attribute to them any unchanging characteristics), notes that she does treat maternity as an irreducibly biological and physiological process, that is, as a process that is unaffected by socio-political factors and, as such, is essentialist.

It is not only Kristeva's account of maternity and femininity that has been criticised as essentialist but also her notion of the semiotic. According to this view, as Tina Chanter observes, the semiotic is 'equated with the biological, instinctual motility of the body'.[15] In other words, it is treated as something natural, pre-cultural and unchanging in contrast to the symbolic, the realm of culture and history. One of the difficulties with Kristeva is that her thought oscillates between different poles (just as language and subjectivity also oscillate between the semiotic and symbolic). So, whilst it is difficult to refute the claims of those who spot essentialist elements in Kristeva's account of maternity and femininity, even possibly in the semiotic, these essentialist moments have to be read against the alternative strand which also runs through that account, a strand which is radically anti-essentialist. Thus, alongside the equation of femininity with maternity, there is Kristeva's insistence that women, as such, do not 'exist', that femininity is a fiction. Similarly, in relation to the semiotic, Kristeva is clear that it only acquires meaning through expression in symbolic language, and thus in trying to make sense of the semiotic we symbolise it (we submit it to culture).

Political conservatism and anti-feminism

One of the reasons that Kristeva's theory has been seen as politically conservative, and thus of no use to feminism, concerns what critics see as its lack of an effective political agent to bring about change in the symbolic order. For some writers, the problem lies with Kristeva's conception of the speaking subject as a split subject. According to Fraser, for instance, the subject of the symbolic is 'an oversocialized conformist, thoroughly subjected to symbolic conventions and norms' who cannot therefore act to overhaul the system, whilst the 'semiotic "subject"' is disabled on three counts. First, it operates outside of culture and thus, outside of the political realm proper; second, it operates transgressively to disrupt the symbolic, but not creatively to transform it; and lastly, it threatens identity, which means it cannot contribute to the generation of new forms of political solidarity based on identity.[16] Each side of the split subject thus cancels out the other, and neither offers a sufficient model of political agency.

This suggests that any politics deducible from Kristeva's work will necessarily be a pessimistic politics, since the symbolic order is not amenable to political intervention and change. Since all that occurs is that semiotic forces disrupt the social order through the return of the repressed then, as critics note, the best that can be achieved is a form of anarchic disturbance of it. This has severe repercussions for feminism as a political movement. It implies that male power can be disrupted but not transformed. It undermines, therefore, feminism conceived as a collective revolutionary politics aimed at the overthrow of patriarchy, at the dissolution of oppressive relations between the sexes, and at the construction of an alternative non-oppressive future. Instead, feminism is recast as a sort of persistent thorn in the side of the symbolic, 'where', as Dorothy Leland surmises, 'the only possible revolutions are temporary transgressions',[17] and where if feminism has a function it is an entirely negative one, of rejection and refusal. Moreover, since Kristeva herself explicitly rejects feminist calls for universal equality, as well as feminist attempts to assert women's radical difference from men, albeit in favour of feminism as a form of ethics (see above),[18] it is unsurprising that feminists have been so suspicious of the politics her work entails.

Applications

However valid these criticisms may be, Kristeva's work has, nevertheless, been very influential in a number of areas. Feminist literary critics have drawn upon her earlier work in order to try to expose elements of the semiotic at work in specific literary texts. Her focus on the maternal function and her examination of the pre-oedipal semiotic has been influential within feminist psychoanalysis since it added a dimension (associated with femininity) neglected within Freudian and Lacanian psychoanalysis. Cultural theorists have utilised a range of Kristeva's ideas (the archaic mother, the semiotic, negativity and abjection) in various ways to explore the psychic underpinnings of the social order. Here the idea of the 'monstrous-feminine'[19] in horror and science fiction film is a good example of how the maternal figure needs to be controlled or repudiated so that patriarchal order can be protected and maintained. Finally, Kristeva's discussion of the subject-in-process has been important in recent debates, within feminism in particular, around identity. By acknowledging the unconscious forces at work in the construction of the subject, she has helped to challenge the notion of the autonomous masculine subject assumed by many schools of philosophy and political theory.

Two ideas, in particular, have been especially influential: abjection and Kristeva's discussion of the stranger. The concept of abjection is, as noted, important as a way of apprehending otherness. Linked into the idea of exclusion, abjection offers a way of understanding the dynamics of oppression. Thus, for instance, Judith Butler in her recent work on gender borrows and amends Kristeva's idea of abjection and the abject in order to understand how viable subjects are produced. The constitution of 'normal' sexed and gendered subjects, Butler contends, is based upon the simultaneous creation of a 'domain of deauthorised subjects, pre-subjects, figures of abjection, populations erased from view'.[20] In other words, for certain kinds of people to be seen as normal and viable, others have to be treated as beyond the pale, as worthless or unintelligible. They have, that is, to be repudiated. Likewise, Iris Young utilises the notion of abjection in her account of justice to describe how the bodies of certain social groups come to be perceived as 'ugly or fearsome'. Abjection thus represents one of the ways in which groups are oppressed. 'Racism, sexism, homophobia, ageism and ableism, are', she contends, 'particularly structured by abjection'.[21] They represent what is unconsciously expelled in order for the dominant culture to operate. An adequate theory of justice needs, therefore, and here Young's approach is distinctive, to move beyond an exclusive focus on conscious or intended acts of injustice and oppression to one that can also encompass unconscious forms of behaviour, bodily reaction and unthinking aversion.

The second broad area of influence concerns Kristeva's discussion of the role of the stranger or foreigner in contemporary society. Given the influx of foreigners into many countries (through asylum seeking and immigration), one of the most pressing questions politically is how to accommodate or live with difference. This is a topic that has exercised much recent political theory. Kristeva offers a distinctive take on the question, applying her own insights about split subjectivity to the questions of nations and national identity. According to the logic of Kristeva's argument national identity, like any other form of identity, excludes certain things, which are then unconsciously projected onto strangers and foreigners. These excluded elements are, however, actually internal to national identity. Toleration for strangers thus requires tolerating the otherness within the national self. For Kristeva such toleration offers an ethical challenge (to recall our earlier discussion) to violence against the other. Whilst perhaps not as well used as her account of abjection (to which it is, of course, related), it suggests an alternative understanding of ethnicity, with implications for how nationalism is understood.

Notes

1. My references are to the version reprinted in Toril Moi (ed.), *The Kristeva Reader*, pp. 25–33.
2. Ibid., p. 25.
3. Ibid., p. 26.
4. Ibid., p. 28, original emphasis.
5. Oliver, *Reading Kristeva*, p. 3.
6. *Revolution in Poetic Language*, p. 30.
7. The signifier is the actual image, object, word or sound and the signified is the concept or idea with which the signifier is associated.
8. 'Julia Kristeva', p. 257.
9. *Powers of Horror*, pp. 1–2.
10. Ibid., p. 4.
11. Ibid., p. 1.
12. 'Stabat Mater', pp. 260, 261. One of the things that are most interesting about this essay is its typographical layout. The essay contains two texts: one that is theoretical and the other that is more personal and experiential. This uneasy juxtaposition of texts may be seen as a representation of the uneasy juxtaposition of the symbolic with the semiotic.
13. 'Women's Time', p. 206.
14. Fraser, 'Uses and Abuses', p. 190.
15. Chanter, 'Kristeva's Politics of Change', p. 183.
16. Fraser, 'Uses and Abuses', p. 189.
17. Leland, 'Lacanian Psychoanalysis', p. 131.
18. See her 'Women's Time'. It should be noted that this essay is concerned specifically with feminism in France, rather than with feminism as such.

19. Creed, 'Alien and the monstrous-feminine'.
20. Butler, 'Contingent Foundations', p. 13.
21. Young, *Justice and the Politics of Difference*, p. 145.

Major Works by Kristeva

About Chinese Women, trans. Anita Burrows (London: Marion Boyars, 1977 [1974]).

Black Sun: Depression and Melancholia, trans. Leon S. Roudiez (New York: Columbia University Press, 1989 [1987]).

Powers of Horror: An Essay in Abjection, trans. Leon S. Roudiez (New York: Columbia University Press, 1982 [1980]).

Revolt, She Said: An Interview by Philippe Petit (Los Angeles: Semiotext(e), 2002 [2002]).

Revolution in Poetic Language, trans. Margaret Waller, extract in Toril Moi (ed.), *The Kristeva Reader* (Oxford: Blackwell, 1986), pp. 90–136.

'Stabat Mater', in Julia Kristeva, *Tales of Love*, trans. Leon S. Roudiez (New York: Columbia University Press, 1987 [1983]), pp. 234–63.

Strangers to Ourselves, trans. Leon S. Roudiez (Hemel Hempstead: Harvester Wheatsheaf, 1991 [1988]).

'The System and the Speaking Subject', in Toril Moi (ed.), *The Kristeva Reader* (Oxford: Blackwell, 1986 [1973]), pp. 25–33.

'Women's Time', trans. Alice Jardine and Harry Blake, in Toril Moi (ed.), *The Kristeva Reader* (Oxford: Blackwell, 1986 [1979]), pp. 188–213.

Suggestions for Further Reading

Becker-Leckrone, Megan, 'Julia Kristeva', in Paul Hansom (ed.), *Dictionary of Literary Biography: Twentieth-Century European Cultural Theorists* (Farmington Hills, MI: The Gale Group, 2001), vol. 242, pp. 248–63. Useful overview of Kristeva's philosophical, psychoanalytic and literary writings.

Butler, Judith, 'Contingent Foundations: Feminism and the Question of "Postmodernism"', in Judith Butler and Joan W. Scott (eds), *Feminists Theorize the Political* (London: Routledge, 1992), pp. 3–21. This exacting article, although not explicitly about Kristeva, deploys the idea of the abject.

Chanter, Tina, 'Kristeva's Politics of Change: Tracking Essentialism with the Help of a Sex/Gender Map', in Kelly Oliver (ed.), *Ethics, Politics, and Difference in Julia Kristeva's Writings* (New York and London: Routledge, 1993), pp. 179–95. Excellent coverage of the debate around essentialism as it pertains to Kristeva.

Creed, Barbara, 'Alien and the Monstrous-Feminine', in Annette Kuhn (ed.), *Alien Zone: Cultural Theory and Contemporary Science Fiction Cinema*

(London: Verso, 1990), pp. 128–41. Utilisation of the concept of abjection for an understanding of horror film.

Fraser, Nancy, 'The Uses and Abuses of French Discourse Theories for Feminist Politics', in Nancy Fraser and Sandra Lee Bartky (eds), *Revaluing French Feminism: Critical Essays on Difference, Agency, and Culture* (Bloomington and Indianapolis: Indiana University Press, 1992), pp. 177–94. Extremely critical appraisal of, *inter alia*, Kristeva, which focuses on agency and politics.

Grosz, Elizabeth, *Sexual Subversions: Three French Feminists* (St. Leonards, NSW: Allen and Unwin, 1989). A comprehensive, if now slightly dated, introductory exploration of Kristeva, Irigaray and Le Doeuff that contextualises them in relation to modern French philosophy and to psychoanalysis.

Leland, Dorothy, 'Lacanian Psychoanalysis and French Feminism: Toward an Adequate Political Psychology', in Nancy Fraser and Sandra Lee Bartky (eds), *Revaluing French Feminism: Critical Essays on Difference, Agency, and Culture* (Bloomington and Indianapolis: Indiana University Press, 1992), pp. 113–35. A challenging account of the psychoanalytic dimensions of, *inter alia*, the thought of Kristeva, specifically with respect to the political potential of this work.

Oliver, Kelly, *Reading Kristeva: Unraveling the Double Bind* (Bloomington and Indianapolis: Indiana University Press, 1993). The most thorough assessment of Kristeva's work to date, though it doesn't deal with Kristeva's most recent writings.

Smith, Anne-Marie, *Julia Kristeva: Speaking the Unspeakable* (London: Pluto Press, 1998). A short, extremely sympathetic and accessible introduction to the work of Kristeva that integrates consideration of her writing, teaching and analytic practice.

Young, Iris Marion, *Justice and the Politics of Difference* (Princeton, NJ: Princeton University Press, 1990). Chapter 5, in particular, offers an adaptation of the idea of the abject in relation to group identity and oppression.

10

Jean-François Lyotard (1924–98)

Simon Tormey

Jean-François Lyotard is probably the most notorious of the so-called postmodernists. 'So-called' because the term postmodern as Lyotard means it is less a particular position or ideology with which one is supposed to identify (as the 'ist' in postmodernist would suggest) than the description of a mood or stance within the modern. More pointedly, it is a stance in relation to the idea of the modern as project, as period, as emblem, as 'a style of writing'. Nonetheless, it is true not only that Lyotard is the French thinker most readily associated with the term but also that he has encouraged that association by publishing a number of works in addition to *The Postmodern Condition* (*PMC*) in which he defended the concept, perhaps recognising that in 'postmodern times' notoriety guaranteed a certain kind of celebrity and, thereby, immortality.

Lyotard was born in Versailles, France, in 1924 and studied in Paris before taking up a variety of teaching posts including stints in Algeria and at the universities of Paris and Nanterre. It was the experience in Algeria in particular that radicalised the young Lyotard and encouraged him to become an activist in the ferment that was French left radical politics. In 1954 he joined the Socialisme ou Barbarie group whose other noteworthy members included Cornelius Castoriadis and Claude Lefort. The group, a neo-Trotskyite-cum-libertarian communist ensemble, was united beyond the opposition to 'bureaucratic' forms of organisation of the sort represented by the French Communist Party. After various disagreements, however, Lyotard left the group in 1963 and aligned

Jean-François Lyotard (1924–98)

himself with the Mouvement du 22 Mars which was to be closely associated with the May 1968 uprisings in Nanterre where Lyotard was a teacher. In the aftermath of 1968 he moved to the University of Vincennes where he was to produce some of his most startling and iconoclastic work, including most notably *Libidinal Economy* (*LE*). It was, however, during the late 1970s and early 1980s that he secured his global 'celebrity' with the more sober and measured analyses such as *PMC*, *The Differend* and *Just Gaming*. Towards the end of his life Lyotard joined that small band of intellectuals whose omniscience seemed to transcend the limitations of time and place. As well as continuing to write prodigiously he held a number of visiting positions in North America, remaining to his death in 1998 a model of the engaged intellectual.

Between the Real and Symbolic

Given the nature of Lyotard's political attachments in the 1950s and 1960s, his early work of this period seems barely 'political' in the sense of manifesting an obvious critique of the given. Yet, it becomes apparent (contra his leftist critics) that his entire oeuvre is intensely political, signalling as it does how and under what conditions critique and resistance can take place. This is a very 'French' kind of radicalism, which stems from the sense of complicity between the writer and the reader. It is a radicalism that holds that ideas matter and thus the defeat of one idea and its displacement by another has implications for political action, assuming for a moment that writing is discounted as a kind of praxis. Given the link between discourse and the political it is perhaps ironical to reflect that if there is a single thread running through Lyotard's work then this would be the centrality of the aesthetic over language and the 'word'. In Lyotard's first major work, *La Phenomenologie* (Phenomenology) published in 1954 Lyotard had, unfashionably, defended the notion associated with the work of Merleau-Ponty that perception cannot be reduced to language or symbolisation, and thus that there is a layer of reality prior to symbolisation and thus only accessible in some extra-linguistic fashion. This is not the same as the Lacanian view with which it has a tendency to be conflated, namely, that the Real is constructed via a 'failure' of language. The 'reality' in which Lyotard was interested was not an absence or 'lack' which could be construed through the gap between language and the world it seeks to 'represent'. Rather, he was interested in exploring the space between the perception of something and its symbolisation, the implication being that there were things we could perceive but not articulate: sensations, experiences and feelings that could not be reduced to words, but which might, in contrast, express themselves in art. Here we have a clue to the distinctiveness of Lyotard as a thinker which the appellations 'post-structuralist' or 'post-modernist' tend to obscure. Language, he wanted to say, is not all there is; and all there is could not be rendered in language. There were forms of experience and perception that eluded language and thus which underpinned the need for thinking of linguistic representation as somehow incomplete or limited. Such a view would of course bring him into conflict with the dominant intellectual fashion of the late 1950s and 1960s: the idea of language as co-existence with reality and thus of 'reality' as constructed via the 'play of signs'.

In *Discours, Figure,* his next major work, this problematising of what will become the basis of the post-structuralist approach to symbolisation is stated in more direct terms and indeed in terms that highlight the 'political' nature of the debate. Here, he argues that the world is constructed 'in language'; but – contra Derrida and others – in some sense the world resists reduction to language. There is always an excess or a layer, the 'figural', which resists symbolisation or, rather, which is prior to symbolisation. Thus, contra Lacan, he could not posit the unconscious as 'structured like a language', from which it would follow that the figural had little place in the 'structuring' of the unconscious, being merely a secondary influence. Instead, argued Lyotard, the unconscious had to be seen as primarily mediated by phantasy and by the deep flows of desire that lay within, flows that were more likely to 'escape' in the process of artistic production which on this view was less susceptible to manipulation and containment than discourse. It is on this ground that Lyotard, like many of his generation, was encouraged to invest considerable hope in art as a mode of resistance. Discourse could never shrug off its origin in a symbolic order that is always already mediated by the forces of repression. Art, in contrast, allows the subject to vent her frustrations on the world, to give 'voice' to that which would otherwise be sublimated or repressed. On this view resistance is not theorised as the posing of one social logic to another. Rather art becomes the political in the sense of a resistance to capital whose logic demands efficiency, orderliness, discipline. Here in germ are what were to become constants in the Lyotardian political refrain: the importance of art as a potential source of disruption to the given; the necessity for resistance in and for itself as opposed to the 'promise' contained within; and in particular the necessity for opposition to capitalism as a form of puritan 'counter-aesthetic'. All this was to be considered less the prelude to the construction of some other world, than the basis upon which the thinking 'after' of capitalism could take place. It was such ideas that formed the basis of the programme and activity of the Lyotardian 22 Mars group which made such an impact in the events of May 1968.

From Freud to Nietzsche: From Art to Life

In the wake of the trauma of 1968 the focus of Lyotard's energies was on the underlying structure of subjectivity in advanced capitalist society and the critical or emancipatory potential contained in the aesthetic. In *LE* this project came to full fruition albeit, so it seemed, at a price. Lyotard was later to describe *LE* as a 'scandalous' work and it is easy to see why he might, given the direction of his mature work. Stylistically, it is free flowing, unencumbered and mesmerising. It obeys few rules and endorses even fewer principles, oscillating wildly between (relatively) sober critique and flights of energetic fantasy. Ostensibly a fusion of currents from Marxism and Freudianism, *LE* is actually a highly original critique of both, going well beyond superficially similar works of 'synthesis' produced by earlier critical theorists such as Herbert Marcuse (*Eros and Civilisation*) and Erich Fromm (*The Fear of Freedom*). Underpinning the text is the same concern that one finds in Deleuze and Guattari's *Anti-Oedipus*, a similarly vigorous 'synthesis' that appeared within months of Lyotard's work. The problematic common to both books was, very generally, the place of desire in animating action. More specifically, both texts can be read as a postmortem on the nature and origins of May 1968, the common consensus being that the sociologically driven class analysis of Marxism was wholly inadequate for explaining why middle-class students led the rebellion rather than the *soi-disant* 'alienated' workers, the majority of whom seemed only too pleased to see 'authority' restored after the heady utopian days of 1968. Here, however, their analyses diverged.

Whilst Deleuze and Guattari attempt to delineate between positive, productive desire, desire which is not constituted as in Lacan as a 'lack', Lyotard insisted on the unity of desire as intensity. The underpinning assumption of Lyotard's analysis was that under advanced industrial conditions desire had become an analogue of capital (and vice versa). Just as capital valorises exchange, so the libidinal could be seen as a valorisation of intensity. Capital and desire were thus held to mirror each other in promoting the exchange of equivalents in an anonymous process of 'circulation' and 'flow' with the object of circulation regarded as accumulation in and for itself. In the case of capital this is an accumulation of money, in the libidinal economy an accumulation of intensity. All of which implied that there is no distinction to be made between desires or, more accurately, within desire. In Lyotard's view it was impossible to distinguish between, as Deleuze and Guattari put it, a 'fascistic' and an emancipated form of desire, but only between relative intensities. Just as capital is neutral in regards to what is circulated (butter, money or guns) so desire can be read as neutral with regard to intensity. Intensities cannot be read outside themselves but only in terms of the overall quantum of effects produced. The more intensity we experience, the better we 'feel'. The implication was that if we 'feel better' with de Gaulle than with Debord then there is nothing more to be said. Desire cannot in this sense be a false witness to itself. There is no inauthentic or alienated desire.

There is, at best, a very personal politics to be found here: seek that which enhances, which affirms one's own being in all its intensity. Seek not the transcendence of the given or some other redemption. *LE* thus endorsed the conclusion of the 'post-political' wing of Situationism. May 1968 on this reading was not the beginning of something new, any less than it was the end of some *dépassé* order of things. It was a moment, a pure 'event' or spectacle whose intensity for its participants (including Lyotard) had to be treasured for itself and for the feelings it induced, not because it pointed towards some possible 'space' beyond itself. This was May 1968 as the ultimate aesthetic experience, as the ultimate 'high'. *LE* was the consecration of the search for highs; but like most such quests it can be read as a markedly narcissistic and apolitical stance. Almost in spite of himself Lyotard had transcended what appeared at one level to be the aim of his critique, a reconciliation of Freud and Marx, finding himself instead in the midst of the nihilistic vitalism attributed to Bergson and Nietzsche.

LE thus marked the realisation of a particular conception of critique, of self, of the social. It was also, as he himself was to argue, a cul-de-sac on all these terms, necessitating some sort of turning back or recuperation of a critical perspective, even if this was not to be achieved by anything as grand as the elaboration of 'critique'. This, it quickly became apparent, was to be led by the concern for the very object that had so recently been surrendered in the baroque excess of *LE*, namely, justice. *LE*, as Lyotard later argued, was at best an apolitical text and at worst a deeply individualistic one. It was evidently this sense of a 'betrayal' of the political that convinced Lyotard of the necessity to turn away from his preoccupation with a libidinally focused politics of subjectivity towards a pluralistically centred philosophy of subjects which was to become the basis of the texts in the late 1970s and early 1980s. In contrast, what remains in the work that immediately follows *LE* is the sense of a final 'drift' from the problematic and form of critique associated with Marx and Freud towards Nietzsche who had loomed so dramatically in its unfolding (hence the title of one of Lyotard's works of the period *Derive à partir de Marx et Freud*, translated as *Driftworks*). Lyotard might have felt the need to temper the Nietzschean thrust of *LE*, but Nietzsche became an ever-more important figure in Lyotard's unbundling and repackaging of himself. What remained pertinent for Lyotard in Nietzsche is the suspicion of critique as grounded in the beyond or, worse, the 'above' of experience, of being, of life. This in turn brought him back into the orbit of Foucault, Deleuze and Guattari, who, like Lyotard, were convinced of the undesirability and indeed impossibility of 'total' critique of the form associated with Hegelian and Marxian discourse, favouring instead 'localised' strategies of resistance. The essays marking the transition from *LE* to *PMC* (most notably *Dispositif pulsionnel* and the 'pagan' writings) suggest that a total critique of the sort offered by Marx and his followers implied totalisation and the desire to dominate. Critique thus had to be informed by a sense of its own limitations and context, and the potential it contained for imperialism and the subjugation of the other. Critique had to be local, delimited and contingent. Above all, it had to acknowledge the speculative, incomplete and thus imperfect quality which Lyotard now attributed to the theoretical endeavour itself. Theory, Lyotard now held, could aspire to nothing more than *theorie-fiction*, a kind of writing that, in renouncing the claim to know, persuades by means of qualities other than writerly authority: style, playfulness, affirmation. Gone, in other words, is the drive to comprehend existence within some over-arching narrative. Gone too is the meta-politics of redemption, reconciliation, and an end to the struggles hitherto epitomising the human condition. From here onwards, localised forms of critique would support localised, plural, diverse forms of struggle and resistance.

Attractive though such a position may have been to a generation of intellectuals wearied by the sectarian battles which progressively divided and subdivided the Left, the difficulties of maintaining a politics built on the 'fact of plurality' haunted post-structuralism's attempt to translate itself from a theory of difference to a politics of resistance. Nietzsche, the dominant intellectual figure behind this rethinking of critique, was, ostensibly, unembarrassed about what the deconstruction of truth and authority meant in 'political' terms. For him, the exposure of the ground of authority as essentially fictive, and as a mask covering over the 'will-to-power', meant in turn an endorsement of a politics of power, strength, of the *aristoi*, in which the 'birds of prey' were indeed to be unleashed on the 'little lambs'. As Lyotard recognised, in order to save a 'minoritarian' politics of resistance from itself it could not rely upon something as flimsy as the goodwill of those engaged in the process of resistance. Such a politics had, rather, to be grounded on some-thing, and in particular on a notion of justice. It was this search for the ground of the just which animated the most important works of the 1980s, and in particular *Le Différend*.

From 'Pagan' to Postmodern

Before the question of justice, however, Lyotard needed to provide a more substantive basis for his account of the problems of grounding knowledge. The pagan works (*Rudiment Paiens*; *Instructions Paiennes*) are suggestive in this respect, but the conclusions of Lyotard's rumination on the ground of knowledge were only fully announced in *PMC*. As should be clear, once the project of a meta-theory of the subject had been shelved, as it was shortly after *LE*, Lyotard's thoughts turn to the status of theory more generally: what could be believed, what was authoritative, how did what we believe come to have established itself as believable? Lyotard's Nietzschean conclusions to the questions left him with the sense that what we believed we did so contingently, and certainly arbitrarily; moreover that what we believed we did so lightly. In short, we had become pagans: unconvinced of the necessity, let alone the desirability, for some bedrock of certainty beneath our contingently held opinions and beliefs.

In *PMC* the historical account of the decline in the basis of belief is conjoined with an analytical account underpinned by Wittgenstein's later philosophy in particular and a pragmatist account of language more generally. The issue concerning the origins of a decline in belief is supplemented by an account of why the problematisation of the ground of knowledge should be regarded as a logical development from the emergence of a pragmatist paradigm. The problem of 'foundations' should not be seen as a mere irrationalist response to a more general crisis of authority, but as an entirely reasonable stance grounded in developments elsewhere in the philosophical firmament. This move supplements the historical account that lies behind the double-meaning that 'postmodern' has in *PMC*. When Lyotard offers his now standard definition of 'postmodern' as 'incredulity towards metanarratives' what he has in mind is not merely that we have become incredulous towards metanarratives, but also that we ought to be incredulous towards them. 'Postmodern' is thus not a mere descriptor for a kind of scepticism that emerges in the course of modernity; it is also a philosophical and political position to be defended against those who would maintain the legitimacy and credibility of metanarratives in any particular domain of knowledge and discourse.

The historicised 'sense' of the term postmodern is relatively easily rendered. In Lyotard's view Enlightenment gave rise to an intense optimism about the degree to which increasing knowledge leads to increasing well-being, to the point where we can imagine an end to all obstacles to human flourishing and self-realisation. Science would empower the species to rise above its current miserable condition. As Lyotard sees it, this thesis requires us to believe in the infallibility of two propositions:

1. the status of science is something different to the status of any other form of discourse in that it is in some ultimate sense 'true'. This differentiates it from 'narrative' forms of discourse which are only true by virtue of the fact that a given group of people holds a particular story to be valid;
2. liberation can be equated to the realisation of some state of self-knowledge, to 'Absolute Spirit' in Hegelian terms. This requires us to think that the achievement of liberation is a 'scientific' undertaking as opposed to a narrative undertaking, in which 'being liberated' is akin to accepting certain contingent premises about the nature of the good life.

The problem as Lyotard sees it is that the claim of science to extra-narrative validity has been undermined as much from within the science camp as without, namely, by the development of new 'narrative'-based scientific disciplines (cybernetics, informatics) and also by the efforts of philosophers of science to explain the difference between science and other kinds of undertaking (Popper, Kuhn, Gödel). As Lyotard sees it, a consensus has now formed around the view that science needs some extra-scientific argument concerning the nature of truth to demonstrate that it is capable of supplying 'truths'. In this sense science is no different to any other kind of discourse in that it requires us to be predisposed to the kind of truths it seeks to develop. Without this predisposition, faith in the certainty and rationality of the undertaking will be lost. The 'postmodern condition' is thus a description of the progressive sense of loss of certainty experienced over the course of the previous two centuries.

More controversially, Lyotard defended this sense of incredulity by explaining why it was a rational response to the all-pervasive crisis he documented. Here he drew directly on the work of Wittgenstein, a thinker who would loom over much of his subsequent work. In Lyotard's view, Wittgenstein had convincingly shown in his later work (particularly *Philosophical Investigations*) that the function of language was not, as earlier philosophers (including himself) had held, to 'describe reality'. As Wittgenstein attempts to show, language does not have a function or a purpose as such. What we call 'language' is rather an infinite set of overlapping and distinct 'games' that we deploy in different contexts for all manner of purposes and uses. None of these games has an ultimate grounding in 'reality' such that we could say that some games are more 'real' or meaningful than others. It is the players of the game who determine the 'meaningfulness' of any given practice, belief or discourse.

Lyotard was evidently deeply struck by these insights and more generally by the contextualisation of language associated with the pragmatist turn in philosophy led in the Anglo-American context by Charles Peirce and John Dewey. Given the absence of an extra-narrative basis for legitimating forms of knowledge Lyotard falls back upon this rich contextualisation to provide an account of how some discourses come to be regarded as valid whereas others fall by the wayside. What seemed clear to Lyotard is that narrative validity is internally self-referential, which is to say that 'validity' is a description of a performative act of consent on behalf of those who are being asked to believe in the validity of a proposition. On this reading it would be legitimate to say 'witches can fly' if we can point to a community of people who accept the proposition that witches can in fact fly. It is irrelevant, in other words, whether such a group can demonstrate to others' satisfaction that (1) there are witches and (2) that they can fly – which would be the 'traditional' modernist demand. If such a group believe the 'narrative' then the narrative is 'true'. If we accept this account then it follows that truths are relative, contingent, 'local' and merely dependent on some sort of consensus for its 'validity' to be maintained. From this premise emerges an account of the 'postmodern' that is much more contentious than the mere description of a pervasive scepticism would otherwise allow, in that Lyotard argues that postmodernism represents a maturing of our stance vis-à-vis authority and truth more generally. Scepticism was not to be combated, but celebrated as a sign of our capacity to see the deeper meaning or significance in the production of knowledge. For his critics Lyotard seemed to be revelling in the chaos of authority, in the lack of ultimate referents and in the 'unholy' mess he documented (some would say unleashed). But then he was celebrating it, though his reasons for celebrating remained opaque and removed from the 'scene' of the initial opening in *PMC*. Lyotard's thesis was an extension of the Nietzschean perspectivism he had been advocating over the previous decade. The difference now was that unlike *LE* and the pagan writings, *PMC* was not only widely read, but widely read by an Anglo-American audience unused to the idea that the Emperor (science) lacked not only clothes, but subjects willing to avert their eyes from his evident nakedness.

Language Games and the Problem of Justice

In view of his own equanimity concerning the question of the postmodern, perhaps the examination of the condition of knowledge in modernity was intended merely to serve as a back-drop for those issues Lyotard considered genuinely compelling and relevant. These were the nature of the 'political' which he addressed directly in *Just Gaming* and *The Differend*; and also the nature of the sublime or incommunicable, which he discussed in his final major works *The Inhuman* and *Lessons in the Analytic and Sublime*. Although Lyotard went on to plough further the furrow of the 'postmodern', one senses that he did so in response to 'market' demand rather than because he felt there was anything interesting to add to the account in *PMC*. The genie had been let out of the bottle; but Lyotard, now at the height of his powers, was less interested in playing the genie than in looking for other bottles.

One of the paradoxes in considering the reception accorded to the idea of the postmodern was that the very quality others perceived to augur the death of the political was regarded by Lyotard as the condition upon which politics could now take place. In his view the earlier dominance of metanarratives as part of the self-understanding of the modern banished the political to the realm of irrational and unsightly behaviour. If science (or any other discourse claiming certainty for itself – such as Marxism) gave us 'insight' into the nature of the liberation to come then politics is reduced to the realisation of some foreordained path towards the 'rational society'. Surely this approach suffocated politics, denuding the political of the 'agonistic', contingent character that in turn stood for the human-all-too-human. Lyotard was trying to rescue politics from the hands both of those who would reduce it to a mere sub-domain of administration (such as systems theorists) and those who misguidedly saw consensus and the end of conflict as the goal of rational human endeavour (such as Jürgen Habermas).

In arguably his most impressive work, *The Differend*, Lyotard draws again on Wittgenstein and also Kant to show how such moves must be resisted. The core of the argument rests on similar premises to those articulated in *PMC*. This is to say, the realm of human activity is a realm of language games, of diverse and plural forms of engagement. Each 'game' has its own rules of conduct and norms of procedure, so that we can talk about different 'regimes' of activity governed by different systems of 'legislation'. Art criticism has one set of rules, international law has another, family disputes another and so on. Within each regime there are 'litigations' or disputes, the resolution of which is determined by an application of the pertinent rules in operation. If I say that this artwork is 'rubbish' then this calls for a justification in accordance with the rules and 'phrases' of art criticism ('it is poorly executed'; 'badly conceived'; 'kitsch'). Others may disagree or contest my judgement; but in order to do so effectively they too must remain within the domain of the litigation, which is to say the language and vocabulary of art criticism. As Lyotard argues, not all disputes have this litigious quality in which there is a certain agreement on the rules and phrases to be deployed. There are disputes that question the basis of the dispute itself and thus which concern the logic of what he terms 'the Idea' underpinning the particular activity in question. One example is the relationship between capital and labour. Many labour disputes can be resolved as a litigation in the sense that both parties tacitly endorse the basic legitimacy of the private ownership of the means of production. Labour thus presents its demands in a fashion that is consistent with the maintenance of the overall system rather than in terms that challenge it, that is, via the demand for more pay, better health-and-safety provision and so on. However, where labour confronts the right of ownership of capital then this indicates a different kind of dispute, one that points towards the legitimacy of capitalism itself. It is this kind of dispute that Lyotard terms a *differend*. This is a silence or brute incommensurability between regimes or Ideas each convinced of its own invincible view of the world. Here we have a clash of metanarratives, of holistic systems of thought or, as we would say today, 'fundamentalisms'. Such clashes cannot be resolved by mediation, compromise or an open-ended conversation, but on the imposition of a particular 'totality' or view of the world.

Merely to describe the character of a *differend* is to get a sense of the political import of the analysis for Lyotard. For him a world of competing differends is a world of mortal combat, not a world of reciprocity or respect for the other. This is the politics of ideologies, of redemption and damnation and ultimately of the Gulag and the concentration camp. To be postmodern in this political sense is to turn one's back on the 'totality', on total solutions to problems which by definition have an immediacy and a context that is excluded from the 'big picture'. As he puts it, 'the totality is not presentable'.[1] There is no Platonic Idea, no recourse or access to the grand narrative of redemption but only 'little narratives', local narratives of desert, merit, happiness and fulfilment for this person, this community. To ask for anything more is to deny that we are bounded, 'local', contextual creatures. It is to think of ourselves as gods, which as pagans we are now bound to resist. Lyotard found it more difficult to answer why we have to accept that liberal-capitalism provides a 'reasonable' or compelling basis for the playing out of these localised struggles. This would be the case if it could be shown that a 'radical democracy' of the sort he came to advocate in his later work mapped directly onto the institutions of liberal-democracy. But as he himself recognised, they do not and would not unless such institutions were themselves transformed on the basis of a rival Idea that posited the necessity for more open and participatory forms of engagement. In short, Lyotard's own political instincts seemed at odds with the conclusions of his 'political philosophy'.

Silence, Presence, Art

This idea of the ineffability of the *differend*, of the necessity and desirability of 'passing over in silence' is a refrain not only of Lyotard's politics but also of his aesthetics – if it makes sense to separate the two domains. In fact, the political and the aesthetic are closely tied in Lyotard's thought and remain so in his last major works *The Inhuman* and *Lessons on the Analytic and Sublime*. It is also in these works that Lyotard reminds us of the critical thrust of his approach, particularly as regards the pernicious and dehumanising character of capitalism and thus the importance of an active avant-garde to combat the worst excesses of commodification. In an echo of Marx, Lyotard describes the logic of capital in terms of 'gaining time'. Capital is constantly at war against the lag between idea and production, manufacture and commodity. It is thus at war with the human itself, since as bounded, finite creatures capable of 'only so much' we are in our very being an obstacle to the boundless energy of capital itself. Yet, in a gesture more reminiscent of Heidegger than Marx, Lyotard announces that art is a key weapon in the war against 'gaining time'. Modern art, in particular, is a game of questioning and thus implicitly of inducing the pause or lag. Art inserts itself into conversation, play, reflection where capital wishes to eliminate it. Art thus confronts capital since, as an example of a primarily 'useless' kind of activity (particularly in its conceptual, high-modernist guise), it queries the logic of gaining time over thought, critique, decision. Lyotard does not deny that art is itself a commodity and thus implicated in the fetish character of modern life; he merely wishes to restore the sense of the importance of an avant-garde in art which in turn means non-realist forms of art that inherently resist reproduction as commodity. The very irritation many feel at Tracy Emin's *Unmade Bed* is thus on a Lyotardian view an entirely compelling reason for regarding it as avant-gardist: it resists, it queries, it annoys, and thus evades reduction to the machine. And for those who stand irritated in its presence, it promotes the very thing capital seeks to extinguish: thought, reflection, laughter, as well as irritation.

Lyotard's defence of the Kantian concept of the sublime is premised on similar terms. The availability of the sublime, the ineffable, that which defeats representation, is seen by Lyotard as a form of resistance to the monochrome world of capital where everything can be subsumed within everything else and thus where the *differend* is in danger of erasure. In contrast to those who regard the 'postmodern' as characterised by the celebration of kitsch, or playfulness induced by the juxtaposition of style over 'substance', for Lyotard the postmodern is characterised by invention rather than nostalgia, by turning away from the reductive realism of transavant-gardism and its desire to contain the excess of what is genuinely avant-gardist, namely, that capacity to induce feelings of the sublime, the unspoken, the unrepresentable. Thus, far from being complicit in the reproduction of capital or merely the face of 'late capitalism', as Fredric Jameson argues,[2] Lyotard's view is that contemporary art can and does have a critical function in these otherwise compromised times. It must bear witness to that which cannot speak; it must induce thought, reflection on that which cannot be spoken; it must slow the passing of time. Above all, it must assert the primacy of the human over the dull, machinic reproduction of life to which we are all otherwise subjected.

Lyotard's Legacy

Lyotard seems condemned to be remembered for arguably his least likeable work, *PMC*, and for giving some intellectual substance to a term, the 'postmodern', that before his intervention could scarcely be regarded as a philosophical concept. Instead of a straw man to aim at, the defenders of modernity or the 'Enlightenment project' had a real person to focus their blows upon, who was, moreover, more than happy to trade punches with them. However, 'Lyotard' has himself become something of an empty signifier since the intellectual case he put forward seems to have become so bowdlerised as to be unrecognisable. Thus it is likely that his 'legacy' will live on (to paraphrase Habermas) in terms of the 'neo-conservative' thinker who 'surrendered' Enlightenment.[3] And of course there are many who wholeheartedly pour into the breach created by Habermas's high-profile assassination of Lyotard. Indeed one could say that where there is a leftist critique of the 'resignation' and 'complacency' of 'postmodernism' so the figure 'Lyotard' will inevitably form the centrepiece of the analysis.[4] One of the ironies that seems to have escaped the mountains of commentary on Lyotard is that he himself would be hostile to the excoriated figure of 'Lyotard'.

Lyotard rejected the idea that to 'be' postmodern meant to be resigned to the status quo; to defend uncritically the institutions of liberal-capitalism; to query or question the achievements of science in all its manifestations; to see the function of art as essentially the production of kitsch designed to dull our senses into conformity. Lyotard remained a critic of the time in which he lived, be it considered modern or postmodern.

Notes

1. Lyotard, *The Differend*, p. 95.
2. See the chapter on Jameson in this volume.
3. Jürgen Habermas, 'Modernity Versus Postmodernity', *New German Critique*, 22, 1981, pp. 3–14.
4. See, for example, Alex Callinicos, *Against Postmodernism* (New York: St. Martin's Press, 1990); and Chris Norris, *Reclaiming Truth: Contribution to a Critique of Cultural Relativism* (London: Lawrence & Wishart, 1996).

Major Works by Lyotard

Phenomenology, trans. B. Beakley (New York: SUNY Press, 1991 [1954]).

Discours, Figure (Paris: Klincksiek, 1971).

Libidinal Economy, trans. I. Hamilton Grant (London: Athlone 1993 [1974]).

The Postmodern Condition: A Report on Knowledge (Manchester: Manchester University Press, 1984 [1979]).

Just Gaming, trans. V. Godzich (Minneapolis: University of Minnesota Press, 1985 [1979]).

The Differend: Phrases in Dispute, trans. G. van den Abeele (Manchester: Manchester University Press, 1988 [1983]).

Lessons on the Analytic of the Sublime, trans. E. Rottenberg (Stanford: Stanford University Press, 1994 [1991]).

The Inhuman: Reflections on Time, trans. G. Bennington (Cambridge: Polity Press, 1991 [1988]).

Suggestions for Further Reading

Benjamin, Andrew (ed.), *Judging Lyotard* (London: Routledge, 1992). Insightful collection of critical essays.

Best, Steve, and Douglas Kellner, *Postmodern Theory: Critical Interrogations* (New York: Guilford Press, 1991). Critical yet informative summary of Lyotard's work and its relation to postmodern theory.

Browning, Gary, *Lyotard and the End of Grand Narratives* (Cardiff: University of Wales Press, 2000). Brief, well-written overview of Lyotard's main writings.

Dews, Peter, *Logics of Disintegration: Post-Structuralist Thought and the Claims of Critical Theory* (London: Verso, 1987). A valuable attempt to situate Lyotard's thought in relation to post-structuralism.

Williams, James, *Lyotard and the Political* (London: Routledge, 2000). A useful attempt at a 'rehabilitation' of Lyotard's thought generally and *Libidinal Economy* in particular.

11

Gilles Deleuze (1925–95) and Felix Guattari (1930–92)

Philip Goodchild

Introduction

Gilles Deleuze, while writing of Baruch Spinoza, once characterised the life of a philosopher as: 'a life no longer lived on the basis of needs, of means and ends, but according to a production, a productivity, a potency'.[1] Such was the thinking of both Deleuze and Guattari; moreover, the entire aim of their work, their teaching and their writing was to change perceptions so that others could live such a life.

For Félix Guattari, this was a life lived as a therapist among psychiatric patients at the clinic La Borde from 1953 until his death. Guattari had abandoned studies of pharmacology under the influence of Jean Oury, and together they co-founded the clinic. In the early years, Guattari underwent a training analysis with Jacques Lacan, but his therapeutic practice and experience led him towards a critique of psychoanalysis, replacing it with 'schizoanalysis', an analysis of institutional and subjective structures that takes seriously the perspectives of schizophrenics. Of equal importance to his anti-psychiatric activities were his political activities, where he was involved in a number of experimental left-wing and ecological political groups and publications. Guattari's emergence as a prominent critical theorist, however, came after his encounter and collaboration with Deleuze in 1969.

Deleuze, by contrast, was an academic historian of philosophy. His early work reacted against the formal philosophical curriculum of post-war France which concentrated on Hegel, Husserl and

Gilles Deleuze (1925–95) and Felix Guattari (1930–92)

Heidegger, for Deleuze was heavily influenced by the empiricist David Hume and the philosopher of science, Henri Bergson. A profound encounter with the work of Friedrich Nietzsche led to the publication in 1962 of *Nietzsche and Philosophy*, a defining moment for the French re-appropriation of Nietzsche and the emergence of post-structuralism. Deleuze's most enduring philosophical influence, however, was Spinoza, on whom Deleuze published his professorial dissertation, *Expressionism in Philosophy: Spinoza*, in 1969. Deleuze's two main philosophical texts 'in his own name' were published around the same time, *Difference and Repetition* in 1968 and *The Logic of Sense* in 1969. A notable break occurred in his writing from this time onwards: in the aftermath of the popular uprising of May 1968, when Deleuze was appointed as a professor at the experimental department of philosophy at Paris Vincennes, Deleuze and Guattari met and began collaborating. Their writing adopted an experimental and eclectic style, constructing a new philosophy involving a prodigious invention of concepts.

The first major collaborative publication was the *Anti-Oedipus* in 1972, an attack on the alliance between psychoanalysis and capitalism, which embodied the spirit of May 1968 and became a bestseller and dominant influence in radical French thought in the early 1970s. During this time, Deleuze and Guattari were close friends with Michel Foucault, and there was much cross-fertilisation of ideas. A change in French politics and fashions, however, meant that their second major collaboration, *A Thousand Plateaus* in 1980, was less well received. Each undertook independent work during the 1980s: Deleuze published a major innovative study on the cinema, while Guattari continued to develop the theory of schizoanalysis. They came together for a final collaboration with *What Is Philosophy?* in 1991. Subsequent to their deaths, Deleuze is one of the few radical French intellectuals of the second half of the twentieth century to retain the status in France of a significant philosopher, while Guattari is remembered as one of the few radical activists who remained committed to social change. Together, their work anticipated the discoveries of complexity theory in science as well as the loosely associated forms of political action that characterise 'anti-globalisation' protestors, lending it an enduring and growing influence.

The New Materialism

In their whole way of thinking, Deleuze and Guattari project an image of a positive, affirmative life which stands in opposition to the semblances produced by human consciousness, for in order to comprehend the human relation with matter, as well as human society and culture, they offer a new materialism that does not start from an imposition of human values, meaning and culture upon material processes, but explores the role of material processes in the formation of the 'three ecologies' of environment, society and subjectivity. At the start of the third millennium, we are acutely aware of human limits, as well as the limits of humanism. Three elements characterise the modern Western attempt to dominate the unruly forces of nature: the scientific revolution aimed to extract the ideal form of physical law from the behaviour of matter, in order to subject matter to abstract prediction and control; the technological-industrial revolution aimed to subject production to the force of the combustion of preserved organic power, together with management by rational recording, calculus and communication, in order to maximise efficiency and output; and the capitalist and free-market revolutions aimed to liberate human choice from subordination to traditional or natural ends. In each of these domains, the progress of humanism has run up against insuperable limits. The new sciences of chaos and complexity demonstrate how the behaviour of matter frequently exceeds all powers of prediction. The ecological crisis demonstrates how economic production is dependent upon a broader framework of ecological cycles to supply its resources and absorb its waste, cycles which can easily become unstable. The globalisation of the capitalist free-market economy demonstrates how social and personal choices are governed by autonomous processes driven by debt, profit and control of consumer desire, rather than ordered by humane values and a substantive rationality.

The slogan of this new materialism or affirmation of life is that 'life is not determined by consciousness, but consciousness by life'.[2] It takes from Marx the notion that laws, institutions and consciousness are directly interwoven with the material activity through which they are generated and sustained. The link between matter and thought is no longer one of representation, whereby thought conforms to the essence of matter, or domination, whereby matter is conformed to the essence of thought; it is one of production,

Gilles Deleuze (1925–95) and Felix Guattari (1930–92)

whereby human and material activity contribute to the existence of specific arrangements of thought and matter. The new materialism takes from Freud the notion that the production of thought is not driven by representations of ideals and goals, or libertarian choice, but by a pre-personal process of desire. Belief in the sovereignty of subjective consciousness or its products is undermined in favour of the interventions of an unconscious. The new materialism takes from Nietzsche the notion that each body or product is a synthesis of forces, a sign or symptom of a mode of existence. Desire is never something that is missing, forbidden, or signified: desire is a power of synthesis that constructs an assemblage in order to increase its power of acting. The new materialism takes from Spinoza an ethics and ontology of power: power that delimits, inhibits, or represses always diminishes life and produces sadness, whereas power that adds new possibilities of life always enhances life and produces joy. The new materialism takes from Bergson the idea that life is manifested in tendencies towards differentiation and creation, and the role of thought is to understand such tendencies through science, philosophy and art.

What is important to appreciate about such a materialism is its self-distancing not only from phenomenological and existential philosophies of the subject but also from the cultural-linguistic turn of later twentieth-century thought characteristic of most critical theory. An appeal to matter may seem naive from the point of view of a historical consciousness that regards all knowledge as either produced by the interpretations of an intentional subject, or produced through the possibilities of meaning provided by language and culture. Such an approach to critique, however, depends on an image of thought as representation: the theorist speaks on behalf of a common sense, a generalisation of the perspective of a specific epoch, culture or minority. It relies on a model of thought as recognition, or the good sense whereby thought naturally approaches the true when a perspective identifies its objects, senses and values. There are two central weaknesses here. In the first place, representation cannot attain the real forces that form thought as such; it ignores or disciplines the thoughts of individuals to produce the conformity of a generalisation. In the second place, recognition cannot produce any new senses and values; it focuses on being, overlooking the becoming through which everything comes into being. Deleuze and Guattari distance themselves from a conception of thought as communication of opinions based on affections and perceptions, the 'Western democratic, popular conception of philosophy as providing pleasant or aggressive dinner conversations at Mr Rorty's'.[3]

Critique, for Deleuze and Guattari, is a clinical practice which aims at the liberation of life. For life is constrained by human consciousness and institutions to the extent that the means of production, whether of thought, practices, or artifacts, are separated from the process and work of production and held constant. When our concepts aid us to think through and tackle our problems, then they enhance life. Yet when new problems emerge, our old concepts may inhibit our ability to address them. New concepts and new ways of thinking are required: philosophy enhances our powers of thinking, living and acting because it consists in the creation of concepts.[4] The method of critique, therefore, in no sense consists in an outright rejection of dominant institutions, patterns of thought, or representative senses and values; these may dissipate under their own lack of force. In this respect, Deleuze and Guattari distance themselves from much critical theory which relies on a dialectical method to produce a critical perspective based on the negation of a prior one. For negation produces the illusion of progress; in reality, it adds nothing to what it negates. Revolution, in both thought and politics, proceeds through an enterprise of demystification that is accompanied by escape and creation:

> To criticize is only to establish that a concept vanishes when it is thrust into a new milieu, losing some of its components, or acquiring others that transform it. But those who criticize without creating, those who are content to defend the vanished concept without being able to give it the forces it needs to return to life, are the plague of philosophy. All these debaters and communicators are inspired by *ressentiment*. They speak only of themselves when they set up empty generalizations against one another. Philosophy has a horror of discussions. It always has something else to do. Debate is unbearable to it, but not because it is too sure of itself. On the contrary, it is its uncertainties that take it down other, more solitary paths.[5]

Deleuze and Guattari simply leave behind a large proportion of the philosophical debates and concepts of their era; citations of the main positions of their contemporaries are comparatively rare. Inspired by Nietzsche's evaluation of becoming above being, and Bergson's differentiation of a time of flow and process from a time cut up into fixed instants, modelled on space, they develop a way of 'thinking otherwise'. Thought no longer cuts up matter simply

Gilles Deleuze (1925–95) and Felix Guattari (1930–92)

according to its own categories of species, genera and organisms; thought no longer expresses the states of the human subject according to its perceptions, affections and opinions. Philosophy will no longer be modelled on the grammatical structure of the sentence, concerned with propositions about what is the case, or the linguistic structure of the signifier, concerned with the conditions of possibility of meaning. The image of thought is no longer based on the hierarchical model of a tree. For such approaches to thought simply reproduce established senses and values through representation and recognition, senses and values which gain their significance from something transcendent to thought. Instead, Deleuze and Guattari construct philosophy upon a plane of immanence, composed of signs, events, intensities, multiplicities and folds, where there are no fixed identities or totalities. Concepts are simply composed of other concepts, and respond to problems. Instead of a tree, Deleuze and Guattari appeal to a rhizome (unfortunately, they have borrowed the wrong word, but one should think of the spreading of couch grass or a fungal mycelium), characterised by connection, heterogeneity, multiplicity, asignifying rupture, cartography and experimentation.[6]

There is a massive revolution in thought effected here. It is one thing to think of events and processes; it is another to make thought into an event or process. It is one thing to turn from the objects of thought to the structures that make meaning possible; it is another to make meaning possible. While many of Deleuze and Guattari's contemporaries were concerned with the location of thought in history, temporality, structure, textuality and culture, few took the more radical step of turning thought into a becoming that responds to a sensation. A new set of problems and a new field for thought emerges. The life of matter, and what it makes us feel through sensation, has a direct impact upon thought, and thought is liberated to respond to the life of matter.

Capitalism and Schizophrenia

Nowhere is the activity of critique as demystification expressed more powerfully than in the *Anti-Oedipus*. Here, Deleuze and Guattari develop a concept of desire liberated from our representations in terms of an object that we want or something a subject lacks: to desire is to assemble. As Deleuze says, one never desires simply a person or an object, but an entire scenario: a skirt, a sun ray, a street, a woman, a vista, a colour. One desires, not simply another person, but a landscape, a possible world, an episode, or a mode of existence expressed through that person. In *Anti-Oedipus*, Deleuze and Guattari speak of 'desiring-machines' composing the unconscious: these are not mechanistic, but assemblages that function, producing a flow. This concept of desire arises from the problem of schizophrenia: what desire is manifested in the delirium of schizophrenics? This is a problem that psychoanalysis has never been able to answer. The solution of schizoanalysis is to reject the psychoanalytic postulate that the unconscious functions as a theatre of representation, whereby desire is formed around objects of conscious representation or the structure of language, through which 'normal' and 'neurotic' desire can be described. Instead, the unconscious is treated as a factory that produces intensities, and the representations of desire result from a process of repression that stops the movement. Whereas psychoanalysis tends to interpret all fantasy material in relation to infancy, the family, or the oedipal structure of repression, the desire expressed in schizophrenic delirium relates to everything: history, geography, tribes, races, climates.

At stake in Deleuze and Guattari's attack on Oedipus is far more than a revision of psychoanalysis. The figure of Oedipus, whether considered as a real family romance, a myth, or a signifying structure, embodies the way in which authority, repression, power and desire were conceived and configured within French post-war intellectual culture. This was not simply a matter of intellectual fashion, any more than explaining one's psychological make-up by childhood relations with one's parents is all simply illusion. Deleuze and Guattari argue that the social form of the nuclear family, specific to capitalism, isolated infants so that little other than parents were available for childhood fantasy. The oedipal family prepares the child for integration into society, where the desire for pleasure is a repetition of one's desire for one's mother, and the reality-principle that postpones pleasure is embodied in the authority of one's father. Those who successfully resolve the oedipal complex through castration of their productive power become obedient citizens who will work for an employer so as to attain the fulfilment they are permitted. Those who do not resolve the complex by themselves become neurotic, requiring psychoanalysis to aid in their adaptation to society.

Deleuze and Guattari do not simply object to psychoanalytic

interpretations of the oedipal complex, but to the current of intellectual fashion running from structuralism to postmodernism. For the structuralist revolution assumes that all is interpretation, or else that everything corresponds to the semiology of language. The result is a generalised logic of the equivalence of perspectives, where only fashion, consensus, the market or the media can control opinion, leading to ethical and aesthetic abdication. Guattari's objection is that the material dimensions of life, such as its ethological, ecological, economic, aesthetic and corporeal components, do not function like the semiology of language: formations of subjectivity, society and environment are primarily non-linguistic.[7] Then Deleuze and Guattari call for a breath of fresh air, and a relation with the outside: 'A schizophrenic out for a stroll is a much better model than a neurotic lying on the analyst's couch.'[8] They move on to produce a political analysis that is not dependent on ideology, on states of opinion, or the structure of language. For it became evident after May 1968, when the Gaullist regime was re-elected, that people understood a repressive formation all too well, but actively desired it. Responding to the problem posed by Spinoza and Wilhelm Reich, 'Why do men fight for their servitude as stubbornly as though it were their salvation?', Deleuze and Guattari trace the libidinal forces operating within politics in terms of paranoia and schizophrenia.[9] Fascism is paradigmatic here, not simply because of its historical proximity, but because they regard it as a movement that emerged from the masses without being imposed from above. Everybody has their own paranoia, their own love of repressive authority, their own resentment of others judged as bad, in contrast to which one identifies oneself as good. Each different, 'molecular' paranoia resonates with all the others, adding up to a 'molar' aggregate of fascism as a large-scale political organisation. Since we all have our own Oedipus, our internalisation of imperialism that has colonised our subjectivity, then the potential for fascism is continually reproduced within capitalism, and microfascism may be encountered anywhere. Political formations do not arise from molar aggregates of states, classes, sexes and armies, so much as from molecular aggregates of gestures, manners of speaking, habits, obligations and expectations through which desire is expressed and reproduced.

These individual, molecular actions and intentions are less significant for their content than for the kind of desire expressed through them. Here, Deleuze and Guattari make a move that parallels the structural revolution and the work of Foucault: formations of power may be distinguished according to their organisation, and the way in which they produce representations. Several points need bearing in mind here. First, at the time that structuralism was turning to mathematics for formulae to express the constant relations of exchange that it discovered, Deleuze was studying the philosophy of mathematics, including in particular differential calculus. Instead of being concerned with scientific functions that describe the behaviour of individuals within the structure of society, Deleuze was concerned with a logic of events composed of multiple rates of change or differentials measured in relation to each other. For example, if a population increases at a certain rate, then it may pass a threshold beyond which an entire system changes.[10] Organisation is at a virtual level, beneath that of individuals, where it is composed of tendencies and their relations of connection, intersection and disjunction.

Second, Deleuze's logic of difference is not simply concerned with the mathematics of change in extension: it is also based on Bergson's philosophy of the virtual where time is distinguished from space. Deleuze distinguished three 'passive syntheses' of time as tendencies or movements of time itself: a tendency to repetition as habit or obligation, a tendency to preserve the past as memory, and a tendency towards change.[11] These tendencies can be marked or represented by codes, territories and lines of flight, respectively, and such codes, territories and lines of flight map the social unconscious, the sites and paths of desire.

Third, Deleuze and Guattari's theory of affects and intensity is not simply concerned with forces and tendencies as such, but in evaluating their modes of composition. Their social analysis of power and desire is based on Nietzsche's genealogy of morals, related to active and reactive forces, social identity and economy. There is an ethology of desire expressed through modes of social formation.

Fourth, for Deleuze and Guattari, 'thinking takes place in the relationship of territory and the earth'.[12] The earth is 'the primitive, savage unity of desire and production', not merely an object of labour or the precondition of all production, but the precondition of representation, the 'surface upon which the whole process of production is inscribed', where the divisions of production and appropriation are inscribed as so many territories.[13] Thought has a direct relation with its social milieu, from which its territory is drawn, and in relation to which it draws lines of deterritorialisation towards an absolute plane of immanence or 'Nature-thought'.

Deleuze and Guattari's analysis of capital invokes each of the preceding dimensions in the successive layers from which it is composed. Building on Marx's periodisation of history into tribal societies, barbarian empires, and capitalist civilisation, they distinguish between differing social formations. Instead of regarding society as a milieu of exchange or circulation, however, they regard it as 'a socius of inscription where the essential thing is to mark or be marked'.[14] For the creation of the social as appropriation or inscription occurs through marking as the creation of debt. Whether it is the coding of flows of production and the assigning of tasks, the collective investment of organs with desire, or the direct marking of bodies to designate social status and role of a member of a tribe, the essential feature is an inscription that creates debt. For the production of a painful mark is also the production of an expectation of repetition, 'a surplus value of code': debt is not owed to those who give, but to those who take. That such debt is inequitable, and thus constitutes an unstable and unworkable basis for society, is precisely the point: social machines only work by breaking down. Tribal societies, ordered around kinship alliances and filiations, must constantly ward off the appearance of an emperor who possesses all, while also warding off the threat of decoded flows. Yet the network of alliances and filiations takes place in a territory, where the earth appears as the undivided source of all life; because of the limitations of locality, an emperor can only emerge from without, as a deterritorialised body.

This next stage of social organisation is characterised by a different mode of representation: tribal society is overcoded to be incorporated into an empire. Its gods, names and language are translated into those of the empire; its territory is owned by the State, divided up and apportioned; its flows of production are appropriated as tribute or taxes; its collective fantasy is invested in the body of the emperor. None of this would be possible without the invention of writing, a new, deterritorialised form of inscription whose locality and surface are irrelevant to the chains of signifiers. Instead, signifier refers to signifier, and all signifiers centre on the name of the emperor. The emperor replaces the earth as the apparent source of all production by virtue of his power to issue law, a form of writing which appears to issue from a transcendent voice. Production may be subject to prohibitions and permissions; in the form of science, law is extracted as the essence of production itself. This imperial power is especially evident in the creation of money. Money may be created by emperors for distribution, including the cancellation of debts, before being reclaimed in the form of taxes. Thus production and exchange are no longer oriented around the primitive social machine, but around a debt of gratitude to the emperor. Nevertheless, the imperial regime of the State is perpetually threatened by the escape of decoded and deterritorialised flows.

A meeting between decoded and deterritorialised flows provides the opportunity for the emergence of the capitalist social machine. The capitalist social machine begins when money begets money, and money replaces the State as the apparent source of all production. Money only gains this power when it becomes industrial capital, allied to the commodified labour of deterritorialised workers who have left their land and place in society as a result of enclosure, poverty or aspiration. Capitalism thrives on decoded and deterritorialised flows, whether of workers, money, technological invention or consumer desire. Nevertheless, it is entirely dependent on the State to enforce laws of property and the market, just as it is dependent on a more primitive coding and localisation of labour; capital builds on the previous regimes. Yet while previous regimes of representation may be operated by the social machine of capital, the social machine of capital itself has no intrinsic meaning. Deleuze and Guattari distinguish between two forms of money: 'alliance capital', merchants' capital that is used for payment in exchange, and 'filiative capital', industrial capital that is used in finance and investment:

> [I]t is not the same money that goes into the pocket of the wage earner and is entered on the balance sheet of the commercial enterprise. In the one case, there are impotent money signs of exchange value, a flow of means of payment relative to consumer goods and use values, and a one-to-one relation between money and an imposed range of products ('which I have a right to, which are my due, so they're mine'); in the other case, signs of the power of capital, flows of financing, a system of differential quotients of production that bear witness to a prospective force or to a long-term evaluation, not realizable *hic et nunc*, and functioning as an axiomatic of abstract quantities.[15]

There is a new mode of representation at work here, whereby abstract quantities are related to each other via differential rates and equations. If the relation between abstract quantities seems

Gilles Deleuze (1925–95) and Felix Guattari (1930–92)

arbitrary in the first instance, an axiom can be invented which determines the starting points of the calculation. The essential move, in this dissimulation of two kinds of money, is the conversion of a surplus value of code (excess production) into a surplus value of flux (increase in capital). This is enough

> to ensure that the Desire of the most disadvantaged creature will invest with all its strength, irrespective of any economic understanding or lack of it, the capitalist social field as a whole. Flows, who doesn't desire flows, and relationships between flows, and breaks in flows? – all of which capitalism was able to mobilize and break under these hitherto unknown conditions of money.[16]

Who doesn't desire the conversion of all things into gold, and an increase in money? Under these conditions, production, recoding and reterritorialisations will be produced, all for the purpose of maximising profits. There is no intrinsic location of power in this field of immanence of desire, although the whole system passes through the banks who control the conversion of the two kinds of money; even here, the mass of economic transactions, the desiring flow of money, escapes the power of the banks.[17] There is no limit to production, for mechanisms for the massive absorption of production, mechanisms of antiproduction such as advertising, civil government, militarism and imperialism can restore lack and the demand for production. There is no limit to capitalism, no tendency to the falling rate of profit, for abstract quantities of credit are separate from the mass of economic transactions; recessions and depressions are good for the capitalist economy, for unemployment weakens the position of labour with respect to capital. Capital is the social machine that works by breaking down. Only as such can it inject lack back into desire, and demand back into production.

There is, however, an exterior limit to capital: the conjunction of decoded and deterritorialised flows may produce their own desiring-machines, external to capitalist production. This process of desire which Deleuze and Guattari name 'schizophrenia', while protesting that they have never seen a schizophrenic, is composed simply of populations, intensities, abstract quantities and lines of flight. Schizoanalysis, then, is a form of social analysis according to abstract machines, lines of flight or deterritorialisation, regimes of signs, the stratification of molecular elements or their destratification, and planes of consistency. It maps the social unconscious according to its movements and intensities of desire. For the purpose of such mapping is no longer to identify or interpret the capitalist system, but to map its dominant strata, so that lines of experimentation or becoming may be constructed through a reassembling of the abstract machines that lie between the strata and produce them. There is no definite political programme here, but merely an attempt to transform subjectivity, society and ecology through collective experimentation with production and desire. This is the task accomplished in *A Thousand Plateaus*, which is so strange in tone and in prodigious invention of concepts that it admits of no simple summary.

Critical Assessments, Applications and Developments

Many critical assessments of the work of Deleuze and Guattari miss the nature of their thought and the modality of their discourse, and thus fail to engage with their project. It is difficult to engage with a body of thought that repudiates judging on the basis of its escape from representation and recognition:

> Judging is the profession of many people, and it is not a good profession, but it is also the use to which many people put writing. Better to be a road-sweeper than a judge ... It is the same in philosophy as in a film or a song: no correct ideas, just ideas ... You should not try to find out whether an idea is just or correct. You should look for a completely different idea, elsewhere, in another area, so that something passes between the two which is neither in one nor the other.[18]

It is not surprising, therefore, that Deleuze and Guattari have been repudiated by those who wish to maintain the significance of representation and recognition, especially by feminists and minority groups who struggle for rights.[19] Similarly, those who seek a more concrete social and historical analysis, or a more specific political project, may be disappointed by Deleuze and Guattari. A further line of criticism comes from those who fasten onto Deleuze's retrieval of the concept of the 'univocity of Being' from scholasticism, and thus accuse Deleuze of either a 'monism of desire' or else an ascetic monotonousness whereby the immense variety of cases are all taken as illustrations of the single ontological proposition: Being is univocal.[20] That these are 'erroneous' readings of Deleuze and Guattari, insofar as they miss the sense produced, is in itself significant: that such erroneous readings should be possible suggests that 'the illusions of transcendence' arise 'like vapours from a pond',[21] and a continual effort is required to dispel them.

This suggests a more subtle critical angle: that in attempting to confine philosophy to the 'creation of concepts', Deleuze and Guattari restrict the function of philosophy more narrowly than the modes of thinking they employ, which include reference to specific abstract machines, practical assessments of when it is best to escape, the selection of problems to consider, and the expression of affects and percepts within thought. Although Deleuze and Guattari maintain that philosophy must be embedded within and utilised by a nonphilosophy, some of the specific distinctions which they construct are somewhat arbitrary. A more direct challenge to their work is to claim that its concentration on differential functions, intensities and abstract lines concedes too much to capitalist representation, of which it is a product, and which it will reproduce: every line of escape offers the opportunity of recapture. Thus its affirmative and ascetic ethos, derived from Spinoza and Nietzsche, is only acquired at the cost of eliminating alternative possibilities of 'thinking otherwise'.

Deleuze and Guattari's work has been frequently applied in cultural and aesthetic criticism, particularly film and literature, to which it lends itself very well, not least in virtue of the numerous studies produced by Deleuze himself.[22] Similarly, it has also been applied in the study of information, virtual reality and artificial life, because of its concern with materialism and the mechanics of the production of representation. There has been some appropriation of their work by feminists, although this has usually been ambivalent, particularly in regard to the loss of the identity of 'woman' in favour of singularities and becomings.[23] In terms of a significant project that takes off from their work, two have recently achieved prominence: Manuel DeLanda's work on rethinking history and ontology in terms of populations, rates of change and complexity theory is very effective and original.[24] It shows the possibility of drawing on Deleuze and Guattari to provide an ontology for the new sciences of the twenty-first century. Michael Hardt and Antonio Negri's work, by contrast, builds on the Marxist political analysis of Deleuze and Guattari to construct a materialist analysis of empire and biopolitics, advocating resistance by the 'multitude' of differing groups and special interest movements. It draws out the contemporary relevance of Deleuze and Guattari's work in the era of globalisation.[25]

Notes

1. Deleuze, *Spinoza: Practical Philosophy*, trans. Robert Hurley (San Francisco: City Lights, 1988), p. 3.
2. Karl Marx, *The German Ideology*, in Christopher Pierson (ed.), *The Marx Reader* (Cambridge: Polity Press, 1997), p. 99.
3. Deleuze and Guattari, *What Is Philosophy?*, p. 144.
4. Deleuze and Guattari, *What Is Philosophy?*, p. 5.
5. Deleuze and Guattari, *What Is Philosophy?*, pp. 28–9.
6. Deleuze and Guattari, *A Thousand Plateaus*, pp. 3–25.
7. Guattari, 'The Postmodern Impasse', in *The Guattari Reader*, pp. 109–17.
8. Deleuze and Guattari, *Anti-Oedipus*, p. 2.
9. Deleuze and Guattari, *Anti-Oedipus*, p. 29.
10. Deleuze, *Difference and Repetition* and *The Logic of Sense* develop this mathematical logic of multiplicities, differentials and events. Manuel DeLanda's recent commentary is an excellent exposition of the significance and relevance of this dimension of Deleuze's thought.
11. See Deleuze, *Difference and Repetition*. Dorothea Olkowski gives an excellent account of this aspect of Deleuze's thought.
12. Deleuze and Guattari, *What Is Philosophy?*, p. 85.
13. Deleuze and Guattari, *Anti-Oedipus*, pp. 140–1.
14. Deleuze and Guattari, *Anti-Oedipus*, p. 142.
15. Deleuze and Guattari, *Anti-Oedipus*, p. 228.
16. Deleuze and Guattari, *Anti-Oedipus*, p. 229.
17. Deleuze and Guattari, *A Thousand Plateaus*, p. 226.
18. Deleuze, *Dialogues*, p. 8.
19. See, for example, Alasdair MacIntyre, *Three Rival Versions of Moral Enquiry* (London: Duckworth, 1990), or Rosi Braidotti, *Patterns of Dissonance* (Cambridge: Polity, 1991).
20. See Alain Badiou, *Deleuze: The Clamor of Being*, trans. Louise Burchill (Minneapolis: University of Minnesota Press, 2000 [1997]).
21. Deleuze and Guattari, *What Is Philosophy?*, p. 49.
22. See, for example, Barbara M. Kennedy, *Deleuze and Cinema* (Edinburgh: Edinburgh University Press, 2000), and Gregg Lambert, *The Non-Philosophy of Gilles Deleuze* (London: Continuum, 2002).
23. See Olkowski, *Gilles Deleuze and the Ruin of Representation*.
24. See Manuel DeLanda, *A Thousand Years of Nonlinear History* (New York: Zone, 1997), and *Intensive Science and Virtual Philosophy* (London: Continuum, 2002).
25. See Hardt and Negri, *Empire*.

Gilles Deleuze (1925–95) and Felix Guattari (1930–92)

Major Works by Deleuze and Guattari

Anti-Oedipus, trans. Robert Hurley, Mark Seem and Helen R. Lane (London: Athlone, 1984 [1972]).

Kafka: Towards a Minor Literature, trans. Dana Polan (London: Athlone, 1986 [1975]).

A Thousand Plateaus, trans. Brian Massumi (London: Athlone, 1988 [1980]).

What Is Philosophy? trans. Graham Burchill and Hugh Tomlinson (London: Verso, 1994 [1991]).

Some Major Works by Deleuze

Nietzsche and Philosophy, trans. Hugh Tomlinson (London: Athlone, 1983 [1962]).

Proust and Signs, trans. Richard Howard (London: Continuum, 2000 [1964, rev. 1971]).

Bergsonism, trans. Hugh Tomlinson and Barbara Habberjam (New York: Zone, 1988 [1966]).

Expressionism in Philosophy: Spinoza, trans. Martin Joughin (New York: Zone, 1990 [1968]).

Difference and Repetition, trans. Paul Patton (London: Athlone, 1994 [1968]).

The Logic of Sense, trans. Mark Lester and Charles Stivale, ed. Constantin V. Boundas (London: Athlone, 1990 [1969]).

Dialogues, with Claire Parnet, trans. Hugh Tomlinson and Barbara Habberjam (London: Continuum, 2002 [1977, rev. 1995]).

Cinema 1: The Movement-Image, trans. Hugh Tomlinson and Barbara Habberjam (London: Athlone, 1986 [1983]).

Cinema 2: The Time-Image, trans. Hugh Tomlinson and Robert Galeta (London: Athlone, 1989 [1985]).

The Fold: Leibniz and the Baroque, trans. Tom Conley (London: Athlone, 1993 [1988]).

Some Major Works by Guattari

Molecular Revolution, trans. Rosemay Sheed (London: Penguin, 1984 [1972/1977]).

The Three Ecologies, trans. Ian Pindar and Paul Sutton (London: Athlone, 2000 [1989]).

Chaosmosis, trans. Paul Bains and Julian Pefanis (Indiana: Indiana University Press, 1995 [1992]).

The Guattari Reader, ed. Gary Genosko (Oxford: Blackwell, 1996).

Suggestions for Further Reading

Genosko, Gary, *Felix Guattari: An Aberrant Introduction* (London: Continuum, 2002). The first major overview of Guattari's work as a whole.

Goodchild, Philip, *Deleuze and Guattari: An Introduction to the Politics of Desire* (London: Sage, 1996). An introduction to Deleuze and Guattari's combined work.

Hardt, Michael and Antonio Negri, *Empire* (New Haven: Yale University Press, 2000). A work of contemporary political analysis that takes off from Deleuze and Guattari.

Holland, Eugene W., *Deleuze and Guattari's* Anti-Oedipus*: Introduction to Schizoanalysis* (London: Routledge, 1999). The best account of *Anti-Oedipus*.

Olkowski, Dorothea, *Deleuze and the Ruin of Representation* (Berkeley: University of California Press, 1999). A most insightful feminist appropriation engaging with psychoanalysis.

12

Michel Foucault (1926–84)

Jon Simons

The Refusal of Who We Are

Michel Foucault is recognised as a key figure in the intellectual scene of the late twentieth century, whose influence is likely to be felt well into the present century. He characterised his work as a philosophical critique of the present, especially of the modes of subjectivity or forms of identity to which we are tied. He urges us to 'refuse what we are', meaning that we should refuse to remain tied to the identities to which we are subjected.[1] He associated his own project with all those who struggle against the ways they are individuated, that is, rendered into the sort of individuals who they are. For example, he linked his work to prisoners who refused to be delinquents and to gays who resist their definition as homosexuals. Foucault's refusal to be what we are flows from analyses of the limiting conditions that subjectify us. Retrospectively, he perceives three axes of subjectification: truth, power and ethics. We are subjects of the truths of human sciences that constitute us as objects of study (such as delinquents) and define norms with which we identify (such as heterosexual). This essay will follow Foucault's self-interpretation by looking at those themes in turn.

To be a subject can be understood in the sense of being subject to something, such as the power of a sovereign. This meaning bears a connotation of being dominated or constrained by something else. In another sense, though, as in grammar, the subject of the sentence is attributed with agency and is empowered to act on the object. According to Foucault, the subject is neither wholly subjected nor entirely self-defining and self-regulating. The subject is indebted to the limits, however oppressive, imposed on him or her for the possibility of being anyone at all, having an identity and capacities to act, including the capacities to resist subjectifying power relations. However, only under certain circumstances can the subject successfully transgress the limits to which he or she is partially indebted and fashion new forms of subjectivity.

Foucault's key criticism of the modern era is that the three axes of subjectification are so closely entangled that the only subjectivities, or modes of being a subject, available to us are oppressive. Refusal of what we are entails resisting the truths that human sciences pronounce, the modern forms of government that subjectify us, and even our apparently autonomous self-definitions. Yet, Foucault also proposes an affirmative project, to promote new forms of subjectivity. He indicates in his writing and life that it is possible to exist as subjects in ways other than those defined by modern government, transgressing its limits to give impetus to 'the undefined work of freedom'.[2]

It is in part through writing as an art of the self that Foucault produces himself as an individual who resists current modes of subjectification. He was interested not in the academic status of his work but the changes his knowledge wrought in himself and in others. Consequently, there is no single adequate classification of his writing according to academic disciplines, as history, philosophy, sociology or cultural criticism. In 1970 Foucault named his chair at the Collège de France 'History of Systems of Thought' to refer to his research into madness, punishment and sexuality.

Foucault's intellectual trajectory exemplifies a French post-war pattern of trying to escape the legacy of the philosophical education provided at the elite École normale supérieure, focused on Hegel, Heidegger and phenomenology. Foucault's earliest work and teaching as philosopher of psychology leant in existentialist and Marxist directions, but he later distanced himself from both Jean-Paul Sartre's existentialism and the structuralist Marxism of his tutor, Louis Althusser. The predominant affinity of the first book he considered a part of his oeuvre, abridged in English as *Madness and Civilization*, is to the Annales school of history, particularly the historian of science Georges Canguilhem, which focuses on trying to grasp the principles of the realities, generally taken as long periods of continuity, being interpreted. He was also deeply interested in avant-garde literature and culture which, along with long periods spent abroad, fed into his strategies to think differently and break familiar patterns of thought. Foucault attributes to Nietzsche the main role in his break with the predominant Hegelian and phenomenological philosophy of the subject.

Politically, Foucault was first radicalised by his experience of student protest in Tunisia (1966–8), then briefly involved in student demonstrations in France in 1968. His most radical period began in 1971, through involvement in unorthodox left politics on issues such as prison revolts, anti-racism and immigration, when he associated politically and philosophically with Gilles Deleuze. By the late 1970s Foucault often visited American universities, also enjoying the gay subculture. There is thus a clear link between his life and his major works such as *Discipline and Punish* and *The History of Sexuality*. His writing is a practice in which he constantly demands of himself and others that they question the limits that have made them what they are.

Truth and Discourse

On his way to analysing the form of power that makes individuals subjects, Foucault analyses the limits of our discourse, especially the discourses of the human sciences. This led him to concentrate further on the historical and political conditions of possibility for knowledge, which are also limits that subjectify humans. The first axis of critique of subjectification, truth, refers to the sciences which offer objective knowledge about humans. Foucault engages in historical critiques of the discourses of psychiatry, medicine, criminology and sexuality. His sustained attempt to analyse the conditions of possibility of discourse, independent of its context, appears in *The Order of Things*. There he claims that there are sets of presuppositions, which Foucault calls epistemes, that elevate perception to the level of objective knowledge. These epistemes are historical, changing suddenly over time. Rather than being identified by their reference to essential objects (such as madness), by a style of descriptive statements (such as clinical discourse), by the permanence of the concepts used (as in grammar), by the persistence of themes (as in political economy), an episteme can be said to exist when there are regular relations between its objects, style of description, concepts and thematic choices. Foucault designates this mode of analysis of the regularities that make true statements possible as 'archaeology'.

Foucault identifies the systemacity of relations between different elements of discourse. Rules of formation are conditions of existence for a particular discourse. They constitute a system that enables statements to become intelligible or significant. '"Truth" is to be understood as a system of ordered procedures for the production, regulation, distribution, circulation and operation of statements.'[3] The rules of regulation of discourse are not only limits that enable the truth to be told but also constraints. They govern what may be said, in what mode (scientifically or not), what is considered valid, what is considered appropriate to be circulated and who may say what in a given setting. As the conditions of possibility of true discourse are historical and contingent, Foucault suggests that knowledge about the human subject that is taken to be objective is itself contingent. There are other subjugated truths to be told about the insane, delinquents or perverts.

Foucault's archaeology is also a philosophical critique of humanism. The modern episteme, beginning at the end of the eighteenth century and perhaps disintegrating by the 1950s, has an 'anthropological' character, focusing on the study of 'Man'. 'Man' is both the subject and object of the discourses about labour, life and language. Foucault's analysis of the systematic arrangement of the elements of discourse leads him to conclude that the existence of 'Man' is contingent on the rules of regulation and systematic relations that constitute the modern episteme. So 'Man', the subject or the author, cannot be considered as the foundation, origin or condition of possibility of discourse. Rather, the subject and especially the author can be defined as a particular space from which it is possible to speak or write and which must be filled if the discourse is to exist. For example, the subject of a discourse such as medicine is a function of legal rights, criteria of competence, institutional relations and professional hierarchy. There are a variety of subject roles in different positions. Archaeological analysis, according to which discourse is governed by its own rules of systemacity rather than by a sovereign subject, endangers apotheosised 'Man', as the figure that replaced God in modern philosophy. In 'Man's' place Foucault expects a resurgence of literary language, functioning autonomously, which he associates with avant-garde writers and madness, and above all with Nietzsche. Foucault's decentring of the author in order to focus on the functioning of language has inspired, with others, a tendency in literary analysis to do likewise. His work has also been central to the whole interdisciplinary field of discourse analysis.[4] Edward Said drew on

Foucault's notion of episteme to analyse critically the regularity of 'Oriental' discourse, which constitutes the West by constructing the Orient as its Other, in his ground-breaking book for postcolonial studies.[5]

Power

Power/knowledge

The task of archaeology is to describe how political practice transforms the conditions of existence and functioning of a discourse. But the larger costs of the modern episteme and the extent of Foucault's critique of modernity become apparent only when the limits of discourse are considered along with non-discursive conditions of possibility, such as institutions, economic processes and social relations. To be politically relevant, discourse analysis must address the conditions of exercise and institutionalisation of scientific discourses. Foucault shifts from archaeological analysis to genealogical critique, a term borrowed from Nietzsche, to characterise his historical studies of the intertwining of power and knowledge, and of the different ways in which subjectification occurs. Foucault's interest in Nietzsche was aroused by the latter's writing on the will to truth and as a historian of truth and rationality. In Foucault's account, desire and power are at stake in the will to truth, disrupting the humanist trajectory of the gradual emancipation of truth from power. In the context of the truths of the human sciences and their notions of human subjectivity to which people are tied, Foucault developed his notion of the mutual constitution of power and knowledge.

One advantage of genealogy over archaeology is that it includes power relations in the ordered procedures that make true discourses possible. Specific genealogical analyses show how contingently certain rational discourse became true by presenting historical versions of the systems of exclusion that determine what is true or false. Modern power disguises itself by presenting the truths of the human sciences as advances in objective knowledge about human beings. Foucault denies that such progress occurs, arguing instead that certain forms of knowledge are replaced by others as discursive arrangements and power/knowledge regimes shift. There is a will to truth because a vast range of social practices, such as economics or punishment, seek to justify themselves by reference to a true discourse, yet should be subject to a politically motivated critique. It is because 'we are subjected to the production of truth through power and we cannot exercise power except through the production of truth' that 'the political question ... is truth itself'.[6]

Foucault analyses the simultaneous emergence in the early nineteenth century of the modern human sciences and of certain new 'technologies' for the governance of people. 'Power and knowledge directly imply one another ... there is no power relation without the correlative constitution of a field of knowledge, nor any knowledge that does not presuppose and constitute at the same time power relations'.[7] As a general formula, Foucault's power/knowledge thesis argues that power relations and scientific discourses mutually constitute one another. Foucault does not attempt to break down the elements of that mutual constitution systematically, deliberately entangling power and truth.

Knowledge, as human or social sciences, and power relations constitute each other by rendering the social world into a form that is both knowable and governable, each being dependent on the other. Power can only be exercised over something that 'techniques of knowledge and procedures of discourse were capable of investing in. Between techniques of knowledge and strategies of power, there is no exteriority.'[8] Methods of government render phenomena (such as an expanding number of people) into objects (such as population), amenable to scientific study. Simultaneously, scientific methodologies provide knowledge of these objects that renders them amenable to government. In *Discipline and Punish* and elsewhere, Foucault describes programmes of government, or models for the rule of society such as Bentham's panopticon. These programmes presuppose a knowledge of the field of reality they act upon and render reality into a programmable object.

Foucault's approach to truth rules out a humanist emancipatory politics which is grounded in a truth purified of all error and illusion. His argument that modern power and human sciences are always entangled precludes the possibility of freeing truth from power. The genealogical approach provides historical rather than epistemological answers to the questions of what constitutes knowledge and truth. In the view of some critics, such as Charles Taylor, Foucault's historical nominalism in relation to truth is relativist, leaving Foucault without a notion of a liberating truth, and hence without the means to judge between different modes of government. According to others, notably Jürgen Habermas, Foucault's analyses must, if Foucault is correct, also be expressions of a will to truth. These criticisms certainly make sense from within the philosophical perspectives of the critics, but they do not rebut the counter-claim that if truth is immanent to power relations, then a critique of oppressive power relations cannot be made in the name of a truth that transcends power.

Discipline and Bio-Power

While Foucault put much effort into analysing the relation between power and knowledge, he also focused on power itself, as the second axis of genealogy. Power is the most amorphous axis, as it includes political structures, systems of rules and norms, techniques and apparatuses of government, dividing practices, and strategic relations between subjects who act upon each other. Power relations are conditions of possibility for subjectivities. Confusingly, sometimes Foucault uses the word 'power' to invoke the negative connotations of 'power over', such as coercion, constraint, and domination. Yet, one of Foucault's main innovations in his analyses of power is to reject the view that power is merely repressive. Even when power is experienced as restriction, as in the case of imprisonment, it is also productive. 'Power produces; it produces reality, it produces domains of objects and rituals of truth.' It also produces people: 'Discipline "makes" individuals.'[9] Power in its positive sense is enabling, constituting subjects, even though the forms of subjectivity constituted may not be desirable. The first meaning implies power as coercion and domination by others, while the second refers to the constraint of being limited yet enabled by one's identity. This second sense includes 'power to' as well as 'power over'. Genealogy examines how subjects are constituted by others and how we participate in constituting ourselves as subjects.

In *Discipline and Punish* Foucault offers an analysis of a specific mode of subjection of humans according to scientific definitions, discipline. 'Discipline ... is the specific technique of a power that regards individuals both as objects and as instruments of its exercise', producing docile yet productive bodies, the work force for industrial capitalism.[10] Discipline involves a range of detailed, meticulous techniques for the subjection of the individual through training, functioning autonomously of regimes and institutions and transferable across them. They constitute the 'micro-physics' of power.

The particular individual produced by the techniques of the

penal system is the delinquent, who fits into a typology of deviancy, as a character who will not or cannot conform to the norm. The delinquent is not simply the author of a crime, but a member of a sub-species whose crimes can be explained as part of their being, character and upbringing. Although the penitentiary system was intended to rehabilitate criminals, recidivist delinquents were not its failure but its successful product. Belonging to an under-class, delinquents embodied a useful illegality that could be deployed to frighten the proletariat away from political illegalities, to police colonies, and to sustain the cycle of police–prison–delinquency.

Discipline would be of merely local interest if it were not that its 'penitentiary' techniques of government were applicable in other institutions that assumed a carceral character, especially schools and factories. 'The carceral archipelago transported this technique to the entire social body', punishing deviance from bourgeois legality through the power of normalisation.[11] The norm is both a statistically determined standard of behaviour administratively required by disciplinary institutions, such as schools, hospitals, armies and prisons, and what is considered as moral law. Moral-legal norms are colonised by the administrative and statistical norms determined by power/knowledge regimes. Judgement is not purely juridical, in that the condemnation of proven acts according to true or reasonable criteria of the licit is colonised by an assessment of the offender in the light of scientific knowledge of the normal. Legal punishment has become the framework for a care or cure of the individual, legitimised as much by knowledge as by right. As its purpose is not merely to punish illegal acts, this 'normalising judgement' is appropriate to the fields of education, health and production too. Deviations from the norm are punished as if they are violations of the law, which in turn appear to be offences against objectively known human nature. Not only the excluded and abnormal pay the cost of normalisation but also everyone who suppresses any part of themselves that is Other in order to remain normal. Modern Western society is not disciplined, but it is disciplinary. As the realm of right and morality is colonised by scientific disciplines (or bio-power) there can be no recourse to right that is not already defined scientifically. This view is rejected by critics such as Habermas, who argues that Foucault must either appeal unintentionally to the humanist norms he rejects in his critiques of domination or be left without normative grounds to justify resistance.

Michel Foucault (1926–84)

Foucault most dramatically asserts that power is productive as well as repressive in regard to the domain of sexuality. He counters the opinion that the modern West has repressed or concealed all sexuality other than legitimate marital relations, and that the interests of industrial capitalism were served by confining human energies to economic reproduction. In contrast, Foucault argues that an objective, scientific truth about sexuality emerged, while the Victorian government of sexuality caused a proliferation of what it considered to be perversions. The bourgeoisie of the mid-eighteenth century affirmed itself as a class in its efforts to overcome these implanted perversions, asserting its own health and hygiene.

The power associated with sexuality is also productive because it enhances life forces. Whereas the paradigm of pre-modern sovereign power was its right to take the life of whoever challenged it, thus being a merely extractive and subtractive power, modern power is exemplified by the development of the life of the social body. If in the past power had been visible in its exercise by the sovereign, in the modern era it became invisible as the application of power to the individual's body and soul. Power is now concerned with the generation and optimisation of life, which calls for regulation of the biological processes of the population as a whole, or a bio-politics. Bio-power deals with social hygiene, rates of fertility and mortality and birth control. Discipline and bio-power are particularly onerous forms of government because they infiltrate so deeply and persistently into the lives of populations and individuals.

Modern power is insidious because of its concealed but effective intercession in daily life. The extent of modern government and modes of subjectivity are obscured by narratives of emancipation that incite us to seek our liberation through strategies that resubject us. Foucault mistrusts the theme of liberation in so far as it refers back to the idea of a repressed human essence. Technologies of power/knowledge have constructed what we know as psyche, subjectivity, personality, consciousness. There is no authentic subjectivity to liberate. For example, bio-power ties us to our sexual identities, leading us to believe that we are our sexuality. In general bio-power aims to optimise all human life forces, such as libido, yet resistance to it is posed in terms of the same life forces that bio-power targets. We embrace our given subjectivities because they promise our liberation through the overcoming of power. Yet, government pursues the same programmes that we do, namely, our salvation through welfare or revolution, or the affirmation of our life. That is why we must refuse to be what we are: because to accept what we are means to accept subjection.

Governmentality

Much of what has been reviewed above under the rubric of discipline, normalisation and bio-power can also be analysed in terms of what Foucault calls 'governmentality'. This term refers to the link between the technologies of domination of others and techniques of the self. One governs one's own conduct, while government guides the conduct of others. Government is the conduct of conduct. Foucault's research into government of the self and the state as a general problem at the beginning of the modern era allows him to supplement his 'micro-physical' analysis of practices of (disciplinary) power with a 'macro-physical' consideration of governmental rationality, partly as a response to criticisms that his work ignored political questions about relations between state and society. The micro-programmes of government in prisons, hospitals or asylums are to be seen to work alongside a wider disciplinary or 'police' rationality.

Foucault claims that the modern art of government is the consequence of a combination between the pastoral thinking inherent in a generalised notion of police and reason of state. Pastoral power is a devoted, individual, kindly power which aims at individual salvation and requires both knowledge and obedience of each member of the flock. Reason of state took as its aim the enhancement of the state's strength in a competitive framework, relying on knowledge of the state to measure its success. It was interested in population and welfare only in so far as they contributed to state power. The care of the individual becomes a duty for the state. Reason of state relies on the technology of police to make individuals useful. The main dilemma of police is presented as the need to increase the happiness of citizens in a way that also enhances the power of the state. This, according to Foucault, is what defines modern political rationality. It is through disciplines, normalisation and bio-power that welfare can be improved and populations governed. At the same time, these forms of government enhance the power of the state. The integration by pastoral power of concerns of state or collective strength with those of individual life makes the modern state a formidable machine of individualisation and totalisation. It augments individual capacities as it augments its own power. 'The modern Western state has integrated ... pastoral power' by reorganising it as 'individualising power'.[12]

Foucault's analysis of governmentality extends from the sixteenth century problematisation of government of self and state, through the interventionist models of 'police' such as mercantilism, through to early and contemporary liberalism, which he defines as a practice as much as a philosophy. Foucault's work on governmentality, most of which was not published until after his death and is still being translated, has proved to be a fecund example for research into contemporary forms of government such as welfare and neo-liberalism.[13]

Resistance

Foucault does not mean to give the impression that we are trapped by modern forms of government, though critics accuse of him of portraying a world without hope. First, Foucault suggests that resistance is possible because all subjectifying power endows subjects with some capacities required to be agents, even when it is oppressive. Secondly, Foucault understands power relations to permeate the whole social body and all human relations. Power is defined as 'a mode of action upon the actions of others'.[14] As each society is a complex, ongoing structure governing the way some actions act upon other actions, then it would be nonsensical to conceive of a society without power. Foucault's definitions make it possible for him to state that: 'Where there is power, there is resistance.'[15] Each power relation generates an adversary reaction on the part of others. Resistance is possible when power pushes toward its limits. Power relations should always be analysed in terms of adversarial struggle and confrontational strategies. There are points of insubordination at which it is possible not to escape power per se, but to escape the particular strategy of power relation that directs one's conduct.

Yet, in his substantive historical works Foucault tends to depict the operations of power from the perspective of the programmes of the power/knowledge regimes, such as Bentham's panoptical scheme, which he analyses. As he does not analyse power from the perspective of the prisoners who revolt, he often induces the sense that power relations cannot be changed. He remains confident, however, that resistance is possible because power relations do not solidify into states of complete domination. Power arises from below in its micro-physical forms, composed of different tactics and heterogeneous techniques, which are not principally coordinated with each other. He denies that either the state or capital are at the centre of systems of domination, which for some critics means that he fails to grasp the underlying structure of power. Other critics, including Habermas, are concerned that Foucault lacks normative reasons to resist or distinguish between oppression and the legitimate exercise of power. In contrast, Foucault implies that no such philosophical motivations or justifications are necessary. He judges between regimes according to the extent to which they minimise domination and enable individuals to transform the system. Practical critique of power in the form of resistance, not philosophical critique, limits its excesses. For Foucault, there is no state of liberation beyond power relations, but liberty is exercised in constant, active resistance to whichever power relations subjectify individuals in ways that provoke their resistance.

Ethics

Resistance in Foucault's perception is not merely a negative operation, in that by resisting contemporary forms of subjectivity we strive to affirm alternative modes of subjectivity. This more affirmative mood in Foucault's later work brings us to ethics, the third axis of genealogy. Ethics involves a relationship to oneself, recognition and self-constitution as a particular type of moral agent. There are techniques or technologies for government of oneself just as there are for the government of others, so in that sense governmentality is the connection between ethics and politics. Ethical self-formation involves four aspects: the substance or part of oneself which is considered problematic for moral conduct, such as desire; the mode of subjection, such as obeying a universal moral law or conforming to a scientific norm; ascetics or the means of working on oneself, such as confession; and the goal of self-formation, such as self-fulfilment.

Foucault advocates an ethical relation to oneself, whose corresponding mode of subjectification is an aesthetics of the self, which has recourse neither to knowledge nor to universal rules. Given that there is no essential subject, 'that the self is not given to us ... there is only one practical consequence: we have to create ourselves as a work of art'.[16] One relates to oneself as an object of art which one must create. Most of Foucault's work on aesthetics of the self focuses on the Classical Greek and Hellenist eras, which gave him the idea of life as material for a work of art, in *The Use of Pleasure* and *The Care of the Self.* He endorses only the formal or conceptual conditions of the Greek and Hellenist relation of self to self, that is, the loosening of the connections between the three axes of subjectification: power, truth and ethics. Foucault insists that we must detach our ethical relations with ourselves from the government of others, from universal moral rules and from scientific (especially psychological) knowledge.

Foucault affirms an aesthetics of existence and care of the self as transgression of the limits of Western humanist culture. He does not direct us to a certain subjectivity or a preferred identity but focuses on the process of subjectification as an art. There are three central features to Foucault's aesthetics of the self: the demands of style; artistic practice as a source of empowerment; and work with present conditions and limits. The general principle is that arts of the self are stylisation of conduct by means of practices of the self. Foucault's aesthetics of existence designates artistic practices and techniques of self-empowerment. It is through artistic, creative activity that we experience ourselves as agents with power. Foucault's aesthetics of existence works on the limits of the present.

Habermas criticises Foucault from several angles, all of which lead to the conclusion that Foucault's total critique of reason is incoherent because it relies paradoxically on the very structure of rationality it opposes. Foucault's critique is particularly partial in so far as it is inspired by aesthetic modernism whose critical standards are derived from the unspoken language of the body in pain. Although this tradition identifies rationalisation as the enemy, the autonomy of its aesthetic discourse rests on the rationalised differentiation of the life world into three spheres, including art. While Foucault's critics may accept that art expresses some legitimate protest against the exclusion of human creative and libidinal qualities, they cannot accept what Habermas calls the terrorist over-extension of the aesthetic cultural order into domains such as politics. As there is no aesthetic logic of social interaction, counter-cultural forms of life are unstable, having to rely on other values, or to fall into the irrational, relativist trap of having no reason for preferring any values. But even if Foucault cannot satisfy his critics with the normative grounds they demand, he does at least express his preference for a world in which the aesthetics of existence are possible for everyone.

Other critics complain that aesthetics of existence and concern for the self induce a withdrawal from politics. However, not only does Foucault look for the connections between government of the self and of others but also his later work is relevant to identity politics and queer theory. Foucault's conception of an aesthetics of existence may well be drawn from his understanding of the transgressive potential of becoming gay. Foucault refused his subjection as a homosexual, bound to an identity that was defined scientifically in the nineteenth century according to a supposedly sexual nature. An art of life rather than science is needed for the conscious choice to be gay. The promise of the gay community and culture lies in its invention of ways of relating. The wider significance of gay friendship is not simply sexual pleasure but the proliferation of new forms of relations between people beyond those currently sanctioned, namely, marriage and the family.

The strategy of 'desexualisation' that Foucault proposes for gays is also relevant for feminism. The general aim of this strategy of resistance is to detach people from their sexually defined identities, such as 'hysterical' women. The validity of Foucault's position for feminism rests on an argument that women in particular are constrained by oppressive sexual subjectivities. Effective desexualisation requires an analysis of how sex and subjectifying power are linked. Feminists who have found Foucault useful thus propose a *'feminist genealogy* of the category of women'.[17] But other feminists are rightly suspicious of Foucault's inattention to power relations between men and women. Others argue that the genealogical critique of 'woman' undermines the solidity of the female subject, which they take to be the grounds of feminist politics. The debate within feminism is whether it need such grounds, or is hindered by appeals to essentialism.

Conclusion

Foucault consistently understood his role as an intellectual to support those who are engaged in refusal, 'all those on whom power is exercised to their detriment, all who find it intolerable'.[18] He holds that his archaeological and genealogical critique can 'separate out from the contingency that has made us what we are, the possibility of no longer being, doing, or thinking what we are, do, or think'.[19] His work has had an impact not only in the areas he researched such as the history of the human sciences but also across the humanities, from literary theory to criminology. In particular, his analyses of the power that makes individuals subjects have been taken up and adapted across the social sciences. Although preoccupied by the West and male subjectivity, Foucault has had an impact on postcolonial studies and feminism. But perhaps all that would have concerned him would have been whether he had helped anyone else practise liberty.

Notes

1. Foucault, *Power*, p. 336.
2. Foucault, *Ethics*, p. 316.
3. Foucault, *Power*, p. 132.
4. See David Howarth, *Discourse* (Buckingham: Open University Press, 2000).
5. Edward Said, *Orientalism* (New York: Pantheon, 1978).
6. Foucault, *Power/Knowledge: Selected Interviews and Other Writings, 1972–1977*, ed. Colin Gordon (Brighton: Harvester, 1980), pp. 93, 133.
7. Foucault, *Discipline and Punish*, p. 27.
8. Foucault, *History of Sexuality*, Vol. 1, p. 98.
9. Foucault, *Discipline and Punish*, pp. 194, 170.
10. Foucault, *Discipline and Punish*, p. 170.
11. Foucault, *Discipline and Punish*, p. 298.
12. Foucault, *Power*, pp. 332, 334.
13. See Foucault, *'Society Must Be Defended'*, trans. D. Macey (London: Allen Lane, 2003); and Graham Burchell, Colin Gordon and Peter Miller (eds), *The Foucault Effect: Studies in Governmentality* (London: Harvester Wheatsheaf, 1991).
14. Foucault, *Power*, p. 341.
15. Foucault, *History of Sexuality*, Vol. 1, p. 95.
16. Foucault, *Ethics*, p. 262.
17. Judith Butler, *Gender Trouble: Feminism and the Subversion of Identity* (New York: Routledge, 1990), p. 5.
18. Foucault, 'Intellectuals and Power', in Donald Bouchard (ed.), *Language, Counter-Memory, Practice: Selected Essays* (Ithaca: Cornell University Press, 1977), p. 216.
19. Foucault, *Ethics*, pp. 315–16.

Major Works by Foucault

Aesthetics, Method and Epistemology, The Essential Works, Vol. 2, ed. J. Faubion, trans. R. Hurley et al. (Allen Lane: London, 1998).
The Archaeology of Knowledge, trans. Alan Sheridan (New York: Pantheon, 1972 [1969]).

The Birth of the Clinic: An Archaeology of Medical Perception, trans. Alan Sheridan (London: Tavistock, 1973 [1963]).

Discipline and Punish: The Birth of the Prison, trans. Alan Sheridan (New York: Vintage, 1979 [1975]).

Ethics, Subjectivity and Truth, The Essential Works, Vol. 1, ed. P. Rabinow, trans. R. Hurley et al. (Allen Lane: London, 1997).

The History of Sexuality, Vol. 1, *An Introduction*, trans. Robert Hurley (Harmondsworth: Penguin, 1978 [1976]).

The History of Sexuality, Vol. 2, *The Use of Pleasure*, trans. Robert Hurley (Harmondsworth: Penguin, 1987 [1984]).

The History of Sexuality, Vol. 3, *The Care of the Self*, trans. Robert Hurley (New York: Penguin, 1988 [1984]).

Madness and Civilization, trans. Richard Howard (New York: Pantheon, 1965 [1961]).

The Order of Things: An Archaeology of the Human Sciences, trans. Unidentified collective (New York: Vintage, 1973 [1966]).

Power, The Essential Works, Vol. 3, ed. J. Faubion, trans. R. Hurley et al. (New Press: New York, 2000).

Suggestions for Further Reading

Barker, Philip, *Michel Foucault: An Introduction* (Edinburgh: Edinburgh University Press, 1998). Good for showing Foucault's key ideas at work in his main texts and the possibilities opened up by them.

Dreyfus, Hubert L., and Paul Rabinow, *Michel Foucault: Beyond Structuralism and Hermeneutics* (Brighton: Harvester Press, 1982). An excellent analysis of Foucault's methodologies and innovations in relation to his philosophical context.

Gutting, Gary (ed.), *The Cambridge Companion to Foucault* (Cambridge: Cambridge University Press, 1994). In addition to valuable essays on various aspects of Foucault's work, includes a useful bibliography of secondary literature.

Hoy, David Couzens (ed.), *Foucault: A Critical Reader* (Oxford: Basil Blackwell, 1986). A handy collection of critical essays by Habermas, Said, Taylor, Walzer and others.

Simons, Jon, *Foucault and the Political* (London: Routledge, 1995). An introduction to Foucault that focuses on the political ramifications of his work.

13

Jean Baudrillard (1929–)

Paul Hegarty

In terms of subject matter, style and attitude to ideology, Jean Baudrillard is seen as the archetypal postmodernist. Because of his high-media profile and willingness to address contemporary events and phenomena in a polemical but not overtly political way, critics attack his apparent 'celebration' of the postmodern world and uncritical readings of contemporary events and politics. Some (such as Douglas Kellner) allow that in his early work Baudrillard provided a strong and original critique of the world of late capitalism. Others would insist that his important work lies in the style, new theoretical concepts and focus of his later work (Mike Gane, Arthur Kroker). Many, particularly in the English-speaking world, see him as a charlatan complicit with contemporary structures of power (notably Christopher Norris and the English-print media). Most would agree, though, that Baudrillard's big idea is 'simulation', whose appearance marks the move from his earlier, more traditionally critical position, thereby dividing his work roughly into two periods: 1968–76, and 1976 onwards. There are many more theoretical ideas and considerations that come after simulation (the virtual, seduction, the fatal, the event, the fractal, Evil) or indeed against it (symbolic exchange, seduction, the fatal), but these essentially lie within Baudrillard's theoretical world-view of the mid-1970s.

Early Baudrillard and Marxism

Baudrillard emerges as a writer in the aftermath of 1968, his early work being marked by a strong, essentially Marxist, ideological critique of late capitalist consumer society, which he frames in a structuralist approach to signs and a pseudo-psychoanalytic reading of consumer desire. He gradually brings in references to writers such as Georges Bataille, Marshall McLuhan, Marshall Sahlins and Friedrich Nietzsche. These references are crucial for understanding Baudrillard's later notions, as they not only provide the background to his critique of society, thought, politics and culture but also, in the case of Bataille and Nietzsche, suggest the way in which the critique is to be conducted. His shift from offering or seeking an alternative to near-nihilism is attributed by some to general disillusionment with the 'project' of May 1968 that distanced him from the Situationist critique of Guy Debord, for whom the 'spectacle' of consumer society was a conscious ideological strategy to maintain control of the masses. The open-ended utopianism of the student and worker revolt seemed to have brought nothing, save some terrorism. The involvement of Marxist thinkers and trades unions in the movement was also held responsible for its failure. Marxism seemed to be complicit with 'the system', merely the other side of the coin of repressive, conservative power. Intellectuals felt obliged to move on from earlier models for change that were now seen as dogmatic. However, Marx pre-empted some of Baudrillard's ideas (notably on the spectral, magical nature of the commodity), so critics think his arguments would improve if he were more Marxist.[1]

Baudrillard's early books analyse the significations of objects, lifestyles, the use of fashion as an ideological tool and the prevalence of codes into which we are encouraged to buy. Although they might seem obvious to us now, Baudrillard's observations on credit's role in expanding and promulgating late capitalism and on the fallacies of liberation through consumption were timely and systematically argued. His early work, up to *Mirror of Production*, also emphasises alienation (from a more authentic way of living, owing to capitalism's all-pervasiveness). Baudrillard moves gradually but clearly away from Marxism, into a world-view that does not rely on a centralised agency of oppression and alienation, which opens the way for the simulation/symbolic exchange confrontation to come. In *For a Critique of the Political Economy of the Sign* Baudrillard builds a critique of capitalist society on the basis that the commodity form mirrors the sign form, and that they reinforce each other. In the case of the sign, the signifier and signified need each other to work, both being invented values. The same goes for exchange value and use value, where, contrary to Marx, Baudrillard argues that utility, general or particular, is as much a construct of a system of meaning

Jean Baudrillard (1929–)

and signs as exchange value. This is a significant diversion from Marxist notions of 'fetishism', where real value is lost in phantasmagoria. In terms of Baudrillard's oeuvre, this book is significant in that we see his shift towards a rejection of the realness of the real world – nothing is outside of signification, least of all something called 'materialism'. The slight glimmer of an outside does persist, in the form of 'the symbolic' (paralleling Kristeva's 'semiotic') – a destructive, playful moment where codes are broken down, as in the revolt of May 1968 where a new radical community had formed, even if only briefly. Just as the real disappears, however, so the symbolic becomes something less utopian as Baudrillard progresses.

Baudrillard extends his critique of utility to production in *The Mirror of Production*. Marxist critique is caught within 'production', extolling it as both enemy and liberator. The individual subject is created by his or her relation to the means of production, being obliged, whether for or against the system, to produce himself or herself as an individual subject. Self-production is governed by 'the code', Baudrillard's term for the inherently ideological signifying systems that define us (according to class, gender, race, sex, language or role within production). Neither Marxism nor psychoanalysis – the other supposedly radical discourse of the 1970s – can offer a way out. Instead we should look to revolt and insurrection; we should be machine breakers rather than freeing ourselves by making the machine better. Perhaps surprisingly for those familiar with his problematic later stances, or hasty critiques of them, Baudrillard argues that women, blacks and homosexuals are all major challenges to 'the code'.[2]

All that resists, or that is forced outside, can be seen as 'symbolic exchange'. We can see Baudrillard beginning to develop this key notion in opposition to economic exchange and Marxism's apparent misunderstanding of early societies. According to Baudrillard, Marxism's belief that early societies are based on subsistence is a moral judgement that misunderstands the need, for example, to sacrifice the first and/or best produce. In misunderstanding (or presuming too much about) 'primitive', sacrificial societies, Marxism proves itself incapable of getting out of capitalist economy. In fact, the 'surplus' might come first, while expenditure might be more important than accumulation. An economy of sacrifice is one version of symbolic exchange (already hinted at in *The Consumer Society*). At this point Bataille's influence over Baudrillard outweighs that of Marx.

Simulation and Symbolic Exchange

If simulation is Baudrillard's key idea, then symbolic exchange, or something like it, is never far away, as that which is outside of simulation. Both ideas are central to *Symbolic Exchange and Death*, Baudrillard's most substantial theoretical work. The argument is deceptively simple: reality is increasingly removed as we move through history, a process that culminates in simulation replacing reality with 'hyperreality', the more real than real. Symbolic exchange is presented as an alternative form to which the West has largely lost access. The 'reality', though, is more complex. Baudrillard argues that we have had 'three orders of simulacra':

- the *counterfeit* is the dominant schema in the classical period, from the Renaissance to the Industrial Revolution
- *production* is the dominant schema in the industrial era
- Simulation is the dominant schema in the current code-governed phase.

The first order simulacrum operates on the natural law of value, the second-order simulacrum on the market law of value, and the third-order simulacrum on the structural law of value.[3]

The way we view the world affects the world, such that eventually it disappears as a concrete entity, while the way we view the world is utterly historicised and culturally determined.[4] This raises the question of who lives in simulation, when they do, and where. It is only the third order that results in a shared world-view, such that the world disappears. The first order, working on the 'natural' value of things, belongs to the West before the early modern period, consisting of the presumption of a natural link between sign and thing. The counterfeit plays on this presumption, strengthening it even as it undermines the system. The second order reiterates the link between capitalism and modern forms of signification: meaning is produced, as are commodities. In practical terms, this means representation rather than symbolisation: that is, there is a gap between signifier and signified, a thing to be represented on one side, a thing representing on the other. Reality is produced by making the link. In the third order, simulation is no longer even a copy, as there is nothing left to copy, which is where we are now – the 'structural' form of value is one where values exchange against each other, not against a real world (as in late capitalist stock markets).[5]

This third order takes over gradually, with the Stock Market crash of 1929 a key moment, standing for the shift to pure speculation and its pre-emption of depression in the 'real world'. As simulation 'precedes' reality (here in the form of the simulated economy), the realness of the real world diminishes.[6] Also central in this story are the mass media. Baudrillard takes McLuhan's 'the medium is the message' to its logical extreme, as, ultimately, there is nothing left to mediate, nothing that has not already been pre-empted. May 1968 also marks a shift from the politics of the modern period, exposing ideology not only as a tool of the ruling class but also as suffusing all ideas. The accumulation of such tendencies (including the disappearance of the Left–Right distinction in electoral politics), gradually brings 'hyperreality'. At an everyday level, there can be no better example of this theory than 'reality TV' (which Baudrillard wrote on in the mid-1970s). Reality TV prevents the real from occurring – in framing the content as real, it begins to simulate the reality rather than showing it. The behaviour we see is 'as it would be without cameras', but is nothing of the sort. The people selected, in being 'representative', are already a spurious cross-section of a society that itself is subject to simulation. Reality TV goes beyond its shows, infiltrating the real world, illustrating that it has always already supplanted the old type of reality.

The concepts of simulation and symbolic exchange have each been criticised. Simulation could lead to quietism, relativism, even nihilism. Philosophically, Baudrillard's world is indeed nihilist, but, following Nietzsche, the nihilist world requires a further nihilism to be understood.[7] Baudrillard's writings of the last few years persist in their view of the simulated world, yet maintain a critique of contemporary politics. We can see his position as an echo of Nietzsche, or of Jean-François Lyotard, in *The Differend*, where it is the absence of truth that demands we argue a version of it. Simulation is arguably too neutral in its conception, given that some people have more access to the 'means of simulation' than others. Would people with access to hi-tech communications be worse or better off than those outside? Does simulation apply to everyone because of the global economy and mass media? Perhaps not all the world is simulated just yet.

According to Baudrillard, only 'symbolic exchange' is outside of all simulacra – forms of interaction which involve the loss of self, giving, death, sacrifice, refusal of 'the code'. 'Primitive' societies do not exclude death as we do, thereby maintaining a sense of reciprocity and reversibility. The increasingly simulated world knows only the unilateral: life, the real, economic gain, clear meaning.

When death or the other is brought in, as with initiation, sacrifice or the way in which the dead are treated, then symbolic exchange occurs and opens a space for community.

Symbolic exchange might seem utopian, a nostalgic view of a natural community. But Baudrillard is clear that he does not mean 'fusional utopias', as symbolic exchange is 'a social relation which puts an end to the real'.[8] Whilst it is 'other' to simulation, we cannot easily attain it, as it occurs only fleetingly, before being incorporated into the system. As a result, any radical event or attempts at critique become caught in simulation. The anti-globalisation movement relies on the worldwide spread of media, physical communications networks, technological literacy. Its protests are advertised events. In Baudrillard's terms, this is not simply irony – there is no way out of these traps. The movement itself is spawned by what it protests against (as with all protest movements). Equally unironic is Naomi Klein's *No Logo* being classified as a business book by a leading UK retailer. Symbolic exchange is itself only a fleeting moment of success, as simulation prevails. Except that Baudrillard argues that there has never been a real world, only the assumption that there was one, so it remains a question of how to respond in the particular order in which you find yourself.

The Fate of Politics and the Event

Simulation has proved a useful tool for Baudrillard, and has, arguably, been proved correct in its assumptions. Simulation is far from being a retreat from the world, but is an engagement that maybe more 'realist' discourses are not able to match. Baudrillard comments extensively on contemporary politics, discussing particular events and trends rather than ideologies. He eschews analyses of power that assume power is still held by sovereign leaders of sovereign states on behalf of (or despite) a sovereign people.

Baudrillard's most controversial statements have been on war, such as his infamous claim that 'the Gulf war did not happen', which for many who had not read the book attentively, was grounds to cease paying any attention to him.[9] This claim is rooted in an argument made in 1976, that the Vietnam war did not occur at the level of the real.[10] It had been pre-empted then supplanted by its media form. That the war is simulated does not lessen the actuality of death and suffering, as 'events continue at ground level'.[11] In fact, simulated war could be worse for those directly involved because its directors operate with long-distance weapons, computer projections, directing media coverage. The Gulf war, then, does not happen, because its reality has been subsumed into the media, into technology and models of warfare.

The conduct of war is affected significantly by changes in the politics of hyperreality, a world where appearance is more important than anything, in which Saddam Hussein, the one-time ally of the West, is compared to Hitler. Baudrillard, though, does not generally attribute a source to, and therefore responsibility for, 'hyperrealisation', but mostly offers a kind of functionalist view that it simply happens, the main actors being subject to the force of simulation. So, for example, the farce of the US presidential elections of 2000 would not suggest conspiracy or incompetence, but the precedence of simulation (beyond the obvious level of the mediatisation of the campaign), such that the 'real result' was not deemed to be the actual one. Not only that, but the way a result was achieved took priority over actuality.

Politics benefits from simulation, but it too is disappearing as ideologies are carefully removed. Neo-fascism would seem to be an exception, but in Baudrillardian terms we might say that the rise of the extreme Right in Europe provides an alibi for the rest of politics – look at Chirac's record score in the French presidential elections of 2002, achieved on the basis that he would save the Republic from fascism.[12] Even power fades as it is identified as all-pervasive (that being the thrust of his *Forget Foucault*, which he regards as an extension, not a rebuttal, of Foucault). Once power is everywhere, it is effectively nowhere, having left behind its possible reversal (that is, non-existence).

Traditional models of politics are replaced by simulated power (more dangerous than its 'real' counterpart), the masses, terrorism and the 'transpolitical'. Political models based on ideology, or even liberal-market models which claim an absence of ideology, are all transposed into a world where they cannot function as before: classes are replaced by the masses, the economy of production by an economy of self-generating, self-referring values, and a 'world order' renders national politics local, managerial.

Baudrillard is not the first to talk of the masses, but, from Marx onwards, the masses are considered to be awaiting conversion into a cohesive agent. In the world of simulation, though, the masses provide an unexpected resistance: their power lies in their inertia. They are produced by 'the social' (a simulation of society or community),[13] but they also resist it. They are simulated society's unexpected byproduct – they are too mass-ive, too unlikely to respond. Having been complicit in establishing the simulation we live in, power now pays the price in (it claims) a more troublesome, unpredictable, violent 'youth', for example. 'The masses' are usually assumed to be passive, and also, as a result, highly receptive to populist ideology. According to Baudrillard, it would be a category mistake to make such a case, as 'the mass and the media are one single process'.[14] Even their conformism is an ultraconformism, an acceptance too far. The masses, whether created purposively or not, usher in the implosion of power, which has nowhere to go. Without classes (which is not to say there are no divisions) or real power, or Left–Right divide, we are in the 'transpolitical'. Introduced in the late 1970s, this concept is still invoked in Baudrillard's terminology. It is accompanied by terms such as 'transaesthetics', 'transeconomics', 'transsexuality' and, above all, 'transparency'.[15] The 'trans-' in all of these terms signals not a radical or consciously new politics, but a move made in the simulated world, the world of objects which elude and increasingly exceed us. The transpolitical is politics without politics (and the transsexual the world without sex as everything is sexualised). Even recent fascisms are part of this, as they represent retro-politics.

Transparency is a word that, at institutional level, has positive connotations, implying openness and visibility. For Baudrillard, our era of visibility is one where we are made visible, monitored, recorded on videotape, made to account for our actions. It is a panoptical world where power, as it loses its realness, inflicts its visibility on us. Transparency and the transpolitical are intimately linked in the spectacle of politics – elections are game shows, sports events. In both, means and ends become displaced (so winning the election is the goal), while what matters most is the appearance of working well. (This point is illustrated when we hear of 'the economy' doing well – instead of being a means to an end, all our claims must be tested against the ultimate goal of 'the economy'). A recent sign of the all-pervasiveness of the transpolitical can be seen in the 'Clinton–Lewinsky' affair – not only in terms of the coverage, or strange notions about what 'not having sex' includes, but in terms of the fact that, after all that attention, it did not matter.[16] This analysis might show that Baudrillard is a cynical ultra-Leftist, but the implication that all this 'just happens' might indicate that he is a conservative.

Jean Baudrillard (1929–)

Whatever his own position on what he claims occurs in the simulated world, Baudrillard continues to identify phenomena that elude or undermine simulation. One such is seduction. Seduction is artifice that challenges stability of meaning, undoing the production of same. Seduction, though, is intertwined with simulation: simulation seduces, while seduction simulates. If the two seem complicit, we need to remember that simulation is about the reproduction of reality, insisting on its realness, truthfulness and so on. Seduction prevents the world from closing and being only the real world. The book *Seduction*, however, is also notable for Baudrillard's odd views on women, Woman and feminism. To caricature slightly, he claims that Woman should stay out of the world of Subjects, truth production and equality, thereby eluding the 'real' of simulation. Baudrillard often seems to suggest that the association of seduction with Woman and the feminine is inherent. So, women are doubly marginalised: first, in being excluded from 'the means of production' of meaning; and second, in being instructed to remain outside full subjectivity. Alternatively, *Seduction* could be understood to posit Woman as a tactical other, as she has historically been seen as the site of seduction. On that reading, despite Baudrillard's explicit criticism of Luce Irigaray in *Seduction*, there are resonances with her work. However, later writings that foreclose such readings are full of complaints about women's liberation and increasingly strange, reactionary assertions about women.

Despite his suspect position on gender (and also race, notably in *America*), Baudrillard challenges facile positive evaluations of difference in respect of gender, race, even postcolonialism. He advocates alterity rather than difference, as difference, he argues, is a device that merely allows the other back in, on terms decided by the powerful (males, the West, Europe).[17] He argues that the other should be seen as irreducibly Other. To illustrate, he argues that deserters and mutineers of the First World War should not be pardoned, as that denies the validity of their acts for a second time, in that the pardon says 'you were wrong and you're now forgiven'.[18]

Resistance, though, only has limited opportunities: it is the Object, the world outside agency, that resists. Viruses of all sorts are a form of resistance. Terrorism, although politically motivated, is also a product of a system attacking itself as system, a form of auto-resistance. Baudrillard's version of the end of history illustrates this inertial, ironic resistance. From the early 1980s on, he has referred to Canetti's idea of history ending but no one noticing.[19] Events occur, but are devoid of meaning. Unlike Fukuyama's claim for a meaningful end of history, thanks to the triumph of liberalism and capitalism, Baudrillard estimates that after such an end, the reality of events and their historical nature is emphasised more than ever. After a while, when events will cease to occur, the non-event will take over. Instead of an end of history, this means the end of history is impossible, as we witness a slowing down, such that the end is in sight, but only as vanishing point.[20]

The complicity with the system of alternatives to simulation (those being seduction, symbolic exchange, the object and/or image as resistance) leads Baudrillard finally to the 'perfect crime' and 'the impossible exchange', both of which posit the world as a manifestation of its own non-existence. In the first, the perfect crime would be to replace an actual (essentially unobtainable) reality with the different forms of the 'real' we have actually seen in history. Luckily, he writes, the crime was not perfect, as there is something other than 'the real'. But according to the notion of the 'impossible exchange' this infinitely small 'other' to simulation shrinks even further, because the real has nothing to exchange against – all has become 'same'.

In this setting, events both disturb the flow and are never allowed merely to be events: instead they are subsumed into a mediatised form to such an extent that they become 'non-events' (as exemplified by Princess Diana's death).[21] Terrorism is a non-event, a transpolitical strategy (seemingly emerging from the system rather than from specific groups), yet also an attempt to revitalise the moribund real of simulation, an attempt to offer an Other to the system, a recognition of the 'impossible exchange' simulation has given us. The more real simulation has become, the less it can provide external evidence of this realness; all becomes self-fulfilling prophecy, when the real is real because it looks real. Terrorism mobilises this impossibility. In both *The Perfect Crime* and *Impossible Exchange*, Baudrillard suggests that we need the simulacra of reality, as actual reality is only void, violence and death.

This 'actual reality' is a form of the symbolic, he argues in *The Spirit of Terrorism*, such that 9/11 constitutes an attack not only on America, or 'the free world', but on a system of simulation which attempts to exclude death (hence, even in wartime, the insistence on 'clean' war, 'surgical strikes'). The attack on the World Trade Centre is a sacrifice that the system cannot handle, committing suicide in the collapse of the towers. Even more controversially, Baudrillard writes of a secret pleasure in seeing the attack, not only in the minds of those with grievances against America.

Theory, Style, Aesthetics

From the organised sociological thinking of his early works, Baudrillard moves in the mid-1970s to a more polemical approach, almost always taking a counter-intuitive line, even in terms of his own theorising. Whilst there is clear continuity in his main ideas, the way theory is to be written comes into play, particularly from the mid-1980s. From then on, his writing becomes more aphoristic, even more intentionally provocative (perhaps spurred on by 'political correctness'), spreading itself out to address a seemingly endless set of cultural events, phenomena and products.

This shift is first seen in *America*, in which Baudrillard looks at the place that would seem to offer itself as the heart of the simulated world. However, the book is not a deep analysis, but knowingly superficial, addressing the obvious and always already mediatised manifestations of 'America' – New York, California, Death Valley, Las Vegas, the road, the desert and 'have a nice day'. America is a giant film set, Hollywood the alibi for the rest of the country's unreality.[22] This approach allows Baudrillard to skate above any possible depth, and to work at the level of surface, in short bursts of thought on often banal subjects (such as joggers). His musings on everyday cultural phenomena always feed back into a model of simulation, culminating in the controversial 'Utopia Realised' section.[23] For some, this section illustrates Baudrillard's acceptance of simulated hyperreality, and, by imputation, of the politics of those in power. Others read this chapter as ultra-cynical: America's giant error being the belief that it already is utopia. According to Baudrillard, for Europeans, utopia is unattainable, an aspiration, whereas Americans' aspirations are driven by the 'fact' of already being the best possible society. In any case, the 'utopia' Americans live in is a cynical yet naive, and ultimately totally shallow society, being something of a joke as a result. Baudrillard can certainly be criticised for presenting a monolithic version of America, one that attains hyperreality only through a wilful ignorance of any realities of the place. But France and Europe are as much the objects of his ire here (as elsewhere), and because America was born into modernity, it will always be ahead of Europe. America, in a strange way, becomes a utopia through its rejection of all 'old European' values (tradition, critique, History, 'depth'). This 'loss', which we might imagine a problem, Baudrillard estimates as a sign of vitality (as in later books when he writes of violence, of viruses that protect us through saving us from a greater evil).[24]

At around the same time as writing *America*, Baudrillard compiled the first volume of *Cool Memories* (covering the period 1980–5). These texts consist of short observations, often written, it would seem, while en route to another talk, given the references to travel and conferences. The *Cool Memories* are somewhere between diaries and books of aphorisms. As in *America*, Baudrillard explicitly writes from a personal perspective but without revealing much about himself directly. In these books, he covers any and every topic imaginable – from architecture to political corruption to the Pope as special effect.

The writing is very free, often poetic, speculative and highly politically charged. Baudrillard's strangely conservative views on sexual difference and 'Woman' are undisguised. He attacks political correctness and the ecology movement with a mix of ironic approval and exposure of the logical difficulties of their positions (seeing ecological concern as maintenance of humans at the top of the food chain, for example).[25] In these books Baudrillard also rehearses ideas about 'Thought' in general, and his own theoretical approach. The third and fourth volumes show deep disgust with contemporary thought and art. As the style of these texts gradually filters into those that are more overtly theoretical, readers of the recent Baudrillard are challenged by his refusal to play by the rules of 'proper' analysis or academic discourse. Instead of a cohesive, substantiated argument, Baudrillard offers assertions, imagined scenarios, diversions and polemic. Thereby asking: what is a theoretical text? and what is it good for?

Baudrillard's later work also ventures into the aesthetic, outflanking those who accused him of merely offering an aesthetics. In the 1990s he was not only more directly interested in art, but also in the status of 'the image' – notably in his attention to photography. Photography, as the height of simulation, offers, if not a way out, then a way on, a position from which to make some sort of statement that is paradoxically less simulated. Baudrillard's insistence on the importance of the Object rather than the Subject reaches a culmination in photography. At first glance, he seems to simply argue that photography captures something of the object world.[26]

Jean Baudrillard (1929–)

As he develops the idea, though, he approaches a 'deconstructive' position, according to which the photograph is a trace of what is not (otherwise) there. But whilst 'deconstruction' reveals something 'always already there', Baudrillard's method is more actively destructive, as he suggests that in making the trace you destroy the real – a real that, of course, was not there anyway.

Baudrillard extends this interest into practice, taking reasonably successful photographs of, on the one hand, obvious locations in America, and, on the other, insignificant details, without comment. This involvement seems to have given him more freedom to attack contemporary art, with which (after Duchamp and Warhol) he does not wish to engage. Notwithstanding this rejection of most contemporary art, art has always been interested in Baudrillard.[27] Baudrillard's work can equally be applied critically to much contemporary art – community art, art about identity, art about (but trapped in) simulation, art interested in the everyday, for example.

The question of aesthetics raises a fundamental question: is there something other than simulation? If so, is there some sort of obligation to pursue it? Increasingly, Baudrillard has returned to a minimal utopianism: there is a way to play the system, by outdoing it, in emphasising illusion and the lack of reality (as shown in ultra-realism). What he does not tell us is why we would bother, thereby allowing his ideas to be appropriated and applied, faithfully or otherwise.

Conclusion

Baudrillard's work has reached out beyond the world of the Academy and professional protesters, generating interest in and beyond 'the West', notably in South America and Japan. His thought will prove to be of lasting use in the advancing domains of technology, information, media and contemporary science. Yet, no one has really taken up his style, perhaps because his world is so self-contained, if not self-completing. It is very hard to take his ideas and apply them, except at a fairly general level, though writers such as Arthur Kroker, Gary Genosko, Victoria Grace and William Bogard have sought to work within a Baudrillardian paradigm. Writers such as Derrida, Foucault or Deleuze and Guattari have been taken up as models, with the latter pair, in particular, proving more popular with 'radicals' as they seem to offer ways of escaping the system. But Baudrillard is relentlessly accurate in his analyses of contemporary culture. His approach allows him to take on genuinely contemporary phenomena, such as terrorism, developments in mass media, artificial intelligence and cloning. However, there is a tiredness about some of the recent work, perhaps because he has been ahead of developments for a long time. He was already theorising cloning, for example, in the late 1970s, while his article on 9/11 could have been extrapolated from *Symbolic Exchange and Death*.

His work is increasingly hermetic in terms of other writers, referring still to Nietzsche, while favouring writers such as Canetti and Borges. Among contemporary theorists, he has little time for anyone but Paul Virilio (the writer closest to him in style and subject matter) and Peter Sloterdijk. This disinterest might be one of the reasons for a degree of repetition creeping into his work. In contrast, maybe that makes a better read, and it may be theoretically appropriate to refer to actors, novelists, films, buildings and so on as theoretical devices as well as 'objects of study'. In this distancing and estrangement, Baudrillard seeks to go beyond theory, leaving it beached on the real – or maybe the corpse of the real is washed up on theory.

Notes

1. Such is the view of Douglas Kellner, Alex Callinicos, Peter Dews, Steven Connor and Mark Poster. For some, nothing can save Baudrillard (Terry Eagleton and Christopher Norris). Arthur Kroker is more interesting in observing that Baudrillard builds on Marx (see Kroker and Cook, *Postmodern Scene*).
2. Baudrillard, *Mirror of Production*, p. 151.
3. Baudrillard, *Symbolic Exchange and Death*, p. 50. Compare with the 'four phases of the image' in *Simulacra and Simulation*, p. 6.
4. Baudrillard will later refer to this removal of the real, leaving only its trace, as 'the perfect crime'. See especially *The Perfect Crime*.
5. Baudrillard has subsequently added a fourth order, 'the fractal', where value becomes viral, ever shifting. See *The Transparency of Evil*, p. 5 and *passim*. In my opinion, this new stage occurs within the third stage, rather than replacing it.
6. The phenomenon identified as the 'Precession of Simulacra' (*Simulacra and Simulation*, pp. 1–42).
7. See 'On Nihilism', *Simulacra and Simulation*, pp. 159–64. For Nietzsche's take on nihilism, see *The Will to Power* (New York: Vintage, 1968).
8. *Symbolic Exchange and Death*, pp. 144, 133. This aspect of symbolic

Jean Baudrillard (1929–)

exchange is strikingly misinterpreted by Lyotard, in *Libidinal Economy* (London: Athlone, 1993) (as noted by Julian Pefanis).
9. Notable in this respect is Christopher Norris, *Uncritical Theory* (London: Lawrence and Wishart, 1992).
10. Baudrillard, 'Precession of Simulacra'.
11. Baudrillard, *Simulacra and Simulation*, p. 36.
12. This echoes his view of Disneyland, which exists to hide the fact that the US is Disneyland. *Simulacra and Simulation*, p. 12.
13. The social is built on 'the ruins of the symbolic and ceremonial edifice of former societies' (*In the Shadow of the Silent Majorities*, p. 65).
14. Baudrillard, *In the Shadow of the Silent Majorities*, p. 44.
15. See in particular *The Transparency of Evil*.
16. Baudrillard, *Cool Memories IV*, p. 101.
17. *The Transparency of Evil*, p. 133; also *The Illusion of the End*, p. 108.
18. *Cool Memories IV*, p. 113.
19. See *In the Shadow of the Silent Majorities*, p. 95.
20. Baudrillard, *Illusion of the End*, p. 3.
21. Baudrillard, *Impossible Exchange*, p. 137.
22. Baudrillard, *America*, p. 56.
23. Ibid., pp. 75–105.
24. This idea can be found in all texts since *The Transparency of Evil*. In that work, see the chapter 'Prophylaxis and Virulence', pp. 60–70.
25. On this, see also 'Maleficent Ecology', *Illusion of the End*, pp. 78–88, which also proposes a model of human ecology.
26. Baudrillard, *Transparency of Evil*, pp. 146–55.
27. Baudrillard's significance is often taken as a given in the art world. For example: 'in the 1970s, artists reacted critically to the onslaught of secondary images and illusions in which the Baudrillardian simulacrum came to replace primary tangible reality' (*Art of the 20th Century* (Cologne: Taschen, 1998), vol. 2, p. 561).

Major Works by Baudrillard

America, trans. Chris Turner (London: Verso, 1988 [1986]).
The Consumer Society, trans. 'C.T.' (London: Sage, 1998 [1970]).
Cool Memories, trans. Chris Turner (London: Verso, 1990 [1987]).
Cool Memories II: 1987–1990, trans. Chris Turner (London: Polity, 1995 [1990]).
Cool Memories IV: 1995–2000 (Paris: Galilée, 2000).
Fatal Strategies, trans. Philip Beitchman (London: Pluto, 1990 [1983]).
For a Critique of the Political Economy of the Sign, trans. Charles Levin (St. Louis: Telos, 1981) [1970].
Forget Foucault, trans. Nicole Dufresne, Philip Beitchman, Mark Polizotti and Lee Hildreth (New York: Semiotext[e], 1987 [1977]).

Fragments: Cool Memories III: 1991–1995, trans. Chris Turner (London: Verso, 1997 [1995]).

The Gulf War Did Not Happen, trans. Paul Patton (Bloomington: Indiana University Press, 1995 [1991]).

The Illusion of the End, trans. Chris Turner (Cambridge: Polity, 1994 [1992]).

Impossible Exchange, trans. Chris Turner (London: Verso, 2001 [1999]).

In the Shadow of the Silent Majorities, trans. Paul Foss, John Johnston and Paul Patton (New York: Semiotext[e], 1983 [1978]).

The Mirror of Production, trans. Mark Poster (St. Louis: Telos, 1975 [1973]).

The Perfect Crime, trans. Chris Turner (London: Verso, 1996 [1995]).

Screened Out, trans. Chris Turner (London: Verso, 2002 [1997]).

Seduction, trans. Brian Singer (London: Macmillan, 1990 [1979]).

Simulacra and Simulation, trans. Sheila Glaser (Ann Arbor: University of Michigan Press, 1994 [1981]).

The Spirit of Terrorism, trans. Chris Turner (London: Verso, 2002 [2002]).

Symbolic Exchange and Death, trans. Iain Hamilton Grant (London: Sage, 1993 [1976]).

The System of Objects, trans. James Benedict (London: Verso, 1996 [1968]).

The Transparency of Evil, trans. James Benedict (London: Verso, 1993 [1990]).

The Uncollected Baudrillard, ed. Gary Genosko (London: Sage, 2001).

Suggestions for Further Reading

Bogard, William, *The Simulation of Surveillance* (Cambridge and New York: Cambridge University Press, 1996). Applies Baudrillard to issues of contemporary vision and power.

Butler, Rex, *Jean Baudrillard* (London: Sage, 1999). Strong introduction.

Debord, Guy, *The Society of the Spectacle* (Detroit: Black and Red, 1983). A revolutionary Marxist critique of simulation.

Gane, Mike, *Jean Baudrillard: In Radical Uncertainty* (London: Pluto, 2000). Strong thematic reading, especially good on recent writings.

Genosko, Gary, *McLuhan and Baudrillard: The Masters of Implosion* (London: Routledge, 1999). Locates both writers in the context of the transmission of ideas about communication.

Grace, Victoria, *Baudrillard's Challenge* (London: Routledge, 2000). Unique feminist interpretation – not always successful.

Kellner, Douglas, *Jean Baudrillard: From Marxism to Postmodernism and Beyond* (Cambridge: Polity, 1989). Important early in-depth critical analysis.

Kroker, Arthur, and David Cook, *The Postmodern Scene: Excremental Culture and Hyper-Aesthetics* (Basingstoke: Macmillan, 1988). Where to go after Baudrillard? Combines theory with older philosophies and new aesthetics.

Levin, Charles, *Jean Baudrillard: A Study in Cultural Metaphysics* (Hemel Hempstead: Harvester Wheatsheaf, 1996). Engaged and detailed study. Occasionally fawning. Excellent glossary.

McLuhan, Marshall, *Understanding Media: The Extensions of Man* (London: Routledge, 1964). How technology and perceptions affect cultural reality.

Pefanis, Julian, *Heterology and the Postmodern: Bataille, Baudrillard, and Lyotard* (Durham and London: Duke University Press, 1991). An advanced theoretical work that establishes Baudrillard's link to Bataille.

Plant, Sadie, 'Baudrillard's Women: Eve of Seduction', in Chris Rojek and Bryan S. Turner (eds), *Forget Baudrillard?* (London: Routledge, 1993). An account of Baudrillard 'on women', comparing him with Irigaray.

Zurbrugg, Nicholas (ed.), *Jean Baudrillard, Art and Artefact* (London: Sage, 1997). Focuses on Baudrillard's aesthetic theory and photography. Thin on applications.

14

Pierre Bourdieu (1930–2002)

Cheleen Mahar and Christopher Wilkes

Introduction

Pierre Bourdieu has always worked against the grain. In an era beset with anxiety about 'Grand Theory', he became a master thinker of our age. Bourdieu combined the disciplines of philosophy, sociology and anthropology into a theoretical understanding of modern Western society and its habits. He actively engaged in the sociology of class reproduction, of colonialisation and post-colonialisation, gender relations, economic and political hierarchy, and of the process of artistic production. In doing so he rewrote the way we understand Western societies.

In an early article on French sociology, Claude Lévi-Strauss argued that sociology had long suffered from the gap between its bold theoretical premonitions and the lack of concrete evidence.[1] Bourdieu has forever changed this situation. His work combines a massive theoretical apparatus and an extensive empirical enterprise. He has constructed a devastating critique of domination by the power of the state and by the international grip of capital. By the end of his career, which was sadly cut short by his death in January 2002, Bourdieu was actively engaged in many layers of political life, in publishing, in television interviews and in political rallies, all activities which encouraged resistance to domination by societal structures.

From the beginning of his academic career, Pierre Bourdieu had been involved in acts of resistance. Born in the Gascon region of Béarn in rural southwestern France, Bourdieu did not come from a background that would have predicted scholarly success, much less that he would come to hold the chair of sociology at the Collège de France, the most prestigious academic institution in France. While Bourdieu actively sought academic accolades and worked in a strategic fashion towards his position in the academy, he never left his earlier self behind, always distrustful of elites and their institutions. As a result of the uneasy relationship between his background (and its connection to the suffering of those who were not entitled) and his powerful position as an international scholar, he was never at rest with his achievements, continuing to argue against the powerful and the suffering that they imposed upon ordinary citizens. It was this ability not only to perceive but also to, in a sense, feel such suffering that led to the substantial political contributions of Bourdieu's work.

Digging through the archaeology of Bourdieu's work is a little like following a tree diagram which spreads its branches out in all directions. The intellectual journey began with his early training in school as a scholarship student, to Paris and his work in philosophy at the École normale supérieure, to Algeria where he conducted ethnographic research (*The Algerians* and *Algeria 1960*), thereby breaking with the structuralism (scientific ethnology) of Lévi-Strauss, and then into his work in education during which he investigated the links between the French educational system and the reproduction of social class (*Reproduction in Education, Society and Culture*). This intellectual background was the structure upon which Bourdieu came to create his major theoretical and methodological body of work.

Work on broad theoretical and epistemological issues is spread throughout Bourdieu's contributions. He never left philosophy alone, returning to it repeatedly in times of disquiet, and then reinventing his own approaches as a result. Bourdieu had revolutionary views on how sociology was to be practised, views which are outlined in work which stretches from *The Craft of Sociology* (1968) to *The Logic of Practice* (1990) and from *Leçon sur la leçon* (1982) to *Pascalian Meditations* (2001). The genesis of Bourdieu's later work in art, politics, television, gender studies, class and poverty is the fundamental break that he made with traditional sociological thought, which posited as irreconcilable the perspectives of objectivism and subjectivism. Bourdieu's early theoretical work, *Outline of a Theory of Practice*, transcended this opposition, which he termed a false dichotomy, transforming it into a dialectical relationship between structure and agency.

Bourdieu's earliest ethnographic work was focused around the question of social transformation in Algeria, and Bourdieu continued with his commitment to empirical research in such works as *Distinction* and *The Weight of the World*. Later in his life, Bourdieu overcame his natural tendency to shy away from public political spectacle. Bourdieu wrote and spoke in public against the spread of global corporatist television, and the dangers inherent in global capitalism. He also came out in support of French railway workers when they went on strike in 1995 and defended immigrants, *les sans papiers*, who could not legally justify their presence in France. The thread that connects this activism with his method is his understanding of society as a struggle of symbolic and material forces, in which the truth of 'reality' is one of interpretation and structural recasting imposed by a dominant symbolic structure, which treats its particular version of reality as natural.

The Method

Bourdieu argued that fundamental to good sociological analysis was the method of doing social science. His methodology is deeply joined to theory, and can be conceived of as a series of conceptual categories which, when connected by the investigator, can account for practice in everyday life. These concepts are to be used in a relational fashion, rather than as instruments of separation. When asked what he considered to be the core ideas around which his work has been established, Bourdieu answered,

> The main thing is that they are not to be conceptualised so much as ideas, on that level, but as a method. The core of my work lies in the method and a way of thinking. To be more precise, my method is a manner of asking questions, rather than just ideas. This, I think, is a critical point.[2]

As evidenced below, this method is such that it routinely questions relations of power and domination. The central conceptual categories are analytic tools which have been endlessly reworked by Bourdieu in his successive books. The idea of reworking his methodology is deeply embedded in the way Bourdieu thought about his work; everything was a work in progress towards an increasingly clear account of the genesis of practical life. This orientation implies a self-consciousness on the part of the investigator, so that the work itself is never to be disassociated from the practice of sociology. The theory and practice of sociology, which are embedded in political and powerful forces of the disciplinary field, are never innocent. Bourdieu comments,

> In the case of social science, to understand the progress of knowledge supposes a progress in the knowledge of the conditions of knowledge; it therefore requires a stubborn return to the same objects which offer opportunities to objectify more completely, the objective and subjective relation to the object. And, if it is necessary, we must retrospectively reconstruct in them the stages, because this work tends to make its own traces disappear.[3]

For Bourdieu, nothing is written in isolation. He said that he uses the 'tools' around him with 'humility but also with discernment'. Bourdieu considered his own work to owe a great deal to a long list of predecessors, as if he had never invented anything at all himself.[4]

Habitus and the Field

The two central concepts embedded in Bourdieu's method are 'habitus' and the 'field', which he combines with notions of capital, strategy and struggle in order to explain the practice of everyday life. The use of these concepts allows us to link class and social space with family, individual dispositions and personal agency. Fundamental to all sociological analysis is the decision about how to talk about constraint and freedom, constraints which result from the hold institutions have over us, and freedom resulting from the actions of agents, of individual people who live within these constraints. As Wacquant suggests, 'The concepts of habitus and field allow Bourdieu to forsake the false problems of personal spontaneity and social constraint, freedom and necessity ... and to sidestep the common alternatives of individual and structure'.[5] The use of habitus and field further provide a method which interrogates class trajectories over time, as well as individual lives in the ethnographic present.

Bourdieu first used the notion of habitus, (an old Aristotelian and Thomist concept rethought by Bourdieu),[6] to break from the structuralism of both Louis Althusser and Lévi-Strauss. Neither the position of Althusserian structuralism, in which people were mere 'bearers' of history, nor that of the Lévi-Straussian structural unconscious, in which myths and rituals were the source of final causes, though independent of the conscious wishes or actions of people, were adequate methods to account for the genesis of social practice. Bourdieu's interest in using habitus was in understanding what we call the 'individual' is shaped by social structure. By that, he referred to the internalisation of social structure, which then serves to act as a generative system within the individual. By using habitus as a structuring mechanism, Bourdieu analyses the relationship between individual practice (permanent dispositions) and the world in general, thus bridging the gap between structuralism and phenomenology.

Habitus also refers to social structures which operate as they are internalised by a person through their bodily incorporation. As an instance of this: 'Thus the submissiveness of Kabylian women is embodied in the curvature of their spines towards the ground. It is not just that social learning is ingrained on the body ... rather it is imitated unconsciously through specific bodily actions'.[7] Habitus, then, refers to the durable dispositions which agents have in the world and which reflect the action of the world on the body and the self. It is also a system of models of perception and appreciation, and, as such, it results from learning in the world and from acting in the world. It is given, but it is also created, and it provides the major source of ideas and practices. Habitus provides a sense of one's place in the social world, as well as an account of our *sens de jeu* (feel for the game), to use Bourdieu's oft-quoted phrase. Habitus embodies our understanding of the logic of society and what place we have in it. By reconstructing the dialectic between structure and agency through the development of this new concept, Bourdieu hoped to reconcile the levels of the abstract structures with the actions, feelings and mental states of individual persons.

The notion of what Bourdieu called the field is one that reflects the space of social interaction, conflict and competition. For him, society was a system of fields which are autonomous but which exist in relationship to one another, and which collectively exist within a larger social space (defined as the overall conception of the social world). Each field has its own structure and field of forces organized around specific capitals, which are used in competitive and strategic ways. Fields are dynamic, as Wacquant says; fields are not dead structures or sets of 'empty places' but a space of play.[8] Fields identify areas of struggle, and therefore can be imagined as fields of forces, because they constitute the dynamic spaces of social practice. The struggles for positions (through capital) act to transform fields; this means that they can never be imagined as merely static social structures. Fields are further defined by a system of objective relations of power that lie between positions in the field. These

Pierre Bourdieu (1930–2002)

positions also correspond to a system of objective relations between symbolic points, such as works of art, artistic manifestos, political declarations, and so on. Bourdieu says,

> One of my lectures at the Collège is about the relations between habitus and field, and how action (practice) is a product of the relationship between habitus (which is a product of history), and field which is also a product of history, and at the same time, a product of the field of forces. In a field, there are stakes, there are forces, and there are people who have a lot of capital and others who do not ... However I would like to stress that in every different case, you must study how the situation works. So my ideas are not a general theory but a method.[9]

The active principle here is the strategy by which people move within a field and use or transform capitals in order to reach or maintain particular positions. For Bourdieu strategy, struggle and the field are completely interrelated.

Capital

Bourdieu rejects the ordinary and purely economistic meaning of the word capital, and adds to it the notions of 'symbolic' and 'cultural' capital as avenues through which class positions and power are manifested. Capital is broadly defined as a socially valued good, but it has many specific meanings. Most generally, symbolic capital has been defined as a sense of honour, reputation, dignity, prestige or power. Symbolic capital is the most critical form of capital as, for Bourdieu, both pre-capitalist and capitalist societies are organised around symbolic capital. Indeed, one of Bourdieu's principle endeavours was to show how the symbolic and the apparently non-material are profoundly important in structuring our lives. For example, he revealed how the divisions and subdivisions based on tastes, aesthetic judgement, social hierarchy and methods of discernment act in powerful ways as mechanisms of social classification. This is apparent in the establishment of hierarchy, and in the maintenance and struggle over the most material of systems: class structures.

Cultural capital, itself symbolic, refers to such relationships as are embedded in social and kin groupings, one's educational and professional qualifications and the like. However, the critical point about capital is not so much the definitions of the different types of capital, but the relationship between capital as a symbolic structure and as a social structure. While Bourdieu does not argue that symbolic structures create social structure, he does argue that the symbolic is much more than an instrument of knowledge. These social forms are to be understood as principles of vision and division, which allow us not only to create a reality but also to believe in that reality, even before it may exist. Within certain limits, symbolic structures have an extraordinary and, Bourdieu argued, underestimated power of constitution. Such power is realised in philosophy as well as in political theory.

Connected to power, the state, class privilege and the domination of masculine ideology is Bourdieu's use of symbolic violence, which constitutes an extension of the concept of symbolic capital. The power within symbolic capital resides in its ability to constitute the given by stating it, while symbolic violence in the exercise of symbolic capital is 'the power to impose ... instruments of knowledge and expression of social reality ... which are arbitrary (but unrecognized as such)'.[10] The power of symbolic systems and the domination that they impose over the construction of reality is perhaps the most critical as well as one of the most creative aspects of Bourdieu's work. Such symbolic forms of power as language, dress and body postures, as well as symbolic forms of power such as the law, are vital in understanding the cognitive function of symbols in the life of an individual. In addition, they reveal the social and cultural function of symbols as instruments of knowledge and domination. Such systems make possible a 'given' consensus within a community and contribute to the reproduction of the social order.

In Bourdieu's later work, these ideas were used in a more obviously political way: in his critique of the media, *On Television*, and of international capital, *Acts of Resistance*. In these later works Bourdieu revealed the struggles for capital through the insidious control of the powerful over the disenfranchised, who, while they understood their position as an underclass, were compromised by the suffering and degradation which they found in their day-to-day experiences. Such suffering took too much of their lives for them to have an effective political voice. Bourdieu took on this suffering, and tried to be a voice for them and for us.

Criticisms

Bourdieu's deep forays into the fields of anthropology, sociology, education, philosophy and aesthetics, not to mention his extended influence among all the human sciences, have brought him up against many dissenters. The stakes of the debate are considerable. Central to this struggle is the fact that theorists have to decide how much freedom individuals have to create their social practice, and how far they are constrained by social structures. Bourdieu makes no a priori claims about this debate, preferring instead to allow empirical work to provide answers. In what follows, we concentrate on four major areas of concern.

First, Bourdieu's work is thought to lack an account of history.[11] Jenkins is especially sharp in his critique,

> his theory becomes a machine for the suppression of history, banishing it with an eternal ethnographic present that is indistinguishable from the past and prefigures the future. It is a world where behaviour has its causes but actors are not allowed their reasons.[12]

There is little doubt that Bourdieu's work dwelt largely in the ethnographic present, and in the politics and semiotics of institutions, social structures and social movements. While his studies of art and literature (*The Field of Cultural Production*) sought to establish the historical origins of the field, for example, in his discussion of Flaubert and Manet, it is also true that Bourdieu did not foreground historical analysis. In part, this is a reaction to the ruthless historical determinism found in a form of structural Marxism which he had long ago rejected, as he avoided the imagery of the machine of history clanking inexorably forward. Habitus is, of course, an embodied history, but this still gets us no closer to a history of societies, or a history of social groups.[13] Therefore, Bourdieu's work does stand guilty as charged with not privileging history above contemporary forms of analysis.

Yet, history is everywhere in his work, and some critics have mentioned his close relation to the 'New Historicism'.[14] Wacquant, in discussion with Bourdieu, argues that Bourdieu was engaged in a radical historicism, while Bourdieu himself claimed to be engaged in a double historicity of mental structures.[15] In his discussion of Heidegger, Bourdieu argued quite clearly for a historicised account of the emergence of ideas, even though this suggestion is not always taken up in his empirical work. He was also critical of philosophy's refusal to confront historical issues. Indeed, he claimed that the separation of history from sociology had been catastrophic.[16] One must not forget that, with Foucault, he was deeply influenced by Georges Canguilhem, who, along with Gaston Bachelard, suggested to a generation of French thinkers the possibility of a new way to realise the role of the philosopher in intellectual life. Epistemologically, this concerned the move from the mimetic models of science to a model which apprehends the hidden principles of the realities being interpreted. Thus, for Bourdieu, social science must reveal the hold of the past on the models of the present. Therefore, the separation of sociology from history is a disastrous division which has no basis in epistemology. Nonetheless, historical analysis has played a limited role in the empirical work for which he is most famous.

This charge of a lack of a theory of history is closely tied to a second charge, this time of Parsonian functionalism. Talcott Parsons, the iconic theoretical figure in American sociology in the 1950s and 1960s, famously ignored Marx while celebrating Durkheim and Weber, and established a theoretical account based on stability, equilibrium and the need for the social institutions of inequality to maintain the social order. Central to the functionalist view is the circular argument that because certain social institutions exist in many societies, they must be functional for societies. Their necessity is determined by their existence. Such a view is sometimes said to exist in Bourdieu's work. Within the 'Sacred Trinity' of habitus, capital and field,[17] we find an entirely persuasive apparatus, which explains social practice. What is capital? Capital is a socially valued good, with complex qualities. It is that for which people struggle. Habitus provides the sources of motivation; field the terrain of struggle, the social context in which this occurs. Functionalism can therefore be implicitly read into this story.[18] However, the antidote to functionalism is found in Bourdieu's work in two ways. For Bourdieu, the world was not rule governed (as demonstrated by his break with Althusser and Lévi-Strauss), but rather organised around the notion of strategy. Struggles and strategy enable the social actor not only to function purposively in the social arena but also to challenge, collectively or individually, the very structure of the rule, thus altering the shape of the game itself. Thus, successful practice is not merely enabled by gaining a *sens de jeu*, but in attempts to resist and reconfigure the very structure within which strategy performs. In his later work, which is most openly political, it is also hard to substantiate the charge of functionalism, since the emphasis here is so decidedly aimed at the rupture of present circumstances.[19] What does remain, however, especially in his earlier empirical work, is a sense that the structure of domination in late capitalist societies is so brutal and so complete that determinism, social constraint and reproduction are all but guaranteed for most people, and thus a functionalist and fatalist vision of social practice comes into play.

Third, Bourdieu is accused of engaging in universal theorising in an era when such efforts have largely been discounted.[20] Bourdieu, of course, would not have seen it that way. In 1990, he argued in an interview that his attempt was to provide universal methods of analysis, rather than theoretical dictates.[21] His approach was to ask questions in a particular fashion, rather than establish a priori some unyielding structure of explanation. However, this does not solve the problem. Whether we call the theoretical apparatus a series of questions, a methodological universalism, or a particular form of analysis, it still works as an account of social practice. This leads us to consider where he stands epistemologically. Clearly, Bourdieu has little time for the postmodernist project in whatever form it comes. In the end, Bourdieu must count his 'generative structuralism' as a form of sophisticated realism; tendencies, rather than laws, govern the social world in his analysis. In Fowler's felicitous phrase, Bourdieu's project is probably best described as a 'rational utopianism', which 'represents a realistic assessment of the potential for transformation given a better grasp of the many obstacles to reason'.[22]

Fourth, the serious charge has been made against Bourdieu that his work culminates in an act of 'bad faith', which, following Sartre, means saying one thing and doing another.[23] Bourdieu is accused of building an elaborate edifice of theory, woven around with the spells of philosophy, and guarded forever by the continually more complex defences he gave of his work. Using Bourdieu's own arguments against him, Jenkins sees Bourdieu's use of an elevated style, an overly demanding vocabulary, and his negation of the 'labeling' of positions, as sources of this problem. Certainly, Bourdieu, more than anyone in sociology, was aware, through his method of epistemic reflexivity, of how it is that the intellectual is created and consecrated. And certainly again, in a unique way, his own trajectory is explained by his own method. Whether a claim of bad faith can be sustained in his work is open for discussion. There is no doubt that Bourdieu's fundamental interest in sociology was in its use as a mode of scientific interpretation that should be tied to the possibilities of liberation from domination. At the same time, he certainly and systematically tried to avoid having his ideas dismissed too easily, labeled in order to be ignored, or falling prey to intellectualist or hierarchical errors in his strategic decisions. In this he was perhaps more successful than most.[24]

Bourdieu's Influence

It is in the field of education, with which Bourdieu was preoccupied during the early 1960s, that he first became famous. The two relevant texts, *The Inheritors* and *Reproduction in Education, Society and Culture* were at the centre of debates in the student-driven social uprisings of that era, and have had profound effects on research concerning the social reproduction of poverty and neglect through schooling. Most well known, perhaps, in the United States, is Jay MacLeod's *Ain't No Makin It*[25] which has been widely used as a textbook, and which debates with Bourdieu's 'reproduction' theory directly. Bourdieu's central critique was of the 'naturalism' which always accompanied merit, thus making eternal those qualities that had been created through power. Meritocracy thus became simply a cover story for domination, enabling the reproduction of elites through the apparently objectivist strategies of testing and evaluation. His story of the reproduction of cultural capital as a parallel system to the reproduction of economic capital is one of the most powerful accounts of the relation between education and hierarchy that exists.

His influence, which is widespread in the literature in a variety of countries, also set the scene for what has been called the 'Reproduction Debate'. Bourdieu resolutely rejected a model in which education simply reproduced hierarchy. Instead, complicated processes involving history, habitus, social structures, and the shape and nature of the social field, form the practice of agents. Critics such as Henry Giroux have argued that Bourdieu had no faith in the dominated classes to resist.[26] And Willis suggested that Bourdieu had no place in his work for 'cultural production', that is, forms of resistance in the classroom and outside which resist educational domination.[27] But Bourdieu's analysis trod the awkward path of denying the infallibility of reproduction, while refusing its alternative, the leftist populism of the 1970s. His sophisticated theory of practice has found favour in several hundred ethnographic studies, which have applied his broad methodological framework to a wide variety of educational sites throughout the world. What results is a picture of symbolic power which goes far beyond France and Europe to offer up an account of a globalised empire of scholastic domination.

Pierre Bourdieu (1930–2002)

Bourdieu's argument that sociological practitioners ought to be ruthlessly self-conscious about their location in the enterprise of empirical work resonates strongly with themes developed in advanced circles of anthropology. The approach avoids the narcissism of objectivity and the radical liberalism of sanctifying the subjectivity of the subject. His new questions about social scientific practice had to be answered, and through this intervention he created a following of critical scholars, though others found his epistemological critique intensely difficult and annoying to confront.

Perhaps most important are Bourdieu's theories of hierarchy and domination, which find expression most particularly in his masterwork *Distinction*, and in his studies of the state and intellectual hierarchisation, to be found in *Homo Academicus* and *State Nobility*. These studies led to a profound break with, and an enrichment of, the established ways of thought about privilege and domination, and have been widely invoked. His reworking of theories of class in *Distinction* raises serious questions for the traditional ladder-like models of class hierarchy which have routinely been championed by American stratificationists. As with education, his work in *Distinction* serves to denaturalise the taste of the dominant order, and to make evident the elaborate structures of hierarchy and repression embedded deep in the heart of the social and cultural choices we make each day. He claimed that structures of inequality are deeply rooted in the basis of social life, widely glossed as social necessity and material inevitability. Elaborating, as he did, on the complexity of the Marx–Weber synthetic models of capital produced a highly sophisticated general theory of capital across several fields of understanding, thus providing the research community with a profoundly innovative and insightful theoretical armature. His intervention has changed the way we do class analysis forever.

While Bourdieu's has always been a political voice which spoke for the dispossessed (as in his work on Algeria, on education and in the house journal which he started in 1975, *Actes de la recherche en sciences sociales*), his most strongly political works appeared the 1990s. The influence of these latest texts has yet to be judged. Bourdieu had been requested by the Socialist government of the 1980s to produce two reports on the state of education. By the 1990s, he became more directly active, turning his attention to a variety of organising strategies involving academics, unionists, activists and cultural workers. He was at the centre of a group of progressive social scientists, Raison d'Agir, who launched a publishing house of the same name. In *On Television* he attacked the mainstream media as cultural fast-food, while in *Masculine Domination* he looked at androcentrism. Bourdieu worked in many ways to protect the dispossessed and the unheard: he fought for pensions, for full employment, and against racism. He became a major figure in the fight against neoliberal globalisation, which he wrote about in *Acts of Resistance*, and in the posthumously published *Interventions, 1961–2001*. He commented on the world of suffering in the vast ethnography *The Weight of the World*, continuing a heavy programme of teaching and more traditional publishing until his death. The intensity of his political thrust in the last years gave a certain poignancy to a life in which the urge to confront domination through science was brought finally into stark relief.

Notes

1. Claude Lévi-Strauss, 'French Sociology', in Georges Gurvitch and Wilbert Ellis Moore (eds), *Twentieth Century Sociology* (New York: The Philosophical Library, 1950).
2. Cited in Cheleen Mahar, 'Pierre Bourdieu: The Intellectual Project', in Harker, Mahar and Wilkes (eds), *An Introduction to the Work of Pierre Bourdieu*, pp. 26–57, p. 33.
3. Bourdieu, *Questions de sociologie*, p. 7.
4. See Honneth, Kocyba and Schwibs, 'The Struggle for Symbolic Order', p. 39.
5. Bourdieu and Wacquant, *An Invitation to Reflexive Sociology*, p. 23.
6. See Erwin Panofsky, *Architecture gothique et pensée scholastique*, trans. Pierre Bourdieu (Paris: Les Éditions de Minuit, 1967 [1955]).
7. Fowler, 'Situating Bourdieu', p. 17.
8. Bourdieu and Wacquant, *An Invitation to Reflexive Sociology*, p. 19.
9. Bourdieu cited in Harker, Mahar and Wilkes (eds), *An Introduction to the Work of Pierre Bourdieu*, p. 36.
10. Bourdieu, 'Symbolic Power', p. 115.
11. See Harker, Mahar and Wilkes (eds), *An Introduction to the Work of Pierre Bourdieu*, p. 215; and R. W. Connell, *Which Way Is Up: Essays on Sex, Class and Culture* (Sydney, Boston: Allen and Unwin, 1983), pp. 140–61.
12. Jenkins, *Pierre Bourdieu*, p. 97. Jenkins's treatment is especially critical. He accuses Bourdieu of, among other things, functionalism (81); determinism (82); a lack of novelty (89); a lack of clarity (89); a weak theory of institutions (89); the charge that the concepts of habitus and field are poorly related (90); and functionalism again (90). Much of this commentary stems from a narrow reading of Bourdieu, especially of his empirical work. Elsewhere, the criticism is extended to include

objectivism (91); empiricism (92); determinism (96); an oversocialised conception of man (*sic*); a failure to deal with subjectivity; a failure to understand classes (148); condescension to the working class (148); reductionism; (149); overly complex language (164, 169); and, finally, 'bad faith' (169). Jenkins's book is an excellent antidote to the process of canonisation that has too often accompanied the response to Bourdieu's work.
13. While a focus on social struggle was implicit but never fully developed early in Bourdieu's work, the emphasis shifted in the last decade of his work, particularly in *Acts of Resistance* and *The Weight of the World*.
14. Bourdieu, *The Field of Cultural Production*, p. 1.
15. Bourdieu and Wacquant, *An Invitation to Reflexive Sociology*, p. 139; and Bourdieu, *Political Ontology*, p. 153.
16. Bourdieu, *Political Ontology*, p. 156, fn. 112; pp. 157 and 90–1.
17. A phrase introduced by Fowler in her essay 'Pierre Bourdieu', p. 321.
18. See Jon Elster, *Sour Grapes: Studies in the Subversion of Rationality* (Cambridge: Cambridge University Press, 1983), pp. 68–71; Jenkins, *Pierre Bourdieu*, pp. 81–2; Harker, Mahar and Wilkes (eds), *An Introduction to the Work of Pierre Bourdieu*, p. 217.
19. While the charge of functionalism is widespread, it refers generally to Bourdieu's writing before his more openly political work of the 1990s.
20. Joseph Margolis, 'Pierre Bourdieu: Habitus and the Logic of Practice', in Richard Shusterman (ed.), *Bourdieu: A Critical Reader* (Oxford: Blackwell, 1999), pp. 64–83, p. 65.
21. Mahar, 'Pierre Bourdieu: The Intellectual Project', p. 33.
22. Fowler, 'Pierre Bourdieu', p. 325.
23. Jenkins, *Pierre Bourdieu*, pp. 158–62.
24. Bourdieu and Wacquant, *An Invitation to Reflexive Sociology*, pp. 58–9.
25. Jay Macleod, *Ain't No Makin' It: Aspirations and Attainment in a Low-Income Neighborhood* (Boulder: Westview Press, 1987).
26. H. Giroux, 'Power and Resistance in the New Sociology of Education: Beyond Theories of Social and Cultural Reproduction', in *Curriculum Perspectives*, 2, 3, 1982, pp. 1–26.
27. P. Willis, 'Cultural Production and Theories of Reproduction', in L. Barton and S. Walker (eds), *Class and Education* (London: Croom Helm, 1983), cited in Harker, Mahar and Wilkes, *An Introduction to the Work of Pierre Bordieu*, p. 104.

Major Works by Bourdieu

Acts of Resistance: Against the Tyranny of the Market, trans. Richard Nice (New York: New Press, 1998 [1998]).
Algeria 1960, The Disenchantment of the World, The Sense of Honour, the Kabyle

House; World Reversed: Essays, trans. Richard Nice (Cambridge: Cambridge University Press, 1979 [1977]).

The Algerians, trans. Alan C. M. Ross (Boston: Beacon Press, 1962 [1958]).

(with Jean-Claude Chamboredon, Jean-Claude Passeron), *The Craft of Sociology: Epistemological Preliminaries*, ed. Beate Krais, trans. Richard Nice (Berlin, New York: Walter de Gruyter, 1991 [1968]).

Distinction, trans. Richard Nice (Cambridge: Harvard University Press, 1984 [1979]).

The Field of Cultural Production: Essays on Art and Literature (New York: Columbia University Press, 1993).

(with H. Haacke), *Free Exchange*, trans. Richard Johnson (Stanford: Stanford University Press, 1994 [1994]).

Homo academicus, trans. Peter Collier (Stanford: Stanford University Press, 1998 [1984]).

The Inheritors: French Students and Their Relation to Culture (Chicago: Chicago University Press, 1979).

In Other Words: Essays towards a Reflexive Sociology, trans. Matthew Adamson (Stanford: Stanford University Press, 1990).

Interventions 1961–2001: Science sociale et action politique, eds Franck Poupeau and Thiery Discepolo (Marseille, Agone, Montréal: Comeau et Nadeau, c. 2002).

(with Löic J. D. Wacquant), *An Invitation to Reflexive Sociology* (Chicago: University of Chicago Press, 1992).

Leçon sur la leçon (Paris: Éditions de Minuit, 1982).

The Logic of Practice, trans. Richard Nice (Stanford: Stanford University Press, 1990 [1980]).

Masculine Domination, trans. Richard Nice (Stanford: Stanford University Press, 1998 [1998]).

On Television and Journalism, trans. Priscilla Parkhurst Ferguson (New York: New Press, 1998 [1996]).

Outline of a Theory of Practice, trans. Richard Nice (Cambridge: Cambridge University Press, 1977 [1972]).

Pascalian Meditations, trans. Richard Nice (Stanford: Stanford University Press, 2000 [1997]).

The Political Ontology of Martin Heidegger (Stanford: Stanford University Press, 1991 [1988]).

Questions de sociologie (Paris: Les Éditions de Minuit, 1980).

(with Jean-Claude Passeron), *Reproduction in Education, Society and Culture*, trans. Richard Nice (London: Sage, 1977 [1970]).

State Nobility: Elite Schools in the Field of Power, trans. Lauretta Clough (Cambridge: Polity Press, 1996 [1989]).

'Symbolic Power', in D. Gleeson (ed.), *Identity and Structure: Issues in the Sociology of Education* (Driffield: Nofferton Books, 1977 [1977]), pp. 112–19.

(with Alain Accardo), *The Weight of the World: Social Suffering in Contemporary Society*, trans. Priscilla Parkhurst Ferguson (Stanford: Stanford University Press, 1999 [1993]).

Suggestions for Further Reading

Fowler, Bridget, 'Pierre Bourdieu', in Bryan Turner and Anthony Elliott (eds), *Profiles in Contemporary Social Theory* (London: Sage Publications, 2001), pp. 315–26. A brief, succinct summary of Bourdieu's work.

Fowler, Bridget, 'Situating Bourdieu: Cultural Theory and Sociological Perspective', in Bridget Fowler (ed.), *Pierre Bourdieu and Cultural Theory: Critical Investigations* (London: Sage, 1997). Full of insights and thoughtful analysis.

Harker, R., C. Mahar and C. Wilkes (eds), *An Introduction to the Work of Pierre Bourdieu: The Practice of Theory* (London: Macmillan, 1990). The first book in English on Bourdieu. Begins with a review of key concepts, an interview with Bourdieu, and then chapters on each of the key areas of Bourdieu's work.

Honneth, A. N., H. Kocyba and B. Schwibs, 'The Struggle for Symbolic Order – an Interview with Pierre Bourdieu', *Theory, Culture and Society*, 3, 3, 1986, pp. 35–51. A very insightful exchange, recommended as an early read on Bourdieu.

Jenkins, Richard, *Pierre Bourdieu* (London: Routledge, 1992). A sharp, acerbic critique of Bourdieu. Jenkins pulls no punches and takes Bourdieu to task for many weaknesses.

Robbins, Derek, *The Work of Pierre Bourdieu: Recognizing Society* (Milton Keynes: Open University Press, 1991). An excellent early book about Bourdieu, very well written and especially strong on educational issues.

Wacquant, Löic, 'The Sociological Life of Pierre Bourdieu', *International Sociology*, 17, 4, 2002, pp. 549–56. A succinct and incisive account of Bourdieu's life, written as an obituary at the time of Bourdieu's death. It offers an insightful account both of Bourdieu's individual writings, and a sense of his overall accomplishment.

15

Jürgen Habermas (1929–)

Martin Morris

The Turn to Language in Critical Theory

Jürgen Habermas became widely regarded as the leader of 'second generation' Frankfurt School critical theorists following the death of his mentor, Theodor Adorno, in 1969. While deeply indebted to his predecessors at the Institute for Social Research, Habermas developed his own distinct approach. The later generation have substantially transfigured critical theory in response to new empirical social conditions and philosophical problems. In particular, Habermas rejects Adorno's philosophical orientation for its 'paradigmatic' limitation by the so-called 'philosophy of consciousness' (a criticism that applies to all first-generation critical theory).[1] The philosophy of consciousness refers to a vast and highly differentiated modern tradition, that is unified only in its inability to get beyond the view that the subject relates to the world exclusively through knowledge and action. For Habermas, the need to switch from consciousness philosophy to a communication theory paradigm offers critical theory more secure normative foundations.

It was during the 1970s that Habermas began systematically to incorporate communication theory and linguistic philosophy into his critical theory via 'universal pragmatics', which drew on the speech pragmatics of John Austin and John Searle and the formal pragmatics of his own colleague Karl-Otto Apel. Also significant during this period was Habermas's growing appreciation of systems theory (or media theory), which emerged from his debate with the German systems theorist Niklas Luhmann.[2] The result was an attempt to rethink historical materialism in terms of increasing systems differentiation, on the one hand, and stages of normative development that reflected the successful creation of new institutions of communicative competence, on the other.[3] In this formulation, the development of the forces of production created pressures on social and political institutions but were not, as Marx thought, the primary source of the dynamic of development. Indeed, for Habermas, the potentials lying latent in the forces of production could only be released after new institutions of communication were created which established and legitimated a new normative context. It was the new normative context that then allowed the development of the forces of production rather than it being the forces of production that generated such a context.

Language brings forth worlds of experience and knowledge – it has a 'world-disclosing' function, as the phenomenological tradition from Husserl and Heidegger has argued. But it also has a logical function: it makes sense of things. Habermas emphasises this historical sense-making capacity that produces understanding and knowledge and socio-cultural learning at the individual and collective levels. Language, for Habermas, entails a differentiated form of life that always includes normative structure, world disclosure and self-formation. Only through language do we come to know anything, which suggests that the order of our subjectivities will also be found in the structure and practice of language. The starting point of his analysis, however, is not the facticity of the knowing and acting subject but the relations between communicating subjects and the operation of communication as a system. For Habermas, any adequate philosophy must account for the communicative context in which all speaking subjects become capable of knowing and acting, recognising meaning and taking responsibility for their knowledge and action. This context is possible owing to the consensus-generating power of human language itself. 'What raises us out of nature,' Habermas states in his inaugural lecture at Frankfurt University, 'is the only thing whose nature we can know: *language*. Through its structure, autonomy and responsibility are posited for us. Our first sentence expresses unequivocally the intention of universal and unconstrained consensus.'[4] Habermas's first programmatic statement of the linguistic turn in critical theory expresses its core normative orientation. This chapter focuses on Habermas's communicative paradigm as the normative basis for his social analysis and theory of deliberative democracy.

Universal Pragmatics and Communicative Rationality

The idea at the core of speech pragmatics is that we do things when we use words. It has been common since the ancient study of rhetoric to recognise that a speaker can achieve certain strategic effects on a hearer with the use of compelling speech – that is, with eloquence, poetics, passion and so on, as well as persuasive reason. Speech pragmatics, however, analyses the action of sentences themselves independent of the style of the speaker or the aesthetic affects and effects that the words or speaker may elicit. It does this by analysing the pragmatic achievements that accompany and, indeed, provide the communicative context within which the semantic content of sentences appears and is grasped. Drawing on Austin's distinction between 'illocutionary' speech acts, which do things in the saying of something, and 'perlocutionary' speech acts, which produce consequential effects from the saying of something, Habermas develops his distinction between the communicative action of language and the institutional, strategic or instrumental power of language. As long as communicative action is distinguished in this way, a normative level of language can be analysed apart from the various effects discourses have.

The theory of universal pragmatics directly links communication and normative action by reconstructing the universal presuppositions of speech that are activated in every utterance. The pragmatic assumptions that speakers and hearers make whenever they communicate have a normative content and force that are, according to Habermas, non-transcendable and unavoidable. To act communicatively is to seek understanding and agreement with another speaker in language, which means that a 'discourse ethics' can be reconstructed in speech action.[5] A discourse ethics seeks to clarify the communicative presuppositions of speech that identify the precise social bonding achievements enacted in every communicative exchange. As an ethical or normative pragmatics, it is distinguished from all forms of objectivist or naturalist ethics and from instrumentalist approaches to action. To act strategically or instrumentally indicates an orientation toward ego's success through objectification of speech, interlocutors and situations without the need for understanding or agreement in language with another speaker.

Communicative action thus aims at 'reaching understanding and agreement', which indicates a cognitive achievement that is more than merely epistemological. It is an essentially intersubjective event that entails consensually oriented action by both parties to the communication. Consequently, it means much more than simply acknowledging or responding to the symbolic meaning of an utterance. Communicative action involves the raising and redeeming of validity claims in speech, which is why it is an action oriented toward reaching understanding and agreement. The pursuit of valid knowledge, for Habermas, is in this way immanent to society itself – indeed, dependent on it. 'It is part of understanding a sentence,' Habermas explains, 'that we are capable of recognizing *grounds* through which the *claim* that its truth conditions are satisfied *could be redeemed*'.[6] Unless we raise truth-claims and pursue truth, speech capable of possessing meaning and coordinating action would be impossible. The notion of validity, which is to be strictly distinguished from power or coercion, requires intersubjective consensual agreement on truth as part of its meaning.

Habermas's contribution to the development of interpretive social science also turns on his analysis of communicative action. The key distinction between the 'objectifying' natural sciences and the 'interpretative' social sciences consists in the 'double hermeneutic' of the latter. Social science's objects are already constituted by pre-interpreted symbolic meaning in communicative practice and the social scientist must bring his or her interpretive context to bear in understanding these objects. Habermas thinks the resulting 'hermeneutic circle' can be broken by recognising that the methodological rationality of the social sciences is based upon the internal relation between meaning and validity (a metatheoretical insight). In approaching a text, it is the interpreter's grasp of the '*reasons* that allow the author's utterances to appear as rational' that allows him or her to 'understand what the author could have *meant*'. In other words, it is precisely the same structures that make possible reaching understanding in everyday speech that also allow 'a reflective control of this process' (that is, as social science).[7] While social scientists and their knowledge are always constituted through historical 'interpretive communities', it is not the context or concrete social relations that finally explain the understanding of social science but the extent of its reconstruction of the structure of meaning and validity. By reconstructing the universal pragmatics of meaning, one can get beyond the fateful dualism of particularism and objectivism.

Communication, Validity and Lifeworld

With every utterance, a speaker raises claims to validity, some of which, at least, must be already accepted by the hearer if communication is to occur at all. That is, in order for a speaker and hearer to communicate, there must be a set of reciprocal expectations regarding the use of symbolic expressions as well as an assessment of their appropriateness in a given context.[8] The achievement of sameness in meaning occurs with the ability to follow a rule, which logically depends on intersubjectively established meaning contexts. With every utterance, then, speakers and hearers bring forth a cultural, social, and normative space of shared meaning contexts that serve as the largely unquestioned background against which the act of speech occurs.

This familiar background is what is known as the 'lifeworld': the 'social space inhabited in common that emerges in the course of dialogue'.[9] The lifeworld is the phenomenological terrain of sedimented tradition, shared contexts, knowledge and competencies – a complexity on which every communicative act depends. The lifeworld is always historical, in the sense that its existential experience depends on practice and active reproduction in communication. Communication communities 'bring forth' worlds of meaning in this sense. Particular lifeworlds depend on actual communication occurring every day in a dynamic and spontaneous or free way, since active human subjects generate their worlds of sense-making experience and social cooperation by using their constitutive language. The 'always already' givenness of the lifeworld, which makes it unknowable as a totality, arises from the requirement that participants in linguistic communication must always bring forth their lifeworld as a matter of successful communication itself.

There are numerous consequences that follow from this insight. The phenomenological terrain of the lifeworld cannot be rationally administered as a whole much less organised according to an overarching ideology without severe domination and restriction of communication. One would need Orwellian control over all mass and private means of communication – complete surveillance, censorship and propaganda along with the manipulation of desire and fear. Totalitarianism is no longer on the political agenda in Western mass societies, yet significant and systematic manipulation and restriction of mass media remain. While the spectre of

Jürgen Habermas (1929–)

Germany's fascist period haunted much of Adorno's work, it is worth noting in passing that Habermas's theoretical and political positions also reflect an on-going concern with Germany's – and Europe's – ability to work through this past. In 1987, Habermas began a fierce attack on conservative German historians who argued Germany should 'get over' Nazism by understanding it largely as a misguided reaction to Bolshevism.[10] In the debate over German reunification, Habermas defended the idea of 'constitutional patriotism' as the only kind of political sentiments worthy of the new Germany that would prevent the repetition of past political errors.[11] Habermas maintains a strong presence as a public intellectual in Germany, regularly commenting on social and political issues, intellectual controversies, international affairs and, recently, human genetic engineering.

The political system can, however, intervene on behalf of the lifeworld and enhance or protect specific forms of life without totalitarian implications. Multiculturalism or cultural nationalist policy are examples of the political system responding to democratic demands or perceived social indicators by regulating cultural reproduction processes. Regulation of mass media in the interests of an effective public sphere is another example. But there are clear limits to the effectiveness of solutions driven by the political system without significant and ongoing involvement of the lifeworld actors and institutions themselves. Cultural policy cannot treat living cultures like endangered species for just this reason, Habermas believes.[12] Cultural ways of life are capable of surviving in a democratic modern society only to the extent that they are self-reflectively constituted through the active communicative participation of their members. State regulation should not simply protect cultures by decree but instead should provide adequate possibilities for the articulation of marginalised interests within a broad political culture capable of supporting communicatively achieved public opinion and communicatively affirmed traditions.

Participation is always required for cultural forms to reproduce themselves. In any utterance, only a segment of the lifeworld can ever be brought forth – the situational definition that is relevant for the specific communication in question. Such situational definitions need not be identical but must overlap sufficiently for mutual understanding to be possible. Any communication, no matter how complex or comprehensive (for example, a canonical text), can illuminate only a portion of the lifeworld, which entails that the lifeworld as a whole always remains at the backs of communicating participants.

To illustrate the 'thematisation' of lifeworld contexts that occurs in every utterance, let us consider an example. At a city work-site, a worker says to another worker, 'Go get us some beer'. The time happens to be lunchtime with the speaker an older worker and the hearer a recent, younger worker. The success of the utterance, 'Go get us some beer' will depend on both workers (along with any others in attendance) mutually recognising: (1) the intersubjective context of validity in which an older worker can assume that such an imperative directed at a younger worker is appropriate (it's lunchtime not work-time, older workers enjoy some authority in the workplace); (2) the younger worker understands the objective (constative) validity claim of the utterance that he or she is to fetch the beer and all objective conditions for such action exist; and (3) that the older worker means what he says such that the hearer will give credence to what is said.[13] There are thus three phenomenologically distinct validity claims being made simultaneously: the claim to 'normative rightness' that concerns appropriate intersubjective relations, a 'truth claim' about the objective world, and a claim to 'truthfulness' or the sincerity of the speaker. In all of these dimensions, an appropriate claim to validity is made by the speaker which can be accepted, rejected or left undecided by the hearer. It is thus immanent to an utterance that a speaker seeks agreement and understanding from others because of the claims to validity that are always raised therein. The communication in our example will be judged fully successful if the younger worker 'redeems' the validity claims and fetches the beer within the context of the situation: action will have been coordinated communicatively.

This describes the achievement of autonomous speech oriented toward mutual understanding. The imperative form of the utterance by the older worker is thus not an institutionally bound utterance. That is, the utterance is not governed by formal institutional rules as are, for example, the command, 'Fire!' given by a captain to the troops, the declaration 'I now pronounce you husband and wife' uttered by a minister in a marriage ceremony, or 'Write this report' said by a manager to an appropriate staff member. All such utterances are bound by their formal institutional contexts such as protocol, ritual or employment contract and are determined by the explicit expectations and interpretation of rule-following that constitutes action within these fields. The action coordinated by institutionally unbound speech acts requires and expects far more consensual achievement. The 'beer' example illustrates the non-institutionalised, informal communication of everyday speech that draws on culturally and socially established contexts that must be brought forth in the dynamics of the communication. Bringing forth such situational definitions that draw upon normative, social and cultural assumptions by raising and redeeming of validity claims are thus necessary conditions for successfully coordinated communicative action.

A social coordination problem occurs, however, when the assumptions necessary for communicative action become uncertain. When this uncertainty is pursued, a specific aspect of the lifeworld background is questioned and subjected to argument that seeks to restore understanding and agreement on the situational definition. To continue our 'beer' example, the younger worker may object to the cultural or unofficial hierarchy between older, more experienced workers and younger workers in this kind of matter – that younger workers ought to do such lunchtime errands for older ones. If so, he may argue that he is not the other's servant, that workers should be responsible for their own lunches, or, on a less confrontational tack, that another worker is the more appropriate choice for undertaking the errand. Whether or not such arguments will be successful in altering the situational definition will depend on many contextual and dynamic factors. But irrespective of these, the fact that such arguments can be made and can change the situational definition is evidence that the mutual recognition of the validity claims is necessary for the success of the communication, whether these are sedimented in tradition, institutionalised or generated in the moment of intersubjective communication. The key insight, for Habermas, is that argument is the only free and autonomous way of restoring disrupted consensuses that are required for affirming the 'normal' operation of communicative coordination.

Validity, Power and Deliberative Democracy

Communicative motivation differs fundamentally from empirical motivation. If a speaker utters threats or offers rewards to induce cooperation, there is no requirement for the participants to orient themselves toward validity claims. Such empirical force or motivation cannot secure validity nor communicative coordination because the success of power claims is independent of the acceptance or rejection of validity claims. The recognition of validity requires a special kind of consensual action and understanding at a different level to empirical force.

While Habermas believes that communicative action has always occurred in human societies, the specific communicative competencies associated with criticisable validity claims have only been fully developed in the modern world. Indeed, modern learning processes are dependent on raising and redeeming validity claims that bind speakers and hearers in a co-operative search for truth. This can be seen in the fact that, as the condition for claiming validity, it must always be possible to offer reasons that demonstrate validity. This has nothing to do with the quality or content of the claim to validity but everything to do with the action entailed by the claiming. To accept a validity claim is to understand that valid reasons can be given that both speaker and hearer will accept. Such a condition is, Habermas argues, immanent to the concept of validity and underlies the political hope attached to deliberative democracy. It is just this 'warranty' that is offered and redeemed in the validity claim and that binds speakers and hearers rationally: 'a speaker owes the binding (or bonding: *bindende*) force of his illocutionary act not to the validity of what is said, but to *the co-ordinating effect of the warranty* that he offers'.[14] A reflective speaker is able to place himself in the position of the potential hearer of his utterance and take up the hearer's perspective on himself as the utterer of validity claims.[15] In this way, the speaker anticipates a negative response to the claim he raises and is prepared to argue. By internalising this relation, the speaker becomes capable of self-criticism and criticism of others.[16]

This perspective can be developed in normative practical-political directions, for the use of public reason presumes a '*co-operative* competition for the better argument' where 'the goal of a communicatively reached agreement unites the participants from the outset'.[17] This normative model is sometimes described as the 'ideal speech situation' that is implicit in all communicative interaction. The ideal speech situation is not, for Habermas, a regulative ideal like Kant's Categorical Imperative, but indicates a pragmatic set of presuppositions that every speaker anticipates in communicative speech. A speaker anticipates the freedom and equality of an ideal communication community every time he or she engages in argumentative discourse. The agreement that results when a claim to

Jürgen Habermas (1929–)

validity is recognised in an argument makes sense only if it is assumed that it has been achieved freely, without coercion, and with an equal capacity for counter-argument. This is what Habermas means when he speaks of the 'unforced force' of the better argument. The ideal communication community never actually exists in real-life argument situations, yet every performance of argumentative speech invokes the ideal communication community. Thus a crucial social bond is found in the reconstructed presuppositions and practice of communicative action that aims at consensus. Such consensus is not mere accord or the de facto consensus of like-minded souls but an agreement that enjoins participants through their rational convictions. In rational argument, one must wish to convince by using good reasons and not rhetoric, (mere) authority, lies, deception, exclusion or coercion. The pragmatic presuppositions of the discourse ethics approach to the process of argumentation are:

> (i) that nobody who could make a relevant contribution may be excluded; (ii) that all participants are granted an equal opportunity to make contributions; (iii) that the participants must mean what they say; and (iv) that communication must be freed from external and internal coercion so that ... participants ... are motivated solely by the rational force of the better reasons.[18]

The normative core of the theory of deliberative democracy is thus found at the level of everyday speech and argumentation in the call for widespread access to information, relevant reasons, and participation in the informal and formal processes and institutions of public opinion- and will-formation. No one with an interest in any particular decision should be excluded from equal participation in the argumentation process. It is through such a process that the validity of binding decisions is established. In short, modern law (public will) can be said to be democratically legitimate if it is created (or reproduced) under institutional conditions that actualise the informal and formal processes of communicatively reached agreement. It is because of this practical-political necessity that Habermas can claim to solve the fundamental problem of democracy posed since at least Rousseau: namely, that people may act autonomously and freely 'only insofar as they obey just those laws they give themselves in accordance with insights they have acquired intersubjectively ... [and] that *for us*, who have developed our identity in such a form of life, it cannot be circumvented'.[19]

Habermas's strict distinction between power and validity claims is at the root of his rejection of postmodernist or post-structuralist critical theories. For Habermas, postmodernist theory is, despite its self-understood discontinuity with modernity, nevertheless caught within the 'aporias' of the philosophy of the subject that are evident in the various reductions and 'leveling' moves produced in its methodologies. Habermas associates post-structuralism with irrationalism because of its rejection of the cognitive claim associated with the pragmatic presuppositions of rational speech. Post-structuralists are caught in a 'performative self-contradiction' because they deny the binding nature of the performative presuppositions of argumentative speech at the same time as they use argumentative speech to do the denying. He accuses post-structuralism of conservatism for its positivist dissolution of subjectivity into knowledge–power complexes in which no distinction between validity and power can be made.[20] By contrast, Habermas believes that the normative content of modernity found in the communicative orientation to mutual understanding can be clarified independently of power–knowledge claims. The moral-practical learning processes that have ushered in a post-conventional moral consciousness indicate definite possibilities for a society yet to be liberated from domination and myth (or ideology) – in short, a freer and more equal society is suggested by discourse ethics. A postmodern turn is premature, for Habermas, since the 'project' of modernity that turns on developing its rational potentials is incomplete – it ought to be fully tried.

Post-structuralists have in turn criticised Habermas for his rationalist emphasis, which supposedly implicates him in the totalising 'Enlightenment project'. His marginalisation of aesthetic communication in favour of rational (or reasonable) communication is a more important problem, however, since he fails to acknowledge or find an adequate place for the 'communicative body' in his theory. Feminists have similarly found fault with the gender-blindness of Habermas's rationalism. According to Habermas, the aesthetic dimension cannot be decoded for political liberation as earlier critical theorists thought, which means that it must be subordinated to rational discourse. Many critics are uncomfortable with his reliance on the cognitive power of reason to the exclusion of the 'speech' of the body. While many Habermasians consider post-structuralism's positions either incoherent or, remarkably, tending toward Habermasian theory itself, the recent ethical move of deconstruction toward a 'politics of friendship' (Derrida following Levinas) cannot be incorporated into the theory of communicative action and hence poses a major challenge to its universalist ambitions. Marxists, in contrast, generally find Habermas's emphasis on rational speech undialectical and his political theory mere social-democratic reformism. But even Jameson regards Habermas's formula of 'modernity as an unfinished project' as 'usefully ambiguous' – compared to, say, the 'radicalised modernity' of Anthony Giddens – for it allows one to think that the middle class and its economic system are incapable of completing it.[21]

Communication, Society, Democracy

Modern societies are characterised by substantial social differentiation that has vastly increased their complexity. The transition to modern society destroys stratified and exclusive social orders, replacing them with a functionally differentiated order. The mode of legitimation also changes radically, as Marx was among the first to recognise, with 'ideology' taking on a decidedly critical function. The development of functionally differentiated spheres of action is indicated most generally in the rise of the political state, which deploys political power according to increasingly rationalised administrative goals, and a capitalist economy, which coordinates activity according to the calculation of individual self-maximising goals. Political administration and economic activity develop according to rationalisation processes that are relatively independent of cultural values and beliefs. Culture, society (morality, ethics) and identity (personality), in contrast, become more differentiated from one another and, in the absence of natural law, 'relative' to historical context.

But unlike many systems theorists, Habermas does not regard the cultural, social and personal spheres of life as functional in the way that political and economic systems are. This is because one is socialised into a world in which one must be capable of recognising cultural and moral values and making judgements that cannot be reduced to the requirements of social function. In 'communicative' action, actors must recognise the validity of what is being said, which for Habermas requires an orientation toward mutual understanding and agreement. In strategic or instrumental action, by contrast, actors need only recognise relative advantage, costs and benefits, practical capacity, appropriate means and so on, and 'agreement' is secured empirically. The strategic and instrumental rationalities of administration and economy are, for Habermas, quite different from the communicative rationality that constitutes cultural life.

As a consequence, Habermas recognises two great quasi-ontological spheres of social action: a functionalist 'systems' sphere that is distinguished from the communicative sphere of the 'lifeworld'. The lifeworld is in turn internally differentiated according to different cognitive spheres of meaning: it gives place to the shared object world of things, the social world of intersubjective relations and the inner world of the individuated self. The system sphere is differentiated according to the 'delinguistified' or non-communicative media of money and power that facilitate the relatively autonomous subsystems of the economy and state. The key difference is that systems media coordinate (or 'steer') social action without the need for reaching understanding and agreement, since their rationalities are entirely based on ego's empirical measurements such as calculation (economy), threat or reward, or formal regulation backed up by coercive force (law). Social coordination in the lifeworld of communicative relations depends instead on an orientation toward validity, critical judgement and consensus. These two great spheres of action are thus distinguished according to their modes of communication.

In modern market societies, instrumental labour, strategic action, technological control and administrative organisation involve necessary objectifications of the lifeworld that remove action coordination from communicative contexts. Following Lukács, such processes may be understood as reification processes.[22] But there is also an objective need for such reification: certain levels and forms of labour, technology and organisation are always required to reproduce the lifeworld's material basis. Marx describes this as the 'metabolism' of society but does not explain how it will be regulated in a future society. The great threat to modern society, which Frankfurt School critical theory recognises, is that instrumental reason and its attendant reifications will extend to dominate the totality of social relations. Without distinguishing the functional rationalities of the systems sphere from the validity and meaning-giving rationality of communicative interaction, social science has little purchase on how functional or instrumental rationalities can be brought under control. Habermas maintains that systems of instrumentalisation and strategy must be distinguished from and subject to democratic, communicative processes of reaching understanding and consensus-making if the former are to be prevented

Jürgen Habermas (1929–)

from unwarranted (creative) destruction.

A critical theory, for Habermas, therefore must continue to recognise the ambivalent and violent development of modernity that lacks adequate democratic control. The rationalisation of the lifeworld has brought the raising and redeeming of validity claims more to the fore in everyday life as well as in politics, which has eroded and undermined previously unquestioned traditions and beliefs. This has allowed challenges to the 'structural violence' of ideology and opened up political mobilisation of social movements. Yet reaching mutual understanding in everyday life has become 'riskier', for Habermas, precisely because of the higher cognitive and social demands entailed by rationally motivated agreement.[23] As a result, there is a heightened potential for disagreement and conflict in modernity. Happily, however, this heightened threat of instability in the communicative sphere is offset by the simultaneous development of the delinguistified media of the system that effectively compensate for the increased risks and demands of communicative action by removing the need for communicative understanding and agreement. As mentioned, systems media of money and power replace language by using symbolic forms that do not require a communicative attitude to understand their meaning. The generalisable codes of money and power relieve actors of the responsibilities associated with communicative speech because they require only an orientation toward the 'facticity' (that is, the sheer empirical reality) of economic life and legal regulation. These increasingly complex systems of communication do not require subjects who must back up their claims with argumentatively defensible reasons. The 'uncoupling' of modern political administration (the state) and economic interaction from the lifeworld thus enables actors to gain new and greatly improved degrees of freedom of action oriented to success,[24] which Habermas sees in principle (at least) as complementary to the communicative rationalisation of the lifeworld.

The facticities of economic life and political administration acquire their own life because systems are dynamic (a system is, by definition, always in motion). The relatively autonomous subsystems of the economy and political administration, by necessity, treat the lifeworld, its institutions and actors as 'environments' from the point of view of the totality of their internal functions. The rationality of the whole always has logical priority over the elements of any system. When one participates in a social system, in this sense, one must objectify oneself as well as one's perception and 'understanding' according to the rules and goals governing the operation of the complete system in relation to its environment.

However, when the autonomous subsystems experience 'steering problems' – fiscal crisis in the state or accumulation crisis in the economy, for example – the resources and operation of lifeworld institutions come under threat. Capitalism is still inherently crisis ridden, in Habermas's view, and it may displace its own systemic crises onto everyday lifeworld processes as well as the political system. That is, difficulties in accumulation may be solved by extending market relations into previously uncommodified spheres of social life – the mass media are clearly key to such extensions today. The transfer of such systemic problems onto communicative and legal domains through processes of 'internal colonisation' distorts and undermines these spheres of social reproduction and generates individual and social pathologies. The technological media culture is at best highly ambivalent in its 'empowerment' and is in any case overwhelmingly oriented toward manipulative entertainment and a politics of spectacle that stimulates consumerism and legitimates only limited democratic control.

Habermas's critique of mass welfare-state democracy also draws attention to the contradictions of the 'monetarisation' and 'bureaucratisation' of the lifeworld.[25] The welfare state comprises the fourth general wave of 'juridification' – the transfer of social regulation to legal regulation – that follows the development of the democratic constitutional state by extending 'freedom-guaranteeing juridification' from political rights to social rights. But the form of welfare-state intervention compatible with the system of bourgeois law requires individualist determinations of legal entitlement. It is the need to deal administratively with the life-risks indemnified by social rights that entails a 'violent abstraction' from the concrete contexts of the life histories and forms of life that gave rise to the problems in the first place. The dominant consumerist form of monetary compensation for such risks is generally inadequate for addressing the social (that is, lifeworld) problems, so therapeutic social services are required as a supplement. Yet the expert–client relationship of the 'therapeutocracy' contradicts the aim of therapy, which is to promote the client's independence and self-reliance. By reducing complex social relations and citizenship to legalistic client relationships, the welfare state ironically promotes their disintegration since 'the consensual mechanisms that coordinate action ... are transferred over to media such as power and money'.[26]

For Habermas, a better response would be to prevent the colonisation and deformation of the lifeworld by the system in the first place, which entails a project of radical democracy and an enhancement of processes of mutual understanding at every level of society. For example, research applying Habermas's model supports dialogical responses to doctor–patient communication in general practice, health promotion and education in primary prevention of disease, improvement of intercultural communication in multicultural and anti-racist education, and better citizen participation in administrative processes. These examples are but a few of a vast and expanding secondary research on Habermasian practical applications. His current intellectual influence is broad in the social sciences and humanities, since his concept of communicative action has significant interdisciplinary appeal.

Within such a modern socio-political context, we must therefore understand democracy as describing the social and political institutions and culture that facilitate and strengthen communicative interaction in the face of economic and administrative pressures and the circulation of 'unofficial' social power. The core normative experiences of freedom and equality that are essential for democracy can be realised only if the system's operation is successfully subject to control exercised through the communicative processes of democratic opinion- and will-formation mediated by language. It is, in other words, the same 'natural' communicative power that reproduces selves and societies at the level of everyday action that can also be drawn upon to control the colonising tendencies of the subsystems given the appropriate institutions and cultural space.[27]

Notes

1. For a detailed analysis of the claims concerning the paradigm shift to linguistic philosophy, see Martin Morris, *Rethinking the Communicative Turn: Habermas, Adorno and the Problem of Communicative Freedom* (Albany: State University of New York Press, 2001).
2. See Jürgen Habermas and Niklas Luhmann, *Theorie der Gesellschaft oder Sozial-Technologie – Was leistet die Systemforschung?* (Frankfurt a. M.: Suhrkamp, 1971).
3. Jürgen Habermas, *Communication and the Evolution of Society*.
4. Jürgen Habermas, *Knowledge and Human Interests*, p. 314.

5. Jürgen Habermas, *Moral Consciousness*, pp. 43–115. See also Benhabib and Dallmayr, *Communicative Ethics Controversy*.
6. Habermas, *Theory of Communicative Action*, Vol. 1, p. 317.
7. Ibid., pp. 132, 121.
8. Jürgen Habermas, *Theory of Communicative Action*, Vol. 2, pp. 17–22.
9. Jürgen Habermas, 'A Reply', in Axel Honneth and Hans Joas (eds), *Communicative Action: Essays on Jürgen Habermas's Theory of Communicative Action* (Cambridge, MA: MIT Press, 1991), pp. 214–64, p. 218.
10. Jürgen Habermas, *The New Conservatism: Cultural Criticism and the Historians' Debate*, trans. Shierry Weber Nicholsen (Cambridge, MA: MIT Press, 1989).
11. See Jürgen Habermas, *The Past as Future*, trans. Max Pensky (Lincoln: University of Nebraska Press, 1994); and Jürgen Habermas, *A Berlin Republic: Writings on Germany*, trans. Steven Rendall (Lincoln: University of Nebraska Press, 1997).
12. Jürgen Habermas, 'Struggles for Recognition in the Democratic Constitutional State', in Amy Gutman (ed.), *Multiculturalism and 'the Politics of Recognition'* (Princeton: Princeton University Press, 1994), pp. 107–48.
13. See Habermas, *Theory of Communicative Action*, Vol. 1, pp. 307–8.
14. Habermas, *Theory of Communicative Action*, Vol. 1, p. 302.
15. Jürgen Habermas, *Postmetaphysical Thinking*, pp. 149–204.
16. Habermas, *Theory of Communicative Action*, Vol. 2, pp. 74–5.
17. Jürgen Habermas, *The Inclusion of the Other*, p. 44.
18. Ibid.
19. Jürgen Habermas, *Between Facts and Norms*, pp. 445–6.
20. This is an argument and conclusion that some commentators think overstated.
21. Fredric Jameson, *A Singular Modernity: Essay on the Ontology of the Present* (London: Verso, 2002), p. 11.
22. Georg Lukács, *History and Class Consciousness: Studies in Marxist Dialectics*, trans. Rodney Livingstone (Cambridge, MA: MIT Press, 1971).
23. Habermas, *Theory of Communicative Action*, Vol. 1, p. 70.
24. Habermas, *Theory of Communicative Action*, Vol. 2, pp. 263–4.
25. Ibid., pp. 356–73. But Habermas's critique does not imply that the principles of social equalisation and freedom are themselves contradictory.
26. Ibid., pp. 362–4.
27. See Habermas, *Between Facts and Norms*, ch. 7.

Jürgen Habermas (1929–)

Major Works by Habermas

The Structural Transformation of the Public Sphere: An Inquiry into a Category of Bourgeois Society (Cambridge, MA: MIT Press, 1989 [1962]).
Knowledge and Human Interests, trans. Jeremy J. Shapiro (Boston: Beacon Press, 1971 [1968]).
Communication and the Evolution of Society (Boston: Beacon Press, 1979 [1976]).
The Theory of Communicative Action, 2 vols, trans. Thomas McCarthy (Boston: Beacon Press, 1984, 1987 [1981]).
The Philosophical Discourse of Modernity: Twelve Lectures, trans. Frederick G. Lawrence (Cambridge, MA: MIT Press, 1987 [1985]).
Moral Consciousness and Communicative Action, trans. Christian Lenhardt and Shierry Weber Nicholsen (Cambridge, MA: MIT Press, 1990 [1983]).
Postmetaphysical Thinking: Philosophical Essays, trans. William Mark Hohengarten (Cambridge, MA: MIT Press, 1992 [1988]).
Between Facts and Norms: Contributions to a Discourse Theory of Law and Democracy, trans. William Rehg (Cambridge, MA: MIT Press, 1996 [1992]).
The Inclusion of the Other: Studies in Political Theory, trans. Ciaran Cronin (Cambridge, MA: MIT Press, 1998 [1996]).

Suggestions for Further Reading

Calhoun, Craig J. (ed.), *Habermas and the Public Sphere* (Cambridge, MA: MIT Press, 1992). A fine collection of essays by eminent scholars discussing the continuing relevance of Habermas's early controversial book. Includes further reflections by Habermas on the idea of the public sphere and a response to critics.
Benhabib, Seyla, and Fred R. Dallmayr (eds), *The Communicative Ethics Controversy* (Cambridge, MA: MIT Press, 1990). A philosophically advanced collection of programmatic statements and defences of communicative ethics, along with critical responses.
White, Stephen K. (ed.), *The Cambridge Companion to Habermas* (Cambridge: Cambridge University Press, 1995). A collection of generally accessible essays covering the heritage of critical theory, social science and discourse ethics, discursive democracy and modernity. Includes a select bibliography of Habermas's work and secondary literature.
von Schomberg, René, and Kenneth Baynes (eds), *Discourse and Democracy: Essays on Habermas's* Between Facts and Norms (Albany: State University of New York Press, 2002). A set of critical discussions of Habermas's most important book since *Theory of Communicative Action*. Includes an interview with Habermas on political theory.

16

Fredric Jameson (1934–)

Nick Heffernan

The Marxist as Critic

Fredric Jameson is commonly regarded as the most important and influential Marxist cultural critic of the last three decades. His principal achievement over that period has been threefold. First, his work and indefatigable presence have kept Marxism as a critical tradition alive in the United States through long and often hostile stretches of political and intellectual conservatism. Second, he has adapted this tradition to meet the new intellectual and political challenges posed by continental European theory on the one hand and the globalised, media-based capitalism of the postindustrial period on the other. Third, his startling theorisation of postmodernism has ignited and set the terms for an epoch-defining debate about the significance and value of contemporary culture which continues to reverberate through the humanities and social sciences. After Jameson, no discussion of contemporary culture that aspires to be the least bit systematic can avoid an engagement with the nature of modern capitalism or the claims of Marxism as both analytical tool and critical social philosophy.

For his admirers Jameson is not just a profound thinker but 'a great writer' whose breathtaking scope of interests transcends the merely political, ranging with equal fluency across the highest and lowest of cultural objects and discourses, from German idealist philosophy to punk rock.[1] For his detractors he is a jargon-spouting ideologue whose gloomy pronouncements on some abstract foe called 'late capitalism' emanate from one of the most comfortable and privileged positions that system can provide – that of the

Fredric Jameson (1934–)

tenured professor at an elite university.[2] Whichever perspective is adopted, however, it is undeniable that in his work and career Jameson has been guided by an imperative to which any intellectual with avowedly leftist political convictions must respond: Marx's injunction not simply to interpret the world but to change it.

Born in 1934, Jameson came to maturity in the United States of the 1950s, a period characterised by what sociologist Daniel Bell called 'the end of ideology'.[3] The crises of capitalism and of democracy represented by the Great Depression and the Second World War had apparently resolved themselves into a new age of stability and prosperity. Anti-communist conservatism prevailed in politics, bland consumerism in social life and anti-political technicism in the academy. Capitalism was unassailable, at least in the West, and the old communist left of the 1930s was busily denouncing Stalinism and accommodating itself to the new realities of American world power. These were unpropitious years for the formation of a Marxist intellectual. However, as a graduate student in French at Yale, Jameson spent crucial months in France. Here he experienced a society that was not (yet) in thrall to the material comforts of consumer capitalism, a polity in which the Marxist left was still a vital and determining force, and a culture in which the politically committed intellectual was able – indeed, was expected – to play an important public role.

Jean-Paul Sartre was the 'role model' in this latter respect.[4] Yet Jameson's study of Sartre – his first book, published in 1961 – dwelt on matters of literary style rather than politics. Only later in the decade, while teaching at the University of California at San Diego, did Jameson fully engage with the European Marxist critical and philosophical tradition, sometimes called Western Marxism, of which Sartre was the most recent and visible protagonist. In California, too, Jameson lived and worked close to the epicentre of the cultural and political revolution of the 1960s. The new forms of lifestyle, political activism and aesthetic practice, such as pop art and rock music, that comprised this revolution influenced Jameson's developing outlook as profoundly as did scholarly immersion in the canonical texts of Western Marxism. Already well into his thirties and an established career academic, Jameson did not fully embrace the anti-bourgeois libertarianism of radical sixties youth. He did, though, in 1968 – the year of the May uprising in Paris and the Days of Rage in Chicago – establish the Marxist Literary Group, a theoretical forum for left-inclined university teachers; and the sense of having lived through 'the momentous transformational period' that was the 1960s had profound implications for his later work.[5]

Marxism and Form, published in 1971, was the fruit of these experiences. In it Jameson reappraised the Western Marxist tradition, finding there uncanny echoes of the impasse faced by the radical movements of the 1960s as they collapsed at that decade's end. For Western Marxism had been born of a similar experience of political defeat on the left two generations before. The failure of the communist revolution to spread across Europe from the Soviet Union in the period after 1917 and the subsequent rise of fascism out of the ruins of the various European workers' movements shattered the orthodox Marxist belief in the historical inevitability of socialism and the spontaneously revolutionary convictions of the working class. These setbacks seemed to arise as much from failures of consciousness and ideology as of political strategy and organisation. Disenchanted revolutionary intellectuals thus turned their attentions to the sphere in which consciousness and ideology were formed and expressed — that is, to culture — in order to account for political defeat and formulate responses to it.

The Western Marxist approach to culture was complex and double-sided. On the one hand, bourgeois culture was dominated by ruling-class ideas and structured by the logic of capitalism; it was therefore the realm of ideology understood as misrepresentation or false consciousness. Cultural analysis was, then, a matter of negative critique or demystification, of exposing the realities of oppression and exploitation concealed within cultural forms, of reading through their alluring surfaces to delineate the ugly contours of the capitalist system beneath. On the other hand, though, culture was the realm of illumination, delight and imaginative transcendence of the given; it thus had an educative, even utopian dimension. Cultural analysis thus also involved the positive, constructive work of identifying and promoting those utopian and potentially progressive elements that foreshadowed a liberated society and educated consciousness to anticipate it.

All Jameson's work since *Marxism and Form* springs from this Western Marxist conception of culture and of the dual role of the cultural critic. But Western Marxism had been a response to political defeat in conditions shaped by the economic crises and overt class antagonisms of the industrial capitalism of the 1920s and 1930s. The American oppositional movements of the 1960s, however, fell apart in the face of an affluent 'postindustrial capitalism' from which class politics and industrial labour had all but disappeared and whose most striking feature was for Jameson its 'false and unreal culture', a consumerist 'dream world of artificial stimuli and televised experience'. While this made the Western Marxist prioritisation of culture and aesthetics all the more relevant in so far as capitalism was now as much a system of symbols, signs and images as of sweated labour and heavy machinery, it also required that this tradition be renovated to take into account these new conditions. Thus, Jameson set about elaborating what he called a 'postindustrial Marxism' for postindustrial times.[6]

His first move in this project was to confront the new methodologies based on the model of structural linguistics which had come to dominate the intellectual landscape in Europe since the 1960s. This was necessary for two reasons. First, structuralism and its offshoots had displaced Marxism as the method of choice among the radical intelligentsia; second, the linguistic model promised insights into contemporary capitalism that Marxism could not afford to ignore. Jameson detected 'a profound consonance between linguistics as a method and that systematised, disembodied nightmare which is our culture today'.[7] Structuralists insisted that any object of analysis, from literature to fashion, from the unconscious to the social system, was organised like a language, a self-referring system of signs. Signification was therefore constitutive of reality, not a second-order reflection of an already existing real. There could be no direct, unmediated access to reality, to truth, only an indirect approach through signifiers, language, texts. Furthermore, human agency and subjectivity were to be seen as effects, rather than causes, of signifying structures which were the absent cause and invisible limit of consciousness: language 'spoke' the human subject rather than vice versa.

Jameson drew on these elements of structuralism and poststructuralism to enrich what he saw as orthodox Marxism's tendency towards a somewhat naive, positivist understanding of reality and of human agency. If postindustrial capitalism was a system of signs and images, postindustrial Marxism had to become a science of signification. Moreover, the structuralist method of conceiving its object as a total system comported with the Marxist conception of capitalism as a complex totality. But structuralists and their ilk were unable to account for change or transformation in their systems, wedded as they were to the static linguistic model. Only Marxism, Jameson insisted, could combine the systematic analysis of signifying structures with a sense of history as a process of change, rupture and transformation driven by conflict and struggle.[8] With Marxism thus modified and reaffirmed, Jameson turned not, strangely enough, to the signifying systems of the postindustrial present, but to those of the precapitalist and industrial past: he produced a history of literary forms.

Marxism and Literature

Literature is central to Marxism, Jameson proposed in *The Political Unconscious*, published in 1981 after his return to Yale from California, because it is the supreme form of narrative. And narrative matters because it mediates between consciousness and history; it is our only conduit to the vast, impersonal structures and temporal processes of which human social and subjective life are effects. Understood in this large, abstract sense, History (with a capital 'H') is an 'absent cause'; it is thus 'inaccessible to us except in textual form', Jameson argues, and 'our approach to it and the Real itself necessarily passes through its prior textualisation, its narrativisation'.[9] The study of narrative and its changing forms, then, provides an understanding of and critical purchase upon the motive forces of History which determine and structure the social and the subjective worlds alike.

But narrative is not merely a symptom or reflex of otherwise occluded historical forces. It is also an active process of engagement through which consciousness seeks to come to terms with these forces and manage their intrusion into lived experience. In this respect narrative, and by extension all cultural activity, works by 'inventing imaginary or "formal" solutions to unresolvable social contradictions'.[10] Its function is to provide symbolic answers to intractably real social problems by suspending these latter in aesthetic form. Thus, as misrepresentations of the real, such forms are profoundly ideological. Yet they also contain a critical 'moment of truth' in so far as they must identify and expose the social contradiction before they can wish it away; indeed, this very wishfulness is utopian in its implicit longing for a condition liberated from social contradiction and the burden of historical necessity.

Paying due attention to this 'dialectic of utopia and ideology' in narrative forms, Marxist analysis works outwards in three stages from the social contradiction 'contained' by a particular text: first to the level of the political at which the contradiction is seen as a localised problem or event; thence to the level of the social where it is understood in terms of a struggle between contending social groups or classes; finally to the level of history where it is grasped as a determinate expression of the structure of the social totality, the mode of production. For example, Jameson maps the contradiction between desire and duty in Balzac's novels onto the social tensions between the *Ancien Regime* and the newly prominent bourgeoisie in the author's France. This latter conflict in turn leads to the as yet not fully achieved historical transition from a residual feudalism to an emergent laissez-faire capitalist mode of production which turns out to be the true content of Balzac's texts, their structuring 'political unconscious'.

This presence within Balzac of antithetical capitalist and feudal impulses is manifested in an unresolved switching between contrasting realist and non-realist formal registers, each of which implies a distinct model of character and psychology, of selfhood. Thus Balzac's texts also illustrate how different modes of production generate narrative forms and sign systems peculiar to them, whose effect is to organise consciousness and experience into patterns appropriate to the historical moment. The history of cultural forms, then, is bound not only to the development of modes of production but also to the construction of the various modes of human subjectivity to which they give rise.

The cultural forms of precapitalist societies – myth, ritual and what Jameson calls 'magical narratives' – are collective in character and therefore do not contain any notion of autonomous selfhood or individual, psychological subjectivity. Fully integrated into the practices and knowledges of everyday life, they are socially functional in a way that the increasingly specialised cultural products of modern societies are not, providing the community with a shared understanding of itself and the universe it inhabits. This vision of an original harmony between culture and a properly collective, co-operative social life serves Jameson as a prototype for the role of culture in a liberated post-capitalist society.

The emergence of capitalist forms of social and economic organisation and the rise of the bourgeoisie as the dominant social class shatter this unity. Culture is subjected to the same processes of reification and commodification – the fragmenting of human activity into separate and increasingly specialised units subject to an instrumental logic of technical development and economic exploitation – as the rest of social life. And the representational system appropriate to this new mode of production is realism. For it is through realism (especially the novel with its focus on individual character, experience and destiny) that the notion of the autonomous human self or subject is elaborated and established. In this way, realist forms embody in the cultural sphere the individuating logic of bourgeois competitive capitalism, actively 'reprogramming' the inhabitants of this new laissez-faire social world 'to the "freedom" and equality of sheer market equivalence'.[11]

If realism represents the first moment of what Jameson refersto as the capitalist 'cultural revolution', modernism constitutes the second. The modernist fragmentation of realist forms reflects the intensified pitch of reification and commodification in the shift from freely competitive to imperialist monopoly capitalism at the end of the nineteenth century; and the disintegration of coherent, autonomous selfhood in modernism expresses the subject's increasing dislocation in this new system. But realism and modernism do not simply serve the logic of capitalism in its successive stages; they protest it too. Realism's characteristic delineations of the relationship between individual and society resist and compensate for the autonomous individual's abandonment to the pitiless currents of the market system. And modernism's emphasis on the embattled interiority of isolated consciousness, as well as its 'difficult' formal repudiations of industrialised popular or mass culture, are attempts to defend the integrity of both individual consciousness and the work of art itself against further reification.

Indeed Western Marxists of an older generation, such as Georg Lukács and Theodor Adorno, had championed realism and modernism respectively as socially critical forms that might constitute the basis of a politically progressive culture of opposition to capitalism. Yet for Jameson, any critical purchase these forms might once have had was neutralised by the shift to a postindustrial order neither was able adequately to represent. Moreover, both were now domesticated, too fully assimilated into the cultural, educational and commercial institutions of late capitalism to have retained any oppositional bite. The defining cultural form of the historic third stage of multinational consumer capitalism was therefore to be found 'beyond realism and modernism alike'.[12] Jameson's next step was to identify this form and isolate whatever progressive seeds it might contain. But the explosion of anti-hierarchical art practices since the 1960s – rock music, pop art, TV and video – demonstrated that literature, perhaps even narrative itself, was no longer the central form of capitalist culture. This task would therefore also involve a move beyond literature to engage with the full spectrum of 'postmodern' cultural activity in consumer society.

Marxism and Postmodernism

What Perry Anderson calls Jameson's 'capture' of the concept of postmodernism can be traced to two precise moments: the lecture 'Postmodernism and Consumer Society', given at New York's Whitney Museum in the autumn of 1982, and the publication of a much expanded version of this talk in the *New Left Review* in the summer of 1984. Prior to this the term 'postmodernism' had been in moderate but relatively uncontroversial critical use as a label for various new styles of thinking and aesthetic practice that self-consciously broke away from an exhausted and lifelessly academic modernist tradition. Surveying these developments in not just literature but architecture, the visual arts, film, music and what he called 'theoretical discourse' too, Jameson observed a number of common formal procedures and characteristics. These new styles were marked by a disregard for generic boundaries, a populist acceptance of 'low' or mass culture, and a tendency toward pastiche or the eclectic recycling of ready made forms all of which flagrantly disregarded the modernist emphasis on aesthetic autonomy, difficulty and originality or 'making it new'. The systematic emergence of such features across the whole spectrum of contemporary cultural production suggested to Jameson that something more than merely isolated stylistic developments was taking place. Rather, these were signs that a new representational system had arrived to accompany the shift to a new stage in the capitalist mode of production. Jameson's seizure of the notion of postmodernism, then, transformed the term from a modish stylistic label into what he called 'a periodising concept whose function is to correlate the emergence of new formal features in culture with the emergence of a new type of social life and a new economic order'.[13] Postmodernism was thus redefined in Marxist terms as 'the cultural logic of late capitalism'.

Drawing on Ernest Mandel's monumental work of Marxian political economy, *Late Capitalism*, Jameson proposes that the beginnings of this new order are to be located in the immediate post-Second World War period and the US's assumption of the role of global leadership. War rescued capitalism from worldwide depression by precipitating the mass destruction of over-accumulated commodities and the development of new technologies which would vastly enhance civilian productivity. Based on computerisation and electronic communications processes, these latter were not traditional industrial technologies of production but rather postindustrial technologies of reproduction; and the affluent, leisure-oriented societies to which they gave rise were less marked by class conflicts at the workplace and more by mass consumption of cultural goods and services, particularly in the media of entertainment.

While this new order is postindustrial, it is certainly not post-capitalist. Indeed for Mandel, and hence Jameson, it is a purer form of capitalism than that of the competitive and monopoly stages that preceded it. The twin processes of reification and commodification attain in it a new level of intensity and spatial reach, eliminating any remaining precapitalist enclaves and making it a more 'total' system than ever. In particular, Jameson argues, nature and the unconscious are at last fully colonised by capitalism. The aggressive export of US style 'modernisation' to Third World countries and the 'green revolution' in which industrial and technological methods replace traditional farming practices reduce nature to the status of a commodity, while the virulent spread of media imagery and discourses through the globalisation of North American entertainment culture penetrates even the deepest recesses of human consciousness, subjecting them to technological and economic exploitation.

Jameson goes beyond Mandel in arguing that the centrality of culture is the defining characteristic of late capitalism. The production of media images and of cultural objects and experiences is as crucial to it economically and ideologically as was industrial manufacturing to capitalism's earlier stages. Culture thus loses whatever autonomy it may once have had and capitalism can now be said to operate according to a 'cultural logic' which is best exemplified by those styles labelled postmodernist. Postmodernism is the new 'cultural dominant' through which the structures and imperatives of late capitalism are both furthered and symbolically expressed, and by which subjectivity is remodelled to meet the new system's distinctive temporal and spatial demands.

Mandel dates the arrival of the social and economic forms of late capitalism from 1945, but for Jameson postmodernist culture does not properly crystallise until the 1960s, when the eruption of anti-hierarchical aesthetic practices produces the shocking sense of a 'radical break' from all that went before. Indeed, postmodernism is intimately bound up with the revolutionary ethos of the 1960s from which it derives its playfulness, populism and disrespect for boundaries; but its accommodating posture towards the market, its sense that to resist commodification (as modernism sought to do) is futile, simultaneously betrays this ethos. In this respect 'postmodernism is the substitute for the sixties and the compensation for their political failure', offering aesthetic sublimations of socially subversive impulses and demonstrating how late capitalism swiftly absorbs opposition into itself via what Thomas Frank calls 'the conquest of cool'.[14] True to his Western Marxist precursors, Jameson finds an explanation for revolutionary defeat in a theory of culture.

Postmodernism's compliance with the market system is manifested in a number of important ways. First, its representative cultural products are marked by a quality of depthlessness, severing them from the kinds of meaningful connection with history which realist and modernist forms struggled to establish. Here Jameson contrasts Van Gogh's painting of a pair of peasant boots with Andy Warhol's *Diamond Dust Shoes*. Whereas the former encapsulates the collective history and continuity of a whole way of life, the latter simply displays its objects as glamorous fetishes for the viewer's consumption. The new prevalence of pastiche is a further symptom of this loss of history. That the historical novel and the 'retro' film are prominent contemporary forms might seem to indicate a 'return' to history in postmodernism; but this is a return that can be managed only through the quotation of received ideas about and stereotypes of the past. No longer available as collective lived experience, history is reduced to a collection of texts, images or period details as in some museum or costume drama.

A second key feature of postmodernism is its peculiar emotional tenor. Whereas realism and modernism were in different ways centrally concerned with registering the depth, complexity and tragic difficulty of subjective experience, postmodernism is in contrast marked by what Jameson calls 'the waning of affect'. The sense of embattled angst communicated by Kafka's fictions or the figure in Munch's *The Scream* gives way to a flat, ironic or playful tone (again best exemplified by Warhol) punctuated only by isolated moments of intensity or 'highs'. This signals for Jameson 'the end of the bourgeois ego' or 'centred subject' and its replacement by a new 'schizophrenic' form of selfhood emptied of any impulse to struggle for coherence or integrity.[15]

This 'postindividual' model of subjectivity is linked to a third key feature of postmodernism: its sense of accelerated temporality. From the discontinuous syntax of 'language' poetry to the quick-fire editing of television, movies and pop videos, contemporary culture both high and low, Jameson argues, demonstrates the breakdown of narrative sequence. We are thus immersed in a perpetual present, dissociated from past and future alike. Narrative's traditional function of binding past, present and future together in order to orient consciousness within time and sustain a sense of unique personal idenitity has decayed.

There is also a spatial dimension to this condition of subjective disorientation. Indeed the fourth key feature of postmodernism is its presentation of a new kind of space, particularly in the fields of architecture and the built environment. The elite designs of A-list architects like Frank Gehry, Michael Graves or Rem Koolhaas, the redeveloped postindustrial cityscapes of Los Angeles, Atlanta or Detroit, and even the mundane proliferation of immense malls throughout suburbia are all examples of a bewildering postmodern 'hyperspace' which exceeds the grasp of the individual's limited perceptual capacities. These confusing spaces are partial, concrete figures for the immense, abstract world system of late capitalism itself which cannot be apprehended in its totality. As attempts to 'map' this totality, postmodernist forms are necessarily faulty and distorted, yet they are accurate in as much as they convincingly render our desire and our inability to grasp it.

In sum, then, the fate of subjectivity in postmodernism is to be emptied of the content invested in it by realism and modernism, severed from history, and cast adrift in space as well as in time. Jameson's characterisation of postmodernism is therefore largely negative and his evaluation of it pessimistic. Its forms provide precious few resources for the orientation of consciousness in history or for a positive understanding of the relation between self and social structure necessary to any kind of transformative political project. This of course reminds us that Jameson's conception of postmodernism was conceived out of political defeat at the end of the 1960s and delivered into a climate of militant neo-conservative and free-market hegemony in the 1980s. Indeed, the Whitney lecture was delivered just as Jameson forsook what he fondly refers to as the 'socialist commune' of Santa Cruz, California, to take up his current position at Duke University in the Republican heartland of North Carolina.[16] But it is important to recognise that his is not a moralising criticism which denounces postmodernist forms for being insufficiently 'good' or progressive. These forms cannot be other than they are in so far as they are determinate expressions of the mode of production; and in the form of globalised, technologically sophisticated late capitalism, this latter has achieved 'a long night of universal domination' which its culture cannot help but powerfully illustrate.[17]

Although fully ideological in this sense, postmodernist cultural forms are not without cognitive value, for they unavoidably (if indirectly) express the historical situation's 'moment of truth', and their faulty, incomplete figurations of the late capitalist world system can be understood as 'peculiar new forms of realism'.[18] In this respect they do not merely reproduce and reinforce the logic of late capitalism but contain at least the potential for a more critical relationship to it; and their presentation of radically new modes of experience and subjectivity can be scrutinised for anticipatory glimpses of what might be to come in some liberated, postcapitalist future. By identifying and enlarging upon these elements the Marxist critic moves from negative critique to a more positive, even utopian, form of engagement with contemporary culture, closer to changing the world rather than merely interpreting it.

The Critic as Marxist

The task of locating, or even envisioning, a postmodernism of resistance forms one strand of Jameson's contribution to what he calls 'a cultural politics'; this, rather than a traditional politics of parties and elections, he maintains, 'must now – at least in the First World – be the primary space of struggle'.[19] Traces of such resistance can be detected in the new, postindividualist models of selfhood that certain postmodern aesthetic forms are beginning tentatively to construct out of the ruins of the bourgeois ego. Contemporary video art and architecture in particular seem to Jameson to demand and partially inculcate new ways of experiencing and understanding the world that could help develop 'the perceptual equipment to match this new hyperspace' of the capitalist world system.[20] It is therefore politically important to bring the critical engagement with these often marginalised forms into the centre of the debate about culture.

But it is through the notion of what he calls 'cognitive mapping' that Jameson most forcefully elaborates the vision of an engaged and socially critical aesthetic practice that would 'be an integral part of a socialist politics'.[21] Here he rekindles and updates the Western Marxist project of elaborating a revolutionary culture, a project which foundered on the stand-off between realism and modernism in the inter-war period. For Jameson such a practice must necessarily go 'beyond realism and modernism alike' in proving equal to the task of representing the global system of late capitalism in its totality. It would thus enable human subjects to grasp imaginatively or 'cognitively map' their position within this totality, providing both a broad understanding of the system and a basis for collective action to transform it.

At various points in his work Jameson has seized upon particular postmodern cultural forms which appear to offer 'hints and examples of such cognitive mapping on the level of content'. These have included: cyberpunk science fiction, whose notions of 'cyberspace' are powerful metaphors for the abstract totality of late capitalism; Hollywood conspiracy thrillers, whose immense shadowy plots are displaced, partial figurations of this unknowable mode of production; and Third World narratives which typically dramatise the relationship of 'developing' or subaltern nations and cultures to the dominant capitalist world system. While none has been judged entirely satisfactory as political art, Third World narratives offer perhaps the most trenchant critical purchase, as they arise out of a geographical and historical condition of what Marx called 'uneven development', that is, the visible persistence in the Third World of precapitalist modes of social life alongside and within globalised capitalism. This renders capitalism less absolute and impenetrable than it appears from the perspective of the overdeveloped First World.

Jameson's qualified advocacy of Third World cinema as a critical form reflects a growing interest in the visual in his work. Indeed, in a culture increasingly in thrall to a near-pornographic obsession with the visual, the key question becomes 'how to escape from the image by means of the image'. While the postmodern elevation of spectacle over narrative is, as we have seen, problematic for Jameson, it nonetheless offers new possibilities for understanding the late capitalist world system. Film especially contains the capacity to represent this system, for film images insert us most forcefully into a spatial universe, and the imaginative command of space is fundamental to the construction of a model of what is now a multinational, geopolitical social totality. However, the cinematic mediation and analysis of space constantly threatens to collapse back into mere decoration and mystification because of the now deeply complicit relationship between the spectacle and the market. If 'the image is the commodity today', Jameson observes, then 'it is vain to expect a negation of the logic of commodity production from it'.[22]

The project of cognitive mapping therefore awaits fulfilment in some future cultural production, and Jameson has conceded the acute difficulty of imagining what form this might take. Yet, he argues, it is politically crucial to keep alive the possibility of imagining it, for the left cannot relinquish utopian thinking in the face of a system which diverts genuinely utopian impulses into the commodified fantasies and gratifications of the marketplace, thereby abolishing the very idea of a radically different future. Paradoxically, then, Jameson's theorisation of the impossibility of Utopia in late capitalism serves to keep it alive.

The second main strand of Jameson's cultural politics is his mission to 'explain and to popularise the Marxist intellectual tradition' and thus to secure 'the legitimation of the discourses of socialism in such a way that they do become realistic and serious alternatives for people'.[23] This is a peculiarly North American vocation, for Jameson's native country is exceptional in so far as it lacks the kind of organised working-class political parties and institutions of the left that are common elsewhere in the world. And his achievement in this respect is ambiguous. He has certainly established Marxism in the American university system, and, as much through the virtuosic power of his descriptions of the existential texture of contemporary life as through his theorising, inspired a generation of scholars to see questions of culture as inseparable from the deepest questions of political economy. Moreover, as an intellectual of impeccably internationalist outlook as well as international repute he has been a stimulus for and focal point in the expansion of cultural debate on the left to truly global proportions.

Yet there is a sense in which this success is also a failure of sorts. For it has been achieved at the cost of the translation of Marxist cultural criticism into a highly specialised and esoteric academic discourse, prevalent in Ivy League humanities departments and scholarly conferences but increasingly remote from the concerns and vocabularies of the street, the union meeting or the daily press. Academic Marxists converse with one another over the heads of the general audience, surrendering the role of what Russell Jacoby calls the 'public intellectual' to the demagogic opinion-mongers of the right; while for pragmatic liberals such as Richard Rorty the fixation of the 'cultural left' with arcane Marxist terminology and rarefied aesthetic matters prevents it from forging meaningful political alliances with groups campaigning on bread-and-butter economic issues such as job protection, wages and conditions of employment.[24]

These kinds of strategic reservations about academic Marxist cultural theory are far more substantial than the strident denunciations of 'tenured radicals' orchestrated by the neo-conservative right over the last decade or so. No doubt Jameson would retort that the confinement of Marxist discourse to the academy is an effect of the current historical situation in the West in which market forces prevail. We might also argue that he of all people has more than convincingly demonstrated how cultural and aesthetic questions can never simply be separated from political and economic ones. All the more reason, then, to persist with what is the primary function of Marxist cultural analysis and the purpose for which the concept of postmodernism was constructed: 'tirelessly to denounce the economic forms that have come for the moment to reign supreme and unchallenged'.[25]

Notes

1. Perry Anderson, *The Origins of Postmodernity*, p. 72. See also Terry Eagleton, 'Fredric Jameson: The Politics of Style', *Against the Grain: Essays 1975–1985* (London: Verso, 1986), pp. 65–78.
2. Jameson took first prize in the *Philosophy and Literature* 1997 Bad Writing Contest. Roger Kimball's *Tenured Radicals: How Politics Has Corrupted Our Higher Education* (Chicago: Ivan R. Dee, 1998) is typical of the neo-conservative denunciations of Jameson and other radical scholars that reached a crescendo during the 'culture wars' of the 1990s.
3. Daniel Bell, *The End of Ideology: On the Exhaustion of Political Ideas in the Fifties* (New York: Basic Books, 1960).
4. Jameson, 'On Aronson's Sartre', *Minnesota Review*, 18, 1982, pp. 116–27, p. 122.
5. Jameson, 'Periodising the 60s', *The Ideologies of Theory Volume 2* (London: Routledge, 1988), p. 207. On the Marxist Literary Group see Dan Latimer, 'Jameson and Post-Modernism', *New Left Review*, 148, 1984, pp. 116–28, and Sean Homer, *Fredric Jameson: Marxism, Hermeneutics, Postmodernism*, pp. 28–30.

6. Jameson, *Marxism and Form*, pp. xvii–xix.
7. Jameson, *The Prison-House of Language*, p. ix.
8. Ibid., p. 216, and Jameson, *The Political Unconscious*, p. 19.
9. Jameson, *The Political Unconscious*, pp. 102 and 35.
10. Ibid., p. 79.
11. Ibid., p. 221.
12. Ibid., p. 11. See also Jameson, 'Reflections in Conclusion', p. 211.
13. Jameson, 'Postmodernism and Consumer Society', p. 113.
14. Jameson, *Postmodernism, or, The Cultural Logic of Late Capitalism*, pp. 1, xvi. Thomas Frank, *The Conquest of Cool* (Chicago: University of Chicago Press, 1997).
15. Jameson, *Postmodernism*, pp. 10, 15.
16. Jameson, 'Cognitive Mapping', p. 352.
17. Jameson, *The Geopolitical Aesthetic*, p. 213.
18. Jameson, *Postmodernism*, p. 49.
19. Jameson, *The Geopolitical Aesthetic*, p. 212.
20. Jameson, *Postmodernism*, p. 38.
21. Jameson, 'Cognitive Mapping', p. 356.
22. Jameson, *Signatures of the Visible*, p. 162, and *The Cultural Turn*, p. 135.
23. Jameson, *The Ideologies of Theory* (London: Routledge, 1988), Vol. 1, p. xxvi, and 'Cognitive Mapping', p. 359.
24. See Russell Jacoby, *The Last Intellectuals* (New York: Basic Books, 2000), and Richard Rorty, *Achieving Our Country: Leftist Thought in Twentieth-Century America* (Cambridge, MA: Harvard University Press, 1999).
25. Jameson, *The Geopolitical Aesthetic*, p. 212.

Key Works by Jameson

'Cognitive Mapping', in Cary Nelson and Lawrence Grossberg (eds), *Marxism and the Interpretation of Culture* (London: MacMillan, 1988), pp. 347–60.

The Cultural Turn: Selected Writings on the Postmodern 1983–1998 (London: Verso, 1998).

The Geopolitical Aesthetic: Cinema and Space in the World System (London: BFI, 1995).

Marxism and Form: Twentieth-Century Dialectical Theories of Literature (Princeton, NJ: Princeton University Press, 1971).

The Political Unconscious: Narrative as a Socially Symbolic Act (London: Methuen, 1981).

'Postmodernism and Consumer Society', in Hal Foster (ed.), *Postmodern Culture* (London: Pluto Press, 1985), pp. 111–25.

'Postmodernism, or, The Cultural Logic of Late Capitalism', *New Left Review*, 146, July/August 1984, pp. 53–92.

Postmodernism, or, The Cultural Logic of Late Capitalism (London: Verso, 1991).

The Prison-House of Language: A Critical Account of Structuralism and Russian Formalism (Princeton, NJ: Princeton University Press, 1972).

'Reflections in Conclusion', in Ernst Bloch et al., *Aesthetics and Politics* (London: Verso, 1977), pp. 196–213.

The Seeds of Time (New York: Columbia University Press, 1994).

Signatures of the Visible (London: Routledge, 1990).

Suggestions for Further Reading

Anderson, Perry, *The Origins of Postmodernity* (London: Verso, 1998). An admiring yet critically acute assessment of the importance of Jameson's intervention into the postmodernism debate.

Dowling, William C., *Jameson, Althusser, Marx: An Introduction to 'The Political Unconscious'* (London: Methuen, 1984). Does what it says on the cover!

Heffernan, Nick, *Capital, Class and Technology in Contemporary American Culture: Projecting Post-Fordism* (London: Pluto Press, 2000). Attempts to place questions of class at the centre of a Jamesonian understanding of postmodernism.

Homer, Sean, *Fredric Jameson: Marxism, Hermeneutics, Postmodernism* (Cambridge: Polity, 1998). A helpful critical survey.

Howard, June, *Form and History in American Literary Naturalism* (Chapel Hill: University of North Carolina Press, 1985). A good example of literary criticism heavily informed by the *The Political Unconscious*.

Kellner, Douglas (ed.), *Postmodernism, Jameson, Critique* (Washington: Maisonneuve Press, 1989). Essays on Jameson's postmodernism thesis from a wide variety of positions.

Mandel, Ernest, *Late Capitalism*, trans. Joris de Bres (London: Verso, 1975). The economic rationale that underpins Jameson's theory of postmodernism.

Pfeil, Fred, *Another Tale to Tell: Politics and Narrative in Postmodern Culture* (London: Verso, 1990). A Jamesonian approach to practical criticism.

Soja, Edward W., *Postmodern Geographies: The Reassertion of Space in Critical Social Theory* (London: Verso, 1989). Studies of globalisation and the new urbanism which flesh out Jameson's notion of postmodern hyperspace.

17

Edward Said (1935–2003)

Patrick Williams

Contexts

In the BBC2 *Arena* programme 'The Idea of Empire' which accompanied the publication of his long-awaited *Culture and Imperialism*, Edward Said says, 'For as long as I can remember, I have had the feeling of being part of more than one world'. This awareness of the possibility of simultaneously inhabiting different overlapping worlds – or indeed of actually being the overlap, if the worlds insufficiently coincided – was an increasingly important dimension of Said's thought, as well as a simple fact about his life. Said was a Christian Palestinian, born in Jerusalem in 1935, brought up largely in Cairo, and definitively separated from his homeland by the *nakba* (disaster), the Palestinian term for the 1947–9 war which established the state of Israel and left Palestinians scattered and homeless. Originally educated in British schools in Cairo, Said was sent to the United States to complete his education, where he remained to become one of the most distinguished university professors and internationally celebrated intellectuals.

Said lived the combination of being part of the centre (the United States) and the semi-periphery (the Middle East); part of the West, and the non-West (indeed, the wrong part of this particular non-West, insofar as Palestinian rather than Israeli); part of (supposedly) one of the great national identities in the contemporary world, and part of a fragmented people, scattered, oppressed and ignored; part of the elite, and part of the undistinguished or indistinguishable mass of the majority world; part of the ivory-tower academy and – as a one-time member of the Palestine National

Council – part of a radical political struggle. Perhaps unsurprisingly, this has profoundly marked both the subjects Said wrote about, and the manner in which he did so; perhaps unsurprisingly – though it is worth noting that there are numerous other academics and intellectuals in Said's position who have made nothing like the same ethical or political stands. Given the conditions of his own life, that of his fellow Palestinians and, beyond that, many millions in the post-colonial world, the idea of exile is one to which Said returned on numerous occasions and will be discussed in more detail below.

Said's intellectual context demonstrates something of the same divisions, overlaps and tensions as the circumstances of his life. On the one hand, all his adult life he was part of the elite university system, formed as a scholar of canonical English literature in the apolitical world of the humanities in the United States. On the other hand, his own intellectual choices or affiliations – to use one of his favourite terms – took him in important directions away from the traditional, the canonical and the depoliticised. The first of these was into – and subsequently in many ways back out of – literary theory. As an early explicator and advocate of post-structuralist theorists (particularly Foucault and Derrida) in the United States, Said marked an important break with the habits of his discipline. Later, however, much theory seemed to him to be insular, inward looking, and to have failed in its radical political potential, so he became very disillusioned with it. His dissatisfaction extended, in general fashion, even to those areas of theory which many people would have considered the most radical, such as Marxism. It is significant, however, that although Said may have been critical of the failures of contemporary Marxist theory and its advocates to be sufficiently engaged with the politics of the real world, he nevertheless retained both affection and respect for a number of Marxist thinkers such as Georg Lukács, Antonio Gramsci, Raymond Williams and, above all, Theodor Adorno.

The other important move was into the texts of the non-West – precisely those writers and thinkers to whom Western universities paid least attention. Novelists such as the Egyptian Naguib Mahfouz or the Kenyan Ngugi wa Thiong'o, and anti-colonial theorists and activists such as Aimé Césaire and Frantz Fanon, together represent some of the most exciting developments in modern literature as well as being an area in which theory has significantly not failed to live up to its responsibilities. In particular, Fanon – who in his elite education, exilic life and radically anti-establishment politics offers an interesting parallel with Said – was a kind of intellectual touchstone. Said's overall approach could be categorised as marked by a deep loyalty to certain ideas and writers (sometimes problematic or unfashionable ones such as humanism or Joseph Conrad) and a remarkable awareness of, and openness to, new work – while scrupulously avoiding the merely fashionable. It is also important to stress that dissatisfaction with the over-academicised turn of theory at this juncture does not make Said either anti-theory or a-theoretical – though it has probably strengthened the tendency for him to be, increasingly, an engaged, eclectic thinker and oppositional critic, rather than the formulator of systematic theories or conceptual models.

Combinatory Concepts: Intertwined Ideas

Although it is not one of his most substantial pieces, the title of the essay 'The Politics of Knowledge'[1] could be seen as encapsulating the most important aspects of Said's work. Again, there is the bringing together of areas often held to be separate: the life of the mind and life in the real world, exemplified by politics. One of the things which some (academic) readers of *Orientalism* found so shocking was Said's unrelenting demonstration of the ways in which the supposedly pure or transcendental life of the mind – literature, philosophy, scholarship in general – far from being somehow above politics was inescapably bound up with the unpleasant facts of worldly existence. A brief list of some of Said's central concerns (several of which will be examined in detail) gives an indication of the interlinked nature of these key areas: culture and imperialism; critical consciousness; secular or worldly criticism; the politics of representation; the nature, role, social and political responsibilities of intellectuals; Orientalism; the historical role of narrative; 'overlapping territories; intertwined histories'; resistance; the limits and possibilities of theory; contrapuntal reading; filiation and affiliation; speaking truth to power. These are very much his own concerns. There are others which he borrows – for example, hegemony and civil society from Gramsci, or discourse and power/knowledge from Foucault – although the amount he uses them varies greatly. The fact that Said dared to combine ideas from the post-structuralist Foucault and the Marxist Gramsci in the same book, *Orientalism*, has greatly exercised a number of critics over the years, though it could of course be regarded as no more than another attempt to make certain kinds of theoretical territory overlap in a productive fashion.

Orientalism

Orientalism marks Said's first sustained attempt to map the politics of knowledge, and in so doing he set himself an enormous task. His focus is the way in which Western ideas about the Orient have been linked to Western military, economic and political acts towards the Orient in the course of the last two centuries. In particular, he is concerned with Western representations of the Orient – from scientific theories to commonsense notions, from pictorial images to literary narratives – and the forms of 'knowledge' which they produce. Here he draws on Foucault's concept of discourse as both an archive-like body of texts and a self-regulating system for the production of ideas about a designated object or field of objects. Although some commentators regard Foucault's model as rather abstract and separated from historical or political circumstances, Foucault himself argued for the need to see discourses 'in terms of tactics and strategies of power ... deployed through implantations, distributions, demarcations, control of territories and organisation of domains, which could well make up a sort of geopolitics'.[2]

Said is at pains to demonstrate two important things in relation to Western representations of the Orient. First, there is the remarkable manner in which they are mutually self-reflecting, self-confirming. In other words, whether the particular area of discourse is scientific, historical, linguistic, anthropological or literary, the same set of ideas about the Orient or Orientals emerge (especially in terms of civilisational stagnation, technological backwardness, limited intellectual attainments, irrationality, despotic systems of government, weakness of character, sexual excess, dishonesty and cruelty, general inferiority vis-à-vis the West). The extreme repetitiousness of the representations produced by this group of apparently separate discourses and disciplines leads Said to treat Orientalism as one enormous discourse producing stereotyped knowledge about the Orient. As he says

> Orientalism staked its existence, not upon its openness, its receptivity to the Orient, but rather on its internal repetitious consistency about its constitutive will-to-power over the Orient. In such a way, Orientalism was able to survive revolutions, world wars, and the literal dismemberment of empires.[3]

An important dimension, then, of the power of Orientalism is the apparent coherence and consistency of knowledge which it generates (regardless of the truth or accuracy of this knowledge). This carefully constructed and maintained image of the inferior Other – here, but by no means always, the Oriental – allows the corresponding construction of a powerful and superior self-identity: cultural, national or even continent-wide. 'In a quite constant way, Orientalism depends for its strategy on this flexible positional superiority, which puts the Westerner in a whole series of possible relations with the Orient without ever losing him the upper hand.'[4]

The second of Said's points in relation to Orientalism concerns what representations and knowledges actually do and what effects they have, which is where the connection between representations and worldly power becomes strongest, as the continued repetition of Oriental inferiority, backwardness and so on works to justify Western military or political intervention or straightforward colonial conquest. More than two hundred years of growing European global expansion, colonial control and economic exploitation required – and received – its ideological justification in the shape of the representations of other cultures. This is what Said has in mind when he talks about the 'material effectiveness' of texts or ideas: namely, their sometimes devastating political, military or economic repercussions.

Importantly, Said highlights the fact that the relation between Orientalism and Western domination (the knowledge and the power) has altered over time. Initially, the knowledge produced by Orientalism was extremely useful for governments, generals and the like, but it was not produced specifically for their benefit. More recently, and particularly in the twentieth century, there has occurred what Said identifies as 'the major shift in Orientalism ... from an academic to an *instrumental* attitude'.[5] In part, this has meant an end to the illusion that universities, for example, might somehow be above politics, as the rise in Area Studies as a discipline, especially in the United States, has been specifically tailored to the production of 'experts' whose knowledge of other cultures would feed, and form, the decisions of policymakers in government.

In this respect, the link between the forms of knowledge and their political effects has never been clearer. At the same time, although more and more knowledge is being produced, its quality does not necessarily improve: 'one aspect of the electronic, postmodern world is that there has been a reinforcement of the stereotypes by which the Orient is viewed'.[6] (If there were any doubt about that, the appalling racist rhetoric which accompanied or justified the arbitrary arrest and incarceration of over one thousand suspected 'Muslims' in the wake of the attack on the World Trade Center on 11 September 2001 should forcibly dispel it – not to mention the rhetoric surrounding the war in Afghanistan, the second invasion of Iraq, the ongoing crisis in Palestine and so on.)

Intellectuals

Another aspect of the process of 'the seductive degradation of knowledge'[7] as Said calls it, is of course the position of those who produce the knowledge. Intellectuals have long been one of Said's key concerns, a fact marked by his decision to focus his 1993 BBC Reith lectures on 'Representations of the Intellectual'. While *Orientalism* is more or less entirely concerned with Western intellectuals, since its purpose is to examine the nature and effects of Western intellectual practices, none of Said's other works has so exclusive a focus. Although, as mentioned, Said draws on both Gramsci and Foucault in *Orientalism*, he surprisingly makes no particular use of their work on intellectuals (all the odder since these are two of the most influential writers on the subject in their respective traditions). The fact that there are more intellectuals in society today, in terms of highly educated individuals working with data, ideas, information and so on, has clearly not resulted in a dramatic improvement in their performance vis-à-vis questions like racial or cultural stereotyping. Why should that be? Part of the answer lies in the power of an ideological or discursive system such as Orientalism, especially in its ability to convince and co-opt intellectuals whose adherence then further strengthens the discourse. As Gramsci argued in class terms, intellectuals originate from, and are based in, different social classes, but the ruling class always tries to win them over.

Another part of the answer lies in the way in which intellectuals are currently formed: both in their education and in their careers they are subject to ever greater professionalisation in the shape of specialisation and the cult of 'expertise', which encourages both narrowness of vision and adherence to an institutionalised way of seeing. All of these tendencies get in the way of what Said regards as the proper performance of the role of the intellectual, which he characterises as 'amateurism', to emphasise the extent to which intellectuals should not be 'in the pay' – literally or metaphorically – of institutions, corporations or political parties. At moments such as this, Said moves from the descriptive to the prescriptive, from analysing the condition of intellectuals at the end of the twentieth century to saying what intellectuals should be or do. For some commentators, this kind of move is problematic; for others it is unavoidable. However, rather than giving in to the forces embodied in institutions or parties, intellectuals have the duty to 'speak the truth to power':

> At bottom, the intellectual in my sense of the word is neither a pacifier or a consensus-builder, but someone whose whole being is staked on a critical sense, a sense of being unwilling to accept easy formulas, or ready-made clichés or the smooth, ever-so-accommodating confirmations of what the powerful or conventional have to say, and what they do.[8]

Adopting this type of attitude inevitably puts intellectuals into a minority or even marginalised position, and Said's favourite figures for them are outsiders or, above all, exiles – estranged or banished from the comfort of their societies. The experience of exile may be a real or a metaphorical one, but in either case the distance or estrangement helps to create the necessary condition for the development of a 'critical consciousness', which Said, following Adorno, categorises as not being 'at home' in the norms of any nation or system.

If descriptions of the behaviour of Western intellectuals are somewhat tinged with gloom – to the extent that they succumb to the blandishments of power – there is in Said's work (though he himself does not draw such a simple parallel) a complementary emergent figure in those non-Western or anti-colonial intellectuals who form such an important part of a book like *Culture and Imperialism*. For these, their historical or cultural location both increases their relative autonomy from sources of Western power and makes them more likely to be critics and opponents of that power. Such opposition is not absolutely – as far as Said is concerned – or should not be based on polarised rejection ('West bad: non-West good'). One of Said's paradigmatic anti-colonial intellectuals is the Trinidadian C. L. R. James – historian, factory worker, novelist, cricket correspondent for the *Guardian*, a lifelong Marxist for whom implacable opposition to racism, imperialism and capitalism went hand-in-hand with a love of Beethoven and the classics of Western literature. James's famous categorisation of the position of black people as 'in, but not of, the West' is a description which could well apply to Said.

'There is no question in my mind that the intellectual belongs on the same side with the weak and unrepresented.'[9] Again, this could or should apply to all intellectuals, though there are reasons why it applies particularly to non-white on non-Western ones. Historically, the power of the West and of discursive systems like Orientalism meant that the West represented its Others, both to itself and to them. In other words, the West told Africans or Asians the 'truth' about Africa or Asia; the West's arrogant assumption being – in the phrase of Marx's which Said is fond of quoting, – 'They cannot represent themselves, they must be represented.'[10] For 'them' – the oppressed or colonised peoples – to begin to answer back, or speak in their own voices, or tell their own stories to the West and the rest of the world, was politically enormously important and therefore the role of intellectuals in this process of emergent self-representation is vital. The politics of representation is necessarily linked to the politics of knowledge, since the oppositional or non-Western self-representations produce very different forms of knowledge about the despised, colonised Others.

Narrative

The political repercussions of telling your own story constitute one form of the power of narrative for Said. In the context of Orientalism, Western representations of the Orient, as we have seen, tend towards the stereotypical. This in turn involves a fixed, static or unchanging Other. Such a rigid representation Said categorises as a 'vision', and in opposition to this he poses 'narrative', which he sees as incorporating the flow of history, change, movement or development – all things which the Orientalist vision must ignore or repress in order to continue unchallenged. The dynamic nature of narrative thus offers a form of resistance to the reifying power of Orientalist discourse and ideology. A specific example of the importance of narrative brings Said closer to home – or his lost home in Palestine. In the essay 'Permission to Narrate'[11] Said analyses the way in which both a specific (Israeli and US) and more general refusal to accept a historically informed narrative of the Palestinian people, their present condition and future aspirations, has an enormously adverse effect on their progress towards self-determination. Narrative, of course, has no essential or inherently progressive identity, and one of Said's main aims in the first half of *Culture and Imperialism* is to examine the relationship between the great narratives of the classic European novel of the eighteenth to twentieth centuries and the growth and maintenance of the European colonial empires. Interestingly, and in some ways problematically, Said suggests that it was part of the purpose of the European realist novel to maintain support for colonialism. It is, however, a large step from demonstrating – as Said so brilliantly does in the book – that the brutal system of plantation slavery underpins the pleasant existence of Jane Austen's *Mansfield Park* to suggesting that a genre as vast and various as the realist novel might have such an ideologically circumscribed purpose. In addition, however, given its non-essentialised nature, the novel is also available as a powerful cultural resource for anti-colonial and post-colonial writers, even if the conditions are not always perfect: 'That is the perpetual tragedy of resistance, that it must to a certain degree work to recover forms already established or at least influenced or infiltrated by the culture of empire.'[12]

The question of a Palestinian narrative or perspective relates to perhaps the most important area of Said's whole body of work – and certainly the area which has been most neglected by critics and commentators. Although more than half of Said's books are now concerned with Palestine, they have received nothing like the attention lavished on *Orientalism* or *Culture and Imperialism*. The partial exception here is *Covering Islam*, no doubt because it is less specifically (uncomfortably) focused on Palestine. As the subtitle 'How the Media and the Experts Determine How We See the Rest of the World' indicates, we are dealing with a very particular configuration of power/knowledge, in some senses the most potent manifestation of Orientalism. Here, the convergent interests and ideologies of government departments and media corporation owners combine to create news agendas and interpretative frameworks, which function to limit informed discussion or appropriate sympathetic understanding, both of Islam and Islamic societies, as well as of the truth of the United States' government actions in relation to them. Said chronicles what passes for knowledge in these fora: at best, shallow, recycling unexamined stereotypes; at worst, fuelled by racist fantasies and wild warmongering. Although the subtitle might make the situation appear gloomy – our views are determined by the capitalist media – Said is aware that there is more to it than that, and he examines the struggle waged by some academics, journalists and others to produce 'antithetical knowledge'. This is a struggle which remains urgent – as Said notes in the introduction to the revised 1996 edition:

> In the fifteen years since *Covering Islam* appeared, there has been an intense focus on Muslims and Islam in the American and Western media, most of that characterised by a more highly exaggerated stereotyping and belligerent hostility than what I had previously described in my book.[13]

As in other spheres, this fragile resistant knowledge is routinely rejected or marginalised by the vested interests it aims to oppose – though that only makes the need for it all the greater.

Identity

One of the uses of narrative – as indicated in the Palestinian example – is the articulation or representation of identity; in this case, national and cultural identity. Identity, and especially the problems relating to identity formation, has been another of the most consistent themes in Said's work. Like other fundamental themes he has approached and analysed the question in different ways. Unlike those post-structuralist theorists who would see the process of identity construction around the poles of Self and Other as inevitably involving the Self's dominatory will to power over the Other, Said downplays such theoretical dominance. What matters for him is when it translates into dominance in the real world:

> All cultures tend to make representations of foreign cultures, the better to master or in some way control them. Yet not all cultures make representations of foreign cultures *and* in fact master or control them. This is the distinction, I believe, of modern Western cultures. It requires the study of Western knowledge or representations of the non-European world to be a study of both these representations and the power they express.[14]

The assertion of identity is not a neutral – still less a purely positive – phenomenon (as, for instance, it is often portrayed in the United States). One of the things which most concerns Said is the way in which assertions of identity can come to reify the identities involved. Static or monolithic conceptions are no more helpful to the Self than they are to the Other. In either case, recourse to a reductive or essentialised identity risks bringing into play 'atavistic passions' which scarcely belong in the secular rational world Said hopes for.

This can be the fate of even the most progressive of movements, while the case of Algeria as analysed by Fanon is paradigmatic for Said here. Writing at the height of the liberation struggle and on the eve of his own premature death from leukaemia, Fanon warned of the dangers of the struggle becoming stuck at the stage of nationalism – a necessary, but for him absolutely insufficient, phase in the process of the self-liberation of the people. In that respect, he was, unfortunately, extremely prescient. Numbers of postcolonial societies have taken a further step – understandable to a degree but unfortunately retrograde – into 'nativism' (as Said terms it), often in the shape of an idealised authentic – and therefore usually pre-colonial – cultural or national identity. 'Nationality, nationalism, nativism: the progression is, I believe, more and more and constraining. To accept nativism is to accept the consequences of imperialism, the racial, religious and political divisions imposed by imperialism itself.'[15] Nativism may be understandable in terms of wanting to repair the ravages of colonialism, or even as a hoped-for kind of resistance to continued Western domination, but the combination of, first, trying to turn the clock back a century or two and, second, positing this kind of essential, pure identity at all, appears to Said as a recipe for disaster (and, he would argue, the contemporary world provides more than enough evidence of the political disasters which follow from the aggressive assertion of essentialised identities).

As always for Said, the theoretically incoherent or untenable nature of such ideas is one thing (and bad enough in their own terms); however, it is the human consequences – ethnic conflicts, the wars in the former Yugoslavia, genocide in Rwanda and so on – which make them tragic, even unforgivable. The ideologies of separateness or difference ('exceptionalism' in the case of the United States) ignore those very Saidian contexts of 'overlapping territories: intertwined histories', as well as all the other forms of mixing, change and hybridisation which contrive to render all identities somewhat less than pure. 'What matters a great deal more than the stable identity kept current in official discourse is the contestatory force of an interpretative method, whose material is the disparate, but intertwined and interdependent, and above all overlapping, streams of historical experience.'[16] Although his starting point is the analysis of literary texts, Said's method of 'contrapuntal' reading – combinatory, historically contextualised, politically informed, culturally sensitive, non-reductive – is equally relevant to interpreting the larger 'texts' of the historical past and the contemporary world.

This returns us to the idea of the 'worldliness' of texts. At its most basic, this for Said is a reminder to us all that literary works are not sublime, transcendental aesthetic creations, floating free of messy reality. More broadly, worldliness refers to the text's location in a potentially global (not infinite) range of connections (intertwinings), as well as its contribution – and that of its contrapuntal reader – to the definition and struggle to maintain human values or rights on a global scale (usually called universal). As Said acknowledges:

> It is risky, I know, to move from the realm of interpretation to the realm of world politics, but it seems to me true that the relation between them is a real one, and the light that one realm can shed on the other is illuminating.[17]

Uses and Abuses of Said

For the last twenty-five years of Said's life, by far the bulk of the academic responses to his writings have been to *Orientalism*. That continues to be the case. On a personal level, it is perhaps unfortunate that the appearance of *Orientalism* coincided with the gradual emergence of critical theory in universities in Europe and the United States. In a purely academic sense, it has made *Orientalism* one of the most written-about and argued-over of comparable contemporary works and helped make its effect far-reaching. The unfortunate aspect of *Orientalism* coinciding with the rise of theory was that a great many early articles were concerned simply to establish their distance from Said, improve on him, or demonstrate his putative theoretical shortcomings. (Sadly, that remains for some their only way of interacting with his work.) There is an obvious irony in the fact that someone who has premised his career on the careful reading of the work of others and called for that as one of the bases of intellectual activity should be the recipient of so much repeated careless attention from his peers, including some of the most eminent. (Whether that kind of response is worse than the personalised abuse from, for instance, aggressively pro-Zionist journalists or critics is a question only Said could answer.)

There is a further irony in that *Orientalism*, as a relentless critique of the recycling of cultural stereotypes by intellectuals, should be the subject of so much recycled stereotyped critical misrepresentation. To take just one example: in an article published as recently as

2002, one of the oldest misreadings of *Orientalism* appears yet again: namely, that Said's historical framework is ambiguous, inaccurate, indeed ahistorical, because his model of Orientalism stretches not only to Dante in the Middle Ages but also to Aeschylus two thousand years ago. In fact, Said clearly differentiates between Orientalism as a broad 'style of thought' which divides the world into 'us' and 'them', Orient and Occident, and can therefore accommodate Dante and Aeschylus as well as contemporary writers such as the academic Bernard Lewis, and Orientalism as it has developed over the last two hundred years as a complex discursive field intimately connected to the massive political, military and cultural power of the West. The 'style of thought' is to an extent transhistorical (though the precise values attributed to Orient and Occident can be historicised); the materially grounded discursive formation is eminently historicisable – and that is what Said does.

Another, no less repetitive, but in some senses more respectable, area of criticism concerns *Orientalism*'s absences: gender and indigenous resistance. In the case of the former, whole books have been written to remedy Said's 'lapse'. It is true to say that *Orientalism* contains no sustained analysis of gender issues, but Said does, for instance, highlight the very masculine nature of Orientalism and colonialism, not only in terms of the gender balance of those involved but also in the way in which the Orient was both feminised and eroticised: seductive, available, penetrable. In the case of the latter, first, *Orientalism* is simply not about resistance – its focus is on the other side of the coin: the spread of the enormous appropriative Western material-discursive complex; and, secondly, Said acknowledged the absence and devoted one third of *Culture and Imperialism* specifically to the discussion of resistance to imperialism.

A similar kind of reading accuses Said of constructing a 'monolithic' Orientalism, unchanging and undifferentiated. That is not the case, since as far as possible Said shows the multiple forms of cultural practice and intellectual activity which Orientalism can incorporate. Also, to accuse him of portraying Orientalism as monolithic, as if that were an intellectual or theoretical failing on his part, is to miss the point completely; nevertheless, part of the reason for what one might call the 'monolithic effect' lies in the practice of recycling and repetition in the representations produced about the Orient, which we have already noted. Decades, even centuries, of repetition can certainly give a very convincing impression of an unchanging (monolithic) body of knowledge. At the same time, although Orientalism is not monolithic, it would certainly like to be: repetition or recycling is precisely the sign of the labour involved in trying to create an absolutely coherent, self-consistent system. As indicated in the quote above, Orientalism's main concern was 'its internal repetitious consistency about its constitutive will-to-power over the Orient'.

In a more specifically theoretical mode, Said, as mentioned earlier, has been criticised for bringing together the post-structuralist Foucault and the Marxist Gramsci in the same book, since their conceptual frameworks are deemed by some not to be compatible. While there may be no absolute answer to this question on theoretical grounds, for Said what matters most is what the theories actually do together, the analytical scope and purchase to be derived from combining their insights, rather than the possible transgression of certain theoretical boundaries. (The purist approach would be a good example of why in Said's view theory can be a hindrance rather than a help.) Although Said has not invoked it in his own defence, the use of Foucault and Gramsci would be a legitimate example of a 'contrapuntal' use of theory, blending different 'voices' in the manner of musical counterpoint.

Probably the most famous – if not infamous – criticism of Said came from someone who might have been expected to be an ally: another politically committed (in this case, Marxist), postcolonial (though he would vehemently refuse the label) academic, the Indian Aijaz Ahmad. The central chapter of Ahmad's book *In Theory* is a wide-ranging sixty-page attack on Said's work.[18] Ahmad was previously best known for a perceptive – if no-holds-barred – article on fellow Marxist critic Fredric Jameson, but his personalised assault on Said is neither coherent nor convincing, so concerned is he to score points at any cost. Ahmad's inability to read Said with sufficient care means that, for instance, he spends pages on the 'Aeschylus to Bernard Lewis' red herring mentioned above. Said is well known for championing 'criticism before mere solidarity', but just a little solidarity to temper Ahmad's kind of criticism would not go amiss.

The influence of Said's work has been enormous. Numbers of critics have argued that without the impact of *Orientalism* in universities worldwide, the important academic field which has now cohered (if that is quite the word for such a disputed terrain) as Postcolonial Studies would probably not have formed (and certainly not in the way it did). Yet, at the same time, there have been literally hundreds of 'Orientalist' articles, essays, book chapters, even entire books, taking issue with Said, 'refuting' Said, 'going beyond' Said, or simply making use of the insights in *Orientalism*. As well as that, and even more importantly, Said's work has enabled (empowered, if that is not too strong a term in the circumstances) many academics and critics to attempt the kind of difficult combinatory, contrapuntal analysis of aspects of imperial culture and history which he has championed.

Whether he is discussing the role of narrative, questions of cultural or national identity, exile and diaspora, lost causes, or the behaviour of international media corporations, Palestine forms the backdrop to Said's analytical activities, the worldly circumstance to which he must return, which grounds and instantiates the theory and the politics. Said's courageous and principled stance on Palestine has helped to focus attention – in constituencies as diverse as the worldwide academic community and US TV audiences – on a people and their plight, a plight which is all too easily overlooked or misrepresented, thereby contributing to or colluding with their continued oppression. In this, he is providing an influential and inspirational example, living by his own conception of the intellectual as someone who must make difficult choices, side with the weak and the unrepresented, speak truth to power, and in so doing advance human freedom and knowledge. A mere theorist could not hope for much more.

Postscript

Between the writing of this chapter and its delivery to the publishers, Edward Said died. Although he had been suffering from leukaemia for more than a decade, the enormous sense of shock and loss voiced in the international academic community and beyond testified to the way in which his remarkable survival had made him seem – as Tariq Ali commented recently in the *New Left Review* – 'indestructible'. Typically, Said continued his principled polemic output to the very end, arguing for justice in Palestine and denouncing the Bush and Blair-led invasion of Iraq. The fact that academics, cultural critics, journalists and politicians have all described him as 'irreplaceable' is one of the most significant tributes to both the form and content of his very special theoretical work, as well as an indication of its enduring importance.

Notes

1. Said, 'The Politics of Knowledge', in Said, *Reflections on Exile*.
2. Michel Foucault, *Power/Knowledge*, ed. Colin Gordon (Hemel Hempstead: Harvester Wheatsheaf, 1980), p. 17.
3. Said, *Orientalism*, p. 222.
4. Ibid., p. 7.
5. Ibid., p. 246.
6. Ibid., p. 26.
7. Ibid., p. 328.
8. Said, *Representations of the Intellectual*, p. 17.
9. Ibid.
10. Karl Marx, 'The 18th Brumaire of Louis Bonaparte', in Karl Marx, *Surveys from Exile* (Harmondsworth: Penguin, 1981).
11. Said, 'Permission to Narrate', in *Reflections on Exile*.
12. Said, *Culture and Imperialism*, p. 253.
13. Said, *Covering Islam*, p. xi.
14. Said, *Culture and Imperialism*, p. 120.
15. Ibid., p. 276.
16. Ibid., p. 378.
17. Said, 'Politics of Knowledge', p. 339.
18. Aijaz Ahmad, *In Theory* (London: Verso, 1992).

Major Works by Said

After the Last Sky: Palestinian Lives (London: Faber and Faber, 1986).
Beginnings: Intention and Method (New York: Basic Books, 1975).
Covering Islam (London: Routledge and Kegan Paul, 1981; revised edn, Vintage, 1996).
Culture and Imperialism (London: Chatto and Windus, 1993).
Orientalism (New York: Pantheon, 1978).
The Politics of Dispossession: The Struggle for Palestinian Self-Determination (London: Vintage, 1995).
Reflections on Exile, and Other Literary and Cultural Essays (London: Granta, 2001).
Representations of the Intellectual (London: Vintage, 1994).
The World, the Text and the Critic (London: Faber and Faber, 1984).

Suggestions for Further Reading

Ashcroft, Bill, and Pal Ahluwalia, *Edward Said: The Paradox of Identity* (London: Routledge, 1999). The first book-length study of Said (other than collections of essays such as Sprinker's). A thematic analysis which takes the question of Said's identity as the key to his work.

Edward Said (1935–2003)

Hussein, Abdirahman, *Edward Said: Criticism and Society* (London: Verso, 2002). A substantial study which, interestingly and in some ways problematically (and unlike Kennedy and Ashcroft), focuses on Said's early work. Not an introductory text.

Kennedy, Valerie, *Edward Said: A Critical Introduction* (Cambridge: Polity Press, 2000). The most accessible book for students and general readers. Locates Said in relation to postcolonial studies more usefully than other studies.

Sprinker, Michael (ed.), *Edward Said: A Critical Reader* (Oxford: Blackwell, 1992). Probably still the best of the edited collections. Contains some insightful pieces.

Williams, Patrick (ed.), *Edward Said*, 4 vols (London: Sage, 2001). Provides a substantial selection of the best critical work on Said over the last twenty-five years.

Names Index

Adorno, Theodor, 2, 13, 15, 234, 239, 258
Aeschylus, 281, 282
Ahmad, Aijaz, 282
Ali, Tariq, 283
Althusser, Louis, 3, 5, 9–10, 13, 14, 15, 16, 19, 51–67, 186, 221, 226
Anderson, Perry, 259
Apel, Karl-Otto, 234
Arendt, Hannah, 13, 15
Aristotle, 19, 91, 105, 106
Austen, Jane, 277
Austin, John L., 97, 234, 236

Bachelard, Gaston, 225
Badiou, Alain, 48
Bakhtin, Mikhail, 135–6
Balzac, Honoré, 75–6, 257
Barthes, Roland, 3, 9, 15, 16, 68–84, 98, 135
Bataille, Georges, 19, 87, 124, 202, 203
Baudrillard, Jean, 4, 13, 14, 15, 16, 201–17
Becker-Lecrone, Megan, 141
Bell, Daniel, 253
Bentham, Jeremy, 190, 195
Benveniste, Emile, 114
Bergson, Henri, 34, 37, 156, 169, 171, 172, 176
Bhaba, Homi, 99
Blanchot, Maurice, 35, 87
Bloom, Harold, 98, 99
Bourdieu, Pierre, 13, 15, 16, 218–33
Brecht, Bertolt, 69, 70, 71
Buber, Martin, 37
Butler, Judith, 148

Camus, Albert, 70
Canguilhem, Georges, 186, 225
Castoriadis, Cornelius, 23, 152
Cayrol, Jean, 70
Chanter, Tina, 146
Chevska, Maria, 131
Chouchani, Monsieur (itinerant Talmudic scholar), 35
Cixous, Hélène, 5, 13, 14, 15, 16, 99, 104, 118–35
Clément, Catherine, 121
Conley, Verena Aldermatt, 127
Culler, Jonathan, 70, 75, 81

Dante Alighieri, 281
De Man, Paul, 99
Debord, Guy, 3, 202
DeLanda, Manuel, 181
Deleuze, Gilles, 4, 15, 16, 155, 156, 157, 168–84, 187, 213
Derrida, Jacques, 4, 7, 13, 14, 15, 16, 22, 48, 52, 85–101, 105, 120, 124, 154, 213
Descartes, René, 19, 37, 41, 98, 105

Dewey, John, 160
Douglas, Mary, 141
Durkheim, Emile, 34, 226

Eagleton, Terry, 65
Engels, Friedrich, 59, 60

Fanon, Frantz, 270–1, 279
Feuerbach, Ludwig Andreas, 52, 54
Foucault, Michel, 4, 13, 14, 15, 16, 19, 52, 53, 69, 98, 157, 169, 176, 185–200, 207, 213, 225, 270, 271, 272, 274, 281
Fouque, Antoinette, 121
Fourier, Charles, 77
Fowler, Bridget, 227
Frank, Thomas, 261
Fraser, Nancy, 145, 146
Freud, Sigmund, 13, 15, 19, 22, 53, 106, 107, 122–3, 138, 139, 140, 142, 156, 157, 171
Fromm, Erich, 155
Fukayama, Francis, 210

Gadamer, Hans Georg, 13, 15, 97
Gane, Michael, 201
Gates, Henry Louis, 99
Giddens, Anthony, 245
Giroux, Henry, 228
Gödel, Karl, 160
Goldmann, Lucien, 135
Gramsci, Antonio, 51
Grosz, Elizabeth, 146
Guattari, Félix, 4, 15, 16, 155, 156, 157, 168–84, 213

Habermas, Jürgen, 6, 9, 13, 15, 16, 97, 162, 165, 190–1, 192, 196, 234–51
Hall, Stuart, 14, 65, 99
Hardt, Michael, 11, 181
Hartman, Geoffrey, 99
Hegel, Georg W. F., 13, 15, 19, 37, 39, 52, 56, 96, 105, 106, 168, 186
Heidegger, Martin, 13, 15, 19, 35, 53, 86, 88, 91, 104, 105, 106, 129, 164, 169, 186, 235
Horkheimer, Max, 2, 13, 15
Hume, David, 169
Husserl, Edmund, 13, 15, 35, 86, 91, 168, 235

Imbeni, Renzo, 104
Irigaray, Luce, 5, 13, 14, 15, 16, 99, 102–17, 121, 122, 135, 209

Jacoby, Russell, 265
Jakobson, Roman, 19, 114
James, C. L. R., 275–6
Jameson, Fredric, 13, 14, 15, 16, 65, 165, 245, 252–69, 282
Jaspers, Karl, 19

Names Index

Jenkins, Richard, 225, 227, 230n.
Joyce, James, 19, 119, 120

Kant, Immanuel, 13, 15, 19, 36, 105, 162
Kellner, Douglas, 201
Kermode, Frank, 98
Kierkegaard, Søren, 94
Klein, Melanie, 142
Kleist, Heinrich von, 127
Klossowski, 19
Knight, Diana, 81
Kojève, Alexandre, 19
Kristeva, Julia, 5, 13, 14, 15, 16, 77, 99, 104, 121, 122, 135–49, 203
Kroker, Arthur, 201, 213, 214n.
Kuhn, Thomas, 160

Lacan, Jacques, 3, 5, 9, 13, 14, 15, 16, 18–33, 53, 69, 103, 111, 123, 139, 142, 154, 168
Laclau, Ernesto, 27
Lacouthe-Labarthe, Philippe, 22
Lefort, Claude, 152
Leland, Dorothy, 147
Lenin, Vladimir Ilyich, 56
Lévi-Strauss, Claude, 3, 5, 13, 15, 19, 53, 69, 92–3, 108, 135, 218, 219, 221, 226
Levinas, Emmanuel, 7, 13, 14, 15, 16, 34–50, 105, 106
Lewis, Bernard, 281, 282
Loyola, Ignase de, 77
Luhmann, Niklas, 234
Lukács, Georg, 13, 15, 51, 246, 258
Lyotard, Jean-François, 4, 9, 13, 15, 16, 152–67, 205

Macherery, Pierre, 65
MacLeod, Jay, 228
McLuhan, Marshall, 202, 205
Mandel, Ernest, 259, 260
Marcuse, Herbert, 155
Marx, Karl, 13, 15, 53, 54–5, 56, 59, 61, 105, 106, 108, 109, 156, 157, 164, 170, 177, 202, 214n., 226, 235, 245, 246, 253, 264, 276
Mauss, Marcel, 124
Merleau-Ponty, Maurice, 19, 87, 105, 106, 153
Merquior, J. G., 74
Miller, J. Hillis, 99
Miller, Jacques-Alain, 20, 29–30
Mitchell, Juliet, 5
Mnouchkine, Ariane, 120, 128
Montesquieu, 52
Mouffe, Chantal, 27

Nancy, Jean-Luc, 22, 98
Negri, Antonio, 11, 181

Nietzsche, Friedrich, 13, 15, 34, 88, 97, 99, 105, 106, 156, 157, 158, 172, 176, 181, 187, 188, 189, 202, 205, 214
Norris, Christopher, 201, 214n.

Oury, Jean, 168

Parsons, Talcott, 226
Patočka, Jan, 93
Pêcheux, Michel, 65
Peirce, Charles, 19, 160
Picasso, Pablo, 18
Plato, 19, 37, 92, 105, 106, 138
Popper, Karl, 160
Poulantzas, Nicos, 65
Prince, Gerald, 98
Proust, Marcel, 80

Queneau, Raymond, 19

Reich, Wilhelm, 175
Robbe-Grillet, Alain, 70
Rorty, Richard, 14, 266
Rosenzweig, Franz, 37
Rousseau, Jean-Jacques, 92

Sade, Marquie de, 77
Sahlins, Marshall, 202
Said, Edward, 13, 14, 15, 16, 188–9, 269–85
Sarraute, Nathalie, 70
Sartre, Jean-Paul, 3, 52, 69, 70, 105, 186, 227, 253
Saussure, Ferdinand de, 19, 69, 70, 72, 88–9, 92, 135
Scheler, Max, 36
Searle, John R., 97, 234
Shakespeare, William, 127
Sollers, Philippe, 77, 87, 135
Spinoza, Baruch, 168, 169, 171, 175, 181
Spivak, Gayatri Chakravorty, 99
Steiner, George, 98

Taylor, Charles, 14, 190
Todorov, Tzvétan, 135

Virilio, Paul, 214

Wacquant, Loïc J. D., 221, 222, 225
Weber, Max, 13, 15, 226
Willis, P., 228
Wittgenstein, Ludwig, 1, 13, 15, 159, 160, 162

Young, Iris, 148

Žižek, Slavoj, 11, 27, 30, 48

Subject Index

abjection, 141–2, 148
Abraham, sacrifice of Isaac, Derrida's interpretation, 94–5
absolute, Hegel's concept, 39
advertising, and the satisfaction of desire through fantasy in Lacan's view, 28–9
aesthetics, as simulation, Baudrillard's views, 212–13, 215n.
alienation, 24, 25, 54, 55
alterity
  Baudrillard's views, 209–10
  Cixous's views, 118, 120
  Kristeva's views, 144
  Levinas's views, 35, 36, 38, 41, 42, 43, 46–7
aporias, 93
archaeology, Foucault's views, 187, 188, 189, 198
art, as political resistance, 154–5, 164, 165
author
  Barthes's concerns with death of the author, 75, 78
  decentring, 188

behaviourism, 5–6
beliefs
  Althusser's views, 63
  Lyotard's views, 158, 160–1
bio-power, Foucault's understanding, 192, 193
the body, Cixous's concerns with, 130
borders, Derrida's concerns with, 95–6, 99

capital
  Bourdieu's views, 223–4, 226
  Deleuze and Guattari's analysis, 177–80
  Lyotard's views, 155–6, 164–5
capitalism, 170
  ideology's function within, 62–3
  Jameson's criticisms, 252, 254–5
  role of credit and consumerism in Baudrillard's view, 202–3
civil rights, Irigaray's views, 111
Clytemnestra, myth reinterpreted by Irigaray, 107, 115n.
the code, Baudrillard's use, 203
cognitive mapping, within postmodernism, Jameson's views, 263–5
communication
  Derrida's views, 97, 99
  Habermas's use of communication theory, 234–45, 247–9
  sexuate communication in Irigaray's view, 103
Communism *see* Marxism
comprehension, 39–40, 41
consciousness, philosophy, 234
contexts, Said's sense, 269–71, 275

contextualisation, Derrida's attitudes towards criticised, 97–8
contradiction, 56–7
critical theory, 1, 2–3, 4–12, 16
  as affected by Lacan's views, 26–31
  Barthes's concerns with, 69, 70–1, 73–8
  critical canon, 11, 12–13
  Deleuze and Guattari's views, 172–3
  Foucault's views, 189–91, 196–8
  influences upon, 13, 15–16
  Levinas's views, 47–8
  Lyotard's practice, 157–8
  recommended approaches to, 14–17
  second-generation critical theory, 234
cultural capital, Bourdieu's views, 223
cultural politics, within postmodernism in Jameson's view, 263–5
cultural revolution, within capitalism in Jameson's view, 257–8, 260–1
cultural studies
  Althusser's influence, 65
  Birmingham School cultural studies, 11–12, 14
  and critical theory, 11–12
  Derrida's influence upon, 99
culture
  Barthes's critical concerns with, 71–2, 73–4
  and the idea of the feminine, Kristeva's influence upon, 147–8
  Jameson's Marxist critique, 254–5
  Western culture's foundations in matricide, Irigaray's views, 107
  within democracy, Habermas's views, 239

death, relation to self-identity in Levinas's view, 42–3
debt, Deleuze and Guattari's concept, 177, 178
deconstruction, Derrida's concerns with, 85, 86, 87–90, 97
delinquents, Foucault's views, 192
democracy, Habermas's views, 242–3, 249
desire, 171
  and capital in Lyotard's view, 155–6
  Deleuze and Guattari's views, 173–80
  Lacan's views, 19, 28–9
différance, 87–90, 97, 120
difference
  and alterity in Baudrillard's view, 209–10
  within language, 121–5
différends, 163–4, 165
discipline, as the exercise of power, Foucault's views, 191–4
discourse
  Foucault's views, 187–90, 272
  sexuation of discourse in Irigaray's view, 103, 113–15

288

Subject Index

discourse ethics, Habermas's views, 244
domination, Bourdieu's theory, 229

ecology, effects on humanism, 170
écriture, 69, 70–1, 76–8, 79, 80–1; *see also* writing
écriture féminine, 104, 113, 119, 126–8, 130
ego formation, Lacan's understanding, 18, 23, 24–5
English-speaking world, influenced by critical theory, 4–5, 6–11
enunciation, Irigaray's views, 112, 114
epistemes, 187, 188
essentialism, criticisms of Kristeva, 145–6
ethics
    aesthetics, Foucault's views, 196–8
    Derrida's views, 93–5
    Kristeva's interests in, 144–5
    Levinas's views, 34, 35, 37, 38–45, 47–8
ethnocentric invasiveness, Western practices, 92–3
exile, Said's sense, 270

'the face', Levinas's concept, 36, 40–1
fantasy, 26, 28–9, 30–1
fascism, Deleuze and Guattari's attitudes to, 175
fashion, Barthes's concern with, 73–4
féminine, 132n.
feminism
    as affected by Deleuze and Guattari's work, 181
    desexualisation in Foucault's view, 198
    French feminism, 5, 119, 120–2
    Kristeva's interests in, 136–7, 146–8
    links with maternity, 145–6
    theorists associated with, 16
    see also women
fetishism, 203
the field, within sociology, Bourdieu's concept, 221, 222–3, 226
the figural, Lyotard's understanding, 154
film studies, Althusser's influence, 65–6
Frankfurt School (Institute for Social Research), 2–3, 4, 7, 12
fraternity, Levinas's views, 35, 36, 43, 44
French Communist Party (PCF), 52–3, 54, 59, 65
Freudianism, 53, 57, 155
functionalism, Bourdieu's uses, 226–7

gender
    Baudrillard's views, 209
    Said's concerns with, 281
globalisation, opposition to globalisation critiqued by Baudrillard, 206
governmentality, in subjectification, 185, 190, 192, 194–5

habitus, within sociology, Bourdieu's concept, 221–2, 223, 225, 226
heresy, and responsibility, 94

herethics, 143, 144, 145
hierarchies, Bourdieu's theory, 229
Hinduism, Irigaray's views, 109
historical causality, Althusser's views, 56–9
History
    accessibility through literature in Jameson's view, 256–8
    Bourdieu's views, 225–6
    Deleuze and Guattari's concept, 177, 181
    end of history in Baudrillard's view, 209–10
human rights, Levinas's views, 46–7
humanism
    Althusser's views, 54–5, 59, 60, 61, 62, 63, 64
    limits as viewed by Deleuze and Guattari, 170
hyperreality, Baudrillard's views, 205, 207

ideal speech situations, Habermas's views, 242–3
identification, as counter to lack within the subject in Lacan's understanding, 23, 24–5
identity
    construction through narrative in Said's view, 278–80
    Foucault's understanding, 185
'identity politics', 10
ideology, 245
    Althusser's concept, 59–65, 65–6
the imaginary, 18, 19, 23–5, 26, 112
imperialism, indigenous resistance to, Said's views, 281
the impossible exchange, Baudrillard's concept, 210
infinity, Levinas's views derived from those of Descartes, 41–2
Institute for Social Research (Frankfurt School), 2–3, 4, 7, 12
institutions, origins, 37
intellectuals
    influence over the character of knowledge, 274–6, 280–1
    political responsibilities, 69, 70
intentionality, and phenomenology, 35
interpellation, 63–4
intersubjectivity, Cixous's views, 118, 120, 125–6, 128–9, 131
inversions, Derrida's views, 98
Isaac, sacrifice, Derrida's interpretation, 94–5

jouissance, 25, 26, 28–30, 31, 77, 124
Judaism, Talmudic Judaism and its influence on Western philosophy, 36–7, 46
judgement, Foucault's understanding, 192
justice
    and abjection, Young's views, 148
    Derrida's views, 99
    Levinas's views, 36–7, 44–5
    Lyotard's concerns with, 157, 158

Subject Index

knowledge
  grounds, Lyotard's views, 158–61
  as power, in subjectification, 189–91
  Said's views, 271–6, 280–1, 282

language
  Cixous's views, 121
  Derrida's views, 88–9
  Kristeva's interests in the structuralism of language, 137–43
  Lacan's use, 21–2
  Levinas's views, 45
  Lyotard's views, 153–4, 162–3
  role in ego formation, 24–5
  Sartre's views, 70
  sexual difference within, 121–5
  Wittgenstein's views, 160
late capitalism *see* postmodernism
liberation
  Foucault's views, 193
  Lyotard's views, 159
lifeworld, Habermas's concept, 238–41, 246, 247–9
linguistic theory, and communication theory in Habermas's view, 234, 235–45, 247
literary criticism, 6–7, 8, 16
  Althusser's influence, 65
  Derrida's attitudes towards, 98, 99
  Said's involvement, 270–1, 276–80
literature
  importance for Marxism in Jameson's view, 256–9
  women's involvement in Irigaray's view, 104–5
logocentrism, 91–2, 125

Man, Foucault's understanding of Man's nature, 188
Marxism, 2, 3, 5, 16
  Althusser's views, 51, 52–4, 59, 60, 61, 62, 63, 64
  criticised in May 1968, 4
  economism, Althusser's views, 56–8
  influence on Baudrillard, 201–3
  influence on deconstruction, 86
  Jameson's views, 252, 253–6, 256–9, 259–63, 265–6
  Lyotard's criticism, 155
  Said's criticisms, 270
  signifiers within, 27–8
  understanding of ideology, 59–62
mass media, Baudrillard's views, 205
the masses, Baudrillard's views, 207–8
materialism
  Deleuze and Guattari's views, 170–3
  historical materialism in Habermas's view, 234–5
maternal function, 138–41, 142–3, 144, 145–6
matricide, as the foundation for Western culture, Irigary's views, 107
May (1968)
  effects on Barthes, 68, 74–5

influence on Baudrillard, 202, 205
influence on Deleuze and Guattari, 169
influence on Derrida, 86
Kristeva's involvement, 136
Lyotard's associations with, 153, 155, 156
popular responses to, 175
meaning, and significance, 78–81
metalanguage, Barthes's concerns with, 69, 70–6, 80–1
metaphors, Derrida's views, 95–6
mimicry, adoption by women for involvement in philosophy, 105–6
mirror stage, 18, 24, 110, 123, 139
modernism, and cultural revolution, Jameson's views, 258
modernity, Foucault's critique, 189
money, role in capitalism, Deleuze and Guattari's concept, 178–9
mother–daughter relationship, Irigaray's views, 111, 112
mythological, concept, Barthes's concerns with, 70, 71–2, 80

narrative
  Jameson's views, 256, 262, 264
  Said's views, 276–80
national identity, Kristeva's views, 148–9
nationalism, as hatred of the Other in Žižek's view, 30
nativism, Said's concept, 279
neo-Marxism, theorists associated with, 16
neurolinguistics, 102, 115n.
the norm, Foucault's views, 192
Nottingham University (UK), Critical Theory group, 8–9, 10, 12

Oedipus complex, 107, 139–40
  resolution of desire, Deleuze and Guattari's concept, 174–5
  role, Althusser's views, 64
ontology, Levinas's views, 38
Orientalism, concept, Said's views, 271, 272–3, 274, 276, 277, 280–3
the Other, 16, 21
  lack, 28, 31
  and the lacking subject, Lacan's understanding, 25–6
  as the object of hatred in nationalism, Žižek's views, 30
  relationship with, 47–8
  and the self in Cixous's views, 118, 120
  and the self in Levinas's view, 41, 42–5

parler-femme, Irigaray's views, 112
pastoral power, Foucault's views, 194–5
patriarchy, 138–9, 142, 144
  Irigaray's criticisms, 105, 107–10, 111
PCF (French Communist Party), 52–3, 54, 59, 65
peace, and war in Levinas's view, 38–41, 45–6
the perfect crime, Baudrillard's conept, 210

Subject Index

personal, and politics, Cixous's concerns with, 132
phallocentrism, and logocentrism, 125
phenomenology, 16, 35, 86–7
phenominalism, Lyotard's involvement, 153–4
philosophy
  Deleuze and Guattari's views, 168, 181
  Irigaray's views, 104–7
  Levinas's views of origins, 38, 44–5
phonocentrism, 92
photography, as simulation, Baudrillard's views, 212–13
plaisir, 77
poetry, links with the semiotic chora, 140
points de capiton ('quilting points'/'nodal points'), 27–8
policing, as governmentality, Foucault's views, 194, 195
political discourse and ideology, and the importance of the symbolic in Lacan's view, 26–31
politics
  Bourdieu's involvement, 229–30
  Cixous's views, 121, 132
  effects of simulation, 206–8, 209–11
  Foucault's involvement in, 187, 198
  Guattari's involvement in, 168, 169
  influence on the lifeworld in Habermas's views, 238–9
  Kristeva's interests in, 136–7, 146–7
  Levinas's views, 37, 38, 45–7
  Lyotard's concerns with, 153, 154–5, 158, 161, 162–4
  Said's views, 271–4, 282
post-Marxism, 16
post-structuralism, 16, 244
postcolonialism, 16, 99
postmodernism, 10, 16
  Baudrillard's views, 201
  Habermas's views, 244
  Jameson's criticisms, 252, 259–63
  Lyotard's association with, 152, 159, 161–2, 165–6
power
  influence, 171
  in subjectification, 185, 189–96, 199
power claims, Habermas's views, 242, 243–4
pregnancy, 142, 143, 144
presence, metaphysics deconstructed by Derrida, 87–8, 90, 91
production, Baudrillard's Marxist critique, 203, 204
psychoanalysis, 16
  Irigaray's criticism, 105, 107–8
  Kristeva's interest in, 136–43
  Lacan's contributions, 18
  and sexual difference, 105, 123–4
psychological reductionism, 20–1
punishment
  Foucault's understanding of legal punishment, 192

penitential systems as manifestations of governmentality, 192, 195

quasi-concepts, Derrida's views, 96

race studies, Derrida's influence, 99
racism, as hatred of the Other, 29–30
reading
  Barthes's concerns with, 75–8
  Derrida's practice, 95
the real, 112
  importance, 30–1
  Lacan's understanding, 18, 20, 23–4, 25–6
  and language, Lyotard's involvement, 153–4
realism, and the cultural revolution, Jameson's views, 258
reality
  access to, Derrida's views, 91
  replacement by simulacra, Baudrillard's views, 204–5
reality TV, Baudrillard's views, 205
reason
  Derrida's views, 88–9
  Levinas's views, 43
relationships, intersubjectvity, Cixous's concerns with, 130–1
repressive state apparatuses (RSAs), 63, 64
resistance
  Baudrillard's views, 209
  within power relations, Foucault's views, 195–6
responsibility, Derrida's views, 93–5

schizoanalysis, 168, 169, 174, 179
science, 62, 170
  Lyotard's views, 159–61
seduction, Baudrillard's views, 201, 209
the self, 16, 118, 120, 196–8
self-identity, Levinas's views, 38, 41, 42–3
semiology/semiotics
  Derrida's views, 89–90
  Kristeva's interest in, 137–41, 146–7
  and metalanguage, Barthes's concerns with, 69, 70–4, 80–1
  theorists associated with, 16
sexuality
  Butler's views of sexual normality and abjection, 148
  Cixous's concerns with the suppression of sexual difference, 129–30
  and disciplinary power, 193, 198
  Irigaray's views, 102, 103, 104–6, 112
  transsexuality in Baudrillard's view, 208
significance, and meaning, Barthes's concerns with, 78–81
simulation
  Baudrillard's views, 201, 202, 203, 204–6, 209, 211–13
  effects on politics, 206–8, 209–11
Situationism, 3, 202
the social, Baudrillard's views, 207–8

291

social sciences, Habermas's influence, 237
socio-political power relations, theorists associated with, 16
sociology, Bourdieu's views, 218, 219–23, 226, 227, 229
Spaltung (splitting), 22
spatial awareness, within postmodernism, Jameson's views, 262
speech, deconstruction, Derrida's views, 91–3
speech pragmatics, Habermas's use, 236
state
  as the means to human alienation, Althusser's views, 54
  reasons, Foucault's views, 194
strangers, role in society in Kristeva's view, 148–9
structural causality, 58
structural linguistics, Jameson's use in connection with Marxism, 255–6
structuralism, 3–4, 16
  Barthes's concerns with, 73, 74
  Deleuze and Guattari's rejection, 175, 176
  influence on Derrida, 87
  Kristeva's interest in, 135–6, 137–41
  Lacan's relationship with, 23
  linguistic structuralism, 23
subject
  alterity, 144
  identity, 138–40, 149
subjectification, Foucault's understanding, 185–6, 187, 188, 189–98
subjectivity
  the lacking subject, Lacan's understanding, 22–6
  Levinas's views, 43
  within postmodernism, Jameson's views, 262
the sublime (incommunicable) nature, Lyotard's concerns with, 161, 164–5
supplément, 92
Surrealists, Lacan's involvement with, 18–19
the symbolic, 112
  Althusser's interpretation of Lacan's notion, 63
  Lacan's understanding, 18, 19, 23–31
  and the semiotic, Kristeva's interest in, 138–41, 146–7
symbolic capital, Bourdieu's views, 223–4
symbolic exchange, Baudrillard's views, 201, 202, 203, 204–6

technology, effects on humanism, 170
Tel Quel (Journal), 68, 77, 135, 136
terrorism, Baudrillard's views, 210–11
textuality
  Derrida's views, 85, 91, 99
  Irigaray's treatment, 106
theatre
  Brechtian theatre movement, 71, 79
  Cixous's contacts with, 120, 128–9, 130

theoretical antihumanism, Althusser's development, 53–5, 61
theory
  Althusser's approaches to, 53
  Baudrillard's views, 211–12, 214
  Bourdieu's use, 227
  Lyotard's views, 157–8
the thetic, 139–40
thought
  context, Deleuze and Guattari's concepts, 176–7
  as representation, Deleuze and Guattari's views, 171–3
time
  Cixous's concerns with in the theatre, 129
  Derrida's critique, 90–1
  passive syntheses, Deleuze's concepts, 176
  within postmodernism, Jameson's views, 262
totality, as ethics, Levinas's views, 39–40
translation, Derrida's views, 89
transparency, Baudrillard's views, 208
the transpolitical, Baudrillard's views, 208
truth
  bearing on justice in Levinas's view, 43
  Foucault's views, 185, 187, 188, 190–1

universal pragmatics, and communication theory, Habermas's views, 236–7
utility, role within capitalism, Baudrillard's views, 202–3
utopia, Baudrillard's concept, 211–12

validity, Habermas's conept, 237
validity claims, in communication, 240, 241–3

war
  and peace, Levinas's views, 38–41, 45–6
  simulation and conduct, Baudrillard's views, 206–7
welfare state, Habermas's views, 248–9
'white mythology', Derrida's views, 95, 98–9
women
  Baudrillard's views, 209
  commodification, Irigaray's views, 108–9
  configurations, Irigaray's views, 110–12
  realisation through writing, 126–8
  subjugation in writing, Cixous's views, 121–5
  see also feminism
women's liberation movement, Irigaray's involvement, 103, 104
writing, 16
  deconstruction, Derrida's views, 91–3
  Deleuze and Guattari's concept, 177
  as realisation of the intersubjective, Cixous's views, 118, 120, 125–6, 131
  see also écriture

EU representative:
Easy Access System Europe
Mustamäe tee 50, 10621 Tallinn, Estonia
Gpsr.requests@easproject.com